The
Bibliographic
Record
and Information
Technology

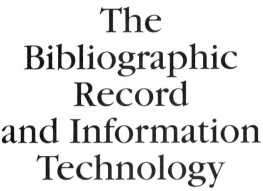

The Bibliographic Record and Information Technology

Third Edition

Ronald Hagler

School of Library, Archival and Information Studies
The University of British Columbia

AMERICAN LIBRARY ASSOCIATION
Chicago and London
CANADIAN LIBRARY ASSOCIATION
Ottawa
1997

While extensive effort has gone into ensuring the reliability of information appearing in this book, the publisher makes no warranty, express or implied, on the accuracy or reliability of the information, and does not assume and hereby disclaims any liability to any person for any loss or damage caused by errors or omissions in this publication.

Cover design by Richmond A. Jones

Text design by Dianne M. Rooney

Composition by the dotted i in Berkeley on Xyvision

Printed on 50-pound Finch Opaque, a pH-neutral stock, and bound in Roxite B cloth over 98-point binder's boards by Edwards Brothers

The paper used in this publication meets the minimum requirements of American National Standard for Information Sciences—Permanence of Paper for Printed Library Materials, ANSI Z39.48-1992. ∞

Library of Congress Cataloging-in-Publication Data

Hagler, Ronald.
    The bibliographic record and information technology / Ronald Hagler. — 3rd ed.
            p.   cm.
    Includes bibliographical references and index.
    ISBN 0-8389-0707-5 (acid-free paper)
    1. Machine-readable bibliographic data.   I. Title.
Z699.35.M28H34   1997
025.3′16—dc21   97-2718

Canadian ISBN: 0-88802-280-8

01   00   99   98   97   5   4   3   2   1

Contents

v

II

- · -

Library Standards   205

Preface

The two previous editions of what my students know as BRIT were published in 1982 and 1991 (the first was co-authored with a colleague, Peter Simmons). BRIT1 was designed to replace the traditional beginning "cataloguing" text in a graduate program in library studies with a text introducing the bibliographic record to prospective reference librarians as well as to prospective cataloguers; to do so in *all* contexts in which a record is used, not merely those directly related to a single library's catalogue; and to describe bibliographic-record processing and searching using computers as well as manual files and the several pre-computer automated techniques which had been developed through the 1950s and 1960s.

In 1997, the computer is the primary, and for many the only, technology used to compile or search bibliographic information. A user now queries a library's integrated user interface, often at home or the office rather than in the library's building, to discover what is owned not only by that library but by many libraries, what is listed and indexed in any of a huge number of commercial databases, and increasingly to access nonbibliographic ("full-text") information in text and graphic formats via the Internet. The "catalogue" of that library, a major focus of so much earlier education in library schools, is a mere mote in the eye of that searcher.

Writing, and now twice revising, a text analyzing these developments has meant keeping apace of radical changes in processes which, in library cataloguing departments, had remained stable for virtually the whole of the twentieth century up to the mid-1970s. The speed of those changes, which seemed frightening in the 1970s, has increased with the 1990s and the latest stage of *interconnectivity*—a term and concept close in spirit but far in technology from the *net-working* just gaining currency two decades ago.

This change has been characterized by increased flexibility for each library, each programmer of a processing system, even each searcher, to tailor technical details to suit an individualized purpose and context. The first edition of this book could describe many practices in detail with assurance that every library would adhere to them, and that every searcher would adopt the same methods and see the results displayed in generally the same way. Most bibliographic principles and many fundamental practices remain unchanged. However, the means of achieving an expected result are now many and varied, largely because the private-sector "business of bibliography" has created a competitive environment in which invention and flexibility in applications are the order of the day as bibliography enters the latest computer age of the graphical user interface and the Internet. As a result, this third edition must be a little more general and a little less specific in treating some issues as it attempts to remain relevant to what might occur during the several years of its lifetime.

In the late 1970s when the first edition was written, the century-old terminology of the cataloguer and the maintainer of cataloguing systems was just beginning to change as a result of computerization and new cooperative practices. By now, much professional conversation of hardly a generation ago between two cataloguers seems an archaic, even almost foreign, language. It becomes ever more, not less, difficult to define and use a terminology of neologisms and an alphabet soup of acronyms which straddle traditional librarianship and computer science; yet to do so and to fix a consistent vocabulary in the beginner's usage are as central to the purpose of this third edition as of the first two. For example, the terms *entry* and *heading* were abandoned in the previous edition, in this one *machine-readable* gives way to *digital*. *Gateway* both entered and left the vocabulary during drafts of this edition!

That this edition must retain some description of manual files and techniques exacerbates the problem of using terminology clearly. Practices retained from the period of manual files, whether or not required by (or even consistent with) digital technology, can only be explained by including some history and older terms throughout the book, not only in chapter 1. For example, manual arrangement (filing) of bibliographic records, with its many eccentricities and non-standardization, is no longer an issue, so chapter 9 can be much briefer in this edition; yet computer-based filing is far from problem-free, and librarians must still be able to locate records efficiently in old manual files.

On the other hand, readers may wonder why some examples used in the figures show books with rather old publication dates. The reason is that it was unnecessary to change examples from previous editions when they remain ideal to illustrate a bibliographic principle—provided their date is inconsequential to the principle under discussion. In the same vein, no effort was made to replace examples using printed books with those taken from other media when the former can illustrate the issue more clearly to a beginner.

This book has never purported to be a how-to manual, yet its two previous editions included an appendix with enough detail about the MARC digital format to enable a beginner to apply all relevant content designators to a bibliographically uncomplicated printed monograph. This was because no simplified teaching version of MARC yet existed to link the format explicitly to a cataloguing code. Teaching aids for the novice do exist now, and the increasing complexity of MARC makes it more difficult to summarize comprehensively in a few pages. The shorter appendix on MARC in this edition is therefore not a detailed summary of coding. Its more limited purposes are to analyze the format's structure and basic features in the context of cataloguing rules and to explain its apparent anomalies by reference to its history.

This is a conceptual treatment of current bibliographic practice in the context of its principles and history. It is neither a survey or critique of existing literature nor an investigation of theoretical advances. It acknowledges primary, rather than secondary, sources in the formulation of that practice. The journal literature in this field remains the follower and describer, not generally the harbinger, of developments. These are the reasons why this book lacks a formal bibliography and why only primary sources and the few direct quotations are documented in notes. To those who wish to trace the development of bibliographic practice in the literature, the following English-language sources are recommended: *Annual Review of Information Science and Technology* (for its topical literature surveys), the journals *Catalogue and Index, International Cataloguing and Bibliographic Control, Knowledge Organization* (formerly *International Classification*), and *Library Resources and Technical Services.* Anyone required to know the details of application must also scan currently the technical publications of the Library of Congress, the British Library, and the National Library of Canada.

This self-imposed limitation is breached here for a particular reason. As the introduction to part I indicates, the scope of this book reaches beyond traditional cataloguing, abstracting, and indexing. However, it stops short of any attempt to characterize practices of describing and organizing electronic resources per se. These are still in the earliest stages of formulation; none can yet be considered a standard. As this book went to press, there appeared a commendable outline of how these practices are evolving, which also places them in the context of what is covered in this book: Jennifer A. Younger, "Resource Description in the Digital Age," *Library Trends* 45, no. 3 (winter 1997): 462–87.

By way of acknowledgement, brief but heartfelt, I repeat verbatim the final paragraph of my preface to the previous edition, which is newly valid for this one:

> My students continue to be my most valued teachers, but two colleagues, Peter Simmons and Mary Sue Stephenson, taught me what I know about automation. The latter read the penultimate draft of this book thoroughly and thoughtfully and greatly improved the organization and expression of the parts dealing with automated database management and file structures. Any remaining ambiguities are my own fault.

I must further acknowledge Dr. Stephenson's help in clarifying, for this edition, issues in the structure and use of the databases of abstracting and indexing services.

Vancouver, Canada
March 1997

PART

I

■ ▪ ■

Principles of Bibliographic Control

The dawn of civilization shines from a distant past when speculation and its communication through language differentiated *Homo sapiens* from other animal species. Human thought and action embarked on a path of evolution as people have examined and analyzed, then built upon, human thought and activity of the past. This remains our means of discovering what was previously unknown and of fashioning social and moral activities through philosophical, religious, and artistic exploration. It is why librarians and other *information professionals* exist: they preserve, store, organize, and retrieve existing information for its practical value in helping people run their lives and for its value in generating further speculation and therefore generating new information.

At one time, the only way to communicate fact or opinion was by face-to-face conversation, using gesture and expression. A community developed its knowledge base and the applications thereof orally and collectively. The communal memory was grounded in the impartial, wise, and probably elderly citizen, the storyteller, a person whose memory we today consider phenomenal—the original information professional. Then, at least ten thousand years ago, humans began to communicate in graphic forms, at first pictures. Although they can still be seen in the dank caves of Lascaux and other sites, it will never be known whether preservation was accidental to their purpose or whether they were *intended* as records of events to be seen

1

and interpreted by viewers in an unknown future. There is no doubt, however, that such pictures came to be used by later storytellers as aids to memory and by the listeners as aids to both memory and understanding. As such, they became protected and revered parts of the heritage of every oral culture.

The strength of the oral tradition to maintain all the information channels needed for societal functioning is still intact among the world's remaining pre-literate cultures. Nor has that tradition ever entirely vanished from the functioning of print-bound society of the industrialized world even at its most literate, just before the advent of electronic communication—say, mid-nineteenth-century Europe, where even Sunday sermons were routinely committed to print. That very example, however, shows that parts of a society's oral tradition are considered useful parts of its literate, or written, record even though the force to inspire and motivate may still depend upon an initially oral presentation.

THE PERMANENT DOCUMENT

Most historiographers consider the people of Sumer around 3500 B.C. to have been civilization's first historians. In the process of adopting a less nomadic and more settled lifestyle, they found it useful to record material events of their existence continually in physical form for later reference by those we now call accountants, lawyers, and administrators. These physical records, created to support later claims to rights and therefore intended to remain in existence at least for a time as evidences of activity or thought, are the beginning of our documentary heritage. Because these records are more permanent (a relative term at best), we call them *documents* to distinguish them from the ephemeral, although still physical, sound waves which comprise oral communication.

The simple but "permanent" graphic representations like the prehistoric cave drawings, created to help keep an oral tradition in mind, could be and were replaced as they deteriorated, or even when their images seemed to need updating, without compromising their unchanging informational value. Their purpose was only to reinforce the content or the memory of an orally transmitted message, not to *be* that message. For a document to serve as irrefutable evidence of an activity, however, it must be tangible and either original or at least a copy made under verifiable controlled conditions. Unlike the oral storyteller, the document does not interpret itself and it can be forged. Indeed, interpretations of the meaning or significance of its content may vary wildly, but each interpretation depends on and can only be judged against the original documentary evidence. This is an entirely different mode of judging and transmitting information from oral-tradition evidence and communication, a major consequence of which is that the documentary heritage is by nature accumulative, even repetitive.

Ever growing numbers of documents demanded more space for their storage and security for their protection against the ravages of both nature and man. More of a problem was the need for increasingly sophisticated organization, both physical and intellectual, so that any specific document required later could be retrieved efficiently. The custodian of information could soon no longer be expected to be the community's storyteller. Its personified collective memory, today's reference librarian, is trained *not* to answer a query from fallible personal memory. As the amount and range of informational detail which might be needed transcended any single person's ability to absorb enough of it, the person charged with managing and retrieving it had to become more and more a *technocrat*, a *designer* of systems and organizations of information control, and an *administrator* who maintains the functioning of these systems and organizations. Thus the earliest Sumerians who consciously gathered and organized shards and tablets recording accounts, promises, and claims originated both the *archive* and the archival theory and service governing the preservation and interpretation of documents within the context of their creation.

As the means of fixing language in written scripts developed in sophistication in the Far East and in the Mediterranean area in the second millennium B.C., it was inevitable that sections drawn out of the context of the oral tradition (snapshots, in a real sense) would be committed to writing as parts of the documentary record: Homer became written history, no longer only sung ballad. Whether later critics interpreted Homer's historical details as legend or as fact has been coloured by how they receive and perceive the context of an oral versus a written tradition as much as on the objective verifiability of the details recounted: "The medium is the message."

Plato cannot have been the first to recognize *dis*advantages in basing the development of knowledge on writing rather than on interactive oral communication. Nevertheless, documents embody the knowledge people need to progress further from the technical achievements of the past; to understand human nature, relationships, and culture; or just to give the emotions a needed lift—the latter at times the most useful purpose of all. Thus, along with the evidentiary document of the archive, the purely communicative document began to pile up as people saved any tangible physical evidence of past thought, and so the institutions and profession of the librarian were launched.

Documents and Personal Uses of Information

People receive information in many ways. We observe natural phenomena and converse with others nearby or at a distance. We reflect
on private matters and on what the print-based and the electronic
mass media bring to our eyes and ears. We contemplate antiquities
and contemporary works of art. We note the influence of actions,
whether of our own, of others, or of nature. We read. As our minds
process and interconnect vast quantities of information, we attempt
to fix in memory bits of it whose later use we can foresee; semicon-
sciously, we store a great deal more for later (and often unexpected)
recollection when it suddenly becomes relevant.

As job and personal needs become more varied and complex, the
information-retrieval techniques of personal memory are less and less
adequate, so we rely more and more on documents. How to go about
finding the right ones is not an inborn skill; much of formal education at all levels exists to hone information-seeking and -interpreting
skills. Furthermore, no work of any kind is best understood in isolation from others, so a major issue in information retrieval is knowing when and how to locate more than just one document that might
meet the information need of the moment.

The storyteller of the oral tradition typifies the creative "thinker"
whose processing of information involves speculation, contextualiza-
tion, prioritization, and emotional processing. The thinker is an originator and may be casual about the connection between a new thought
and its specific sources. The accountant, lawyer, or engineer typifies
literate society. This is the "bean counter" who defines, verifies, and
classifies what is seen as objective fact and, in recombining facts and
drawing new conclusions, justifies each new opinion or discovery by
citing precedent or a source. No slur is intended: much (perhaps most)
thinking is based on bean counting. What is significant here is that the
way they locate, select for significance, and use information constitutes
a major distinction between these two groups.

These are the "two cultures" of C. P. Snow and others, the extremes
of the spectrum bridging the thinker in the humanities and the practitioner of an applied science. Both depend on documents, but while
the most characteristic information-seeking activity of the latter is to
look for particular sources in a specialized index of journal articles or
other "reference" specific to the field of the query, the former is more
likely to profit intellectually from browsing in a large collection of
works or by tracking through works of an individual whose interests
appear close to the inquirer's. It is a wonder that one can even attempt
to serve both types of demand using similar techniques of information management, but they cannot be clearly separated in practice.
What is usually needed is a blend of the two approaches.

Published Information

Much of the information anyone seeks is not original. It has already been processed and interconnected by someone else whose resulting conclusions are fixed in words, pictures, symbols. This reprocessing of information drawn from the "raw" data of archives, artifacts, and artistic expression has, from the earliest period of human communication, been *published,* that is, deliberately made public. Publication does not necessarily imply a documentary format, and a documentary format does not necessarily imply publication. Thus the ballad sung at a mediaeval court and this evening's telecast are both published despite the fact that they originate in a non-permanent, non-documentary method of communication. However, if anyone considers such ephemeral communication important, it has likely been converted to, and probably also published in, a documentary format. For example, lectures and conference proceedings have been printed for centuries, and preserving electronic communication as documents on tape or disk is now commonplace.

Conversely, archival documents are created as a result of the natural functioning of an organization or individual. Letters, minutes, diaries, invoices, etc. are not originally produced with the purpose of being published (that is, open to anyone to see), even if many are published subsequently. Nor is reproduction in many copies synonymous with publication. The most traditionally printed bound book is not published if it was produced only for private distribution to recipients known to its author.

Published information is, by definition, open to the scrutiny and challenge of anyone, and has a special place in the transmission and preservation of information precisely because it *is* scrutinized and challenged publicly, and even continuously. Publication in the academic world is the clearest example of this scrutiny because it is accompanied by a carefully guarded and administered system of prior referencing by peers. The expectation that a journalist will adhere to that profession's code of ethics exemplifies another approach to the constant assessment of published information. Among more popular publications, it is the system of post-publication evaluation through reviews that helps the seeker of information separate the relevant from the irrelevant and the current from the obsolete. Published information is the particular domain of the librarian's functions.

Documenting Time

Written language records words with (some) meaning but divorced from their sound. Any other graphic images on documents over a hundred years old are static pictures. The dimension of duration, or time, is an essential part of the oral tradition; this gives it sound, pitch, rhythm, intonation, gesture, and movement. We call a more formal state of the oral tradition a *performance,* whether of music, drama, poetry, etc. Performances can be described in words and static pictures, so we do have documents which give some notion of what a performance of *Antigone* in an ancient Greek amphitheatre was like, or how Chopin played his own piano music, but at second-hand and in a medium wholly inadequate to convey their reality. Only since the advent of motion-picture and electrical recording techniques, hardly a hundred years ago, can a performance per se be preserved and made available as a physical document.

Advances in technologies of making documents have been so rapid in this century that it comes as a surprise to some young people that their great-grandparents might not have been able to retrieve any performance through an exact copy of it. Even so, as any actor or musician will attest, no two performances even of the same work are identical. Only within the past twenty years is it technically and commercially feasible to preserve images and sounds in the virtually unlimited quantity in which print has preserved words for the past five hundred years and using a technique (digitization) as unified and integrative as the writing of spoken language has been for some thousands of years.

Since hardly a hundred years separate the period when no performance could be committed to a preservable document from the period when it could, it is sometimes forgotten that some performance genres exist only by virtue of their resultant documents. For example, although a rock concert might be recorded without alteration for later broadcast or permanent preservation, a motion picture does not exist "live" independently of a physical document (the acetate or magnetic material from which it is projected) because what has been photographed and recorded is subsequently edited. Thus the motion pictures, sound- and videorecordings, and other physical documents preserving the oral tradition of performance since the late nineteenth century join older types of documents in the archival repository and the library, although not always to a wholly enthusiastic welcome.

THE NEW ORAL TRADITION

The above description of oral communication as the process through which knowledge developed in pre-literate society stresses the essentially transient nature of the communication's content. When a message is communicated orally, that content is both sent and received in a state of some flux. When it is recorded as a permanent written or printed document, it can be stored, physically identified (and therefore located), referred to, and examined closely at any time, retaining an objectivity that transcends time, space, and psychology. However, as a frozen relic, the idea communicated loses at least some of the force of its oral presentation to move, convince, or persuade. Its originator also loses much control over the context in which it will be received. While it can still be moulded dynamically under active scrutiny of an audience through the formal balancing mechanisms of the print world such as letters to the editor and reviews, these do not routinely become one with the original as they do in the oral tradition. Each has a separate life, and there is risk that they may fail to come together as parts of the same concept.

This is why an oral communication can never be completely replaced by a written manuscript, a printed publication, or a sound- or videorecording as a means of shaping the development of knowledge and society. Even librarians and archivists, historically custodians of physical documents, came to perfect reference services based on sources and contacts other than documentary ones. Still, the five-hundred-year hegemony of print in the Gutenberg era fixed and protected the primacy of the physical document and therefore of the theories and information-retrieval services based on the physical document. This foundation remains the focus of this book.

Long before the Internet, librarians had become concerned about the transitory nature of the computer file. In the form in which its content is established, this medium is "physical" or documentary only in the essentially temporary arrangement of electrons. How one should best list (catalogue) or refer to (cite) a file of digital information remains problematic even when the file takes its most tangible form for preservation on a reel of tape or a floppy disk. Both external (physical) and internal (data formatting) practices applicable to its preservation and use have changed with a speed that until now has defeated the necessarily slow progress toward agreed and stable rules for identification, and hence, access.

Now, both scholars and those in the business of communication discern a revitalization of the oral tradition in its purest and therefore most chaotic form in the prevalent use of the Internet. Creating a preservable and citable document appears to be among the least of the users' concerns as the content of a bulletin board or listserv changes by the minute. Even maintaining a reliable index of server locations appears to be a practical improbability in the foreseeable future! Yet the modern academic community, the very group expressing the greatest interest in using the Internet as a medium of scholarly communication, communicates according to rules which demand the accurate citation of locatable sources: traditionally physical documents.

WORK, DOCUMENT, INFORMATION

It is this academic community which expects documentary, not merely oral or hearsay, evidence of any claims of new knowledge (although in some disciplines a conversation might be cited). A reader who trusts in the veracity of the author pursues few citations to their sources, but as a principle, someone—author, archivist, librarian—is expected to be able to produce at least an exact reproduction of any document cited. The philosopher at a mediaeval university and all contemporary colleagues felt satisfied on being told merely that, say, Aristotle was the source of a particular argument. However, modern usage finds such reference to an author alone much too vague if only because it assumes the hearer's knowledge of the author's entire corpus. Although reference to a single *work* (for example, Aristotle's *Poetics*) generally suffices, a need for closer levels of distinction is not uncommon. It pervades such fields as literary criticism, usually because some error has crept into certain documents containing the work. Each subsequent document purporting to embody the intellectual content of a given cited work may vary in some detail, major or minor, from the original. This requires separate identification of the product not only of each different translator, editor, or other intellectual transformer of the work but even of each different publisher or printer. There are even instances where "copies" of the same edition are not interchangeable to answer a particular informational need.

For five hundred years, almost anything deliberately preserved and organized for posterity consisted of printed bound monographs or printed issues of regularly appearing journals. Copies of these existed in many places and were recorded in library catalogues in increasingly standard ways for easy identification and retrieval. Although it might seem redundant to list separately, say, the many reissues by different publishers of the same version of a Jane Austen novel, the fact that most works existed in only one edition and one form—print—kept redundancy to a minimum. More ephemeral printed material such as clandestine political and religious pamphlets constituted a problem less of listing than of finding and collecting.

Then, hardly half a century ago, it became practicable to produce the same intellectual, sonic, or visual content in the form of documents differing from one another only in respect of external format. The reproduction techniques ensured that there would be no change in the original's intellectual content. For example, a musical performance released as both a cassette tape and as a compact disc is the same performance, although there are other reasons why a user might prefer one format over the other. A xerographic reproduction of a text can be made virtually indistinguishable from the original printed product, and a microform copy of it is at least identical, if miniaturized, in its visual image. The useful distinction suggested above between a work itself and any document(s) which embody it was muddied by these developments in reprography. At least some of the techniques capable of reproducing an original "exactly" (always a debatable qualifier) are deliberately used to generate not commercial editions but single copies for isolated purposes. Do these constitute different editions from the copied original? If so, who can be said to be their publisher? Furthermore, some techniques facilitate alteration, for example, omission of unwanted portions, addition of an index, or an updated list of sources prepared by someone other than the work's creator.

Within the past generation, the application of computer techniques to communication and documentary reproduction and the arrival of the new oral tradition through the Internet have further blurred the distinction between work and document and have greatly expanded the implications of the act of publishing. This leads to such questions as:

1) Is the "document" the hard-copy printed output or the floppy disk, tape, or other storage medium which contains the data file?
2) If it is a file of digital data, where does that file primarily exist—in RAM, on a hard disk, on a CD-ROM, or as the back-up data on a floppy?
3) Does a group of screens full of information found "on the Internet," however coherent, focused, and polished, constitute a *document* for a cataloguer to list or is it better treated as a *location* of information for a reference librarian to consult as the latter consults an expert by telephone to answer a question?
4) If indeed a document is at issue, what are its characteristics?
5) More than one person, even in different localities, can alter a "document" constituting an Internet discussion virtually simultaneously; does that make them joint authors of the work it embodies? the editors?
6) One downloading or printout of such a file under active revision may differ significantly from another made only seconds earlier; does each constitute a different work as well as a different document, or does a work suitable to keep track of as a document only exist when someone responsible for it as an "author" signals in some way that it is finished?

Recording the existence of documents is a very different matter from keeping track of the ever changing content of oral communication. However, it is now considered essential for a library's catalogue (which provides information about documents) also to be a link with the new oral tradition (to provide information of any kind). This advance in information services enhances the status of librarians and their institutions, and gives them some voice in determining how the tools for which they are responsible are best used in a new context to gain access to non-documentary information.

At least until librarians approach consensus on the issues this raises, however, this book retains, as its primary focus, methods of identifying documents and locating the resulting document identifications in files. These are the traditional functions of a cataloguer. It is ever harder to distinguish these functions from those of a reference librarian, namely retrieving and interpreting information in general for the end-user. Nevertheless, the integration encouraged—even enforced—by automation is reflected in the fact that it has been harder to stick to that focus in each edition.

FOUR INFORMATION PROFESSIONS

The inscribed clay tablet on which a Sumerian accountant preserved evidence of a debt, the snapshot on which a photographer recorded a smile, the crucifix with which the mediaeval monk-artisan inspired the penitent to reflect on the afterlife, the compact-disc reissue of Caruso's performance of a Neapolitan folk song, the cave painting with which a tribal elder conveyed a blessing or curse, the crystal goblet with which René Lalique communicated one aspect of the joy of wine, the sheet of paper on which a seventeenth-century cartographer printed a bird's-eye view of Amsterdam are *all* permanent documentary forms in which information has been preserved, whether that information was generated as part of an oral or performing tradition, or whether the document was the original form of its creation. Not all were originally created with the intent that they should be preserved indefinitely as evidence of human thought and activities on which to base the future, but that is what has happened. It is only recently that we consciously think of these forms as containers of information.

The physical and intellectual characteristics and the uses and users of each different type of document are distinguishable, so the institutions, theories, and practices of four separate professions have evolved. However, they share the common activities of gathering, organizing, listing, preserving, and retrieving information from documents for known present and hypothetical future needs. Calling their practitioners the archivist, the gallery curator, the librarian, and the museologist puts their English names in alphabetic order, but this happens also to be the order of their differentiation from one another in history. (In the twentieth century, the profession of the records manager has effectively separated from that of the archivist.)

Among the reasons for the continued separation of these professions is the fact that librarians deal primarily with the information in documents existing in many copies. The others deal primarily with original unique objects and must therefore be at least as concerned with the *objects themselves* as with the information they embody. Another reason is that the very close connection of the gallery curator with the discipline of fine arts, and the usual connection of the museologist with anthropology or ethnology, mean that these professionals can involve themselves closely with the intellectual content of their documents. Many become scholars in their fields. Despite a long-standing connection between archivists and the discipline of history, and the fact that many librarians work in closely defined subject specialties, the primary concern in these two latter professions is managing and maintaining the documents themselves while others investigate the meaning of their content.

It is natural for members of any professional group to justify their existence by emphasizing what is unique in their work or goals versus what they share with others. Many of the differences among the four information professions became entrenched through their separate education and training and the separation of the administration of their institutions only over the past century. Still, their differentiation is far from complete, and the lines of responsibility blur. It is hard to predict whether the crafts of a pre-industrial society will be found in an art gallery or in a museum, or whether historical photographs of a community will be housed in its local public or college library or in an archive. Many librarians administer art galleries as part of their institutions. Most archives, galleries, and museums incorporate library departments housing books and journals related to their areas of interest. By 1973, when its library function was separated from it by the establishment of the British Library, the British Museum as a single institution was a repository for archival records, works of fine art, and library materials of all kinds including the current publications of U.K. publishers, as well as the museum objects for which it is most renowned.

Especially at detailed levels of technique, those who work with different types of material once tended to develop specialized methods, including those of description and indexing. Such rules must always reflect differences in intellectual characteristics and uses. However, the information technology of the computer era is now used by all, and learning its applications has suddenly provided much in common in the education of everyone working with information.

Library Functions

Archivists and librarians have more in common than either shares with the other two groups. In the English-speaking world at least, their professional education is now often undertaken under the same academic umbrella. The focus of this book is the activities of the *librarian* in organizing and locating the types of information sources held in libraries.

The primary reason why librarians, more than other information professionals, need the conceptual (even abstract) foundation this book purports to offer is that their mandate is the broadest of the four professions. The librarian is the *generalist* among information professionals, serving information in its greatest diversity (if not necessarily at its deepest levels of meaning) equally in all disciplines in the humanities, the social sciences, and the pure and applied sciences. Those who work with the holdings of archives, galleries, and museums publish materials collected in libraries. The aesthetic experience of being in a museum or gallery is transferred to library users who see illustrations on the pages of art and archaeology books. The concert hall enters the library through sound recordings. An art or craft object held in an archive, gallery, or museum must also be identified in a library catalogue when it becomes the subject matter of a later book or article. Librarians were also the first to take interagency standardization seriously, since it is easiest for them to share and lend their materials.

Shifting from special-purpose private to general public information agencies was a necessary part of society's transition to democratic institutions, a fact seen dramatically in the tax-supported public library movement of the nineteenth century. Even though in practice, a librarian may operate in a particular position with a high degree of specialization as to type of user and the subject area of information service, job mobility is high and education for the profession as a whole cannot be narrow. The present trend back to special-purpose private information-handling agencies does not signal a return to specialization in methods. The ever growing quantity of documents of all types prevents any organization, private or public, from attempting comprehensiveness unless its field of collecting is finely defined and extremely limited.

Institutions are increasingly asked to share information about what they own and even the documents themselves. This is only done efficiently if systems for describing and listing documents of all kinds are fundamentally compatible. This is sufficient reason for librarians to have taken the lead a century ago in developing the most general standards for listing and indexing the documentary heritage and now to repeat the exercise in the context of computerized information retrieval. That all information professionals share the same basic purposes, standards, and even methods in much that they do may become evident throughout what follows.

BIBLIOGRAPHIC CONTROL

Despite this book's title and the heading for this first part, no form of the word *bibliography* is used in what precedes, which is intended to establish a context for considering information and its communication in general, not only in libraries. This is a librarian's word, meaning the study of "books" (published documents) per se: that is, not primarily of their intellectual content but of their very existence and identity as objects. *Bibliographic control* is the sum of all the practical operations a librarian undertakes to organize documents and their descriptions so that relevant ones can be located most directly and efficiently in answer to any user's expressed need. Realistically, it cannot mean assembling and indexing in any one location a copy of every relevant document in existence. In the abstract, its functions may be itemized as:

1) identifying the existence of all possible documents produced in every physical medium
2) identifying the works contained within those documents or as parts of them (including articles within journals, papers published in conference proceedings, the contents of anthologies, etc.)
3) producing lists of these documents and works prepared according to standard rules for citation
4) providing all useful access points (indices) to these lists, including at least some access by name, title, and subject
5) providing the means of locating each document somewhere, either as a physical copy or as a digital file accessible directly or through a librarian's intervention.

This may seem an all-encompassing definition and mandate, so in relation to the scope of this book, two major limitations stand to be repeated: librarians deal with documents, not with information per se, and despite their stance as generalists, they deal primarily with published documents, not with every possible kind.

Part I of this book analyzes the principles underlying librarians' methods of bibliographic control from the points of view of history, the present computer-based information technology, and economics. Part II, introduced by a summary of standards and standardization, describes how, in the context of these principles, librarians produce useable bibliographic records: standardized descriptions indexed for searching in computer-based systems.

1
■ · ■

The History and Language
of Bibliography

The title of this book calls its focus the *bibliographic record,* which is a description of a document sufficiently detailed to identify it uniquely among other documents and specifying where the record can be located in a file of such records.

A search under that term in the subject catalogue of a North American library might lead one to suspect that this is a relatively new topic, as yet unexplored in the monographic literature. It is certainly not new: the term is merely another name for the old library catalogue entry and its near relatives such as the *bibliographic citation:* tools long used in the ancient art of bringing documents to the attention of those who are looking for the information they contain. Accurate and adequately detailed and indexed bibliographic records are the single most essential tool in bibliographic control.

Among previous books on the content, production, and use of bibliographic records, most treat primarily the function of *producing* them in the cataloguing department of a library. The proper subject search term for these treatments is therefore the term **CATALOGING**. Others deal with, or consist of, collections of such records and are therefore to be found under **CATALOGS** or **BIBLIOGRAPHIES**.

In contrast, this book is about both creating and using these records, particularly in digital form, within or outside the traditional library. The librarians addressed therefore include cataloguers, reference librarians, online searchers, interlibrary loan librarians, systems designers, and anyone who helps library users interpret the data in catalogues and bibliographic indices.

Admittedly, few nonlibrarians would be interested in pursuing this topic in the detail and complexity covered herein. Yet by the later grades of elementary school, every educated person uses citations and catalogue listings in the pursuit of knowledge.

This chapter's survey of the principal jargon used in the present and recent past may help put the information in succeeding chapters into a context in which it can be more fully understood. Each term of a technical vocabulary exists to convey a distinction, often subtle, but nonetheless essential.

DOCUMENTS AND INFORMATION

The lay user rarely makes a conscious distinction between the document as a physical object and its intellectual content. A Rubens painting conveys an aesthetic experience; a Chippendale chair supports a seated person. In the popular perception, these only generate "information" when they are the subject of the writing of a critic, an art historian, or a commentator on the material goods of a society. Therefore, people who are not curators or museologists tend to think of the catalogue of a museum exhibition or art collection as nothing more than an inventory of precious objects.

However, communicating information is the *primary* (some would say only) purpose of published books and archival documents. This is so important a purpose that people have always lavished care and creative skill on these as physical objects. As a result, a book or diploma can give as much aesthetic pleasure as a painting or sculpture. Most, however, are of no special physical attraction. Their sheer quantity means that physical qualities cannot be given top priority when the information they contain is the typical user's only goal. The physical container can be an annoyance: hard to locate, expensive, fragile, inconvenient to use—and the library either prohibits its removal from the building or wants it back before the user is finished with it!

Librarians and archivists strive to minimize these inconveniences by divorcing the original document from the information it contains. Photocopying, transmitting by telefacsimile (fax), and storing the entire verbal and graphic content of documents in digital form are all means of doing this. It took two hundred and fifty years after Gutenberg to establish in law the concept of copyright as a means of distinguishing between ownership of the physical object and ownership of its intellectual content. The ethical and commercial concerns associated with the latter, now magnified by the uses of electronic technology in libraries, are beyond the scope of this book.

THE BIBLIOGRAPHIC RECORD
AND LIBRARY ORGANIZATION

A bibliographic record can neither describe a document as a physical object while ignoring its intellectual content, nor vice-versa. As a bridge between intangible information (a work) and its tangible container (a document), it leads users to the informational content but also serves as the inventory identification of a physical item to purchase, borrow, shelve, or lend.

In the days when all its information services were based firmly on what a library owned and housed in its own quarters, the inventory function was at least as important as the information function, and the bibliographic record was an important administrative tool. Its format and characteristics were established in that period and still reflect that origin. The period of the isolated library with its self-contained collection was also the pre-computerized period of manual operations based on handwritten (later typed) records to be read and interpreted through human eyes.

Today, standard numbering and barcoding are the accepted methods of inventory control, a process requiring no human interpretation of these data. The advent of full-text retrieval on the Internet brings the "library without books" or without "walls," an information service involving no more than a person with a laptop computer, closer to reality than to science fiction. In the new context, the value of the record's inventory function diminishes and the importance of the information function increases. Yet the characteristics and uses of the bibliographic record change slowly. Libraries computerize at different paces and with different systems. Physical books and journals are still bought and referred to; not everything can arrive via the Internet; difficulties in serving both parts of the double mandate of bibliographic control cannot be instantly resolved. Technical aspects of consequent problems in the content and format of bibliographic records must be addressed again and again.

With its historical focus on keeping track of a collection of documents, bibliographic control within a library has traditionally been assigned to the *technical services* of selection, acquisition, cataloguing, and circulation. The in-house creation and maintenance of bibliographic records and of the catalogues in which they are displayed were the central functions of these services. Librarians in the *public services,* comprising reference, advisory, outreach, and other document-delivery functions, use bibliographic records to match relevant material to users' requests for information and to locate and deliver it. The bibliographic records used in the public services included not only those generated by the library's own technical services but also those comprising the monographic bibliographies and journal abstracting/indexing services which the library purchased as published "reference books."

TERMINOLOGY

The English-language terms by which librarians name what they create and do in cataloguing were standardized in the last quarter of the nineteenth century largely through the American Library Association's early attention to this area of a librarian's work. This terminology remained essentially stable in both word and meaning until the 1960s. Then it came under the influence of a rapid succession of challenges by terminology used in other places, languages, and contexts. First the involvement of Unesco and other international organizations in bibliographic cooperation brought the language of other cataloguing traditions. Coming on the heels of this, and merging with it, the impact of the computer revolution was much deeper.

The automation of the work of accountants and statisticians, among the earliest to be computerized, was imitated by librarians who began by automating similar inventory operations in circulation control. It is no surprise that the terminology of automating nonlibrary functions then crept into the quite different work of bibliographic control once automation reached the cataloguing function. There, it mingled sometimes confusingly with traditional terminology rather than simply replacing it. Automation's greatest effect was radically to change the very operations and products to which it was applied. When this is the case, it is positively misleading to retain an old term from the manual period. At least totally new terms carry little historical baggage. That computerization also had its international differences still causes problems within the new terminology. Only after a generation is the terminology of library technical services once again reaching a state of common acceptance and stability.

From the time of Gutenberg through the nineteenth century, publishing almost always involved printing. Terms used to describe a library's holdings therefore either had or acquired print connotations; for example, *book, imprint, collation*. Libraries now also collect published films, games, recordings, data files, etc. Their counts are now properly expressed as so many *items*, not books. *Collation* has given way to the more neutral term *physical description*. Specialized terms such as *discography* and *filmography* are coming to be accepted in place of *bibliography* when the medium is a distinguishing issue. (A list itemizing the earlier films of Sylvester Stallone exists and, perhaps with the compiler's tongue in cheek, was entitled a *Rambography*.) However, neither logic nor modernity can be expected always to prevail; no generic term has yet surfaced to replace the print-bound *bibliography* or most of its cognates—*mediagraphy,* for one, never got very far.

Still, the terminology of any field is a living, not a stagnant, thing: new trainees speak a different jargon from those about to retire even when the intended concept is the same. Older librarians who have kept up with changes in practice with total commitment and success may still fall into the use of the technical language they learned at library school a quarter of a century ago despite its inappropriateness to present conditions. "Check the card catalogue" can still be heard at the reference desk in a library where the card catalogue disappeared in favour of computer screens a decade ago. To most people, "Look in the database" implies a search of a digital source, but many reference librarians still automatically think of a purchased product such as a CD-ROM when using that term, rather than the locally produced one. "Consult the catalogue" may seem totally neutral, but when the catalogue was merely a list of the books held in one department or branch, it had a quite different meaning than it has since it started to serve many functions additional to showing what the library owns.

Most of the remainder of this chapter is a survey of terms and their meanings through this generation of rapid change. It is presented to supply a context for terms encountered in the current and immediate past literature of bibliographic control and, even more important, to reveal the necessary but sometimes subtle distinctions among aspects of bibliographic work.

Integration

Information technologies have been around for millennia: inscribing cuneiform symbols on a clay tablet is a communication technology. But to use *information technology* as a collective generic term was impossible before the computer permitted the integration of a multiplicity of previously existing functions.

Preparing clay, papyrus, paper, or vellum to receive writing or print; manufacturing the writing instrument, ink, press, and binding equipment; copy-editing drafts; making and transporting the finished product: each of these processes requires equipment and skills very different from one another. Many different crafts, each with its own context and terminology, were applied to produce a single document.

Now, data enter a computer's central processing unit through linked peripheral hardware, are edited using a software package incorporating typography and page-makeup features, and emerge through other linked peripherals as a finished document on a computer screen or from hard-copy printing equipment anywhere in the world without ever leaving the control of a single office's staff. When previously there were separate and sometimes conflicting operations and terms of a score of trades and crafts, there is now one integrated operation.

In the same way, neither the term nor the concept *bibliographic control* could exist as long as each library's bibliographic operations were conducted in-house and were divided among the staffs of acquisitions, cataloguing, serials, and other technical-service units. Each of these different administrative units used a different system of record management and created its own records for the same objects. Although similar in basics, they were different in detail from department to department and, by extension, from library to library.

Whether fair or not, the perception of cataloguing as nitpicking done only in a cataloguing department and only by people who could or would never meet a user was not uncommon fifty years ago. This led to its rules and practices being scorned by the very librarians who most need to know them: the reference librarians who must interpret the products of these rules and practices to users. As summarized at the beginning of chapter 5, interlibrary cooperation to minimize inefficiencies of this type began over a century ago, but within single institutions it seems to have taken the advent of the computer to overcome administrative and, perhaps more important, some psychological barriers.

It is *process integration,* not merely speed or accuracy, which explains the all-pervasive impact of the computer and in particular the amount of administrative disorientation it causes in every field to which it is introduced. It breaks the shell around the cataloguer, merges the functions of librarians in the technical and public services, and makes everyone a manager and a systems analyst. (To break down the psychology of separated functions was a principal goal of this book's first edition in 1981. The computer revolution made the goal realizable.)

By the late 1960s, this integration was linking the parts into a whole and *bibliographic control* took on generic meaning. Three other reasons help explain the pervasive change in the terminology of bibliographic control accompanying the replacement of manual library practices by automation:

1) Printed materials are far from the only published documents librarians deal with. They no longer necessarily constitute even the principal holdings of a library. A new set of generic terms is replacing those whose etymology and primary meaning connect them too closely with books and print.

2) Librarians share so many automated practices with record-keepers in businesses and other types of institutions that to

retain terms based on older library-specific methods would hamper interaction with others in the field of information technology.

3) As library cooperation grows more international in scope, even established English-language terms have been subject to review because they were often used differently on the two sides of the Atlantic.

Incorporating new terminology so comprehensively into the literature of an essentially conservative practice has not been easy or quick. Students of bibliography must read particularly carefully to understand the intended meaning, regardless of whether an older or a newer term is used. As this is written in late 1996, terms gaining in visibility such as *metadata, text encoding initiative,* and *networked information environment* may or may not become useful replacements for, or additions to, existing terms.

Definition and Precision

Charles Ammi Cutter's statement that cataloguing is "an art, not a science" is applicable to bibliography and reminds us that its terminology must be used with conscious judgement.[1] It takes broad practical experience of a variety of bibliographic situations to understand a technical term in a particular context, especially when automation is changing both the term and the context. The traditional jargon of any profession includes many terms used both by its technical experts and by the general public. A layperson uses a medical term knowing it may have some deeper implication to a physician, but who automatically thinks that a term denoting information or books could be ambiguous? Unfortunately, imprecise lay uses of such common terms as *title, edition, serial, index, work,* and *bibliography* encourage librarians also to be sloppy in using them. Terms most basic to the concepts of any field tend to acquire a variety of meanings over time, hence to lose precision; yet they cannot be wished out of existence in favour of modernized, less ambiguous replacements.

For example, whether an item is a serial publication or a monograph is a critical distinction in many practical aspects of a library's operation. Yet even within the same library, the reference librarian seeking to identify an article in a particular serial, the clerk in the serials check-in unit, the serials cataloguer, the librarian who selects serials for purchase, the administrator who divides the collections budget between monographic and serial purchases, and the bookbinder who sews a year of separate issues into one physical unit each probably has a slightly different working definition of what constitutes a "serial" publication. As another example, figure 1 on page 45 illustrates the potential for disagreement about what is the title of a particular publication.

Documents and Works

A document is a physical object produced on a printing press, tape recorder, computer disk drive, etc. An adjective is often used with the word, as in *government document* or *technical document,* to give it a superficially specialized, but usually not very meaningful, connotation related to its physical form, its issuer, or some characteristic of its content. The printer and binder produce a material object. The creation of an author, composer, or illustrator is its intellectual content, properly called a *work,* a distinction previously noted. That a bibliographic record must describe both the document and the work is a complicating factor in bibliographic control. The priority still given in library practice to the document reflects the primary concern of most librarians, which is not to interpret a work to its users but to *find* that work in the form of, or as a copy of, one or more documents.

Nevertheless, the uniqueness of a particular document—even a single copy of a publication—may be of critical importance to a library or to a user. Someone may request

1) the original printer's manuscript of Thomas Paine's *Common Sense* bearing Paine's final revisions in his own hand
2) the one existing printed copy of *Common Sense* bearing George Washington's autograph on its flyleaf
3) any copy of the first British edition of *Common Sense,* or
4) the text of *Common Sense* in any form, whether manuscript, printed, recorded on a cassette for a blind person, or projected on a screen from a computer file.

In the first two of these situations, a particular unique document is wanted, although the user may possibly be satisfied with a reproduction of it. In the third, the work is the object of the request but in a particular edition of which there still exist copies in many places. In the last situation, the user wants the work per se. To say that the user in any of these cases wants a particular "book" is totally ambiguous.

Processes

Bibliography is a process—in fact, two very different processes: (1) the discovery and listing of documents considered pertinent to a defined area of interest and (2) the detailed study of the physical nature of a document. The former is more precisely called *enumerative bibliogra-*

phy or *systematic bibliography.* The latter, called either *analytical bibliography* or *critical bibliography,* serves to authenticate both the document and its intellectual content. Chemists, historians, and textual critics are more likely than librarians to undertake the specialized investigations of analytical bibliography. Using its techniques, chemists have recently helped determine such things as whether the Hitler diaries or the Vineland map are genuine (the jury is still out on the latter case). Textual critics have determined that Melville's intent was to call his "fish of the sea" not "soiled," as in some editions, but rather "coiled."

Important and fascinating though it be, critical/analytical bibliography as such is not a topic of this book. Enumerative/systematic bibliography is, since it provides the rationale for distinguishing and arranging bibliographic records. It is therefore closely related to *descriptive bibliography,* the process of describing documents and the particular focus of part II of this book.[2] Although bibliographic description and its subset, library *cataloguing,* have changed radically through the computer era, they are still strongly influenced by centuries of development during which printed documents were virtually their only concern.

The verb *to document* implies creating a document, not indexing or locating it. The related noun *documentation* has long meant an assemblage of documents bearing on a given issue. In his early-twentieth-century writings in French, the bibliographer Paul Otlet, a founder of the Fédération international de documentation, added a more specific connotation of process: collecting, organizing, preserving, and listing documents. The baggage of antiquarian bookishness present in any term containing the root *biblio-* was absent, so the French word came to imply the handling of journal articles, new media, and even the theory of information handling in the abstract. These connotations were carried over to *documentation* as an English word by S. C. Bradford, who used that one word as the title of a book published in 1948. It became attached to both the theory and the automation of information processing through the publications of the American Documentation Institute, particularly its journal *American Documentation* (a counterpart to the British *Journal of Documentation*) but has largely vanished from American usage since that organization changed its name to American Society for Information Science in 1968.

Information science remains the fashionable term, but for something more comprehensive than *bibliography* or *documentation.* Its connotation of modern theory and state-of-the-art practice causes it to be used for more than a process. It is now part of the nomenclature of many North American graduate programmes accredited by the American Library Association. In a few cases, it has pushed *library* out of names in recognition of the broadening of the scope of those programmes beyond institutional boundaries. Yet bibliographic control, the most nearly "scientific" part of this field, is not the sum total of what an information professional does. If *information studies* is used as the generic term, *information science* might still describe the theory and the processes of organizing, storing, and retrieving all types of information, not merely bibliographic or documentary, using state-of-the-art techniques involving computers, mathematical modelling, the statistical orientation of bibliometrics, etc.

Whether information science as so defined should be considered a subset of a larger context within which librarians work, whether the work of librarians should be considered a subset of the field of information science, or whether these are two separate, if related, fields of study and work is a matter of more than passing concern in educating entrants to the information professions today. As television, the Internet, and other initially nondocumentary techniques expand the business—indeed, the profitable commerce—of communicating information, the crux of the issue appears to be the degree to which librarians should expand their central focus to include nondocumentary formats.

The People

The information professions are neither self-regulating nor exclusionary. Wherever they work, most people involved deeply in areas treated in this book are trained as, and call themselves, librarians; others are not and do not. To many who seek a new image and status enhancement particularly in the growing field of commercial information services, the connotations of *librarian* seem old-fashioned, clerical, and limiting. Those connotations also include an institutional orientation which is less appropriate as a higher proportion of information professionals become freelancers.

Documentalist and *information scientist* arose with the names of newer processes mentioned just above, the former, like its cognate, *documentation,* having a short life in North America. The latter is being adopted both by some academic theoreticians and, along with *information broker* and *information specialist,* by many private-sector practitioners whose principal business is organizing and finding information (bibliographic or other) in digital form. *Information professional* is generic and abstract but tends to be used only in the context of education for those professions.

Among those employed in a library's technical services, specialized titles are usually given to the acquisitions librarian, the circulation librarian, the cataloguer, the classifier, and the subject cataloguer or subject analyst. As a generic term, *bibliographer* might cover them all, yet it is a job title little used today, except in larger academic libraries where it is still sometimes applied in one of two quite different contexts: either to a person who selects materials or to the curator or cataloguer of a rare-book collection. To the nonlibrarian, a bibliographer seems to be anyone who makes lists of books, articles, etc.

A *cataloguer* does two quite different things:

1) describes a document's physical identity and establishes the names of those involved in its creation, and
2) states its intellectual content both in words denoting its subject(s) and in the logical context of a classification scheme.

These are distinguishable functions because the first involves the use of objective evidences while the second demands subjective judgement concerning a document's potential value to its users.

National bibliographic agencies and some very large libraries still divide these two functions between the descriptive cataloguer and the subject cataloguer, respectively. The term *classifier* refers to a definable operation but has no practical significance in North American libraries where it is almost unknown for a person's work to consist only of applying a classification scheme.

Cataloguer and *catalogue* became terms specific to library organization and operation very early. The cataloguer maintains the inventory, or catalogue, of the documents the organization owns. Because of this, a person engaged in the same kind of work in any other type of organization or as a freelancer, or one who identifies information per se rather than particular documents housed in a particular institution, is more likely to be called an indexer, a bibliographer, or just an information specialist. One who organizes the information contained *within* documents is an *indexer.* Although many are educated as librarians, they work not in a library but for a book publisher or a commercial abstracting/indexing service, for example. The result of their work is purchased by a library and, like the work of an in-house cataloguer, is used in the public services by a reference librarian.

Professionals in libraries, as in other organizations, now spend more of their time on supervision, policy making, and systems implementation, leaving the more routine cataloguing functions to a cadre of paraprofessionals, or *library technicians,* who have formal training in the more routine aspects of automation and bibliographic practices but not necessarily a university education.

The informed *patron, client, customer,* or *library user* (there is simply no one very good term) could always become quite adept in locating needed information in catalogues and bibliographies without professional help. Catalogues and other tools for bibliographic searching, whether manual or computer-based, are made as user-friendly as possible. Nevertheless, the terms *end-user* and *end-user searching* acknowledge that the relationship between patron and librarian changed dramatically when communication techniques enabled a user to see anything from a library's bibliographic data to the full text of desired documents without being anywhere near a library.

The Lists

The best guide to any information, including bibliographic information, is not a list but a person who knows the available resources and with whom the searcher can interact intelligently. Unfortunately, it is the nature of most library collections to be too large for any one staff member to recall the presence and value of each item. So we describe briefly what exists, and organize the descriptions into *lists* according to some searchable system.

Many lay users are amazed to discover how much of a library's "reference" collection consists of lists of documents, rather than of other kinds of information—biographical, statistical, scientific, etc. The former easily comprise half the reference collection of a typical academic library and certainly more than half its cost. When the footnotes and lists of selected readings appended to most noncreative writing are added, a library's total stock of bibliographic data—data pointing to the location, or just the existence, of documents—becomes overwhelming.

Most people use *bibliography, catalogue,* or *index* more or less interchangeably to mean a list of documents. If it takes the form of cards or slips in a drawer, *card file* is still a common generic term focusing on the physical form rather than the use. The first of these terms is unfortunately so casually used as a catch-all that at the end of a term paper or article, a list of any few documents is still routinely headed "Bibliography." If the items cited there, however few, indeed constitute the only sources of further information on the topic, this is the proper term. However, if they are only a casual selection of what was easily located, or only a list of what was actually referred to in the text, the better heading is "List of Selected Readings" or "Sources Consulted." This preserves the proper use of *bibliography* as a more systematically compiled survey of the documents pertinent to a defined field. A list including critical comment on the items or summaries of their content is an *annotated bibliography*. If it appears as consecutive prose it is a *narrative bibliography* or a *bibliographic essay*.

A *catalogue* is properly a list of the items permanently or temporarily in a single collection, as in a bookseller's catalogue or an exhibition catalogue. A combined listing of the holdings of several collections is a *union list* or *union catalogue.* The former term is more likely to be applied to records for serials, as in *Union List of Serials,* whereas the latter is more general, as in *National Union Catalog.*

Automation has markedly broadened the scope of every library's "catalogue." In the card format, it could feasibly show only what that library both owned and had fully processed for use. The library would maintain, on cards or slips, various other manual files listing items on order, items received but not yet processed, items in circulation or at the bindery, etc. Some might be open for public consultation but most were accessible only to the staff. The transition to digital format brought change in both the content and the naming of the library's principal file, the catalogue.

Catalogue and *list*, applied to a group of records, retain the connotation of physical items. *File* and *database*, more generic as to their content but technically preferable terms originating with computer programmers, are now also used by librarians. The latter originally meant a group of files with some common purpose but is now used more and more vaguely. Many librarians now direct a user to "the database" as they would, formerly, direct one to "the catalogue." However, *online public-access catalogue* (OPAC) appears to be the term most commonly used at present for a single library's computer-based bibliographic storage and retrieval system and its abbreviation will be so used throughout this book.

The abbreviation *bibfile* came into use to distinguish a file of bibliographic records (the old manual public catalogue) from other files, many of which were maintained for staff use only in a manual system. The typical OPAC is now a multifile database including all the formerly separate files produced in-house and files acquired in increasing numbers from elsewhere, all searchable in a single process by staff or end-user. It is managed electronically by an integrated package of programs for storing, sorting, searching, and input/output described in chapter 4 as a *database management system* (DBMS). More even than just a database compiled from several sources, the OPAC now typically includes communication links. These lead to specific selected databases maintained outside the library and for which it purchases searching rights for its clientele. It is increasingly common for the OPAC to include a direct link to the Internet and all its resources. An individualized name for a library's OPAC is increasingly common, for example, Orion or Gladys, perhaps originally to attract attention to and support for a technical novelty, but also to invite the user to treat it as something significantly different from the many sets of cards it replaced.

A century and a half ago, the term *index* conveyed only the act of pointing out or showing, without a necessarily bibliographic context. William Frederick Poole therefore used quite a few words in the title of his 1847 *An Alphabetical Index to Subjects Treated in the Reviews and Other Periodicals to Which No Indexes Have Been Published*. In the title of his continuation of Poole's work half a century later, H. W. Wilson simplified it all to *guide* in the title *Readers' Guide to Periodical Literature*; by then any user would understand it was subject-oriented and in alphabetic order. The use of *index* as a noun to refer to any kind of bibliographic file (for example, as a synonym for *catalogue*), as well as to any alphabetic list of names, concepts, etc. without attached bibliographic data (for example, an index at the back of a book), renders the word ineffective as technical jargon.

The Organizations

Whether professionally educated or not, people perform bibliographic control functions in libraries and also increasingly outside that context. Among the major producers of bibliographic lists today, whether only in digital form or still also in print, are the many commercial businesses and nonprofit organizations known collectively as *abstracting and indexing services*, or *A&I services*. They produce the A&I publications: listings, principally but not exclusively of journal articles, in almost every field of knowledge. The *Readers' Guide to Periodical Literature* and the *Magazine Index* (*Magazine Database* in its digital format) are perhaps still the ones best known to the public, although they are less typical of the genre than are topically limited ones such as *Environment Abstracts* (*Enviroline* in its digital format). Indexers who work for the A&I services typically have formal education in appropriate subject specialties; many are also graduates of library schools. In addition to libraries and the A&I services, commercial and nonprofit publishers regularly produce bibliographies covering every possible topic to fill the reference shelves of any library. These may be compiled by members of a publisher's staff but are more often done on contract or even as a labour of love by someone whose direct monetary reward is usually meagre.

An A&I service now typically locates and identifies documents within its defined field, indexes them to access points (see below), and adds to each citation an *abstract* or summary of the document's intellectual content. Many A&I digital databases also include the full text of all the documents listed.

For much of the earlier part of this century, the listing of a book in a library's catalogue was considered only a distant relative of the listing of a journal article in an A&I publication because the two were created in administratively separate environments (the cataloguing department of a library versus a commercial A&I service) and were displayed in different physical media (the library used individual cards; the A&I service used the book format of printed pages). Records for other types of material such as films and sound recordings were also typically gathered into separate files and were compiled according to different rules. The cliché that the catalogue is the key to a library's resources was far from true in the days of manual files. Finding something in an OPAC is much more a situation of "one-stop shopping" now that it incorporates A&I and other databases and links to access the full text of documents retrieved. The current library-without-books and ownership-versus-access debates in the library profession would be incomprehensible without this expansion of the scope and technology of the old "catalogue."

The Individual Records in a File

A description of one document, appearing in a group of footnotes or a reading list, is usually called a *reference* or *citation* because it refers to (cites) a book, article, etc. These terms are part of the jargon not only of librarians but of any educated person. An information scientist may call it a *document surrogate* because it takes the place of, and leads to, the document itself. In fact, the difference between a citation or surrogate and the document itself is no longer distinct when an A&I publication is consulted via computer, and both a citation and the full text of its associated document are simultaneously present.

A citation contains many separate bibliographic details considered useful to identify the related document both objectively and in the context of its potential uses. Each is a *data element*, treated in detail in chapter 2. Such a description of a single document in a library catalogue was long called an *entry* because a document acquired by the library was "entered" into its inventory by a bibliographic record in the catalogue just as a bookkeeper "enters" a financial transaction by an arithmetic record in an account ledger. Both the noun and the verb (*entry* and *enter*) have become the deepest sandtraps in the technical vocabulary of bibliographic control because the computer has changed or rendered obsolete some purposes and functions to which these terms referred in manual systems. They are avoided in this book to avoid confusion.

In the terminology now standard in computer applications, a *file* is a collection of individual records. This usage is the origin of the *bibliographic record* of this book's title, now a jargon term in the technical services. It has not replaced the use of *reference* or *citation* among librarians who serve the public. That record may take physical form as electronic charges on a silicon chip, a piece of magnetic tape, a disk (floppy or hard), or as pits on a compact disk. Nor can a librarian yet ignore bibliographic records written or printed in sequence on a sheet of paper, or each on an individual 3-by-5-inch (or any other size) card or slip, or photographed onto a piece of plastic fiche or film.

Although obsolescent, these manual formats are far from obsolete. They are still in current use in personal files, in smaller, less wealthy libraries, and in much of the less developed world. Even if they were not, librarians will still, well into the next millennium, have to consult and interpret older bibliographic records still available only in some manual form. More significantly, it will be longer yet before bibliographic records at the end of an article or a book are brought within the control of integrated search systems. The manual record still has a long life ahead.

The Searchable Elements of a Record: Access Points

Library catalogues have been compiled at least since the time of the Alexandrian Library, but for centuries thereafter, each book was still a unique manuscript. Especially in the context of a collection of only a few hundred (a large library in early mediaeval times), a single identifying element (for example, an author's name or a style of binding) probably sufficed both to identify it and to distinguish it from the other books in the collection. In the fifteenth century, when (nearly) identical copies of a text were printed, and then editions of the same work were produced in different formats at different places, it became necessary to refine methods of description so that any one specific book could be identified as being a copy of a particular edition.

When the number of different books and editions became large enough that it was no longer feasible to browse an entire list of them to find the desired one, the list had to be organized specifically for access. This involves providing a predictable place or places for a searcher to locate a single description. Both in the earliest large lists of the sixteenth century and in the most recent manual file, the location most frequently used is the last name of the work's author, in alphabetical order. Whatever the location—a title, a subject, a date, a numerical designator, or the name of an author, an editor, an illustrator, a sponsor, a publisher—it is an *index entry* (the popular term), a *heading* (an obsolescent librarian's term), or an *access point* (the term increasingly favoured since its introduction to the librarian's vocabulary in the second (1978) edition of AACR, the current English-language rules for library cataloguing).

Access point is also the term proper to computer processing: *heading* recalls the written or printed header (top line) on a card or preceding a group of records printed on a page to emphasize the filing location. Because an entire access point can be fairly long, it is sometimes desirable to identify only its beginning segment, the one that determines where the access point is to be found in a sequential (usually alphabetic) manual arrangement. This opening part is sometimes referred to as the *lead element, filing element,* or *access element.* For example, the surname is the access element in the typical personal name. The librarian might say, "Search for Smith," while knowing that hundreds of records relating to dozens of persons are accessible via just that surname.

Subject heading, once a generic term for any verbal access point designating a subject, is no longer generic. It is now used specifically in the context of a particular kind of verbal subject identification system, the *Library of Congress Subject Headings.* Terms arising since 1950 to apply to other types of subject access point are *descriptor, index string,* and *uniterm.* The latter term fell quickly out of use (these terms are defined in chapter 7).

Dates and other numeric and coded designations were not common access points in manual bibliographic lists used by the public, so there is no particular jargon of naming them in manual systems. The verb used to describe the action of establishing an access point of any kind is *to index.* Despite its possible ambiguity because it means so many different things, any alternative in this context is too cumbersome. We therefore say a record is indexed (made searchable) under names, subjects, etc.

In a manual file, only the physical arrangement of its individual records ultimately determines access to any of them. Physical arrangement is irrelevant to the way a database management system searches a digital file (see chapters 3 and 4). Therefore, even *access point* connotes something a little too locational to a computer programmer, who is likely to use *search key* to describe the term, code, or number a user wishes to match in order to retrieve one or a group of records sharing that characteristic.

Chapters 6 and 7 describe the thought and care librarians can devote to *authority work.* This is the processes of deciding what are the useful access points, or search keys, for the records in a bibliographic file and of standardizing the resulting access points so that all records sharing the same characteristic (person, subject, medium, series title, language, etc.) are certain to be retrieved in a search. An access point so chosen and standardized, whether it designates a name or topic, is said to be part of a *controlled vocabulary.* Other useful access points can be taken directly from the text of a record. A title or a date needs no manipulation to be useful. These are among the *natural-language* access points often searched. With the fast computers and their capacious random-access and stored memory, it is normally feasible, if not always desirable, to search for *any* single word or other specified character string appearing anywhere in a record, whether that record consists only of a citation or of a citation plus the full text of the document. This, the opposite of controlled-vocabulary searching, is called *keyword searching*. Finally, a *derived access point* is one which can be generated directly from digitized data by a DBMS without ad hoc keying or formatting by a human as an access point.

STANDARDIZATION

The bibliographic structure leading the user to information must be sound; so large an accumulation of such diverse information could easily collapse into complete chaos. The work of many people and the policies of many institutions are involved. The same user may routinely consult a number of different libraries' catalogues, union catalogues, many A&I publications, and other forms of bibliographic file. The user has a right to expect that the transition from one file or database to another be transparent; that is, that all can be searched in essentially the same way.

The ability to mount files from various sources to be searched within the same database management system allows for significant improvement in situations of potential incompatibility, but this technical trend is also applying intense pressure for greater standardization of the source files. In economic terms, it has long been recognized that for each library with a copy of the same document to generate from scratch its own record for the document is wasteful, but cooperative uses demand standards.

First Principles

Standards of bibliographic control are based on the first principles of adequate identification, searchability, and consistency so that

1) no two different documents can be confused with each other
2) the description of a given document within a file can be accessed by any data element or access point (for example, name, series, subject) judged by the creator or programmer to be relevant to users of the file, and
3) the many details comprising each description are presented in a uniform manner so that they can be interpreted without unnecessary ambiguity.

These principles are not absolute but relative. What is bibliographically significant about a particular document depends on the purpose of the list in which it is included and the purposes and operations of the institution housing it, both of which can be stated as matters of policy. However, it also depends on the immediate need of any particular user, which is almost impossible to predict.

Thus, regarding the first principle, two "copies" of a printed document are interchangeable and therefore need not be distinguished for most purposes. However, most (not all) circulation-control practices are based on separate identification of copies, and a user may demand one particular copy because of the most minor difference—say, the presence of an autograph. It is therefore unreasonable to expect every list to describe an item using all the same data elements or in equal fullness of detail.

Models and Rules

As for consistency, one would think that five hundred years after Gutenberg we would have universal conventions for the arrangement and presentation of the data pertaining to at least printed books. Alas, that is not the case: variations continue to appear under the guise of flexibility of access or user-friendliness. They then become entrenched, usually for economic reasons as systems come to be tailored around the variants. The major variations significant for users of libraries are those which separate the conventions of librarians from those of the A&I services, whose products are increasingly incorporated into library OPACs.

Within the framework of the first principles, the day-to-day work of compiling bibliographies, catalogues, and A&I publications requires detailed rules of practice. Bodley's first librarian at the University of Oxford saw this need in the seventeenth century. Then, as now, a large university library encountered complex bibliographic problems but also had expert staff to decide how best to deal with them. Unfortunately, staff members of each large, important library once prided themselves on creating their own "best" rules carefully tailored to the supposedly unique demands of their users. In those days, users did not regularly seek material in different libraries, interlibrary loan was rare, and it was uncommon for a staff member to change jobs during much of a working lifetime. Word of mouth and in-service training, along with a dearth of written policy decisions, reinforced isolated practices. Conferences, workshops, and other modern methods of sharing ideas and learning cooperatively were almost unknown. Yet the variant cataloguing practices of libraries like the Bodleian, the Department of Printed Books of the British Museum, the Library of Congress, and the New York Public Library through the

nineteenth century are more than landmarks in library history because as models often imitated by the less wealthy or creative, they
strongly influenced cataloguing practice elsewhere.

By the end of the last century, different institutions recognized that
by adhering to common rules, they could

1) contribute records to a useful union catalogue, facilitating the
   location and sharing of documents, and
2) lower the cost of bibliographic work by using each other's records
   interchangeably or acquiring records produced centrally.

These perceived benefits have caused librarians, particularly in the
Anglo-American world, to pursue standardization as vigorously as
political, economic, and technical circumstances allowed.

With personnel and financial resources unmatched elsewhere at
any time, the Library of Congress became the acknowledged leader in
standardization throughout this century, particularly in the English-
speaking world. To understand the practices of bibliographic control
anywhere today, one must know the history of developments there. A
power-grab was never the intention of administrators at the Library
of Congress. Regularly at conferences and in print, their position has
always been that their Library does not impose its practices unilat-
erally, but it will assist others to imitate these practices if they wish.
That practices appropriate to the internal needs of one unique institution cannot be totally relevant for other types and sizes of collections is recognized perhaps more clearly at the Library of Congress
than in other institutions whose administrators choose to minimize
expenses by copying its work. Yet a love-hate relationship between
the Library of Congress and other institutions is inevitable.

Acknowledging that its practices are widely imitated, the Library
of Congress began to cooperate with other bodies in creating standards based on them. Since the first years of this century, it has
worked with national library associations in the United States and the
United Kingdom on rules for descriptive cataloguing. After the Second World War, it undertook a more prominent role internationally
through participation in projects of the International Federation of
Library Associations and Institutions (IFLA) and in association with
national bibliographic agencies of other countries. Within the United
States, it cooperates with committees of a large number of professional groups in pursuing the development and practical application
of standards for description, subject access, and automation. The
most pervasive results of these cooperative developments for the bibliographic record are the *Anglo-American Cataloguing Rules* (AACR)

and the MARC format for digitizing the record. These are the topic of all of part II of this book except for the chapter on subject access points.

Conservatism versus Change

The practice of bibliography is extremely conservative both as a whole and in individual applications. Its purpose is access to human documents from all ages, the only permanent means of conserving the thought and values of society. A library's catalogue is an accumulation of records created over a period of decades, even centuries. Records added to any given catalogue must remain basically consistent with one another if the catalogue is to be easily consulted. Any change must promise clear improvement in use, not merely confusion. A change as great as automation has offered both, in abundance.

It may be natural to concentrate attention on the technical revolution of the past generation, but the significant changes of the next generation are likely to arise more from economic and commercial—even political—circumstances. Greater productivity following automation may protect bibliographic services somewhat from the retrenchment demanded in libraries' more labour-intensive public-service functions, but downsizing and outsourcing to the private sector remain the pervasive order of this decade. This trend has repercussions on the application of standards, most of which were developed by and for public-sector agencies, those most open to cooperation.

A less obvious, but equally effective, cause of change lies in the very documents listed in bibliographic files. Serial publications were once few and simple in their titling, patterns of issuing, etc. Published conference proceedings were once restricted to regular meetings of associations. Corporate names once followed a few standard patterns, such as *Department of* [function] for a government agency. Items in other than printed formats rarely appeared in library catalogues. The wording of title pages followed a fixed order of elements and included no gimmicks. As each new complication finds its way into the sources of bibliographic data, some judgement must be made either about how to deal with it within existing standards or about how to expand or alter the standard.

Finally, change itself begets change. As users become accustomed to more access points, quicker searches, and the possibility of more user control over search strategies, they bring increased expectations and more complex demands to all bibliographic services. The simplification and user-friendliness accompanying integration also make users unsympathetic to differences among the files and search programs with which they deal when these differences are based more in history than in logic.

A period of significant change took place about a hundred years ago. Then, following a period of relative stability through the first two-thirds of the twentieth century, several factors arising during a single generation conspired vigorously against bibliographic tradition. In attempts to cope, some libraries simply gave up on old catalogues and systems and started again from scratch. Others bravely attempted some degree of amalgamation of old and new practices. Whenever changes to bibliographic standards, procedures, and products are required, a period of uncertainty and confusion faces all users of bibliographic information. Even policy conflicts among institutions are inevitable. It is too early to tell whether we are yet near the end of the present upheaval, and if not, when stability will return. The very nature of bibliographic control demands stability.

ADMINISTRATION AND FINANCING OF BIBLIOGRAPHIC CONTROL

Despite automation, integration, and cooperation, libraries differ from one another in their collections and users. No bibliography or catalogue is ever entirely correct or complete. Supplements and revisions are being forever compiled, often by people other than those who did the original work. The increasing presence of commercial interests in bibliographic control increases the number of competing services and products with their overlapping content and conflicting features. One may have a choice of many services for searching the same database, but they use different database management systems and user interfaces. Completely contrary to the interests of librarians, competing computer hardware and software companies still have little interest in industry-wide standardization. The field of bibliographic control is active, costly, and challenging.

This book's treatment of concepts and principles holds itself loftily above any consideration of the specific costs of bibliographic services, but some generalizations are necessary to an understanding of the provision of bibliographic services within and outside of libraries. Every administrator of a library or an A&I service, or of the publication of monographic bibliographies, must manage a complex set of interrelated processes, trying to get the best value from a very considerable expenditure. Bibliographic work is a service, not done in hope of significant direct profit. Even as a commercial venture, it is often engaged in by nonprofit organizations, many of which seek grants in support of their work. It might seem easy to measure the cost of the per-unit cataloguing operation in a library, but attempts at comparative statistics are always viewed with suspicion. Administrators claim such differences in their operations that they cannot isolate the same measurement units as others.

Still, there is no doubt that in a larger library with more complex materials to handle, an average cost of cataloguing a single new document from scratch and getting the record into digital form ready for use by others can exceed one hundred U.S. dollars, for reasons explored in chapter 5. This cannot be blamed on the inefficiency of a wasteful bureaucracy; it is the price of the increasing complexity of the job and the care taken.

Has the money channelled into the capital infrastructure of technical-service automation in libraries in the recent past detracted from the value of the collections or the quality of the public services? What is being enhanced or sacrificed in putting money into the other new capital infrastructure: digital databases purchased for local access and the computer equipment placed in public-service areas for their use? Is the library still a necessary intermediary when end-users can pay directly for Internet access to fee-based bibliographic services? Are libraries reaching a degree of efficiency which might please a private company's auditor?

Librarians generally feel unable to answer such questions largely because of the difficulty of assigning a monetary value to specific tasks and services. In addition to compiling catalogues and bibliographies, librarians have long written user guides and given classes and instruction sessions on the use of bibliographic databases and search methods. Such generalized helps for end-users are part of the ongoing cost and administration of bibliographic services. In the pre-computer period, they were systematically budgeted for and provided in some depth only in school and academic libraries because following formal education, the end-user was assumed to have basic competence. However, as bibliographic tools and the information they contain become more complex and as automation is radically changing the search process, public-service librarians in other types of library are also becoming instructors in bibliographic techniques to groups and individual users. Special librarians, whose policy was once to shield their end-users from concern about bibliographic tools and their use by doing the searching for them and perhaps even interpreting the result, are now specialists in bibliographic instruction.

The cost of an end-user's own time spent in bibliographic searching is still typically ignored as a factor in library administration in the public sector. Bibliographic instruction for groups, like the reference librarian's help on an individual query, also tends to be incorporated into the operating budget. However, cost-recovery for individualized service beyond whatever is defined as "basic service" is now becoming a prominent aspect of fiscal administration in all types of library. Now, more and more public and academic libraries advertise enhanced information services for a fee, generally aimed at the small private-sector business which cannot justify having its own special librarian.

The library claims the fee as payment for a nontraditional service not legitimately covered by its ordinary budget, and usually charges by the time spent on the individual request. Is this the best measure of the *value* of the result to the client? The skill and judgement of the searcher are major factors in the time spent, so performance evaluation of librarians engaged in these services must be more rigorous to justify the billing rate to the customer. But the efficiency of the bibliographic tools they work with is another factor. A well-designed tool with an appropriate technology for searching reveals its information to experienced searchers more quickly and even to end-users with less need for help from the library's public-service staff. The inadequate tool is more costly every time it is used whether by a professional or an end-user; worse, it causes the latter to make more demands for help from library staff.

Within a library, three distinct groups of professionals are involved in the production and use of bibliographic tools:

1) cataloguers and systems librarians create and maintain the various in-house files and user interfaces
2) reference librarians choose bibliographic tools produced externally, interpret bibliographic data to users, and create specialized lists based on local needs and resources, and
3) administrators prioritize needs and allocate staff and budget resources to both bibliographic and other competing services.

The faculty members of the graduate professional library schools constitute a fourth interested group of librarians, reflecting the other three in that each tends to specialize in one of those three fields.

There is an unfortunate history of mutual recrimination among all four groups. Those in technical services often do not meet the public directly; their work patterns are different; there tends to be little personnel crossover between technical and public services. Reference librarians claim that cataloguers hide information under obscure access points or classify items for shelving where no user would think to look. Cataloguers complain that reference librarians do not learn the standards and systems well enough to make the best use of them and that they fail to appreciate either the need for, or the benefit of, periodic changes to those standards and systems. Administrators, who may come from either stream, are routinely accused of favouring whichever segment of the operation they know best in applying performance measures and evaluating services comparatively. Their typical complaint about library school faculty is that the latter slight the practical training needed for immediate—even first-day—effectiveness in applying current techniques, an issue which divides instructors and practitioners in every professional field.

Happily, there is a growing tendency, particularly within consortia and associations, to raise the consciousness of each group concerning the activities of the others and to encourage more systematic contacts. At the local level, the integration already described as a major result of automation first helped bridge the gulf between technical- and public-service staff and is now fostering organizational merger of the two functions.

In the late 1960s, an administrator's principal concern with changing bibliographic services was technological. Today, the technology is well past the experimental stage, and the difficult personnel issues arising from the introduction of automation have largely been solved as a computer-literate generation comes of age. However, automation has rarely fulfilled an early promise of cost reduction. Financial concerns remain and are magnified especially in public institutions by more widespread fiscal restraint. Administrators are trying to manage a shift in the traditional budgetary balance among

1) technical- and public-services costs
2) capital and operating costs
3) machine and human labour costs, and
4) permanent staff and owned equipment, and the purchase of equivalent services commercially or from freelance professionals.

Such shifts are never administratively easy; in the face of union contracts they can be devastating. Difficulties in this area have toppled many library administrations.

BIBLIOGRAPHIC JUDGEMENT

The study of bibliographic control is laden with detail, much of which may seem confusing and irrelevant until one acquires through careful observation and experience the context in which to judge the significance of a given bibliographic fact. Designing, making, or using any bibliographic list, particularly a computer-based one, requires constant attention to detail so that no useful fact is ignored, however inconsequential it may initially seem. To be effective, one must develop the detective instinct of a Sherlock Holmes. People are not born with this instinct. It comes more easily to some than to others, but anyone who consciously rejects this type of mental discipline will find neither self-fulfillment nor much success in the information professions. However, no detail is of consequence in isolation. Its *context* is what makes it significant. The reader should consciously attempt to relate what is presented in this book to

1) its application to past personal experiences in looking up information in bibliographic tools of all types
2) practices observed in various types and sizes of libraries, archives, galleries, and museums, and
3) information gained in studying about all other aspects of librarianship.

It bothers many students beginning a graduate programme in librarianship that so little in the study of bibliographic theory or practice appears to be tangible or quantifiable. Everything is presented as relative. This is particularly disturbing to those who had been misguided into believing that bibliographic citation and library cataloguing consist of the application of concrete and rigid rules to situations which fit those rules unambiguously. The author has always found the hardest student question to answer to be the perennial "But what is the *right* way?" The only honest answer is almost always "It depends on. . . ." One of the things it depends on, for better or for worse, is often an administrator's subjective assessment of the issues involved and judgement of the priorities to be applied. Any option is the "right" one if its premises are conceded.

Fewer premises are conceded today than ever before. The recent changes most difficult to deal with have been caused neither by new cataloguing codes nor by the computer but by the fact that it is now rare for a library to act alone in the purchase or creation of bibliographic records. The politics of compromise and consensus-seeking among cooperating libraries, the politics of lobbying government to support expensive cooperative ventures, and the politics of arriving at commercial decisions in an environment of competitive profit-motivated bibliographic enterprises have become integral parts of bibliographic control.

This book cannot usurp the prerogative of practitioners and administrators in deciding what is "right" in a given situation. All it can do is illustrate what circumstances and reasoning have led to certain practical applications. It is concerned to show what *has* been done and what *can* be done, not to presume what *should* be done. Early in this century, Charles Ammi Cutter feared that the influence of the

Library of Congress for standardization might mark the end of what he called the "golden age of cataloging." We are now in a new golden age. Cutter's view of cataloguing (by implication today, all of bibliographic control) as "an art, not a science" is still valid.[3] This view has one overriding implication for the student: one does not learn to deal with bibliographic records so much by studying their construction or reading a book like this one as by *experiencing* their use.

2

■ ■ ■

Bibliographic Data
and Relationships

Bibliographic control begins with many small building blocks: the separate units of bibliographic data, or *data elements*, which together identify either a document or the bibliographic record for that document. Some of these are familiar to anyone who has ever created a footnote; notably, a document's title, publisher, and date of first appearance. Other data elements are relevant to only a minority of documents but, when present, are just as important; for example, facts about reissuing, a plate number on a sheet of music, or the hardware requirements to use an interactive CD-ROM.

Many details of cataloguing practice still treat a manuscript deed, a portfolio of lithographs, or a digital file of census data on a floppy disk as a novelty rather than as a carrier of information co-equal with a printed book or serial. The user of this book is intended to visualize examples in all such media even when the printed book or its language-based (rather than visual) content is used as an example, for familiarity's sake, to illustrate a point.

As a second category of data elements, there are those of little value to the user of the document but necessary to manage documents collected in libraries, etc.; for example, a call number and restrictions on use. Finally, there are data elements needed to keep track not of the document itself but of its bibliographic record; for example, a control number in a digital file or the date of most recent revision.

All these building blocks, assembled and used in the standardized ways described in later chapters, form a cohesive and comprehensible structure for the most efficient location of any document and the most efficient management of the database of records. The purpose of this chapter is to analyze, in useful categories, the most frequently encountered bibliographic data elements considering their occurrence, their form, and their uses. Data elements serve primarily

1) to identify a particular document uniquely in order to distinguish it from others (for example, a date of publication or a count of the number of pages in a printed book)
2) to show how two or more documents are associated with one another (for example, in that they have a common author or that one is a continuation or sequel of the other), and
3) to provide the basis for access points enabling a searcher to locate the record of a document; useful access points may relate to
   a) objective facts about the document itself (for example, its title or the fact that it constitutes the proceedings of a conference), or
   b) the topic(s) and concept(s) treated in its intellectual content; simplistically, the subject(s) of the document.

No creator of bibliographic records can claim to be doing an adequate job if the first of these purposes is not fulfilled. Many ignore one or both of the other two either because their need is not perceived or because they are far more difficult and expensive to accomplish than the first. Librarians generally treat all three as of equal importance in compiling the files they create. The third use of bibliographic data, namely to generate access points, is a direct concern of only the final section of this chapter. It is the primary focus of chapter 3 and all of part II.

Value judgements have no place in the creation of bibliographic files. The price of an item at the time of publication is a bibliographically useful data element only because it can help identify a particular issue or format. Whether or not it is worth that price in any given situation is bibliographically irrelevant. It is up to the end-user or a reader's advisor or collection development librarian to decide that. The bibliographic value of a title is to identify the document by its own name, in the same objective way as a personal name identifies the person in a passport. The average end-user may rely heavily on title words to indicate something else—the document's intellectual content—but this function is irrelevant to the title's primary bibliographic purpose of objective identification.

THE LANGUAGE OF
BIBLIOGRAPHIC STATEMENTS

Bibliographic data are communicated in the words and grammatical structure of a language. The words may seem to be just normal words in, say, English or French, but an additional language is also involved because the syntax is not that of a natural spoken language, but of bibliographic language. Like any other language, this one is nothing but a set of commonly accepted conventions. An editor or a publisher uses this language (sometimes well, sometimes poorly) in composing the statements to appear on a title page, a record label, an opening screen shown by a computer file, a first image in a filmstrip, etc. A cataloguer expresses the bibliographic situations embedded in this title page, etc., and in the rest of the document, as a record written in this language. As with any language, its words and syntax may be misunderstood and misinterpreted, particularly when (as at present) care for the niceties of good syntax is undervalued; so a reference librarian may have to interpret them to a user who initially fails to grasp their implications.

"Bibliographese" is a compact language of concise and often elliptical expression. Its "sentence" and "paragraph" structures are rigidly circumscribed by rules allowing no flexibility for variation or individuality of style. As when learning to understand any other language, a beginner quickly comprehends much of this one, but finds it more difficult to compose it. Before it yields all the subtleties of meaning of which it is capable, the learner needs instruction and experience in using it in the context of bibliographic files for different purposes and in various formats. Its words (the easy part) are the focus of this chapter; its syntax (which can get quite complex) is the focus of chapter 8.

Someone without experience of the layout of title pages or with little knowledge of the English language might look at the pages reproduced in figure 1 and transcribe the titles as, respectively, *The Story of Whaling Harpooned* and *The Conversions of a Bishop.* Anyone who knows title-page layout and English-language style has no doubt that the first of these can only be read as *Harpooned: The Story of Whaling.* Establishing a correct reading of the other is more problematic. If the title is *The Conversions of a Bishop,* what is the function of the preceding words, *Dom Helder Camara?* One interpretation is that they name the book's author. The words are in different typographic style, and positioning the author's name on a title page before the title is not uncommon, especially in British books. On the other hand, there is a strong implication that Camara is the "bishop" in question and hence as much the book's subject as its author. As an

THE STORY OF WHALING

harpooned

by Bill Spence

CONWAY MARITIME PRESS
GREENWICH

Dom Helder Camara

THE CONVERSIONS
OF A BISHOP

☒

an interview with
José de Broucker

Translated by Hilary Davies

Broucker, José de
　Dom Helder Camara, the conversions of a bishop : an interview
with José de Broucker / translated [from the French] by Hilary
Davies. — London [etc.] : Collins, 1979. — [1],222p ; 22cm.
Translation of: 'Dom Helder Camara'. Paris : Éditions du Seuil, 1977.
ISBN 0-00-216460-4 : £4.95
1.Ti 2.Camara, Helder 3.Conversions of a bishop

(B79-17299)

COLLINS

Câmara, Hélder, 1909-
　　The conversions of a bishop : an interview with José de
Broucker / Dom Helder Camara ; translated ₁from the French₁
by Hilary Davies. — London ; Cleveland : Collins, 1979.
　　₁1₁, 222 p. ; 22 cm.　　　　　　　　　　　　GB79-17299
　　Translation of Les conversions d'un évêque.
　　ISBN 0-529-05624-0 (U.S.) : $9.95
　　1. Câmara, Hélder, 1909-　. 2. Catholic Church—Bishops—Biography.
　3. Bishops—Brazil—Biography. I. Broucker, José de. II. title.
　BX4705.C2625A3313　1979　　　　　　　　　78-74858
　　　　　　　　　　　282'.092'4
　　　　　　　　　　　79　　　　　　　　MARC

FIGURE 1.　　Two different bibliographic records were prepared from one of these
title pages: the upper one is from the *British National Bibliography*, the lower from
the *National Union Catalog*.

indication of subject, the three words can therefore easily be considered part of the title.

Both bibliographic records in figure 1 were composed on the basis of the same title page and according to the same cataloguing rules, each by an experienced cataloguer in a national agency where quality control is presumably exercised. How could the two cataloguers interpret the same objective evidence and rules so differently? In the rules followed by both of them, a title is defined as "the name of a work" or, to paraphrase a poet, "A title is a title is a title," which is not a lot of help. The current rules, implemented after the creation of the records shown, define a title proper as "the chief name of an item." This is not much more help but it does recognize the distinction between a work and a document (item). The wording and syntax as presented on the title page being ambiguous, the bibliographer exercises judgement based on context and purpose. The most significant context in which to understand a title is the authorship of the work. The two records show that their choice of different title wording was due to another difference of opinion involving this context, namely who should be considered the *principal* author of the work, since both interviewer and interviewee share authorial responsiblity.

Creating and using bibliographic records effectively therefore depend on good bibliographic judgements on the identification, meaning, and functions of various data elements. In the remainder of this chapter, each element is analyzed in the context of other elements and of its uses in bibliographic control. What a person familiar with basic footnoting practice and library-catalogue searching should already know may have to be reviewed independently because it is taken for granted here. The formal definitions found in current cataloguing rules and glossaries should also be consulted, and for the deepest possible understanding, the following analyses should be reinforced by practical experience of how the data elements are used in actual catalogues and bibliographies. The order in which the elements are treated below may seem familiar, but it is not the order generally prescribed for the syntax of a citation: chapter 8 deals with that. Here, the elements are grouped according to their functions.

TITLING

In myths and fables, one has control over what one can name. This is true also of bibliographic identification. The titling of documents by their producers, and the transcribing of those titles by bibliographers, is the basis of all further activity in bibliographic control. A title is the one indispensable data element. It is of greatest value when it most clearly names the document, not its content, in the same way that "John Smith" names a person. There may be more than one John Smith, but nobody who speaks or writes that name is referring to or addressing just *any* John Smith—but a particular one, distinguishable from the others if necessary by the context of the reference. The same is now true of bibliographic titling but it was not always. Those who first referred to Aristotle's work as *Metaphysics* were only saying that this work was written as a kind of sequel to his *Physics*. Even *Physics,* at the time, said no more than that Aristotle was discussing the physical, as distinguished from the spiritual, world. If the word is used today as the title of either the work or of a single document containing it, it is understood to be a title in a formally identifying bibliographic sense, not as a casual reference. Publishers today normally try to avoid titling likely to be used for another publication.

In the manuscript period, a huge library collection might comprise five hundred documents. Each was unique, there being no two identical copies. Nobody could even conceive of a need to apply a formal, uniquely identifying title to each. A printed document exists in many copies and is therefore necessarily an object of trade and distribution. Each copy must bear the same title (and probably other data elements) in order to be identifiable as one of the group of identical copies which together constitute a *publication* or an *edition*. Different publications, like different persons, may bear the same title/name: exclusive use (copyright) cannot be claimed for a title. There are dozens of publications entitled *Principles of Economics* and more than a few of *The Second World War.* However, like a personal name, even John Smith, a bibliographic title is still the data element more likely than any other single element to define a clear and simple distinction both between different publications and between different works.

The most common type of nonfiction title is one whose words designate subject content, as in the examples of the previous paragraph. Titles of creative works tend to name characters, whether human or not (*King Kong*), set a mood (*The Naked and the Dead*), or make an allusion (*The Robe*). The following examples show that a title may also consist of, or include, words designating an author, a publisher, a date, a form, or other information:

> *The Complete Shakespeare*
> *Macmillan Bible Atlas*
> *The 1995 Proceedings of the Conference on Aging*
> *Selected Poems*
> *The Barbara Kraus Calorie Guide*

Since bibliography deals primarily with the physical document and only secondarily with its intellectual content, a bibliographic title is most properly that of a publication, not of the work it embodies. This is a significant distinction because different publications (editions) of the same work often bear different titles, whether in the same language (*The Holy Scriptures; The Bible; The Old and New Testaments*) or almost inevitably so in different languages (*Die Dreigroschenoper; The Threepenny Opera; The Three Penny Opera*—each of which files very differently).

To most end-users, the most important role of a title has nothing to do with the bibliographic one of distinguishing publications (or works) from one another. The title's value to them lies in its designation (or at least implication) of what the work is about: *Classical Japanese Gardens.* To a publisher's sales staff, a title is increasingly an advertising medium. In popular books at least, titling more evocative than informative is common to tickle the interest of members of the target audience and sell the product: *Steal This Book.* Failure to distinguish between the use of a title to identify a document and its use to describe the intellectual content or advertise the merits of a work leads to considerable complication in effective subject analysis, an issue addressed most directly in chapter 7.

A title may be displayed in any of several locations in a document; for example, in the case of a book, its title page, cover, spine, running heads; in the case of a compact-disc sound recording, the disc itself, the paper wrapper inside its plastic container, the inserted booklet of programme notes; in the case of a digital data file, the image it generates on a computer screen, any printed packaging material, or insert. Cataloguing rules define one primary expected location of a title on each different type of document, as discussed in more detail later.

Unfortunately, the care taken by the traditional publisher of printed material to ensure that the words and their order are exactly the same everywhere a title appears is fading into a sloppy lack of attention or, worse, deliberate variation. The dimensions or purpose of the different parts of the document on which titling appears and their utility for advertising purposes are known to affect the choice of wording on that location. As different editors and art directors are given charge over various parts of a publication, coordination among them seems no longer to be an overriding concern when their judgement on effective title wording differs. This situation appears particularly among nonprint items consisting of more than one physical piece because the whole may actually be a compilation of previously existing parts, each retaining its own original titling. For example, the box container of a particular educational kit bears the title *Regional Geography of Canada, an Economic and Urban Study* while the guide accompanying the filmstrip inside bears the title *Geography of Canada, a Regional Survey.*

For a bibliographic record to have any value in identifying a given publication, *one* title must be chosen for that publication as its principal title, or what cataloguing rules call a *title proper.* Ideally, every cataloguer would choose the same one from among existing variants, usually on the basis of location or typographic prominence. In reality, alas, this is not always the case, as figure 1 and its accompanying discussion show. Even if all cataloguers agree on the same title, different users may remember and search any wording any of them has seen on any part of the item. Recognizing this, library cataloguers include all title variants in their bibliographic record, but this is rarely done in simpler records, such as footnote citations.

Where a title *ends* may be a matter of concern, for example, when creating a title index. How many users are unable to find the magazine *Time* in a library's catalogue because its full title, *Time, the Weekly Newsmagazine,* appears in the file after the title *The Time of Your Life?* How many are puzzled when the computer displays records for two or three books with the one-word title *Time* but not the magazine—and nothing else, because the program is not "browsing"? A title is a grammatical unit; if it can be separated into parts, the first is the title proper and the remainder, including anything once called a subtitle, is now called *other title information.* To pursue the example, does the magazine have a one-word title proper or a four-word title proper? In the following example, there is less doubt that three separable units are present: *Nuclear Plant Emergency Plans, an Administrative Response to the Alarm Bell, a Selected Bibliography.*

When two or more works are published within one document, a *collective title* is usually applied to the latter if it is a print anthology of pre-existing works and invariably if it is an edited collection of scholarly papers, a conference proceedings, or a journal. None of the titles *The Wasteland and Other Poems, Ten Classic Tales of Mystery,* or *National Geographic Magazine,* even the first, merely identifies a single work. (See the section below, "Contents," for further implications of collective titles.) In figure 2, both a collective title of a publication *and* the titles of the individual works contained in it appear on its title page.

Figure 3 shows cases from two different media where collective titling is either absent or ambiguous. The title page lacks a collective title, so the words constituting the titles and naming the authors of the individual works, in the order presented, must together serve as the title of the publication.

Both the physical medium and the involvement of performers complicate the isolation of title wording in a sound recording. Not to provide a collective title is unusual among publishers of printed books, but is quite common among those of sound recordings. The label on each

---

MODERN PLAYS

MILESTONES
Arnold Bennett & Edward Knoblock

THE DOVER ROAD · *A. A. Milne*

HAY FEVER · *Noel Coward*

JOURNEY'S END · *R. C. Sherriff*

FOR SERVICES RENDERED
W. Somerset Maugham

INTRODUCTION BY
JOHN HADFIELD

LONDON J. M. DENT & SONS LTD

FIGURE 2.   A title page bearing both a collective title and the titles of the independent works contained in the book.

face of a two-sided disc containing more than one work typically names only what is recorded on that face. The compact disc shown in figure 3 may have only one label, but the nature of its elements is not immediately evident. Printed material in its case identifies "Pilz" as the publisher, but one has to go further afield to determine that "East German Revolution" is the title of a *series* of discs rather than of this disc uniquely (see the section on relationships, below). Three works are recorded, one each by Haydn, Mozart, and Schubert, the performers being two radio orchestras, the Rundfunk-Sinfonieorchester Berlin and the Rundfunk-Sinfonieorchester Leipzig (their specific identities and official names given in accompanying printed material). Should the cataloguer accept the words "East German Radio Symphony Orchestras" as a collective title for the disc or should the disc be treated as having no collective title because these words merely name the performers? In the latter case, the three words naming the composers must stand as the disc title. In another bibliographically prominent location, the information given within quotation marks just above

FIGURE 3. The label on a compact-disc sound recording and the title page of a book, each containing more than one independent work but no clearly evident collective title.

reads (in English) "Berlin & Leipzig Radio Symphony Orchestras." Does this affect the decision? This case may support the argument for making three separate records—one for each work—rather than a single one for the publication, a practice once common in the cataloguing of sound recordings (see pages 345–46).

The title page of another anthology is shown in figure 4. The title proper is normally expected to appear at the top of the title page of a printed book, but placing an author's name before it is a well-known variation. James Russell Lowell is clearly named as the author whose selections (of what?) comprise the majority of the book. To say that the book's title is *Representative Selections . . .* is therefore reasonable. The single word "Lowell" is stamped on the front cover and the spine reads "Lowell * Clark and Foerster". The majority of undergraduates who need to make a footnote reference to this book would show

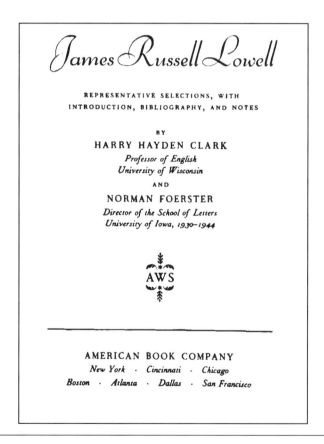

FIGURE 4.   A title page whose typographic layout invites the use of the author's name as the title proper.

Clark as its principal author and *James Russell Lowell* as the title without recognizing the resulting implication that they are citing a biography of Lowell. Every cataloguer would show Lowell as the author; most would transcribe the title as *James Russell Lowell: Representative Selections* more because of the layout of the title page than because of the sequence of its words. These judgements should be compared with those of the two cataloguers who interpreted the similar wording on the Camara book shown in figure 1. Recognition of a title is a matter of linguistic interpretation in the light of knowledge of both publication practices and searchers' retrieval habits.

The presence of a title in more than one language on the same title page, cover, etc. is illustrated in relation to a serial in figure 6, below. It is also common among monographs containing text in more than one language or the text of a literary translation. Cataloguers call a second or later title in a different language from the first a *parallel title*. Those who cite such a document in a footnote are all too prone to ignore all but the first title; admittedly, there can be many in a multinational publication. At least this is an objectively predictable practice and therefore far better than to transcribe only the title in the language most familiar to the person doing the citing. This latter practice results in different citations bearing different titles for the same document: true bibliographic confusion.

The issue of multiple-language titling on the same title page (or other single source) differs from that of a single physical item bearing more than one title page, each in a different language. This typical pattern of the multilingual dictionary is also very common among government publications in a bilingual country like Canada. Sometimes the different-language parts are inverted in relation to each other within the same binding in the so-called tête-bêche format. In these cases, a library in a unilingual setting is likely simply to ignore the existence of the part (and title page) in the nonpreferred language; in the national bibliography, the document may be treated as if it were two separate publications, one in each language, with a linkage between the two resulting records.

Fashions in titles, as in everything else, go through cycles. In one period, publishers tend to apply lengthy titles; in another, brief ones. In nonfiction (particularly monographs in the humanities and the social sciences), there are cycles of preference for explicit titling versus the use of allusion, the latter a little more likely in trade publications than in scholarly ones. It seems currently fashionable to use other title information, which includes any subtitle, to explain something alluded to obliquely in the title proper. The contemporary English-language trade book rarely has more than four or five words in its titling which convey any substantive meaning directly.

Titles of articles in academic journals, particularly in science and technology, typically include many concrete substantive words—among them words denoting a methodological approach—and few allusions. This practice is clearly connected with the long-standing practice among the A&I services of using title words to index the subject content of such articles. Popular journals increasingly follow the newspaper practice of placing at the head of an article a phrase or quotation from the text of the article, to catch the attention of someone scanning the issue, then follow it in slightly different typography with the more serious title. Those who cite the article may unfortunately take this combination to be a title followed by a subtitle.

Although a brief news note, letter to the editor, or review in a journal or newspaper may have an individualizing title by which it can be cited, many others do not. The lack of an explicit title of its own is also common among unique unpublished items such as manuscripts and homemade slide sets, videorecordings, and cassettes which find their way into libraries and archival repositories. Many individual items retrieved when scanning material on the World Wide Web begin "Untitled." People create not only Web compilations but also traditional books by simply piecing together previously published documents, for example, a number of pamphlets, in one binding without any new formal encompassing title page. This practice finds books in libraries for which a cataloguer must compose a title ad hoc in order to list it in a catalogue or footnote. So that such a *supplied title* cannot be mistaken for one transcribed from the document itself, bibliographers long ago adopted the convention of enclosing within square brackets (*not* parentheses!) any data not found on the title page itself.

In some A&I publications, a transliteration (see the end of chapter 9) replaces or is added to a title in a nonroman script. In others, a title not in English may be followed by a supplied translation devised by the indexer. Titles can also be links relating publications and works to one another. In the section below on bibliographic relationships, several more kinds of titles are discussed in this context. All these issues concerning titling are belaboured here at some length because of the critical importance of a title as a document's primary and surest identifier whether on a title page for inclusion in a library catalogue or on a subject line for access by an Internet search engine.

Titles of Serials

A serial (magazine, journal, periodical, etc.) is a publication issued in successive parts and intended to be continued indefinitely. Each article in each issue has its own title, but if one whole issue comprises a number of articles with a single thematic focus, it may also be given a distinctive title, making it quite likely that some users will cite it in a footnote as if it were a separate publication and not just one regular issue of a serial with different titling. There are publishers who apply such single-issue titles for the purpose of advertising and selling each separate issue also as a monograph. Fewer serials than monographs are given a subtitle, but if one exists it is so common for it to be changed frequently that cataloguing rules have always discounted its importance in identification and many brief listings ignore it.

It is the title proper applicable to the run of the serial as a whole which a serials librarian uses to keep track of issues received, subscriptions paid, etc. It is the title by which an A&I service links each indexed article-citation to the journal in which the article appears. It is the one to which each library attaches a record of its holdings in a union list of serials. It should be clear, stable, unambiguous, and as distinctive as possible in view of the high volume of items of a serial nature that come into any library daily.

Many serial titles have none of these good features. Most of the problems they present to the bibliographer stem from two facts. First, the title of a serial is printed on each separate issue produced over a long period of time under the control of a succession of editors and designers. Hence the title is subject to change in major and minor ways from time to time. Its subscribers consider it to be the same journal throughout, but those who search for only one issue or cite an article in it are naturally going to use the titling on that issue without inquiring into the existence of different titles on earlier or later issues. The second troublesome characteristic of serial titling is that far more often than in the case of monographs, totally different serials bear the same (or almost the same) title, vitiating the important function of a title as a means of distinguishing one publication from another.

The latter is a particularly insidious problem. Several monographs are entitled simply *The Second World War* (among them, those of Sir Winston Churchill, Tim Healey, and Charles Messenger), but anyone would cite any of these using both its author *and* its title, so distinguishing them is almost automatic. Among serials, there are thousands whose titles consist of the two words *Annual Report*. Once again, no person citing any one of them would fail to indicate which body's annual report is meant, but as shown in chapter 6, locating the name of a body in an alphabetic file can be much more problematic than locating that of a person. The most troublesome serial titling is not immediately associated with a known person or body. For example, there are dozens of serials entitled *Dialogue,* but while a few of these may be clearly associated with societies or institutions, most are known to their casual users only by that title. These titles require some other data element to distinguish them; no obvious one comes immediately to mind.

Title display on the cover of a serial issue now often seems to be under the control of the graphic artist—someone not generally noted for bibliographic expertise—rather than the editor. It is often deliberately ambiguous. Experienced cataloguers may well disagree on what constitutes the title proper of the two earlier versions of the serial illustrated in figure 5, at least until they read the publication statements transcribed in the caption. Bilingual and multilingual serials exist in

THE BRITISH LIBRARY   BIBLIOGRAPHIC SERVICES

NO. 49 JUNE 1989
ISSN 0268-9707

Newsletter

■■■*SELECT*■■■   NATIONAL BIBLIOGRAPHIC SERVICE

NO. 1 JUNE/JULY 1990
ISSN 0960-1570

Newsletter

THE BRITISH LIBRARY

winter 96
issue 18

s e l e c t

ISSN 0960-1570   the newsletter of the National Bibliographic Service

FIGURE 5.   The publication statement in the June 1989 issue reads "The British Library Bibliographic Services Newsletter is published by the British Library." The publication statement in the June/July 1990 issue reads "Select is published by the British Library." The change of numbering and of the ISSN are also indications of an intended title change, so despite the prominence of *Newsletter* on both, that seems not to be the intended one-word title proper of either issue. In the masthead redesign for the winter [19]96 issue, graphic reality was brought into conformity with the bibliographic reality of the previous six years: while the look is radically different, the one-word title proper *Select,* the numbering sequence, and the ISSN remain as in 1990. The significant words of the other title information also remain but in a changed order; the dating sequence is also different, now specifying season rather than month. The publication statement reads "*Select* is the newsletter of the British Library National Bibliographic Service."

increasing numbers worldwide. The problem illustrated in the top two parts of figure 6 is also found among monographs whose titling and content are in more than one language, as already discussed. Figure 6 also shows the need to inform a user about the various successive titles adopted for a serial publication throughout its life.

In one's own field of study or interest, the same few serial titles are encountered over a long period of time and become very familiar. It is natural to start abbreviating them instead of using the full title every time. This has led to attempts to standardize a unique brief titling for each serial, especially in scientific fields. Covers of the issues of many journals still bear a mnemonic abbreviation as a suggested *citation title,* for example, *Int.j.cir.theor.appl.* for the *International Journal of Circuit Theory and Applications.* In the 1950s, a central agency (later the Chemical Abstracts Service) began to assign a unique designation called a *coden* to each different serial whose publisher would accept and promote it. At first this consisted of four characters taken from

CANADIAN LIBRARY ASSOCIATION
ASSOCIATION CANADIENNE DES BIBLIOTHEQUES

B U L L E T I N

Canadian
library   association bulletin
bulletin de l'association   canadienne des bibliothèques

C A N A D I A N
L I B R A R Y
ASSOCIATION   BULLETIN

CANADIAN LIBRARY

CANADIAN LIBRARY
JOURNAL

Canadian
Library
Journal

FIGURE 6.   Successive titles of the now-defunct journal of the Canadian Library Association, whose numbering continued in an unbroken sequence from the first title shown above to the last. The top two versions of the titling are in two languages; in the top three versions, there is a further question of whether the title does or does not include the name of the association.

the title, but four soon proved insufficient to distinguish the number of journals that joined the programme, so a coden now consists of six characters, the last two not necessarily derived from the title, for example, ICTACV for the journal named above. Coden designations never spread much outside the scientific community and were overtaken, if not entirely replaced, after 1970 when ISDS, the International Serials Data System, began its master file of so-called key-titles. A *key-title* is unique to one serial title and is exactly matched by the unique International Standard Serial Number (ISSN) assigned by a national agency to that serial title.[1]

This summary describes a generation of attempts to standardize abbreviated or codified titling for serials to be used in footnotes, A&I services, etc. As a rather confusing result, the same serial issue may bear a bibliographic title or title proper, a coden, an ISSN with its key-title, and a suggested citation title! Whether this simplifies or complicates the bibliographic control of serial publications may depend on one's point of view. Finally, each A&I service originally adopted its own abbreviation for the journals it indexed. Internally, these were always clearly keyed to the full titles, but when the products of different A&I services came to be combined in the same digital database, the lack of standardization of a title in abbreviated form caused serious problems for searchers.

RESPONSIBILITY FOR INTELLECTUAL CONTENT

In a simpler era, the typical book claimed to be the product of one personal author—occasionally two or three, working in collaboration. This was almost never entirely true and it is rarely the case now. Until very recently, however, the name(s) of only the primary author(s) appeared on the title leaf, recto or verso. Others personally or corporately involved in the intellectual content were discreetly thanked within the prose of a preface or a statement of acknowledgements.

Now, persons involved in even the slightest way are more likely to demand bibliographically prominent recognition in a separate line somewhere on the title leaf, not merely in a thank-you, however fulsome, in prose, and corporate funders ask to have their logos prominently displayed. With academic careers so dependent on recognition of published work and grants more dependent on recognition given to the granting agency, it is no surprise that even some supervisor who has never seen a work prior to publication can demand explicit attribution of a share in its authorship in a form which will be picked up in citation indexing.

An ever higher proportion of works are the intellectual product of acknowledged combinations of persons interacting in various ways, whether as individuals or as members of corporate bodies (committees, institutions, government agencies, etc.). A corporate body—a group of persons acting as a unit under a collective name—is unquestionably the author of such things as its own annual report, even if a particular person(s) had to write the actual words. The statement that a book is "by the editors of Sunset Books and *Sunset Magazine*" identifies no individual who actually composed the words, selected the pictures, etc. Nor does it imply that the corporate publisher takes collective intellectual or legal responsibility for the book's content. However, the statement is far from meaningless: it is a statement of relationship as much as of authorship. To anyone likely to be at all interested in the book, it says that the collective point of view embodied in *Sunset Magazine* is also to be found in this book. Corporate responsibility is often much less clear. One is left in some doubt about the nature and extent of corporate control exercised over the content of the publications whose title pages read as follows; examination of prefatory matter or the text of the item may or may not lead to firmer conclusions.

> *A College in the City: an Alternative.* "a report from Educational Facilities Laboratories. . . . The primary author . . . was Evans Clinchy"

> *The City Fights Back, a Nation-Wide Survey. . . ,* "narrated and edited by Hal Burton from material developed by the Central Business District Council of the Urban Land Institute."

A person designated as an *editor* or a *compiler* may perform any one or more of the following functions:

1) cause a work to come into existence by conceiving its scope, general focus, and arrangement; then convincing others to do the actual writing
2) reconstruct a deceased author's intended text by examining existing editions, manuscripts, and other evidence
3) add critical apparatus (commentary, glosses, footnotes, bibliography, etc.) to an existing work by someone else
4) abridge, revise, paraphrase, bowdlerize, or otherwise modify an existing work by someone else
5) select for inclusion in a new publication material which was created for earlier publication (perhaps orally, as at a conference) by one or by many persons or bodies
6) collaborate with an author in putting the latter's ideas into acceptable verbal or visual form for publication (this activity is

snidely called *ghost writing* or *substantive editing* when it is
done without acknowledgement by a freelance writer rather
than openly under contract or by a member of the publisher's
editorial staff) or

7) go over a writer's work to ensure consistency and correctness
of style, punctuation, orthography, etc., but without authority to make substantial changes (this is called *copy-editing*,
considered an essentially clerical task, and often not formally
acknowledged).

Editing is usually understood to imply more intellectual involvement with the content of a publication than compiling, yet a bibliography is often said to be "compiled" even though every citation in
it is originally written solely by the bibliographer. Cataloguing rules
no longer make the fine distinctions among at least the first five of the
above functions that some older rules did. Distinguishing them from
active authorship in the purest sense is also less easy now that a publisher can sometimes be persuaded to omit the incriminating words
that indicate a lower level of intellectual activity (*compiled by; editor*).
Still, the personal name(s) have always featured prominently both in
the publication and in the bibliographic record at least in the first five
functions and often in the sixth.

A sound recording, motion picture, videorecording, etc. reproduces
a single performance in addition to displaying the work performed—
usually a performance by person(s) other than the work's original cre-
ator(s). Some art forms emphasize the distinction between creator and
performer: a twentieth-century choir sings madrigals by a seventeenth-
century composer. Other forms blur the distinction: a performance
by an avant-garde theatre cooperative *is* the collective creation of the
play. Co-equal with the original creator or not, the performer at least
undertakes functions similar to most types of editing itemized above
and therefore warrants bibliographic recognition in the resulting document. A sufficiently idiosyncratic performance of a piece of popular
music is now readily accepted as a substantially new work.

"Coffee-table" books have always owed much of their success to
photographers, designers, and layout artists. Research assistants, copy
editors, and proofreaders are the heroes of most reference books. Dust-
jacket illustrators are responsible for the sales of many hard-cover novels. All are creative people. All expect more recognition than in days of
demure intellectual modesty. The recto and verso of many a modern
title leaf begin to look like rolling screens of motion-picture credits. It
probably matters little whether even the printer's manager in charge
of colour-separation quality or the audio engineer of a videorecording
is named in the document itself, but how much space need be de-

voted in the bibliographic record and/or its indices to these names and functions?

The expression of the above facts concerning the intellectual origin of the work appearing on a title page, disc label, first-screen display of a computer file, etc. (that is, in a bibliographically significant location on the document) constitutes the *statement(s) of responsibility*, which according to every cataloguing code must be transcribed at least in part into the document's bibliographic record. If the statement is vague or ambiguous, the bibliographer interprets its meaning and may add a note of explanation.

Responsibility for the most basic function(s) of creation is considered so important that it is always recorded when known, even if not mentioned in the document itself (for example, in the case of an anonymous or pseudonymous work). Conversely, in an attempt to keep the length of bibliographic records manageable (a more important consideration when a record ideally occupied one small and perhaps handwritten card) library cataloguing rules have traditionally required mention of only up to three different contributors per function. If four or more are involved in the statement of responsibility, only the first is transcribed into the record. Although totally arbitrary, this "rule-of-three" has been retained in this and a number of other cataloguing practices well into the computer era when record length is a relatively unimportant factor.

What additional names or functions warrant recording depends on characteristics of the works described and on the purposes and users of the type of listing. A citation index published in part for the use of promotion-and-tenure committees lists each of fifteen authors of a five-page article on psychology. Typically of performance media, it would be unreasonable to name only the first (or even the first three) soloists in an opera recording. It is the norm in scholarly and technical publication to name in the book or article not only every author but also every author's affiliation: university, company, laboratory, etc. This essentially temporary information (even tenured academics change jobs) has traditionally been ignored in transcribing statements of responsibility into library catalogues. Yet to reveal what publications derive from work done in a particular academic department or laboratory is a legitimate purpose of other bibliographic tools which not only record, but also index, the corporate affiliations of authors.

An index of "authors" typically includes names of persons and corporate bodies acting in any capacity mentioned above, and others not mentioned. Whether in a manual or an automated system, nothing is accessible, or searchable, unless it has been included in the record or database. In manual systems, however, establishing access points (index entries) was a separate consideration and process. Naming a

person or body within a bibliographic record did not automatically
mean the name also had to be searchable in the index. Now that
computer programs are routinely used to search for *any* significant
word or term occurring in most parts of a record, mere inclusion of
a name itself means access to that name in any system based on the
use of such programs. Implications of this are the focus of chapter 3
and the last section of this one.

PUBLICATION, DISTRIBUTION, AND MANUFACTURING DATA

An *imprint* originally named the place, printer, and date of printing.
The very word betrays its origin in the Gutenberg technology. These
facts were originally printed on the final, not the first, page (as a
colophon, a tail) when the printer completed production, in imitation
of the practice of the earlier writers of manuscripts. Publication and
bookselling functions separated from printing by the eighteenth century, making the printer's name useless to indicate a source for acquiring the book. With that separation, it was the publisher who
wished to display a corporate identity for product identification and
whose name therefore replaced that of the printer in the imprint. The
imprint also assumed a place of greater prominence at the foot of the
title page. The publisher's name and logo, now often divorced from
place and date, are displayed even more prominently on the outer
packaging of items in newer media. Meanwhile, the name of the
printer or other manufacturer may now appear in a colophon, on the
title-leaf verso, or not at all. Even when known, it is ignored in all but
the most detailed bibliographic description except when the publisher is not named and cannot readily be deduced.

After many centuries, it is once again more difficult to distinguish
publishing from manufacturing functions, even in the print media.
Firms exist to make, on demand, single-copy microform or hard-copy
photographic reproductions virtually indistinguishable from the
original of documents no longer available directly from the originating publisher (*out-of-print* is the term used in the book trade). In
some citation practices, the reproducing agent is recorded as the publisher of the reproduction; in others, it is considered merely the
manufacturer of an additional copy of an existing item and ignored in
the citation. Reprint publishers also make reproductions of out-of-
print items but do so as commercial editions.

Desktop-printing techniques now foster the rapid growth of on-
demand publishing, not merely on-demand distribution of previously
published work. The Internet provides the technology for doing such

publishing directly in digital form, so that if the document achieves a physical presence in the traditional sense, that presence is caused by the end-user, not the original publisher or an intermediate manufacturer.

Who produces the physical document is now of little significance. Manufacturers do not influence intellectual content and usually ship only to publishers. But knowing where and by whom it is published helps one characterize the content (the work), distinguish it from other versions of the work, and (at least initially) identify where a copy can be acquired.

Despite the existence of many multinational houses, publishing as a cultural activity still largely reflects particular places and societies. Identifying the place alerts a reference librarian or selector to a possible national or regional emphasis. The publisher's name may also guarantee quality standards (or warn of a lack thereof) and indicate a point of view or emphasis on a subject specialty. Publication information is permanently useful for such purposes. A short form of a major publisher's corporate name is enough to ensure easy location of any of its offices in a directory, but publishing is a very fragmented industry including many small firms with short lifespans—properly so in a democracy where every opinion deserves a platform. Even a street address can therefore sometimes be useful in a citation to help track down a source.

When bookselling activities separated from publishing, any bookseller retailed the products of any publisher but the publisher still handled stock distribution in addition to the intellectual functions of shaping the work as editor, financier, and director of production. Now, all but the largest publishers in every medium are likely to contract out warehousing, stock control, wholesaling, shipping, and invoicing to a *distributor* who supplies the products of the many publishers it represents to libraries, bookstores, and other nonretail buyers. If a distributor is named in the item, this information is useful in any citation intended as an aid to acquiring it. Contractual arrangements for distribution outside a publisher's own country are notoriously unstable, so Canadian cataloguers tend not to include the name of a Canadian distributor in the record for an imported publication even when it appears prominently in the document.

Despite the activity of many multinational firms and a particularly strong presence of United States firms in the Canadian trade, publishing and the distribution of intellectual products are generally treated as cultural industries and therefore nationally based and to a degree protected from excessive foreign competition. They are not immune, however, to the effects of globalization and efficiencies of scale as all communication industries increasingly share common technology and even ownership.

Fifty years ago, any but the most esoteric book published in both the United Kingdom and the United States would be set in type separately in the two countries with consequent differences in spelling, vocabulary, style, the units of measurement referred to, and of course the publisher's name and location. Citations would be different, but the fact that the two editions contained the same work was usually clearly enough indicated by details such as the same title.

Today, it is more likely that a document in any medium is produced in only one place for sale worldwide, using different local publishers or distributors under license. This can mean that more than one publisher is named in every copy, with the likely result that a Briton cites it naming only its British publisher while an American cites an identical copy naming only the American one. This may seem harmless, or even useful in indicating where to acquire it in one's own country, but it can mislead a searcher into thinking there are two editions different in some significant respect. It avoids confusion, therefore, if a citation always indicates at least the first-named publisher.

When copies are separately manufactured in each country or region under license, using printing plates, record matrices, or computer files supplied by the originating publisher, each local publisher is more likely to display only its name prominently on an individualized title page or packaging material. The difference in the imprint causes different citations to be made for what, except for that imprint, are identical copies. This does not bother anyone who never sees but one version, which is usual. However, any library that buys from many sources outside as well as within its country (common practice among academic libraries anywhere) may receive the same item under more than one imprint, particularly if other details also vary.

Sound recordings with their multilingual booklets are a particular problem. In such a case, a cataloguer may choose to ignore principle in favour of economy and not create separate bibliographic records even if significant bibliographic details vary. Treating the one received later as merely a copy of the one received first is cheaper. In view of the complexity of modern multinational publication and distribution practices, statements appearing in a document are to be interpreted, not merely transcribed, so that enough but not excessive information is incorporated into the bibliographic record.

Date

Five different kinds of dating are pertinent to works and publications. These are usually expressed in a citation only as a year, but the significance of the month and day information is created, officially released, or made effective is of increasing importance. For example, a radio bulletin announces that some medical discovery is "to be published in tomorrow's issue of *The Lancet*." With computer files subject to change in fractions of a second, one may expect even more precise chronology in their descriptions.

1) Publication occurs when copies realized from a given set of printing plates, magnetic signals, photographic negatives, etc. are *first* released for distribution by the publisher named in the publication data. The year of this occurrence is the date considered of greatest value in the bibliographic record: it, or a cataloguer's guess at it, is required by current library cataloguing rules.

2) Manufacturing pertains to the object in hand. Dating this act states when the type image was actually inked and transferred to the paper of the copy in hand, the pitted-plastic-and-aluminum compact disk was fused together, the magnetic charges were fixed on the tape's oxide coating, etc. A publisher orders the manufacture of additional identical copies of a document in batches from time to time for as long as it sees continuing demand. The date when any one particular copy was made is only considered significant in the case of some old rare books, or when this date but no publication date is known, or when "copies" manufactured later differ in some notable way from the first batch.

3) The copyright date designates the year when claim is laid to legal ownership of some aspect of the content as intellectual property, of the typographic or other format as design, or of the performance.

4) The date of a work's first publication anywhere, not merely in the publication or manufactured item in hand or even in the same language or version, is significant in the study of the work itself rather than its topic; for example, 1741 in the case of Handel's *Messiah*. For any valued work, it is easily found in a retrospective bibliography or a literary reference source and is therefore not often included.

5) Publication marks the birth of a document, but the work it embodies had a shorter or longer embryonic or pre-natal existence before that. The author-in-a-hurry revises last drafts almost until the pagemaker program assembles the visual image for its first laser-printed proofs. At the other extreme, works have lain complete for centuries before being discovered (or their value recognized) and published. Keeping track to the day of pre-natal stages of a scholarly article is now routine: "Manuscript received [date]; revised draft received [date]; accepted for publication [date]." No citation or cataloguing rule yet requires this information in a bibliographic

record, but one may predict its utility in recording the existence of constantly changing digital documents.

The first two of the above five types of dating relate to documents;
the last three to works. By far the majority of all works are published
and manufactured only once, soon after being completed. It is possible
for a work to undergo all these processes within the same calendar year
and never again thereafter. Such works offer few bibliographic problems
of any kind and certainly none of dating. The small minority of cases
in which some or all these dates differ include anything that could be
called a classic: a work issued, reprinted, translated into other languages
and formats, and edited again and again. *They* are the problematic ones.
So are compilations. An edited symposium, anthology, etc., comprising
different works created or originally published at different times, bears
dates related to the anthology itself and dates for each separate work
within it: sometimes too few dates and sometimes too many.

There is nothing wrong with including more than one of the different kinds of date in the bibliographic record as long as it is clear
which one relates to which function. Cataloguing rules prescribe situations when it is desirable to do so. However, they always give priority to the date of publication as defined above; that is, the date
when the version of the work in hand—the one described in the edition numbering and the publication data—first appeared, not some
other version and not some later reissue from the same source. When
dealing with a pre-nineteenth-century or a particularly rare book, it
is common to try to discover and record the year of its printing. For
newer items, the manufacturing date is considered of little importance unless it must serve as a substitute for an unknown publication
or copyright date. Ignoring it also means that acquisition of a copy
produced later than one already in the collection does not require a
new catalogue record. This may seem inconsistent with the practice
noted earlier of making separate records when only the publisher's
name differs, but a different publisher's name is a more likely clue
than a different manufacturing date to a possible change in content.

Copyright is a complex issue of ever changing national laws and
international agreements in which the statement of claim printed in
a document is of relatively little significance either legally or bibliographically. For example, in the United States prior to 1978, two
copyright dates twenty-eight years apart indicate no more than a re-
newal of the original legal claim without any change in the document's content. The absence of a copyright claim in a work prior to
the mid-1950s is of no significance, because, prior to their adherence
to the Universal Copyright Convention, most of the world's developed countries (but not the United States) recognized ownership of

intellectual property without requiring any formal statement in the publication. In the United States, however, a copyright date has appeared in publications as a requirement for their legal protection for over a century.

Since a copyright claim dates intellectual content more certainly than does a publication date, North American cataloguing practice has been to give both years in the record if they differ significantly and to use the year of copyright as a preferred substitute if no publication date is known. Thus if a 1995 reprint bears a 1910 copyright date, both years are recorded and the informed user knows that the content is old.

Terms of Availability

Data relating to price, conditions of sale or distribution, etc. are valid only in the short term. They are based on the fiction of a fixed retail price and stable marketing conditions and can take no account of special sales or discounts or of changed distribution arrangements. However, some such information can help in selecting and acquiring newly published items. Therefore national and trade bibliographies tend to include such data but not library catalogues or retrospective listings. The constantly changing price of a serial publication is likely to be found only in its own issues and advertisements.

PHYSICAL CHARACTERISTICS

The count and description of the material pieces of which a document consists are the very basis of bibliography as the study of the document-as-physical-object. The amount of such detail it is desirable to ascertain and record varies greatly. Because it has so little to do with the document's intellectual content, the average footnote or basic A&I citation contains little or no data of this kind. A library catalogue usually contains a small amount for pragmatic purposes such as signalling an item of unusual dimensions in separate shelving or alerting the lazy user to which book on the topic has the fewest pages. At the other extreme, a bibliographic record intended to help distinguish from each other two copies in variant states of the same edition of a Restoration drama must include an extremely detailed physical description. Valuable items and those whose authenticity has been questioned are also subjected to detailed analysis of physical components using methods of chemistry, spectroscopy, etc. Finally, physical analysis provides information for the practical needs of conserving collections and restoring damaged items.

Whether a document is in words only or has nonverbal (pictorial) material characterizes its intellectual content and is generally considered significant. For want of a better place to record it, this information is usually treated in the same part of the record as physical characteristics.

The basic physical characteristics of a document are its medium (paper, acetate, etc.), the type and number of its units (pages, frames, reels, disks, etc.), the method by which they are assembled (binding, container, etc.), and dimensions.

Because the unaided human eye cannot discern the image or content on them, or perhaps just because they are less familiar, newer media seem more technically complex than paper-and-ink media and are therefore described in greater detail. The following can all be significant details: the type of magnetic coating on a strip of plastic, the density of the image electronically produced from a videorecording, the transfer process of the emulsion on a piece of photographic film, the maximum number of bytes that can be stored on a disk. Digital documents offer the greatest challenge because the relationship between content and physical format is more tenuous and changeable in this medium than in any other.

A sighted human reads a type image on paper with more or less equal ease regardless of the colour or density of the paper, the height or covering material of the book, etc. In almost every other medium, the user must have equipment (hardware), whether mechanical, electrical, or electronic, just to gain access to the content. Hardware is much less forgiving than the human eye; without an exact match between equipment and document, both remain useless. Most media other than writing and print are still so new that the trial-and-error period of experimental equipment and formats has not ended and true standards are elusive. In a home, there may no longer be any sound recordings other than those on compact discs. A library, and even more so an archival repository, may hold sound recordings in many obsolete and new formats. Technical characteristics affecting access must be noted in their bibliographic records, for example, the turntable speed and cartridge or stylus type needed to play a vinyl recording or the amount of random-access memory needed to process a computer file.

AN ITEM'S RELATIONSHIPS
WITH OTHER ITEMS

A citation presented to the reference or interlibrary-loan librarian is likely to describe only one publication and not related ones. One cannot always expect the user to understand how a publication described in isolation in a footnote may have a complex relationship with other publications or if so, why it matters. To describe an item in terms expressing its relationships is essential to the most efficient use of bibliographic data. Even if the library does not own the exact publication the user has seen cited, it may be able to supply what that user needs in a different edition or format which the experienced searcher or librarian can recognize as relevant from its description. The detail involved in describing bibliographic relationships is what most often causes users to complain about the obscurantism of a library catalogue, but statements which seem unnecessary or ambiguous to the casual user are not trivia to the experienced searcher. Each user is likely searching for an item under only one of its possible aspects.

Information detailing how one document or the work it embodies is related to other documents or works can be quite extensive. Describing useful relationships, both bibliographic and intellectual, involves the most complex and time-consuming work in bibliographic control. It begins with the need to ascertain facts not always evident or even presented within the related documents themselves. As in any detective work, the skill lies not so much in locating the required information as in knowing what to look for. Once the relevant facts are discovered, prior knowledge of possible relationships is usually needed to interpret their significance. When a publication first appears, it is rarely possible to know how it might relate to future publications, so when a related one arrives, it may be necessary to reassess the first one and change its record. Significant types of relationship include the following:

1) Only physical characteristics may differ; for example,
   a) the same content is issued on paper, microfilm, or as digital data
   b) a book is issued with a hard cover, paper cover, or library binding.
2) Other aspects of the bibliographic identity may differ, although the intellectual content remains essentially the same; for example,
   a) the same content is published under different titles
   b) the same digital database is published for searching under different database management systems
   c) the same content is republished later by a different publisher
   d) items which originated independently are later issued together as a new unit; for example, a previously published sound recording accompanies a book on music in a pocket attached to the inner rear cover; ten original Civil War pamphlets are now bound into one book for a collector.

3) The intellectual content of the related documents may differ; for example,
   a) different editions of the same work exist involving revision of text, addition of prefatory or supplementary material, illustrations, colour versus black-and-white reproduction, etc.
   b) publications exist containing some of the same content in common but also some which varies from one to the other (for example, many anthologies or reprint editions containing new material)
   c) different publications are issued in the same series
   d) different publications exist, one being a sequel to another (as in novels based on the same characters), a supplement to another (as in a Christmas supplement to a magazine), or a continuation of another (as when a serial changes its title).

These conditions are not all mutually exclusive: many permutations occur in reality. Publishers are devilishly inventive.

Librarians attempt to inform users about the intellectual content of publications, not merely about their physical manifestation, so they undertake to analyze and describe bibliographic relationships—but to a limited degree. Only a rare-book cataloguer is likely ever to engage in original investigation into textual variations among states and issues of the same "edition." Others merely copy what relevant information can be easily uncovered in existing sources, often those within the item being catalogued. The more complex relationships are topics for lengthy investigation, usually by a subject-area specialist rather than a bibliographer. One consults a study in comparative literature, not a bibliography, to discover the chronology of, and links among, the various Tristan legends. Yet to trace the successive texts is basically bibliographic work, whether its results are a thick volume of scholarly prose on Tristan or a few words sketched on the catalogue record for each link. It always takes skill to state relationships succinctly, unambiguously, and intelligibly.

The most common, easy-to-express, and important bibliographic relationships, those stated in most citations and catalogue records, are normally revealed within the document itself. They are the relationships among:

1) editions of the same work
2) sequels, continuations, etc.
3) items both physically and bibliographically separate from one another but issued and intended to be used together
4) important separately identifiable works contained within one publication and
5) items in the same series.

Cataloguing codes and style manuals vary from one another more in how they treat bibliographic relationships than in other matters. Simpler style manuals tend simply to ignore all but the edition and series relationships. Common to all, however, is the fact that every relationship involves two or more bibliographic entities. To say that a publication is a third edition implies that it was preceded by both first and second editions. To say that a booklet on growing cacti is part of *The Sunset Gardening Series* is to visualize a number of uniformly designed pamphlets of which others are likely to be on topics such as growing shrubs, water plants, etc. Whether or not the library owns, or the cataloguer has ever seen, those other publications is immaterial; their existence is evident, and significant facts about them are known, from the description of the one in hand.

To put it another way, each entity in a bibliographic relationship is the basis for a record which describes it fully but also briefly describes the other related item(s). Thus the typical series statement and the typical contents note on a catalogue record consist of little more than a title and perhaps an author's name of the "related" item. That item may or may not rate its own record in the catalogue, one in which *it* is fully described while the other item in the relationship is reduced to a brief mention. Comments on each of the five most common types of bibliographic relationship enumerated above follow. Techniques for showing the more complex of them in current library cataloguing practice are discussed in greater detail at the end of chapter 8.

Edition

This term probably has a larger number of significantly different and potentially confusing uses than any other technical term in bibliography. It is also misused more than most. An edition is most succinctly defined as the total number of copies of a publication produced from the same master copy by the same publisher. When the author changes the intellectual content of a work of nonfiction, and the publisher agrees to begin the editorial/publication process again, a new print version is called a *revised* (corrected, new, enlarged, etc.) *edition* or is given a higher number in sequence, for example, "sixth edition." In the case of a computer program and generally also of digital databases, it is called a new *version* and bears a number designation one integer higher than the previous version. When more copies are produced without significant change or with only a few typographic errors corrected, the print format is called a new *impression;* minor change in a computer program calls for the addition of a decimal number (for example, "version 2.4").

These are conventions of the honest publisher; they are not legally enforceable. Unscrupulous publishers in any medium have always represented to gullible buyers that the product is improved when it actually has not been. Early in this century, even very respectable publishers were casual about the distinction. A claim to have produced two "editions" of a work in successive years is highly suspect; usually the second turns out to be only a larger printing, with typographic errors corrected, following positive reviews and a sell-out of the first tentative small print run.

The cataloguer neither can nor should attempt to count the quantity or judge the significance of changes between editions; that is the job of the reviewer or critic. One wishes every author or publisher would state how the intellectual content differs in any new edition. To do so as concisely as is illustrated in figure 7 is commendable. The reader usually has to read pages of prefatory material to get less information.

Creative, as distinguished from informational, works are also revised. Few, however, are updated in the sense that a work such as this one must be, alas, every few years; edition numbering is therefore rare in works of fiction, drama, music, etc. Rather, one speaks of, say, the Opera house version of Leonard Bernstein's *Candide*. The Bantam edition of *Bleak House,* or the 1923 edition, or the "Limited Edition,"

First Published 2 November 1922
Second Edition October 1937
Third Edition with an Appendix October 1946
Fourth Edition with further Appendix April 1950
Fifth Edition July 1951
Sixth Edition, revised, 1956
Reprinted 1960

This book, originally published in 1922, consisted of the text of Dr. Einstein's Stafford Little Lectures, delivered in May 1921 at Princeton University. For the third edition, Dr. Einstein added an appendix discussing certain advances in the theory of relativity since 1921. To the fourth edition, Dr. Einstein added Appendix II on his Generalized Theory of Gravitation. In the fifth edition the proof in Appendix II was revised.

In the present (sixth) edition Appendix II has been rewritten. This edition and the Princeton University Press fifth edition, revised (1955), are identical.

The text of the first edition was translated by Edwin Plimpton Adams, the first appendix by Ernst G. Straus and the second appendix by Sonja Bargmann.

FIGURE 7.   From the verso of the title leaf of Albert Einstein, *The Meaning of Relativity,* 6th ed., rev. (London: Methuen, 1956).

may all be identical, word for word, their differences being only in paper, typography, binding, price, and perhaps the publisher's name. On the other hand, publishers do hire (often anonymous) editors to tidy up even a classic text. It is less than helpful to know that "not one word of the original has been omitted" if one is not also informed which version of the *work* is so closely copied in the book in hand. The ease with which digital versions of works can be altered gives one even less confidence in the integrity of a text downloaded at any given time.

When editions are numbered or otherwise designated in a sequence, the titling and authorship usually do not change. The third edition of *Basic Programming* by Kemeny and Kurtz can be assumed to follow a first (but probably unnumbered) and a second edition of the same title by the same authors. Three actual examples show that this is not always the case:

1) The eleventh edition of *Guide to Reference Books* is edited by Robert Balay; earlier ones published under the same title were by Eugene Sheehy and Constance Winchell. Still earlier editions, although numbered in the same sequence, were compiled successively by Alice Bertha Kroeger and by Isadore Gilbert Mudge and bore slightly different titles. All editions are by the same publisher.

2) There is an *Introduction to Respiratory Physiology* by Harold A. Braun, Frederick W. Cheney Jr., and C. Paul Loehnen, 2nd ed. (Boston: Little, Brown, 1980), but there was never an earlier edition bearing that title or issued by that publisher. This book's predecessor is *Physiologic Bases for Respiratory Care* by Cheryl E. Beall, Harold A. Braun, and Frederick W. Cheney (Missoula, Mont.: Mountain Press Publishing Co., 1974).

3) Editions of *Reference Books for Elementary and Junior High Libraries* by Carolyn Sue Peterson appeared in 1970 and 1975. The latter is identified as the second edition. Peterson collaborated with Ann D. Fenton to produce a 1981 revision and the publisher opted to give it a different title, *Reference Books for Children,* and no edition numbering. However, when Peterson and Fenton produced another revision in 1992, the publisher continued the 1981 titling but numbered it as the fourth edition.

It is the cataloguer's responsibility to understand and to express unambiguously all the facts of a work's publication history which might affect the accessibility to searchers of its various editions. Using what the catalogue reveals, the acquisitions librarian avoids wasting money buying a version not significantly different from one already in the collection. Every librarian who serves the public directly must know enough about publication relationships and about cataloguing practices used to record them to realize that an item cited with, say, an American imprint might in fact be identical to a British publication (perhaps even one with a different title in that country), or that an item with a 1983 publication date may contain no information later than 1929 because it is a reprint edition.

Reprint Editions

A *reprint edition* is not simply a new impression or a reprint in the sense of a further batch of copies subsequently produced for the original publisher as steady demand continues. Nor is it a xerographed, tape-recorded, or downloaded single copy made ad hoc (perhaps even without license) by its ultimate user. It is a reissue of a publication by a publisher other than its original one because the latter no longer exists or no longer wishes to keep the work in print. Reprint editions are very common especially in academic libraries since copies of "classics" are always needed long after their original publishers have lost interest in them because of low annual sales.

Reprint publishers have been a distinct subgroup within the publishing industry since the mid-nineteenth century, particularly active when war-ravaged libraries need to be replenished and to stock new ones (for example, in developing countries and during the explosion of post-secondary education in the 1960s). They specialize in bringing back into print publications needed in few copies at a time. The edition reproduced may be in the public domain, meaning that anyone may legally copy it; otherwise the reprint publisher acquires a license to reproduce it.

There are problems of identifying a reprint edition when the publisher fails to give a sufficiently precise bibliographic identification for the edition of the work reproduced. Figure 8 shows how the same content appeared first in 1914, again in 1930, and again in 1971, each time from a different publisher. Each of the 1914 and 1930 publications was issued in a different series; the 1971 publication was not issued in any series. They are, properly, not numbered as first, second, and third editions, since the content was never changed. Not all reprint publishers care to state so clearly that they are selling an old work; it is possible to make a reprint appear to be a newly published or revised text without actually telling a lie.

The body of the reprint is normally visually identical to the original because it was produced either photographically or, now more often, by computer scanning and digitization. However, most reprint editions include something not present in the reproduced original, be it as little

Studies in North Carolina History
Number 3

Ante-Bellum Builders
of North Carolina

By R. D. W. CONNOR
Former Secretary North Carolina Historical Commission
KENAN PROFESSOR OF HISTORY, UNIVERSITY OF
NORTH CAROLINA

Issued under the Direction of the
Department of History

Published by
The North Carolina College for Women
Greensboro, N. C.
1930

First published, in 1914, as the North Carolina State Normal and Industrial
College Historical Publication

This Volume Was Reproduced
From A 1930 Edition
In The
North Carolina Collection
University of North Carolina
Chapel Hill

The Reprint Company
Post Office Box 5401
Spartanburg, South Carolina 29301

Reprinted: 1971
ISBN 0-87152-064-8
Library of Congress Catalog Card Number 70-148342

Manufactured in the United States of America on long-life paper

FIGURE 8.   A complex reprint relationship honestly presented.

as a stick-on label on the inner cover bearing the new publisher's name or as much as new prefatory commentary and an updated bibliography. Only in the case of a *facsimile edition* is the reprint crafted to appear as physically identical to the original as possible. Even then, there is likely to be some new material, often contained in a physically separate accompanying item. A good bibliographic description of a reprint must distinguish bibliographic facts and content relevant only to the original publication from what is relevant only to the reprint. Often only the title and author's name are common to both.

What most concerns the cataloguer is the treatment of the title page. Sometimes only the one in the original publication is reproduced. If so, it may or may not show the name of the reprinter and (less likely yet) the date of reprinting. Sometimes, there is only a newly composed title page. Again, it may contain either or both the original and the new publication data—and perhaps even a variant of the original title or statement of responsibility! Occasionally and most helpfully, there are two title pages: a new one as well as a reproduction of the original one. Both library cataloguing practice and style manuals for footnotes have vacillated over the years on the issue of whether the original or the new publication should take precedence in bibliographic identification. If a library has both the reprint and its original, the former method is an economy if it means that the reprint can be added as a "copy" with little change in the record. This is likely also less confusing for the user, who is normally following up a citation to the original. However, a library is most likely to buy a reprint precisely because it does *not* own the original and in any case may explicitly want it for the new material it contains.

For over half a century, libraries have acquired old, out-of-print, and fragile printed and manuscript documents as complete photographic reproductions in microform. A first frame or a container may mention the producer of the microform and the owner of the original which was photographed. The microfilming industry has much in common with the reprint publishing industry previously described. The significant difference of bibliographic interest is that a microform reproducation rarely if ever contains either substantial content not found in the original or a full newly composed title page. There are also many practical differences in how libraries handle and use microform copies as against reprint editions. They almost always house, and often administer, books and microforms separately. A library housing much older material is likely to own both the original and a microform reproduction so that the former can be preserved while the latter is used by patrons and staff. It is therefore less common to list microform reproductions traditionally in library catalogues, that is, as new, different publications. Much as principle dictates that one list the physical object one owns, librarians persist in listing the original publication with an appended note stating that the library owns a microform reproduction instead of or in addition to it, treating the microform as a copy even if they would not so describe a reprint edition or a print edition from a different publisher.

Continuations and Sequels

When there is more than one title in the sequence of a serial (see figure 6 on page 57 for an example), the record must specify how each title is preceded or continued by, merged into, separated from, etc. another title. To a subscriber, the entire run of a journal is a unit despite the existence of many different titles. On the other hand, each separate title is what identifies the contents of the issues bearing that title in A&I services, footnotes, and any other kind of citation of a single article. That *The Empire Strikes Back* is a sequel to *Star Wars* is also significant. The relationship works both ways, but of course at the time of release of *Star Wars* it was not known what the title of its sequel would be, even though the probability of a sequel was evident.

One cannot prevent a publisher from announcing and even advertising well in advance a forthcoming book, motion picture, recording, etc. Some of these never do make an appearance. This seems particularly true of proposed sequels, continuations, and reprint editions. Yet their ectoplasmic titles and edition numbers, called bibliographic ghosts, float around the world of bibliographic citation haunting acquisitions librarians who may try but will never be able to lay hands on the actual item.

Accompanying Items

When a CD-ROM disk is issued together with a booklet of instructions on how to install and use its search software, it is clear that each was conceived in relation to the whole. The expectation is that at least the same title appears on each physically separate part. A teacher's manual to accompany a language text may be written at the same time as the text, even by the same author(s), but even if it is not, at least it is a dependent item not useable without the text and titled in some way that clearly shows its subsidiary nature. When a travel book and a map are sold together, the latter in a pocket at the back of the book, or tables on a microfiche are inserted in a pocket on the inner cover of an economics text, it is possible or even likely that the two were separately conceived and produced, were brought together artificially after their creation, and are useable independently. A quite different title may apply to each part. In any case, the fact that they have been brought together as a unit still calls for a statement of their relationship to one another in any bibliographic description.

The simplest way of showing a relationship is to make a separate record for each separate part, featuring its own title, physical description, etc., and including a note to identify any related part(s). The use of typed records and manual searching made this seem inefficient, but in a digital database, all records for related items can be linked for easy recall and display. Nevertheless, the closer the use-dependency of one part on the other, the more desirable is a single record for the whole in order to avoid complication in the user's identification of what is wanted.

The latter one-record technique requires the cataloguer to decide which is the dominant part in order to begin the description with it: not always an easy judgement to make. If a filmstrip and a cassette sound recording are produced for use together in a synchronized carousel projector, should the combination be described as a sound recording accompanied by a filmstrip or a filmstrip accompanied by a sound recording? The neutral solution of treating the combination as a single unit, a *kit,* may not solve the problem of which title to begin with if the parts of the kit have different titles. On a card or in a footnote or other printed form, a bibliographic identification is a linear sequence of data, making it inevitable that the description of one part takes precedence over that of the other. In a digital record searchable by any characteristic of any part, that sense of priority can be diminished if not totally eliminated, but any entity treated as a single unit must inevitably be identified primarily by *one* title.

Contents: Parts of a Single Publication

Most longer written material is divided into chapters or parts, musical compositions into movements, plays into acts, etc. This type of component part of a work has no bibliographic significance as long as it is neither separately published nor likely to be isolated for separate attention. Occasionally, a part of a literary, musical, or other creative work does achieve recognition separate from the whole, for example, a hit song from a Broadway musical or the Lord's Prayer from the Bible, whether or not it is separately published.

The component parts of what cataloguing rules call a *collection* are by definition separate works. This is a generic term; *anthology, conference proceedings, Festschrift, kit,* [record] *album,* etc. designate some specialized types of collection. Any issue of a periodical or journal is almost always a collection of separate *articles.* Scholarly nonfiction tends ever more strongly toward the "edited" publication consisting of short separately titled contributions by different authors working more or less independently. A collection as famous as Palgrave's *The Golden Treasury* or the *Anthologia Graeca* is itself, as a collection, translated, issued in different editions, and the subject of study and criticism: it has become a work in its own right, more than the sum of its parts. Some titling problems related to collections are illustrated in figures 2–4 early in this chapter. If a printed anthology has a collective title, it is most usual for its component parts to be listed only in a table of contents. Those parts, the separate works comprising the collection, are described briefly by author and/or title in a *contents note* in the record for the collection. Whether and how to make these authors and titles individually searchable has always been a matter of discussion; now that digital files are routinely searchable under every word in every record, some advocate making a table of contents a normal part of the record not only of any collection but routinely also of nonfiction monographs since words in those tables of contents may be useful indicators of the subjects covered. Formats and uses of the contents note and of the *analytic record* and the *multilevel description* (two other methods of identifying parts of larger bibliographic units) are discussed at the end of chapter 8.

Series

A *series* is any succession of objects or events sharing a common characteristic: a series of novels centering around one protagonist; a series of searches involving a common access point. The bibliographic series is a more closely defined phenomenon, created only by a publisher, who imposes common editorial standards and usually a uniform physical design on each of a succession of publications. Even then, it is only a bibliographic series if each of the resulting publications bears a common title in addition to its own separate (and different) individualizing title. The publisher typically designates as the series editor a noted person to be witness to and perhaps guarantor of quality. The publisher then advertises the series as a unit, hopes that buyers who approve of one publication in it will buy others, and may facilitate this by offering discounts to those who agree to receive all publications in the series as they appear. Establishing a series is more a matter of good sales strategy than of linking publications bibliographically because there is a shared content among them.

Since a library's acquisitions procedures are simplified by receiving series on *standing order* rather than ordering each publication separately, subscribing to the series may be less costly even if some items in it would not individually be selected for purchase. Usually nobody objects provided the level of quality and relevance of the individual publications remains high. The proportion of monographs issued in series was very small less than a century ago. Now, at least the commercial publishers of specialized academic and technical monographs routinely apply series titling to almost everything, each title being associated with a topic and a board of editors.

The characteristic connecting the items in a series is most often their subject content, but that is not bibliographically relevant—topical unity is minimal in a series like *Pelican Books* or *The World's Classics*. Other very commonly applied cohesive criteria are format (*University Paperbacks*) and sponsorship (*IBM Medical Symposia*).

In a bibliographic search, a series title serves

1) to identify the item wanted in a request such as "Give me the *Everyman's Library* edition of Chaucer" and
2) to find an item for the person who for one reason or another knows its series title (often from a less-than-adequate citation) but not its individual title or author.

In the first case, mere mention of the series title in the bibliographic record suffices. In the second, it must also be an access point, preferably in a title index. A citation may provide only the information *University of London Institute of Education. Studies in Education* when referring to the monograph whose title page is shown in figure 9, although its title as a monograph is *The Arts and Current Tendencies in Education*.

If its publisher intends to add items to a series indefinitely, the series is also a serial. Many series are serials, but many others are not. If the number of possible items in the series is finite, the complete series is usually called a *set*. A. B. Paterson's literary writings were published in two volumes under the title *Complete Works*. The volume containing the works written to 1900 is entitled *Singer of the Bush;* the volume containing the later works is entitled *Song of the Pen*. A third volume is unlikely since Paterson is dead. A supplementary volume could appear containing corrections and newly discovered writings. That would complicate the record for the item but not change the nature of the series/set.

Series and contents (see the previous subsection) have an inverse relationship to one another, with consequences for their identification discussed more fully at the end of chapter 8. In a record for the Paterson series, its title is transcribed as *Complete Works*. The other two titles are given, if at all, in a contents note. However, on a record created to describe either of the two individual volumes, the volume-title begins the record and the comprehensive title *Complete Works* appears as a series title. A single "volume" of a series, so designated by its publisher, is not necessarily one physical unit. Figure 10 is an example of two works with different titles which together comprise volume 3 of the thirteen-volume set *Technique of Organic Chemistry*.

UNIVERSITY OF LONDON INSTITUTE OF EDUCATION

STUDIES IN EDUCATION

**THE ARTS AND CURRENT
TENDENCIES IN EDUCATION**

Published for
the University of London Institute of Education
by Evans Brothers Limited, London

FIGURE 9.   A title page illustrating ambiguity as to which is the title of the monograph and which is the title of the series.

TECHNIQUE OF ORGANIC CHEMISTRY

Volume III

Second Completely Revised and Augmented Edition

**PART I
SEPARATION AND
PURIFICATION**

Editor: ARNOLD WEISSBERGER

Authors: Charles M. Ambler   A. Letcher Jones
            Geoffrey Broughton   K. Kammermeyer
            David Craig   Frederick W. Keith, Jr.
            Lyman C. Craig   E. MacWilliam
            A. B. Cummins   Edward G. Scheibel
            F. B. Hutto, Jr.   R. Eliot Stauffer
                        R. Stuart Tipson

1956
INTERSCIENCE PUBLISHERS, INC., NEW YORK
INTERSCIENCE PUBLISHERS LTD., LONDON

TECHNIQUE OF ORGANIC CHEMISTRY

Volume III

Second Completely Revised and Augmented Edition

**PART II
LABORATORY
ENGINEERING**

Editor: ARNOLD WEISSBERGER

Authors: John W. Axelson   Richard R. Kraybill
            Richard S. Egly   Glenn H. Miller
            Richard F. Eisenberg   J. H. Rushton
            M. P. Hofmann   William C. Streib

1957
INTERSCIENCE PUBLISHERS, INC., NEW YORK
INTERSCIENCE PUBLISHERS LTD., LONDON

FIGURE 10.   The title pages of two separate books which together form one bibliographic unit (volume 3) within a yet larger work.

Other Relationships

The following brief statements quoted from particular publications show something of the possible range of relationships other than those already described:

> The dictionary section was taken from *Polygraph Wörterbuch der graphischen Industrie in 6 Sprachen.*

> "Text adapted from *Of Them He Chose Twelve*, by Clarence Macartney."

> Supplement to *Zulu ethnography,* 1976.

Bibliographic relationships can be multidimensional. For example, the second edition of a work may be published in a different series from that in which the first edition appeared; a reissue of a recording of rock music may contain one new song, replacing a single band of the recording as originally issued. It is common for a microform collection to incorporate some of the content of each of a number of previous publications.

The ease with which a digitized document is passed from database to database, often with modifications, does not diminish responsibility for acknowledging explicitly, within its new context, the source of the document and any significant change it has undergone. The ease with which formats can be changed during a transfer also makes any statement of format compatibility a significant data element. Any sighted person can read any printed book in a familiar language; one software program or piece of hardware is typically incapable of dealing with a digitized document designed for other equipment and software.

CODING INTENDED
TO IDENTIFY
AN ITEM UNIQUELY

A judicious selection of the above bibliographic data elements assembled without ambiguity should suffice to identify any publication or work and provide the means of its retrieval from a file via appropriate access points. However, since they are language-based, their use may require judgement and not merely mechanical comparison. The value of computerization—cost-control and reliability—is as great in bibliographic work as in any other stock-control or accounting activity. Its efficient operation requires a separate digital code to designate each item and activity that must be distinguished from all others. Codes for activities (for example, a circulation transaction) are automatically created ad hoc and are useful only for as long as the activity is current or a record of it is needed. It is best to apply a code to the item at the time of its production; later application is costly and complex. Persons and their activities have long been identified by telephone numbers, social insurance and social security numbers, bank account and credit card numbers, etc.

Numbers have been applied in bibliographic work for well over a century uniquely to identify a publication or a single variant issue of one, a work, a bibliographic record, etc. A Superintendent of Documents (SUDOC) number identifies a United States government publication, a serial number in the *Gesamtkatalog der Wiegendrucke* identifies a particular fifteenth-century printing, a Köchel number uniquely identifies a composition by Mozart, and since 1898 a Library of Congress Control Number (LCCN) identifies a single catalogue record created in that library. Computerization increased the pace. It was to automate their inventory systems that British publishers devised the Standard Book Number (SBN) in the mid-1960s. Use of the SBN naturally spread to other publishers in the English-speaking world quickly. When it spread worldwide through the 1970s, its original nine characters were foreseen to be too few so a tenth character was added when it became the International Standard Book Number (ISBN). Librarians devised the International Standard Serial Number (ISSN) in the 1970s to help in the automation of their union lists of serial titles. These two numbering systems appeal over others by not being specific to single-purpose applications. They are applicable to inventory operations at every stage in the book trade and by now are almost universally applied to current publications.

Even within a single computerized operation, different bibliographic numbering systems are likely to be needed. The same number cannot be used for two purposes if any distinction is required for those purposes. A separate ISBN identifies any form of a publication its publisher might invoice separately. Thus a quality paperback, a hardback, and a limited leatherbound edition of the same publication each receives a different ISBN even if all are produced from the same printing plates and would be represented by the same catalogue record in a library. Similarly, a multivolume set is assigned an ISBN for the set as a whole as well as a different one for each volume because the publisher may need to fill one order for a complete set but another order only for volume 3.

Each publisher of a book operates its own inventory system so if the same book has two publishers, whether within one country or in separate countries, the same physical object has two different ISBNs.

A single ISBN cannot be equated with a work, a library catalogue record, or even all copies resulting from one printing or other production process.

The ten characters of an ISBN are conventionally shown in four segments divided by hyphens:

    0-949946-29-X
    3-7825-0052-0
    92-67-10017-3

The final character is a *check digit* used in a verification procedure; it is either a numeral or an X. Each of the other three segments can vary in length and consists only of numerals. The first two uniquely identify the publisher; the third identifies the publication. The first segment alone originally identified a language area rather loosely: for example, publishers in France, Québec, or French-speaking Switzerland adopted a 2, and those in the English-language industrialized world first to join the system used 0 (zero) (a shortage of new publisher-numbers later resulted in 1 also being used among the latter group).

The ISBN system eventually needed central organization, for which publishers and national bibliographic agencies founded the independent International Standard Book Numbering Agency in Frankfurt. The first segment, assigned by this agency, now commonly designates a single country, for example, Ghana is 996, and the country's national library is usually the agency which encourages publishers to participate, assigns a unique second segment to each, and generally oversees quality control in applications of the system.

An ISSN is unlike an ISBN in having no "meaning" except as a unique identifying number; two ISSNs in sequence therefore do not necessarily represent serials in any way related to each other. Both national boundaries and single publishers are less meaningful as identifiers of serial publications. An ISSN consists of seven numerals followed by a check digit (the latter, as in an ISBN, may be a numeral or an X). Conventionally, a hyphen is shown after the fourth digit. An ISSN uniquely identifies all issues of a serial publication while they have the same key-title. When a serial publication changes title, the issues under the new title are assigned a new key-title and a corresponding new ISSN. The Paris headquarters of the ISSN Network coordinates the assignment of ISSNs and key-titles by national agencies, usually based in national libraries.

It was an automatic assumption in the 1970s that the ISBN and ISSN were established for publications in print formats and that separate International Standard Numbering (ISN) systems would be devised for other formats. Music publishers have recently agreed on an

International Standard Music Number (ISMN). However, when standard numbering was proposed over a decade ago for sound recordings of music, the larger producers claimed that an industry-wide unique numbering scheme already exists in that each of them uses a pattern of numbers and letters for its products which does not conflict with that of its competitors and can be used in a variable-field digital format. Companies specializing in language (as distinguished from musical) recordings have generally opted to apply the ISBN system. To date, the ISBN system has been used by many publishers of computer software, slide sets, educational kits, and material in other nonprint formats, but a proposal for an International Standard Audiovisual Number (ISAN) has been recently forwarded to national committees for study.

Finally, one might consider the Internet's Universal Resource Locator (URL) as analogous because like any of the above International Standard Numbers, it uniquely identifies a source in code. It is no longer necessary to consider the limitations of fixed-field formatting (see chapter 8) in devising a code, as it was when the ISBN was devised at the beginning of bibliographic computerization, so the URL is of any length and number of segments. As used at present, it does not necessarily identify just one particular state of the content of a source. However, as people who post documents on the Internet become more frustrated in their own searches for the documents of others, they are taking more care to compose mnemonic URLs capable of distinguishing versions of the same content from one another, thus incorporating something like an edition statement into the locator. Experience in organizing many files and subfiles on a hard disk makes one conscious of both the value and the technique of concise naming. The experimental Persistent Universal Resource Locator (PURL) is an proposed solution to the growing problem of changing URLs for essentially the same material.

INFORMATION PECULIAR TO ONE
COPY OR PROCESS

When listed in a bibliography, a document is usually treated as an abstraction. Whether dozens, hundreds, or thousands of copies exist in the edition and format described, all are identical with respect to the data elements identified so far in this chapter. Libraries do not buy abstractions. They order and pay for single physical pieces which are then individually circulated to users, moved from branch to branch, rebound, etc. Information particular to single physical objects therefore has a place among the bibliographic data recorded in a library catalogue or in any other bibliographic listing of unique objects, such as a sale catalogue of a private collection. Does a copy have a fore-edge painting, a handmade binding, an author's autograph, some association with a significant person or event? Is the copy complete as published or is something missing or damaged?

Answers to these questions are bibliographic data relative to one copy. Whether or not these data are significant enough to record depends on policies and purposes. Where can one expect to find the object at this very moment? in its normal place on the shelves? at the bindery? in the control of a borrower (and if so, when is it expected to return to the library's control)? Answers to such questions may change from hour to hour. They are not bibliographic data, but the best place to record them is in immediate association with the object's bibliographic identification, the catalogue record. Only the computer could make feasible the linking of abstract and copy-specific information, permanent and temporary information, for one-step searching of currently valid facts.

The bibliographic records themselves, as distinguished from the documents they describe, must be under the control of an accounting system. One must be able to identify each access point designated for a record in case any must be changed or deleted (in a manual card system, the access points were listed at the bottom of the card as *tracings*). It is useful to know when and by whom the record was created (in a manual system, such information might only be kept on one copy of the record). In a computer-based system, a unique code identifying the record unites every piece of associated data whether it concerns the record itself or the document the record describes.

SOURCES OF DATA

Any words descriptive of a document's content, wherever they may be found, serve a useful purpose to anyone who wonders about its relevance to a given information need. A *title* has special value not because it describes the content (it may or may not do that very well), but because it *identifies* the document. It can only serve this function if everyone agrees on where to find it; otherwise it is just another group of useful words. Titling consists of characters in a prominent display visibly separate from other wording and in the most obvious possible location closely associated with the content of the document. Traditionally favoured locations are at or near the top of the third page of a printed book (the first two being a protective covering leaf), at the beginning of a magazine article, on the label of a sound recording, on the front of the outer packaging of a kit, and now, in electronic media, on the first screen of information displayed on a terminal when a program and its associated database are activated.

By 1500, a canonic selection, order, and location of the data elements discussed in this chapter (including title) were established as a proper and sufficient identification of a printed book. Even manufacturing data, for centuries written or printed in a colophon at the end, slowly joined the other elements on what came to be known as the *title page*. To print bibliographic information in a colophon, now a rarity in the English-speaking world, is still common in some countries: there are national characteristics even in bibliography!

Whatever the changes in technology, format, and style of presentation of published documents since then, there has been remarkably little substantial change in either the elements or their usual sequence. However, as relevant bibliographic data increased in quantity and had to compete with other advertising/design features on a book's title page, statements of bibliographic importance even for a printed book had to expand to subsequent pages formally designated in cataloguing rules as *preliminaries*. These precede the textual content of the book, which in the case of nonfiction normally begins with a preface or introduction.

Cataloguers (but nobody else) now call the place normally containing the most unified expression of relevant data the *chief source of information* of the type of document in question. In the case of a printed book, this is the title page. In the case of formats lacking something analogous to a title page applicable to the whole, a location less directly attached to the content must suffice. A century ago (fifty years ago in continental Europe), publishers still did not routinely have copies of a book bound before sale: the buyer's taste and wealth determined the covering. Until the 1830s, there was no such thing as a protective dust wrapper; it was not common until the twentieth century. As a result, even today these two covering features are ignored in the standard cataloguing of books. Even if it is no more stable than a binding or dust wrapper, the packaging on other media cannot be so casually dismissed. It is all too likely to be the *only* place where reasonably complete information on the publication as a whole appears.

It took at least two hundred years for printed title pages to settle into a predictable pattern; that producers of newer media are not quickly standardizing where and how they state bibliographic facts should not be a surprise. The cartouche of a map and the title frame of a filmstrip may be close analogies of the title page, but from which source should the title proper of a digital document be transcribed: the image on the terminal screen or the wording found on the accompanying printed booklet? It is a particular problem when sources which seem equally reasonable perversely contradict each other; for example, when the label of a CD sound recording bears the wording *Schubert. Excerpts from Die Schöne Müllerin and Die Winterreise* but the spine label and cover of the booklet inserted into the plastic container both read *Favorite Songs by Schubert*. An example of different title wording on parts of an educational kit is given earlier in this chapter. Since the record for the item can only have one title proper, rules must help define one chief source of information for each medium so that every cataloguer uses the same basis for selecting it and other data.

The positioning of data elements within the same source, particularly names, also matters. A corporate name at the foot of a title page normally designates the publisher. At the middle or top, it sends a more ambiguous signal about what the body has done especially if a personal name also appears there. The whim of a layout artist who knows nothing of bibliographic convention or of a departmental secretary told to get the department head's name on the typescript of a conference proceedings may cause serious puzzlement. Established publishers, including large corporations, and printers who routinely do book work tend to know bibliographic traditions and adhere to them in title-page layout. Familiarity with these traditions helps librarians interpret the results even if they are nonconventional. Traditions are being developed only slowly in nonprint, and particularly electronic, media.

As stated previously, a title is not some abbreviation, paraphrase, or translation of what appears on the item's chief source of information. It is a transcription of *exactly* what is found there. Library cataloguing rules respect the integrity of information taken from the item also in the transcription of statements of responsibility, edition naming, etc. Where abbreviation or truncation is sanctioned, that is also governed by stated rules. No general rule for citation sanctions changing the wording of a title but style manuals tend to be more cavalier than librarians' cataloguing codes about the treatment of other elements, permitting one to summarize or abbreviate what a cataloguer is required to transcribe exactly. For example, a number of style manuals suggest using the formula "ed. J. Smith" instead of copying "John Smith, compiler" from the item's title page or packaging. House rules adopted by single indexing services may go so far as to omit an initial article from a title or even change the spelling of title words from the British/Canadian forms found in this book to American orthography.

Style manuals also show a lack of concern about any data not immediately evident. For example, if a date is not found on a document, one is encouraged to type "n.d." (no date). Library cataloguing rules require a cataloguer to search thoroughly for information on the anonymous work, the undated film, or the serial whose previous title does not appear on the issue in hand. It takes time and skill to locate needed information particularly if secondary reference sources contradict one another.

This means that two records for the same item may differ in the presence or absence of some quite important data element(s). In order to ensure that a searcher is not confused by an apparent discrepancy, it has always been conventional to enclose within brackets any data included in the record but not found on the title page (more recently, on either the chief or some other predictable source). An author may choose to use a pseudonym. A publisher in a country where censorship is a problem may choose to use a fictitious name or place in an imprint. Reference sources may or may not reveal the truth; whether even to consult them is a matter of the cataloguer's instinct.

It is a cliché that a problem does not exist until it is recognized. Unrecognized pseudonyms and fictitious imprints do not vanish: failure of the bibliographic instinct inevitably surfaces to haunt the cataloguer and confound the reference librarian. Perfection is the goal; imperfection the reality. In a smaller institution, how much time to spend on verification and speculative investigation is usually left to the individual cataloguer's professional judgement. In a larger one, some more uniformly applicable policy must be developed and enforced by the administration. Wherever and however the elements are displayed, in sum they constitute a cohesive sequence of bibliographic facts providing unique identification. Every good bibliographic record is based on the copying of data in the order in which they make best sense as a coherent statement. This is the basis for the standard library formats analyzed in chapter 8 and for other rules of citation.

DATA FOR UNIQUE UNPUBLISHED ITEMS

Archivists are in the process of establishing data-element directories and rules for citation and description for the unpublished material with which they work. Less far advanced are standards for describing gallery and museum objects. In all those cases, the fact that the object does not exist in multiple copies means that its creator felt no need to affix to it objectively verifiable information so that it could be sought in many places and identified in many listings of similar objects.

In the case of archives, detailed item-by-item description is not usually accorded the unpublished material comprising most of a repository's holdings. It is listed in contextual groupings, using data elements more relevant to those groups than to individual items. The library cataloguer is unlikely to be able entirely to ignore single unpublished items such as a manuscript or a locally made videorecording of an amateur show. Although its content is certainly published, an Internet bulletin board is part of the new oral tradition mentioned at the beginning of this book, but also has the characteristics of a unique document when it is downloaded by someone for preservation. Such an item rarely has a formalized source of bibliographic data. Data elements to be imposed on, more than extracted from, it are often only partially compatible with those for published items, for example, data relating to the production of the copy replace publication information.

A cataloguer's concise description of the content must typically serve in place of a title either entirely lacking or not useable in the wording scribbled on the case by the maker. That title may be suitably informative about possible uses of the item but cannot serve as a predictable objective identification. How is the prospective user to know whether the cataloguer opted to name it *Recital by music students* . . . or *Student recital*?

HOW MUCH IS ENOUGH?

Whether the text was widely published or not, each copy of a work made before the invention of printing was unique, with its own errors and other idiosyncracies. A student might rely confidently on a teacher's ability to remember the exact wording of a given version of a passage, but the concept of a need to cite that passage to someone else by page in a particular manuscript could not exist. Even citation by a relative location within a text, such as a "chapter and verse" of a sacred scripture, was only common in the case of highly important works likely to be often challenged. The discussion in the previous section may help explain why an exact title even for a work is a concept not formed until about 1500, prior to which a work was alluded to, rather than deliberately and precisely named. That allusion was as often a reference to its author; for example, "The Stygirite [that is, Aristotle] states that. . . ." Even today, it is not uncommon to let the author's name alone identify a work if the person only wrote only one famous work; for example, "Mary Baker Eddy writes that. . . ."

Today's total quantity of documents and the large number of separate publications containing the same work impose much stricter requirements on bibliographic identification. Those who do not see the need, sometimes even writers and publishers, shortcut these and produce footnotes and citations such as the following, which are transcribed from actual publications. Such citations serve only to add to the work and woe of an interlibrary loan librarian:

> *Aristotle.* Columbia University Press
> *Quaternary Research.* University of Washington, 1970.

Nevertheless, some documents are so famous that an even briefer description can elicit instant recognition in an intended audience. Most educated English speakers recognize *The First Folio* or *Shakespeare. Folio. 1623* more immediately than they would recognize a description of the same book compiled according to current library cataloguing rules:

> Mr. William Shakespeares comedies, histories, & tragedies : published according to the true originall copies. — London : Printed by Isaac Jaggard, and Ed. Blount, 1623. — [18], 303, 100, [2], 69-232, [30], 993 [i.e. 299] p. : ill. (woodcuts) ; 33 cm. (fol.)

Complete though it may seem, the latter is still far from adequate for a student of textual criticism. The importance of the First Folio in the establishment of the Shakespearean text and the vicissitudes of its printing occasioned a particularly thorough bibliographic study of it by Charlton Hinman. His two-volume bibliographic description of the known copies of the First Folio is over a thousand pages long: rather too much information to fit on a 7.5-by-12.5-cm. card! It would also challenge the technical size limit for a single digital record in any known library system. Fortunately, not one publication in a hundred thousand warrants such detailed description. Unfortunately, it is impossible to predict when the appearance of a new publication with the same title, a new edition or translation of the same work, another work by the same author, or the need to identify a forgery will cause a previously satisfactory citation to be seen as just a bit *too* brief to serve the principle of adequate identification.

Over the centuries, a different number and combination of data elements have been found useful and have therefore come to be expected in bibliographic records serving somewhat different purposes. A library catalogue record contains more data than a footnote yet is not adequate to the demands of a collector who needs to distinguish the states of an author's first editions. Figure 11 shows descriptions of the same item in six different bibliographies and catalogues. All are very brief, yet they differ in (1) the number of data elements given and (2) their arrangement and presentation.

The target audience of the library's catalogue is the *general* user; the person with specialized bibliographic queries finds them answered not necessarily in the library catalogue but in other bibliographic sources accessible through the library's reference collection and services. A library's bibliographic records are used in more contexts and for more varied purposes than most other types of record. The student who consults them only to find a call number for browsing can ignore the unnecessary detail; the writer of a term paper criticizing textual variants in the editions of Milton is grateful for it.

—— Report of the Tripartite Economic Survey of the Eastern
Caribbean. January–April 1966. [Leader, J. R. Sargent.]
pp. xxi. 278. *London*, 1967. 8°.   B.S. **251/68.**

Report of the Tripartite Economic Survey of the Eastern
Caribbean, Jan.–Apr. 1966. London, H. M. S. O.. 1967.
xxi. 279 p. diagr., tables. 25 cm. £2/10/-
                                                        (B•••)
At head of title: Ministry of Overseas Development.

**Report of the tripartite economic survey of the
Eastern Caribbean [appointed by the governments
of the United Kingdom, Canada and the United
States of America, carried out] January-April
1960. London. H.M.S.O.. 50/-. [dFeb]1967.
xxi,279p. tables, diagrs. 24½cm. Pbk.**

Report of the Tripartite Economic Survey of
the Eastern Caribbean, Jan.-Apr. 1966. London,
H.M. Stationery Off., 1967.
    xxi, 278 p. 25 cm.
    At head of title: Ministry of Overseas
Development.
    "To the Governments of the United Kingdom
of Great Britain and Northern Ireland, of Canada
and of the United States of America".—p. iii.
    50/- pa.

*Report of the Tripartite Economic Survey of the Eastern Caribbean, January-
April 1966*, Ministry of Overseas Development, H.M.S.O., London,
1967.

Tripartite Economic Survey of the Eastern Caribbean, January-April 1966.

Figure 11.   In order, these records are from the catalogue of the British Museum Department of Printed Books; the *National Union Catalog*; the *British National Bibliography* (with a mistranscription of a date); *Canadiana*; Sir Harold
Mitchell, *Caribbean Patterns* (Edinburgh: Chambers, 1967); and Aaron Segal, *The
Politics of Caribbean Economic Integration*, Special Study no. 6 (Rio Piedras, P.R.:
Institute of Caribbean Studies, University of Puerto Rico, 1968). Access points
(see next section) are not reproduced.

Some tolerance is useful in cataloguing codes to permit one library to abridge records more than another would and to permit a cataloguer to use judgement in considering the bibliographic nature and importance of the individual item. Given a choice, it has always been considered wiser to prepare for somewhat more detailed queries than to begin at too elementary a level and have to upgrade later.

With regard to completeness, library practice has changed over time. As an example, early in this century it was considered desirable for a physical description to specify the existence of each leaf within a printed book. In this example, *p.l.* means preliminary leaf:

> 1 p.l., iii-xi, [1], 13-401, [7] p.

AACR requires the cataloguer to record only the highest number appearing on any major sequence of pages. When it is applied, "401 p." replaces all the detail in the above example. At the other extreme, rare-book description may still require collation by (1) format and size, followed by (2) details of each separate signature, and finally (3) pagination, as shown in the following example where these three groups are separated by periods. The signature-descriptions of the second group include their signing, folding, and order.

> Demy $8°$ (227 × 142 mm. uncut). $[A]^2$ B^8 $(-B^8+`B^{8`})$ $C-D^8$ E^8 $(\pm E2)$ F^8 $(-F6+`F6`)$ G^8 H^8 $(-H2,3+H2:3)$ $I-Z^8$ $2A^2$. Pp. [i] title, [iii]-iv preface, 1-356 text.[2]

DATA FOR DESCRIPTION VERSUS DATA FOR ACCESS

The data elements discussed in this chapter describe a document, distinguish it from others, and help the user decide if it might serve a given need. Some of them are also used for the related but different purpose taken up in the next two chapters, namely *finding* or *accessing* the record in a file. For the user, accessing a record must precede any judgement as to whether and how it might prove useful. However, the producer of records must approach it the other way because access results from the data elements described in this chapter. The title-page wording "edited, with an introduction, by Fred Hoyle" is a statement of responsibility. The searcher knows that access is normally provided for personal names and so looks under the personal name within this data element, using the convention of locating not the given name but the surname, *Hoyle, Fred,* to find the item. An ISBN alone is a great access point, much better than an author and/or title because nobody need guess what form it will take in an alphanumeric listing. It serves such practical library purposes as looking for an existing catalogue record to match with a book in hand, but it will be a long time before a reader's advisor suggests that 0-226-81620-6 is a good book to read. A serial is more likely to be referred to by its citation title, which is at least mnemonic: "Where is volume 28 of BAPS?" It is hardly likely to be cited by its ISSN. Among the more meaningful identifications, people still most often rely on a title alone ("Read *Future Shock*"), but common sense indicates that it is not sufficient to tell a friend to look up *Principles of Chemistry* or *Statistical Report for 1981*. Although frequently adequate for both description and access, reference by title along with the author's name must be supplemented by additional information such as an edition number, physical medium, date, or publisher's name if the user is only interested, for example, in the second edition of the *Anglo-American Cataloguing Rules* (not the first), or only a recording in cassette form of Beethoven's *Fifth Symphony* (not one on compact disc), or only the Northwestern/Newberry edition of Melville's *Typee* (not the Bantam paperback). Those designing retrieval systems must consider the desirability of ensuring that any such data element can play a part in access to a record.

It may seem frustrating to a beginner that (1) almost every item presents a slightly different challenge in what bibliographic data elements are relevant to it and how they are stated and arranged within the item itself and (2) almost every different bibliography presents a slightly different combination of data, choice of access points, etc.

This is either the joy or the despair of bibliography, depending on one's point of view. In any case, it is clear that no one universal rule for compiling bibliographic records has ever been, or could likely ever be, accepted. However, libraries are more committed to the exchange of bibliographic data and documents, and therefore need standardization in bibliographic practices, more than other agencies do.

Over the past hundred years, librarians have worked hard to develop rules for national and even international adoption for (1) describing documents using standard data elements and (2) applying name and subject access points to retrieve the resulting records from large files. Librarians' early application of computers to bibliographic work has expedited agreement on standardization if for no better reason than that computer operations require a high degree of technical standardization.

This chapter has concentrated on the definition of data elements. Methods of direct access to relevant elements and their efficient application in manual and automated files occupy the next two chapters.

3

■ ■ ■

Access Points

S heer quantity is the greatest barrier to direct access. Whether one looks for the actual document or for the bibliographic record representing it, the need to find it among thousands or millions of others gives many users the feeling that both a library and its catalogue are impenetrable jungles and that librarians keep things complicated to preserve their jobs as intermediaries in information retrieval. Yet at the same time, every user values the availability of the largest possible assemblage of potentially relevant material. The larger the collection or the file, the more likely something of value to any search can be found there.

Every activity in bibliographic control has the ultimate purpose of providing the most direct possible access to the most relevant particular document(s) which can satisfy a stated informational need. To the impatient beginner, direct access means immediate physical contact: standing at a stack of bookshelves, opening a file drawer or a box of archival records, or signing onto the Internet. Starting to browse gives a feeling of purposeful activity and is often enjoyable, but where does one start and how does one recognize when the browsing has become ineffective? Is some physical marker left to reveal that something is temporarily absent in compact storage, on a user's desk, at a bindery or conservation laboratory? Browsing is not to be rejected as an access technique: serendipitous meandering may have caused the awarding of more Nobel Prizes than purposefully directed experiment. It is occasionally the only way a searcher could possibly find an elusive fact or document.

Even if it adds a step to the search, however, it is usually more efficient to consult a complete and organized file of bibliographic records to discover what is relevant and where to find it. One can browse these records too, and more quickly than the documents themselves. Most people do this from time to time with small files such as bibliographic lists at ends of chapters.

Every compiler of a bibliography, catalogue, A&I publication, or any other kind of index is expected to make the file a consistent and predictable system for accessing the one or few descriptions relevant to each particular search. It is up to the searcher to learn how to use that system.

Librarians have been in the business of both designing and using such search tools longer than any other group. They have always tried to make it possible for others to use them unaided, but if a choice must be made between making a catalogue or index simple to use and making it capable of revealing complex interrelationships of concepts and documents, the latter purpose must prevail. Although only the end-user is competent to define the terms of the search and to evaluate its result, the librarian is the more effective and efficient user of the search tool itself: the index, catalogue, etc. This and the next chapter describe the types and methods of access to records in files. Access implies a mechanism for isolating a single document or its record, or a related group of them, from among many others. The process of isolating, often called "narrowing a search," consists of not one but several steps. In addition to knowing or guessing at specific words, terms, or symbols which may lead to useful documents, a searcher must also know

1) in which file(s) relevant material is likely to appear at all
2) whether the type(s) of data element being considered are included and indexed in that file and
3) in what order the resulting words, terms, or symbols are displayed as that index is consulted by a searcher.

Not every data-element type appears in every file, and although alphanumeric order is common, it is not universal. For example, having selected a bibliography of the publications of a government in order to search for the latest report from the Capilano Fish Hatchery, one finds that documents are arranged chronologically, and their issuing agencies, hierarchically. The document wanted is therefore the last one listed under the Hatchery's name, in the group of agencies found under the Department of Fisheries and Oceans. (That an alphabetic index is likely in such a bibliography is ignored here in order to emphasize the search process and the nature of other useful arrangements.)

The key to the whole process is the individual *access point* (as it is coming to be most generally called in the technical jargon of information retrieval), search term or keyword (in typical user's jargon), or search key (in the jargon of computer-based searching). Three other words once used almost exclusively for this function now confuse more than clarify. *Heading* relates to the filing line(s) at the beginning of a manual record, but is still part of the widely used term *subject heading*, where it has a specialized meaning discussed in chapter 7. *Entry* remains in the vocabulary only of older librarians, as in "The entry is Smith, John." It is better to use this word, if at all, to mean the entire bibliographic record, not just one of its access points. *Index*, whether as a noun or as a verb, is less likely to be misinterpreted than *heading* or *entry*, but is avoided in this book. As a verb, "to provide access" is more awkward but clearer, whether it means to extract data elements from an existing document description as in the above example or to impose appropriate access points as described in the final sections of this chapter.

An access point is a single statement of any one fact (for example, the name of one author, one date of publication, one topic dealt with in the document, even a single word) found in (or considered pertinent to) one or more documents and deemed significant enough to warrant retrieval. The final clause emphasizes that access points serve as answers to *anticipated* user queries, the anticipation being a major factor in determining the significance of potential access points, whether in relation to a particular document or in the context of an entire file.

The remainder of this chapter deals in a general way with the individual access point, of whatever type, in every kind of bibliographic file. The next chapter deals with how it is assembled with other access points in various file arrangements searched manually and via computer programs. Chapters 6 and 7 discuss the rules and practices followed by librarians to choose, structure, and arrange individual name and subject access points in the files they create.

An access point is of limited value if it is considered only as an isolated fact. To select even an access point as obvious as the author or subject of a document can require sophisticated bibliographic judgement. To "index"—that is, to compile a useful list of the access points selected for each document from among its data elements—involves additional operations:

1) structuring these access points for efficient searching of, say, surnames of persons rather than their given names

2) displaying the access points either together or separately by type, in a predictable sequence or set of sequences
3) linking each access point with the record to which it applies and often (but not always)
4) linking related access points with each other.

The three latter functions are particularly technology-dependent. Since the type of file makes a great deal of difference to how they operate, they are also discussed in the next chapter. It is costly to set up systems, especially automated ones, to accomplish them, but adding records to a functioning system is a largely clerical operation which can itself be automated. The first and the last, as well as the initial selection of access points, are particularly cost-sensitive because they are labour-intensive operations ideally using professional expertise in an examination of each document or record involved.

ACCESS TO WHAT?

A potentially useful access point identifies either

1) a characteristic one can remember easily and accurately after seeing the document oneself or
2) a characteristic likely to be part of someone else's oral or written reference (citation) to it.

The most useful characteristics are permanent, associated with the content, and common to relatively few documents; for example, any name, title, inventory number, or precisely stated topic, as found in the document. Anyone who has seen the document is likely to have copied one or another of these from it into a footnote, etc. for future personal reference and for others to see and use. People also remember such characteristics as a red binding or a size but a red (which shade of red?) covering may be changed to a blue one in rebinding and too many objects are 28 cm. high to make the dimension a useful access point in itself. A date is so important a characteristic in determining use that chronologically arranged lists are not uncommon. However, a date is usually not used as a sole or even primary access point because, like a dimension, the same date is shared by far too many documents. It is most useful when combined with another access point in a search as a means of improving the relevance of what is retrieved.

Different types of access points appear in greater variety among monographic bibliographies and the more general A&I publications than among library catalogues. A few, such as author's name, are almost invariably used but there is no particular benefit in indexing all lists in the same way. The compiler of any bibliography or indexing tool covering documents of a narrow subject range or type of materials responds to specialized and particular needs, both of the intellectual content of the documents and of their users' anticipated queries. For example, a bibliography of published reports of sightings of unexplained phenomena includes access points, in separate sequences, of (1) geographic locations of sightings in a geographic (not alphabetic) arrangement by state and city, etc., (2) subjects, using terms governed by a glossary within the bibliography, (3) names of observers, and (4) ethnic groups.

In the catalogue of a general library or in an A&I publication covering all subject areas, there must be a more generalized—even arbitrary—approach to access-point types and choices because the peculiarities of any one subject area or user-group cannot be allowed to take precedence over any other. A good reference librarian or searcher knows when it is better to search a general tool and when to take advantage of the potentially greater precision of a more specialized one.

The cliché is that one can find an item in a library catalogue under its author(s), subject(s), and title(s); that is, under person(s) or corporate body(ies) responsible for its intellectual content, under term(s) denoting what it is about as a whole, and under its identifying name. In the case of titles, the manual catalogue typically provides access only under the first word other than an article; the automated one, under every significant word. Each of the three is a very different type of approach; together, they cover what most end-users are interested in most of the time, with dates of appearance or publication often a close secondary consideration, but rarely a primary one. Automation has introduced the additional numbers and codes described in the previous chapter and has made access to these easy. One might therefore derive the following access points from a particular document: (1) **Eastwood, Terry**; (2) **Bureau of Canadian Archivists**; (3) **1986**; (4) *Toward Descriptive Standards*; (5) *Standards*; (6) **0-88925-680-2**; and (7) **C86-091272-8**, the two numeric codes being its ISBN and its *Canadiana* record-identifier number, respectively. Throughout this book, an access point is shown to be such by the use of the different typeface shown here. **Upper/Lower Case** is used for a personal/corporate/place name; **FULL CAPITALS** for a topical (subject) access point; *italics* for a title or any word(s) taken from a title; and **000** (digits) as relevant for a numeric code. In part I, use of boldface type does not imply that the access point in question is necessarily authorized by any one particular cataloguing code or access-point system; the examination of access-point forms under particular rules of practice is deferred to part II.

HOW MUCH ACCESS?

The most uncomplicated manner of providing access to a single record in a file is the one almost invariably used in the smallest manual files: lists of citations at the back of an article or a book. Only one citation of each document appears in the file. The citations are arranged in alphabetic order by the single access point considered most important for each document, normally its primary personal author (see next subsection). The simplicity and economy of this single-access method is the reason it was also chosen for many much larger bibliographic files produced and consulted manually. The largest such file ever compiled, the union catalogue maintained at the Library of Congress, was designed as a single-access file when it was started as a card file in 1902. This characteristic greatly influenced the development of the cataloguing rules for the identification of works discussed at the end of chapter 6. By 1982, when this file ceased to be a published file in print form, it, like many smaller but similar library-based files, came to include such additional access points as (1) name cross-references and (2) access under the name of each of several co-authors of a document.

Many bibliographic activities are based on document identification: matching a citation brought by a user or in a bookseller's list against what the library owns or can locate, or matching an item in hand with an existing citation for it. All resource-sharing functions are based on document identification, as is administrative stock-control, including acquisitions and circulation. For such purposes, the single-record, single-access manual file remains the ideal search tool it has been for centuries regardless of how many records it contains. The user must only know which file is the best to consult and the rules by which records are arranged in that file, and come with accurate data of the right type.

Information retrieval is a different matter. Its focus is not limited to objectively ascertainable characteristics of particular documents; it includes the world of interconnected topical concepts. Many a searcher seems willing to browse the whole of a small file, whatever the order of its records, to ascertain the presence or absence of something relevant. However, personal motivation and the occasional success to keep one going are the determinants of how large a file one is willing to scan, and such a process would be better described as groping than searching. Automation encourages

1) using a single record for both accounting and information-retrieval functions by integrating into it all data needed for either type of function

2) integrating single files into ever larger databases for separate or combined searching using a common command language

3) replacing confident application of a known search strategy with reliance on a heuristic trial-and-error process ("If I can't find it this way, let's try another") and

4) searching done directly by the end-user (often at the home or office) rather than by or with the mediation of an information professional.

All of these trends have profound influence on the choice of access points and the arrangement and searching of files (the topic of chapter 4). Reassessing manual practices of both creating and searching access points must be an evolutionary process. One cannot wipe away in a stroke either every existing manual file or the ingrained habits of users still familiar with manual processes. The first steps in bibliographic automation, hardly a generation ago, looked back as much as forward and required reorientation. Implementation of what is possible is deliberate and focused but continues to be slow.

Access by Name of Author

Long-standing Western bibliographic tradition opts for the name of the personal creator (or the principal one) of a work's intellectual content—the author, composer, artist, etc.—as the usual access point in any single-access list. This is based on the importance attached in Western civilization to assigning ideas to individuals. The chief purpose of incorporating into a work citations to other works is therefore to enable its user to verify the authenticity of its claims by discovering in context what others think about the topic in question. The content of the work already provides the context, making redundant any further statement of the subject within the citations. The *authors* of the works cited are the primary reason for citation. This explains both why style manuals for academic citation specify the author's name as the normal first element of a citation and why these names are to be given in a filing order for direct retrieval (surname first) only when the references are grouped in one place, not when they are presented in isolation as single footnotes.

For most of the five-hundred-year history of the bibliographic control of printed materials, the purpose of document identification (as distinguished from information retrieval) was also ideally served by access under the name of an author. Since a work's personal author was considered its most important bibliographic characteristic, the name of that person (and usually it was only one person) featured prominently in any document embodying that work and was generally known to those who wanted access to the work. It is no accident that author listings predominate in the history of bibliographic control.

However, an author's name cannot serve in the case of an anonymous work and is an awkward choice in the case of a pseudonymous one. Multiple authorship and committee and corporate responsibility also came to complicate the choice of the author's name as a document's only, or at least most important, access point. Despite complications in deriving this access point from information in the document, librarians still make it the basis for organizing even their multiple-access catalogues for the reasons discussed at the end of chapter 6. They call this the publication's *main entry heading* or *principal access point*.

Other Access Points; Multiple Access

Access via other data elements is clearly desirable for document retrieval and essential for information (subject) retrieval. When no author's name is available for a document, its title (searchable via its first word other than an article) has always been the alternative choice for its principal access point. This emphasizes the theory that a title serves primarily for document identification and retrieval, not for subject access, despite the fact that title words have always been accorded some role in subject access at least for works of nonfiction.

Prior to computerization, when it was impracticable to provide the access now taken for granted to every word of a title, classification and subject headings were considered the only proper means of providing subject (information) access. The shift detailed in chapter 7 toward making title words an integral part of subject retrieval has been the change most visible and valued to the end-user effected by bibliographic automation. However, such words are still normally accessible in a library's OPAC only in a title index. They are thus separated from the access points *intended* for subject retrieval: subject headings in the subject index. Reasons for, and implications of, this distinction are clear to librarians but not necessarily to end-users, who are are as often as not confused by them.[1]

Predictable title access to anonymous classics and folk literature is more necessary (because these have no author to cite) but less certain (because they appear in many versions with different titles, even in the same language). A title adopted by tradition, which does not necessarily appear on the document being listed, is the cataloguer's solution, for example, *Bible*; *Arabian Nights*. Uses of this uniform title are discussed in chapter 6.

There are works largely unknown except by the names of their publishers, for example, a Chilton automobile repair manual, a Sunset garden book, a Time-Life cookbook. Publisher-name access is also useful in lists designed for book-trade and library selection purposes. In a rapidly changing technological field, a date may be the most immediately significant characteristic of a document's content, making a chronological arrangement of citations more useful than any other.

Different access elements serve best for retrieving different categories of documents and for answering different types of user requests. Over the years, the need for multiple access was answered as economics and technological advance permitted. The complex history of the Library of Congress's publication of its major bibliographic service under various titles and in a succession of formats is a useful case study illustrating the problems of single-access lists and the gradual process of adding access points.

Limits to Multiple Access

Aside from any budgetary considerations, to provide access to every possible data element useful to every searcher would render a manual file in card or book form less useful because of its sheer size. Requests considered frivolous have always been ignored in selecting access points to be displayed, even in the context of the greater access possibilities of digital files. The student told to read any three books from a given reading list wants the three shortest ones, but is probably unable to delimit any search by number of pages without looking at the record for each item.

Other demands, if not frivolous, are answered by one type of bibliographic reference tool whose information need not be duplicated in another. The user who wants a novel by a New Zealand author is expected to find some appropriate names and titles (for example, in a monographic bibliography of Commonwealth writing or a literary encyclopaedia) before going to the library's catalogue to see which of them the library has. To search the library's catalogue under **NEW ZEALAND FICTION** might retrieve some critiques but not the novels the user wants. No bibliographic list is an island. Each depends on others for its most productive use.

In addition to reasonable limits on the *types* of access points provided, there are also traditional arbitrary limits on their *number.* For example, of many authors, only the first (or, typically, first three) might be made accessible. Accessibility of a title in a manual file only by its first word other than an article has already been mentioned. If the filing word of a title is generic (for example, *Introduction, Proceedings*), many cataloguing rules of the past suggested that no title access be provided (unless it had to serve in lieu of an author's name as principal access to the document). Similarly, if the title duplicates a subject heading assigned to the same item (for example *Chemistry*), title access was suppressed in a catalogue including authors, titles, and subjects in a single sequence, because the two types of access point would file in the same place. Practical limitations on the size of manual files inspired these and other such limitations, but some were carried over into early OPACs without a full examination of their implications in the context of divided files and separate indices.

That more than one subject-based access point per document must be permitted has always been taken for granted, but various practices were refined to keep the number of subject access points under firm control in manual files, notably:

1) only the one or few topics constituting the focus of the document *as a whole* is represented in an access point, not the many topics treated in its separate chapters and sections, and

2) several concepts are combined, or *pre-coordinated,* into a single access point; for example, **PHOTOGRAPHY OF ANIMALS** is used instead of two separate ones: (a) **PHOTOGRAPHY** and (b) **ANIMALS** (detailed discussion of pre-coordination begins in chapter 4).

Again, these practices are changing, but neither quickly nor completely, in computer-based access to digital files created by librarians.

The desire for more access points led to experimentation as soon as practical limitations could be overcome or minimized. Access to all significant words of any title was welcomed early to enhance the subject access provided by terms selected from a predetermined list. This would also serve in document identification when the searcher could not recall a title exactly or completely. Before computers were applied to the problem, electromechanical sorting and printing devices led to the production of an instantly welcomed type of index, the keyword-in-context (KWIC) and keyword-out-of-context (KWOC) title lists illustrated in figure 12. Each word in a title becomes an access point except designated ones (notably articles) placed on a *stoplist* and therefore bypassed as access points. Computer-based searching immediately incorporated the KWOC technique, making these printed indices historical curiosities now.

As mentioned at the beginning of this chapter, a casual user without a well-formulated specific information need likes to browse. The North American philosophy of library service involves encouraging browsing by having all shelving open to the public, but limitations to

```
   600 Users Meet the COM  Catalog
 Two Years with a Closed  Catalog
        Closing the Card  Catalog          the New York Experience
  Card Catalog to On-Line  Catalog          the Transitional Process
                    Card  Catalog          the On-Line Catalog: the T
      Living amid Closed  Catalogs
    The Effect of Closed  Catalogs         on Public Access
                          Catalogue        Use Survey
     Alternative Forms of  Catalogues       in Large Research Libraries


Catalog      600 Users Meet the COM Catalog
Catalog      Card Catalog to On-Line Catalog: the Transitional Process
Catalog      Closing the Card Catalog: the New York Experience
Catalog      Two Years with a Closed Catalog
Catalogs     The Effect of Closed Catalogs on Public Access
Catalogs     Living amid Closed Catalogs
Catalogue    Catalogue Use Survey
Catalogues   Alternative Forms of Catalogues in Large Research Libraries
```

FIGURE 12.   Above, a portion of a KWIC index; below, a KWOC index covering the same items. In the former, the titles are arranged by the keyword *and* any following words; words preceding it are transferred to the end. In the latter, the keyword is isolated but the complete title is associated with it.

its effectiveness are increasingly serious. Items are in circulation; misshelving is less regularly tidied up; more and more items are placed in storage areas where only staff are allowed. In any case, browsing is only effective under one classification-based access point per item, but not under such multiple subject terms as may be access points in an alphabetically arranged catalogue. Libraries have always kept catalogues consisting of bibliographic records arranged according to the classification symbols under which the documents are shelved but few made this access mechanism available to the public prior to automation. The effective searcher became adept at ways of minimizing the effect of all these limitations to access in the manual bibliography or catalogue.

Before they moved to digital data, libraries and the A&I services adopted approximately the same limitations on access. The latter typically went farther, many providing no title access but only author and subject access. Following automation, the A&I services generally upgraded and modernized access potential much more quickly and thoroughly. That the North American ones are increasingly competitive businesses is one reason. A more persuasive one is that they had no dead weight of an existing catalogue of actual holdings to be incorporated seamlessly into their new systems. An A&I service can make a break with its own past whenever it is ready much more easily than can most libraries.

From this description of multiple access points per record, one may conclude that automation opened the flood-gates of access points, for better or (sometimes, probably) for worse. Some access methods technically feasible before automation were only put into effect as a result of it and the new expectations it created. What is most amazing in retrospect is how librarians made a virtue of necessity in searching manual files. The limitations described here were viewed as positive aids. They restricted the potential for confusion by requiring the user to have formulated a clear search strategy, a defined goal, and a method of reaching it, *before* approaching the file or an organized shelving arrangement. This is still highly desirable for the most productive and relevant, and least costly, computer-based search. "Access" is not hit-or-miss ferreting through the haystack. The cliché "garbage in, garbage out" describes too many searches poorly prepared because a searcher thinks the computer will do the intellectual work. It cannot.

UNCONTROLLED VERSUS CONTROLLED ACCESS POINTS

In the Eastwood example on page 99, seven different access points are suggested for a book on standards in archival work. A cataloguer would call all but the first two *uncontrolled* or in *natural-language* form because, if they are used at all for access, there is no choice but to use them in the exact form in which they appear in the document. The first two, the personal and corporate names **Eastwood, Terry** and **Bureau of Canadian Archivists**, are also in an uncontrolled form except that the personal surname is transposed to precede the given name for filing. The wording used to identify the person and the body in question is wording established by the document's author or producer, not by any later cataloguer. If an access point is expected only to identify and locate a single document, it is most useful in its natural-language form precisely because that is what is commonly copied from the document into footnotes, back-of-the-book lists of citations, and many other bibliographic records.

There are respected bibliographic tools which use only natural-language access points. Compiling these into indices is relatively quick and cheap and very amenable to automation. An experienced clerk can quickly identify those words and terms to be copied from the document or from an existing record and input into a particular data-element index; for example, authors, titles, and dates, all of which are clearly identified as such on title pages or captions. A computer program separates the elements into their types, puts the words of each type into alphabetic order, and prints the result. Many subject indices are compiled from natural-language access points, since title words can provide adequate subject identification in fields whose subject vocabulary is relatively predictable. Now that so much digital bibliographic data is available for other purposes in formats which identify data elements separately by their type (notably the MARC format discussed in chapter 8 and the appendix), a simple program can be used to create a useful inexpensive index by extracting natural-language access points and arranging them automatically.

However, natural-language access points serve neither the needs nor even the expectations of searchers fully. To continue with the above example, the above document might well be sought in an index under a term such as **ARCHIVAL MATERIAL** and perhaps also under **CATALOGUING**, despite the lack of any of those words in its title (admittedly, the latter term is less widely used by archivists than by librarians). It also turns out that the Terry Eastwood of this title page is also known and cited elsewhere as Terence M. Eastwood and that the Bureau of Canadian Archivists has a name in French in addition to this one in English: Bureau canadien des archivistes. In addition, complete access to the *work* in question, and not only this one form of the work's publication, would have to include access to the title and ISBN of its separately issued French-language version. A bilingual catalogue would also require one or more access points designating the subject in French, whether or not taken from the French-language title. In other words, while some of the access points desirable in almost any file can only be natural-language ones (for example, a title as such or an ISBN), access points *not* directly copied from the document in hand may be equally desirable.

Most users expect more of bibliographic access than to find single documents known through citations, etc. They want to locate groups of documents related to each other in order to consult them together. The relationship may be one of those identified in chapter 2; even more commonly requested is a group of material related by subject content. The goal of bringing related items together in a file is difficult to achieve; in fact, perfection is unattainable if subject relationship is desired. Natural-language access points serve the goal better in some disciplines, notably those in the pure sciences and applied technologies, than in others. However, there is inevitably a greater measure of success and searcher confidence if a controlled access-point vocabulary is used wherever it can be.

The first step in achieving this control is to establish which documents share the characteristic under consideration; for example, the same author or topic. This is not always self-evident from the documents themselves. To conclude that a particular work published anonymously or pseudonymously has the same author as another work, one must discover who in fact wrote each of them! In the above example, one must go beyond the title to know anything of significance about the content of the work, and that content is better understood if one can compare this publication with others of the same and similar purpose.

Having identified which documents share the characteristic in question, the next step is to survey all the ways that characteristic is expressed, both within the documents and, outside them, in any reference source. Finally, one formulates actual access point(s) to express that characteristic for predictable retrieval, and if there is more than one, link them so that it is clear that they all represent the same person, subject, etc.

The first of these steps is more problematic in determining subject access points than those for names. For example, in dealing with the openly expressed personal name in the Eastwood example, the cataloguer need only

1) ascertain that the Terry Eastwood of this document is the same person as both the Terence M. Eastwood in his institution's directory (the book's preface mentions where he worked at the time) and the T. M. Eastwood who wrote an article in an archival journal (found in a search of an A&I publication)

2) ensure that the same document is retrieved no matter which of the following forms is searched: **Eastwood, Terry**; **Eastwood, Terence**; **Eastwood, T. M.**

In the context of the small local manual files and databases of the past, these three index forms of the name might be assumed to file immediately adjacent to one another. A user might be expected to assume that they refer to the same person after having browsed enough of the file to ensure the discovery of every potentially relevant "Eastwood." It was therefore common to ignore such seemingly minor variations and make do with only one form of access point for this person. The larger a database gets, the less one can take either assumption for granted. Furthermore, in computer-based searching, it is common for access points to be displayed initially divorced from the full record(s) to which each pertains. This makes it impossible for the searcher to use subject content, issuer, date, or any other characteristic of documents to know whether the three forms identify the same person or not: Eastwood is not an uncommon surname. Superficial redundancy becomes absolute necessity in controlling access in the large digital databases now so common.

Not every person is identified openly in everything by and about him or her, always using exactly the same form of name. Not every reference source and indexing tool uses all the full forms of given names available in what they list or index. Although only a minority of personal names cause the kinds of problem suggested here, it takes effort, time, and judgement just to discover which few are the problematic ones.

If only *some* personal names cause problems of this kind, *many* corporate and place names do, and the naming of subject concepts almost *always* does. This is so important a principle that examples involving a corporate name and a subject concept follow (again, details of rules and practices discussed in chapters 6 and 7 are overlooked).

If a list is to reveal everything created by and written about the animated-film production company started by Walt Disney, one must first discover every different name form ever used in any context to identify this corporate body. Disney Film Recording Company and Walt Disney Productions are two of those used in the past. Corporate reorganization generally accompanies corporate renaming, so one should not be surprised if the transition from one to the other of these names involved more than a name change. Even people generally adopt some different *persona* along with a different name, some of them simultaneous as in the case of Lewis Carroll (the fantasy writer) and Charles Dodgson (the mathematician). Knowing the nature and relationships of a body before and after a name change are as important as knowing the names themselves. The whole company is now Walt Disney Company and is a conglomerate, including the entire formerly independent American Broadcasting Corporation. The animated-film production unit is now only another (smaller) part.

Most users do not actually want *everything* about a corporate entity through all its reorganizations, mergers, etc. However, if it is desirable to provide separate access points for its various *personae* over time, it is equally important to link these because a user may not know or recall the exact name-form applicable to the time period, corporate subdivision, etc. for a given query.

In a subject search, a user may ask for material about rail-based urban transportation vehicles. The first problem is to determine the precise scope of this concept. This is an issue for the user and the reference librarian to resolve. Is it to include all of or be limited to one or a few of: streetcars? cars for broad- or narrow-gauge subways? heavy-rail interurban double-decker commuter cars?

The entity of a corporate body and even more of a person—and therefore its naming—is clearly distinguishable from that of other bodies or persons. A subject, however, cannot objectively define its own bounds or state its own name. Furthermore, a searcher exercises as much control as an indexer over what term is to be applied to the related group of documents requested. Some searchers are taking a broader view of the scope of a topic such as the above at the same time as others are taking a narrower one. Whatever terms are decided upon, the onus is on the cataloguer to have ensured that all the documents listed in the file and which deal with the concept in question *can* be retrieved so that the user at least has the opportunity of judging the relevance of each to the immediate need. This full retrieval must not be limited either by what words happen to appear in the natural language of the documents' titles, etc., nor by which term was selected to begin the search, be it **STREETCAR, TRAM, LIGHT RAIL VEHICLE**, or any other synonym, classification symbol, or code representing the same topic.

If every access point is controlled (except titles of documents, which are necessarily in natural language), a searcher can feel confident that each assembles a group of items related to one another and therefore significantly distinguished from all other items in the file. When only the work of the library's own cataloguing staff was represented in its catalogue, the measure of this assurance was very high.

Now, in the interest of convenient one-stop searching, a library's OPAC is more and more likely to consist of many files available for searching using a common command language. Some of them are created within the library but not by its cataloguing staff and not necessarily according to their rigorous rules. Some are likely to be "imported" from a variety of outside sources, any of which may include uncontrolled access points or ones controlled according to different rules. Any one access point encountered in a search may or may not immediately betray its status in this respect. Librarians do not always stress this important issue while instructing users. However, if the Anglo-American poet appears in a search as **Elliot, T. S.** and **Eliot, Thomas S.** as well in the more usual form, the searcher is right to suspect that even if quality control has been diligently exercised in some of the files, it is lax in other files in the combined database. Even if the access points of all the files in one database are miraculously consistent, every librarian and many users routinely search a variety of different databases, manual and automated, regularly. To use each one efficiently and confidently, it is necessary to take a moment to become conversant with how its access points are controlled, if at all.

Derived Search Keys

Manual indexing offers nothing akin to an access point created by applying a computer program to the content of specified data elements in a record. Because this is generated without ad hoc human intervention, it is called a *search key* in computerese, rather than an access point. If it is derived (from the matter being indexed) rather than imposed (by a cataloguer or indexer), it is an uncontrolled, or natural-language, access point. Yet the computer program gives it the controlled structure which is the predictable factor in a search. This is an administrator's dream: expensive human time is not spent examining each record to decide on each access point to apply. Using a brief key is also economical at the time of the search because it minimizes input-keying time and limits the potential for clerical typing error. How to derive useful access points of many kinds in this manner is the speculation of much of information science. In present practice, the technique may still be described as primitive, if serviceable.

A typical process of deriving a key combines truncation with post-coordination, both treated in detail in the next chapter. The system designer determines which are the most useful data elements and characters to choose for the key, depending on the predicted uses of the file; there are no general standards. A computer program creates the key for each new record from among its data elements as the record is added to the database. Although a key of only a few characters can rarely isolate one record in a file absolutely, a key well designed for its purpose can isolate a mere handful from a huge file, each of which is then easily scanned for relevance by the searcher. As an example, a 4,4 author-title key consists of the first four characters of the author's surname and the first four of the title, excluding an initial article or a word on a stoplist. Thus **BOOR,AMER** retrieves:

> Boorstin, Daniel J. *America and the Image of Europe*
> Boorstin, D. *American Civilization*
> Boorstin, D. J. *An American Primer*
> Boorstin, Daniel *The Americans*

A 3,1,1,1 title key is useful for isolating a book title; for example, **WIL,Q,R,G** can hardly retrieve much more than the *Wilsonline Quick Reference Guide*. However, a searcher must be sufficiently aware not to search this type of key for **PRO,A,T,O** in order to locate a *Proceedings and Transactions of . . .* because that would retrieve far too many different items to scan easily.

Words most common in the data element(s) from which the search key is derived are sometimes excluded in the process, for example, *report* and *proceedings* in title elements. The virtue of a short key is emphasized in the term *compression code* sometimes applied to this kind of key.

Derived search keys were designed in early days of computer-based cataloguing primarily to match books with existing catalogue records. This was the original basis for searching in the OCLC system because at the time, searches in it were primarily to match items in the hands of those doing the searching with records in its database. When only name and title elements are used, the search potential is high for document identification, low for information retrieval.

Although the power of computer searching has long since made searches using the full text of any controlled-vocabulary or natural-language access point routine, it has not necessarily made the results of such a search more precise. Access via a short derived search key remains the most technically efficient, intellectually precise, and therefore economical method of finding something whose bibliographic characteristics are known.

In several examples of personal-name access above, a person's given name(s) may appear in one location in full, in another in initialized form or with some omitted. The person's own preference may vary over time, and an author's various publishers may each impose a house style regarding the use of complete forenames or initials.

Most A&I services consider complete control over name forms too expensive and do not attempt it. Instead, many use a kind of derived search key to bring consistency to different forms and fullnesses of given names. For example, Cecil Heyward Johnson, Cecil H. Johnson, C. Heyward Johnson, and C. H. Johnson may all be reduced by a computer program to **Johnson, C. H.** for both display and as search keys, even though there is a risk that one of the people whose name is so treated is really Charles Henry Johnson. It is not unknown even for surnames to be tampered with by A&I services in using the least expensive data-input methods consistent with the search processes their systems support. Boor is hardly close to Daniel J. Boorstin. In another example, the compound punctuated surname Von Stoltz-Schmidt may appear as the access point Vonstoltzschmidt.

Authority Work

The Johnson example above shows that anything less than thorough attention to identifying and distinguishing each individual name or topic encountered risks a less-than-perfect index and less-than-accurate and confident searching. The activities and processes which aim at (if never achieving total) perfection were outlined in the discussions of the personal, corporate, and subject terms used as examples earlier (Eastwood, Disney, and streetcar). These are collectively called *authority work:*

1) determining whether or not a significant relationship exists between different names or terms and whether the same name or term might refer to more than one different person, concept, etc.

2) establishing and linking all the possible access points which could reasonably express each separate person, concept, etc.

Authority work imposes a cataloguer's decisions on how best to organize and display the identities (of persons, bodies, etc.) and the meanings (of concepts) implicit in the uncontrolled words and terms of natural language. It cannot be reduced to the clerical application of rules. It usually (always, in the case of subjects) requires investigation of many sources and the exercise of professional judgement. It is time-consuming because *every* name and *every* topic encountered must be examined closely whether in the end it proves to be problematic or not.

Despite the considerable expense of careful authority work, largely hidden from and little understood by searchers, it has been a feature of library cataloguing for at least two hundred years in dealing with names and since about the beginning of the twentieth century for the much more difficult case of subjects.

Other bibliographic services engage in it too but not in so exhaustive a manner; for example, some A&I services do authority work for subjects but not for names; others ignore it except in the case of particular names or subjects where its application is clearly desirable to avoid a known potential for confusion. Yet others do it partially; for example, by reducing all given names to initials because this eliminates one of the most frequently encountered differences between various forms of the same person's name, as mentioned in the Eastwood and Johnson examples above. As usual, the compilers of monographic bibliographies vary too much in their individual approaches to this problem to make it possible to be categorical about their work. Much depends on the nature of the material they are listing and the particular problems it presents.

The Controlled Vocabulary: Terms and Links

Carefully done authority work results in *authority control* or, preferably, *vocabulary control,* since it is the words and symbols of access points which are being controlled. An essential part of any controlled vocabulary is the systems of links already referred to. It is not enough to ensure that every document pertinent to the American humorist be accessible via the name **Twain, Mark**. Each must also be accessible via the name **Clemens, Samuel L.** and any of the several other pseudonyms he chose to use. A subject concept must be accessible via any term closely defining it and also via linkages among related but not synonymous terms so that one is led from **VEHICLES** to the fairly remote yet related **STREETCARS** if one feels a need to redirect the search along those lines.

Alternative forms of the same name, different names for the same person, synonyms for the same concept, and various terms indicative of different aspects of a subject field are all valid access points established through authority work. When associated with the document(s) to which they relate, each leads a searcher to the ones most directly relevant to a given request.

For practical reasons of file maintenance, *one* of the several alternative name-forms or synonyms for the *same* person, topic, etc. is usually given technical priority over the others. This is obvious to the user in the most common type of manual system. If one searches elsewhere than at the preferred name or term, one encounters only a *cross-reference,* an access point where there is no information about any document but merely a direction to the preferred access point in order to begin the search anew, for example:

Clemens, Samuel Langhorne
for works by or about this person, look under **Twain, Mark**[2]

How discouraging to be told constantly that one is looking in the wrong place in a library's catalogue!

Most library OPACs make at least the connection between preferred and nonpreferred forms in this relationship transparent to the searcher when dealing with the library's own authority files (see below). The system may recognize, but not betray to the searcher, a preference for either **Twain** or **Clemens**. It displays all the records for the same documents regardless of which one the searcher requested. Such user-friendliness is less common in other search systems. How the cataloguer/indexer chooses the technically preferred name or term depends on rules applied to construct each individual controlled vocabulary. Librarians use the most detailed and complex set of rules for this purpose because of their commitment to a sophisticated level of vocabulary control. Their rules are discussed in detail in chapters 6 and 7.

A controlled vocabulary is therefore the total of all the access points, *and* all the linkages established among them, resulting from all the authority work done on all names, subjects, document types, statements of intended audience, languages, etc. falling within the scope of what the indexer feels is necessary and affordable, that is, cost-effective. A file and its vocabulary may be of very limited scope, say, the bibliography and name or subject index at the back of one book. Created ad hoc, its use is limited to the file which occasioned it. At the other extreme, the two separate controlled vocabularies (one of names, one of subject concepts) established by the Library of

Congress originally for its own bibliographic databases are comprehensive in scope.

Both have been in existence and subject to continuous expansion and revision for almost exactly a century, paid for by the long-suffering United States taxpayer and in the public domain (technically only within that country). The description here of what is involved in constructing a controlled vocabulary indicates the high cost of this work. To copy what is relevant from the work of others is preferable to beginning from scratch for any particular project. The practical application of the Library of Congress vocabularies is therefore now worldwide and their users extend far beyond library cataloguers, even librarians in general, to indexers of all kinds of manual and automated files.

Three different types of relationship are expressed in the linkages incorporated into a controlled vocabulary:

1) the equivalence relationship, in which two or more terms are synonymous (as judged by the indexer and within the context of a given controlled vocabulary)

2) the hierarchic relationship, in which one of two terms identifies a definable part of what is encompassed by the other (a distinction can be made between a generic hierarchic relationship and a whole-part relationship) and

3) the associative relationship, in which terms are related in some different manner than in either (1) or (2) but still closely enough that they should be linked.[3]

In a controlled vocabulary of names, the equivalence relationship is very common because variant forms of any kind of name can exist. In the case of an individual person or place, this is the only type of relationship normally shown, but a corporate body may have parent and subordinate units warranting links to show a hierarchic relationship between them or an earlier/later name sequence warranting an associative-relationship link. All three types of relationship linkage are now considered essential in any controlled vocabulary of subject concepts. Like a person, a subject may be known by different names; for example, **TRAM** or **STREETCAR**. Synonymous subject terms are equivalents to be treated in exactly the same way as pseudonyms and other variant name forms for persons. The equivalence link illustrated above for Mark Twain serves also as an example here. Linking synonyms has few complications and is largely a matter of the technical access strategy outlined above and file structures treated in the next chapter.

Hierarchic and Associative Links

Hierarchic and associative relationships are more challenging than equivalents in both their intellectual and their technical aspects. As the Disney example shows, names of some corporate bodies may be linked hierarchically, but it is in authority work for subject concepts that these two links are most important. Streetcars are one type of public transit vehicle. If the file has documents on both public transit vehicles (in general) and streetcars (in particular), it is usually advisable not to use the same access point to represent both these concepts. Only in the most generalized sense—perhaps in a collection of children's nonfiction—could they be considered terms whose distinction is irrelevant. However, any searcher who locates PUBLIC TRANSIT VEHICLES should be informed that material on a more specific part of the same concept is also available under the other access point. Material whose focus is a part of a larger conceptual entity cannot help but deal as well with aspects of the whole, and vice-versa. A hierarchic link is warranted. Streetcars are not the same things as buses, nor is either of these subgroups of public transit vehicles a part of the other subgroup. Neither an equivalence nor a hierarchic link is warranted. However, a searcher looking for either of these topics might well appreciate being reminded of the existence of the other in the list by an associative link.

In a manual listing, a *see also* cross-reference usually serves equally as a hierarchic and as an associative link; for example,

> PUBLIC TRANSIT VEHICLES
> *for related material, search also under* STREETCARS

> STREETCARS
> *for related material, search also under* BUSES

Smaller files such as monographic bibliographies and A&I publications in very limited fields are now the only ones still kept and searched only in manual form. It is not practicable for one of these to show the user a fully developed authority file with its links, separate from the bibliographic records. The simplified cross-reference method described here serves their users' needs adequately, since browsing is also easier in them. In larger and automated systems, it is now more common to ensure that the searcher can distinguish between a hierarchic and an associative link and, in the case of the former, is specifically told the direction (broader or narrower) of the linkage. How these distinctions are shown in an authority file is discussed in chapter 7.

One retrieves the same records from a file regardless of which of the terms related by an equivalence link one pursues, although this may take a two-step search. Following up a hierarchic or associative link has a quite different result: the search under each additional term reveals more records. The search expands, and nothing in the system limits the result: only the searcher can do that by stopping. However user-friendly an automated search is possible, one does not want automatic retrieval of everything linked hierarchically and associatively. The purpose of these links is not to *require*, but only to *suggest*, that the searcher might wish to expand the search to some or all of the additional topic(s) so identified. Public access to the relevant authority file, whether automated or in print form, is therefore important to users of library OPACs and the major A&I services. The links are shown only in the authority file and the searcher follows up a given link only if it seems worthwhile to do so in the particular circumstances of the individual search.

The computer is making it easier than that to follow links to related destinations. Many library OPACs are programmed in such a manner that, having found one relevant document, the searcher need key only a number corresponding to one of its access points in order to see every other record attached to that same access point in the authority file. This is essentially the same hypertext-search process as clicking on a highlighted term on a screen with a mouse-driven pointer and being transferred directly to a different location containing, or related to, that term.

It is important that the searcher not feel overwhelmed by the number of links provided, particularly in subject searching. The very presence of additional suggested terms leaves a sense of incompleteness in the search if any is *not* followed up. Clear guidelines for limiting the number of hierarchic links are part of the standards cited in footnote 3. The associative relationship is the more difficult to keep under control. There are no specific guidelines, only the injunction that the expressed relationship must be a close one. If one links **STREETCARS** (a type of vehicle) with **LIGHT RAIL TRANSIT** (a type of system using that vehicle), should both these terms also be linked with **COMMUTING** (the purpose of using the system and vehicle)? with [any other term]? There must be limits! These matters are discussed in relation to the principal current subject-indexing systems in chapter 7.

Authority Files

An authority file is the primary product of authority work and the tangible expression of a controlled vocabulary. It is a file containing every established access point determined to be applicable to the names and topics considered. Each individual *authority record* in this file consists of a name or term, all the links determined to be needed, and the nature of each link: equivalence, hierarchic, or associative. In the case of an equivalence relationship, one name or term is designated as preferred and the others as nonpreferred so that all equivalents need appear only once: on the authority record based on the preferred name or term. (The inefficient alternative would require each term in an equivalence relationship to have its own separate authority record.)

An authority file is maintained separately from any bibliographic file; that is, it lists names, subject terms, etc., but none of the documents which are or might be accessible using names or terms in the file. There are authority files, especially of subject terms, created solely on the basis of the terminology and conceptual relationships of the field covered and without reference to particular documents. A separate authority file is not essential in a manual operation, particularly a smaller one, but any cataloguer or indexer finds one useful as a working tool. Even if every access point it contains is also an inherent part of the bibliographic file as part of a record or as a term in a cross-reference, it facilitates keeping track of previous decisions and of links already made. A separate file can hold information needed for its own maintenance in addition to the information needed by end-users. For file maintenance, it is important to have a record of when an access point was created or revised, why and by whom, and what sources were consulted in the process.

An authority file is never finished. New names, terms, and links must be added and obsolete ones dropped, and work already done is always subject to improvement. Continuous revision is one good reason for keeping the authority file in digital form. A better one is that a separate authority file is a necessary part of a totally automated system of bibliographic control, which most libraries now have. How it operates technically in conjunction with its related bibliographic file(s) is described in chapter 4.

Before automation, an authority file could only exist in printed-book or card form. It is hardly twenty years since the name authority file of the Library of Congress could first be consulted anywhere except at a card file in Washington, D.C. A name authority file is now a rarity in any but digital form. As for subject authority files, the four large red volumes of the current printed edition of *Library of Congress Subject Headings* is a familiar aid in any subject search and sits beside the OPAC in any larger library. This authority file is now a searchable file within many libraries' OPACs, but users who need to browse a bit to find an appropriate access point still find it convenient to do so in the printed version. The newest of the very large and quite comprehensive subject/form vocabularies, *Art and Architecture Thesaurus,* was sold in printed-book form before it was published as a digital file.

Although the primary purpose of an authority file is the vocabulary control of access points in bibliographic files, a subject authority file, whether one as general as those mentioned above or as specialized as the *Cosmetics-Perfumery Thesaurus*, is a highly organized and comprehensive conspectus of terminology and the concept relationships of knowledge in the field covered and as such, valuable as a reference source in book form even to people who never consult a bibliography or catalogue. This may be clearer from the more detailed discussion of thesauri in chapter 7.

It is not common for a single authority file to include both names and subject concepts. This is true more for administrative and historical than for intellectual reasons. Traditionally, name authority work is done in the largest libraries, especially the national bibliographic agencies, by people trained as descriptive cataloguers following accepted cataloguing rules. Subject authority work is done in those libraries by people whose qualifications include a graduate degree in an academic subject discipline since their work requires the interpretation of subject reference sources as well as of cataloguing rules. These departments, so professionally separated, are also separated in administrative routines and maintain files which up to thirty years of automated integration have kept distinct.

A typical record from a name authority file is shown in figure 13. Records from two different types of subject authority files are shown on page 290 and page 374.

ACCESS UNDER:	**De Cosmos, Amor, 1835-1897.**
USED FOR	DeCosmos, Amor.
	Smith, William Alexander.
Found in	His Pacific railway. (Amor DeCosmos)
	Wallace. Dates.
	Ency. Canadiana. Born William Alexander Smith.
Verified in	His Speeches of Mr. de Cosmos on the Pacific
	railway.

FIGURE 13.   A record in a name authority file.

ARRANGING ACCESS POINTS

Literate, print-bound people think in words. They are confident in the ability of words to define and express ideas, and in their careful use of words. Words are most easily accessed when arranged alphabetically. During the five hundred years of the Gutenberg period, the alphanumerically arranged bibliographic file predominated. It did not prior to that, and it may become less dominant in the post-literate world of graphic computer communication; but it will not die out. A bibliographic file is less an assemblage of coherent concepts than it is of isolated terms of value in a search either individually or in ad hoc and not easily predictable combinations.

The very neutrality of alphanumeric arrangement is often a virtue in searching. Everyone can be expected to recognize, differentiate, and know the order of the small number of different symbols involved. Therefore, using this arrangement requires minimal effort and offers maximum confidence that what has been sought is either found or proved not to be present. This is not to say that alphanumeric arrangement poses no problems. Before computer filing required its simplification, librarians had introduced considerable complexity, chiefly based on the purposes of different types of access point. A little of it remains (see chapter 9), but what does still causes heated debate.

Most types of information sought from bibliographic files can be alphanumerically expressed; for example, personal, corporate, and place names; titles; dates; subjects expressed in words; and even the symbols of a classification scheme such as Dewey's, whose very purpose is to express concepts in a nonalphabetic sequence. Arranging personal names alphabetically by surname is convenient for locating material by or about individuals. However, if the relationship of persons to historical events is of greater interest to users of the listing, it may be better to arrange them in the equally simple numeric sequence of each person's birthdate, whether in forward or reverse chronological order.

All that said, there are useful nonalphanumeric ways of arranging access points of some types. For example, if family relationships are to be shown, the only arrangement to serve the purpose efficiently is that of a genealogical table, which, being spatial rather than linear, cannot be reduced to an alphanumeric sequence. Direct access to names in such a table could only be provided manually in a separate index, and it was awkward to "point" from the index to a place in the table. Now, computer-based searching of anything that can be shown in graphic mode is commonplace. Names of places are very common access points. Geographically, Alert Bay is very close to Zeballos on the Pacific coast; alphabetically, it is close to Alabama. The subjects **CATAPULT** and **CATASTROPHE** may be causally related on occasion but the relationship is not a deep and meaningful one. One way to locate documents about catapults, howitzers, and other military ordnance together is to arrange either the documents themselves or their bibliographic records according to access points derived from a classification scheme; for example, the group 623 in the Dewey Decimal Classification or **UF** in the Library of Congress Classification. The alphanumeric arrangement of those classification symbols as access points locates material about military weapons together and separates it from material about natural catastrophes.

Still, the *use* of military ordnance is also closely related to such things as economics and politics, which are not part of the the linear juxtapositions reflected in the classification groups just noted. To locate documents on the basis not only of unilinear sequences (alphanumeric or other) but also of multidimensional relationships has always been a goal of information retrieval. Post-coordination was the computer's first notable advance toward this goal; further development of hypertext links, fuzzy-logic searching, and other approaches to artificial intelligence offer possibilities for interdisciplinary searching inconceivable in the sequential files of manual book or card catalogues. Developments in these fields, discussed in the next chapter, will have far-reaching consequences for access to documents. At the moment, however, most automated access to bibliographic files still betrays heavy dependence on the principles and techniques of manual searching. In addition, manual files are still used extensively by librarians and will be for a long time to come. It is therefore first in the context of manual file production and searching that some basic principles of file structure and its effect on access are examined in the next chapter.

4

■ ■ ■

File Structure and
Access Strategy

Technical, psychological, and economic factors refashion the methods of storing and manipulating bibliographic data and of displaying selected data in response to searches. This chapter describes the major methods of organizing and displaying bibliographic data to users both before and since the application of computer techniques.

The benefits of computer searching have rendered obsolete the sizeable manual file of bibliographic data. Wherever typewriters are now obsolete, even small-scale bibliographic compilations, although still published on paper or fiche, begin as digital files in their compilers' computers. Older lists of any size in a manual format will not, however, simply be discarded from library collections. Nor can one expect each useful one to be converted for computer searching or recompiled anew, although updated transfer of older bibliographic data into digital form is being constantly undertaken. Reference librarians must still understand the characteristics of bibliographic files in which information must be located manually. These are analyzed briefly in the next section.

In 1965, few librarians were either programmers or systems analysts. Not many more are in 1997. People who sold the new electro-mechanical and electronic data-processing devices told them that bibliographic data were merely a type of inventory data and as such, readily amenable to automated processing and searching. The truth then, as now, is that the quantity and complexity of bibliographic information are quite extraordinary. A library or an A&I service of quite modest size is easily comparable with any but the very largest business concern in its demands on an information-processing system. However many reservations or stock items an airline or a large retailer must deal with in the course of a year, they are constantly entering and leaving the active file so that the number of items requiring current processing grows slowly if at all. In contrast, any library or A&I distribution service must deal with a constantly increasing amount of bibliographic data.

On learning how to cope with the automation of their local collections, librarians proceeded to try to bring the catalogues of other libraries and the whole publication industry under the single roof of a search system, creating technical and administrative difficulties well beyond those generally encountered in the world of business.

An even more challenging difference between most records used in business and government and any bibliographic record is the inadequacy of fixed-field formatting for the latter. The needs of bibliographic files have generated considerable discovery and invention in the field of information technology, such as programs to deal with the variable-field formats and repeatable fields described in chapter 8. Phototypesetting driven directly from a computer file was designed for the National Library of Medicine and first used to produce the July 1964 issue of the A&I publication *Index Medicus.*

During the hundred years prior to the 1970s, methods of both producing and searching library catalogues had become very standardized and therefore familiar to librarians and library users worldwide. After this long period of stability, the computer revolution challenged every assumption and existing practice. Each library had to choose whether and at what pace to proceed along one of the many forks of the new path, or to wait until the dust settled. The return to slower-paced evolutionary development was inevitable. Despite necessary differences of timing among individual institutions, the library community is now assimilating the changes cooperatively.

The same principles of file organization and management typical of library catalogues have also been generally applied in A&I publications and monographic bibliographies throughout their history, but as described in the brief history in the next chapter, practices in those two fields never became as standardized as they did in libraries.

MANUAL FILE ARRANGEMENT AND SEARCHING

A bibliographic record in a *manual file,* here defined as one searched without using a computer, can only be located via the exact access point(s) assigned by the file's compiler and can only be seen in the exact form in which the compiler assembled its elements. Data resulting from a search can be excerpted from various records and resorted in the searcher's mind and on the searcher's notepad, but only within the ultimate limitation of what the file's compiler predetermined might be useful. That compiler worked within the context of what is practicable in both technology and cost.

Manual bibliographic files are still being produced, but now usually using a computer at least for word processing, text editing, page layout, even for downloading records from digital sources to be incorporated into the new file. Automating file creation results in a digital file, but if the only way it can be consulted is on paper, card, or microform output, the searcher is still faced with a fixed manual file; it is not interactively searchable as defined later in this chapter. From the searcher's rather than the producer's point of view, it might as well be inscribed by a quill pen, as in the Middle Ages.

Some History: Closed and Expandable Manual Files

There are two types of manual bibliographic files. To call them *closed* and *expandable* is not sanctioned by convention but these terms usefully differentiate them. The closed file took shape thousands of years ago. Each document, being a handmade original, was written for and housed in a private collection or institution or for sale as a single object. The lack of identical copies made standardized identification inconceivable, and the only purpose of a listing was inventory control. Since document descriptions, like the documents themselves, were written with stylus on clay or with pen on parchment, a library's catalogue was another "book"—its name, *book catalogue,* does not mean a catalogue of books.

The outpouring of new works following the reinvention of printing in Europe changed more than just the number of records in a typical bibliographic file. Versions of a work came to be available in different editions, and identical (or almost identical) copies of a publication existed in different places. A person who wanted to locate any one of these editions or copies suddenly found searchable finding lists useful to help identify and locate a copy of a wanted book, wherever it might exist. Early union catalogues were an extension of the inventory list, but Gesner's mid-sixteenth-century attempt to list every printed book he could discover would have been inconceivable and largely useless in the manuscript period. Soon no one list could encompass the whole. Enumerative/systematic bibliography was launched on a course of dividing the work into genres and types: national bibliography, library catalogues, bibliographies of topics, places, and persons—and all the smaller-scale work of documenting sources of individual pieces of scholarship.

A specialized list is a snapshot of what existed at the time of its compilation within the scope determined by its compiler. These range from the few citations at the end of a chapter, a book, or an article to the comprehensive bibliography on a person, place, or subject. Monographic publication in print remains a convenient way to publish such specialized lists. They are too diverse in their record and index formats and individually usually too small to be collected in groups in a common format and distributed on CD-ROM. Yet as digital files in their compilers' computers, they can also be shared electronically via the Internet.

It is too early to tell when predictable and reliable routines for locating and downloading useful bibliographies via Internet connection may be developed. The lack of format standards will undoubtedly ensure that, for a long time, any downloaded output will only prove very useful as hard copy on paper: another closed file. In almost every type of library, listings of the most current, the most used, and the most difficult-to-access material are constantly being prepared for public relations and as a reader's advisory service when a librarian is not available. These are typically still reproduced on paper, although libraries' Web home pages will undoubtedly be the new location of thumbnail bibliographies of "What's Hot!" "What's Cool!" and "What's New!"

Finally, the curator of any significant specialized collection still aspires to a separately organized book-form listing where its items can be described in depth and in its own proper subject context, with commentary. That standard bibliographic records for items in the collection appear in the library's digital database does not necessarily ensure its fullest use by a scholar.

No closed bibliographic file is ever perfect as originally compiled, nor can it be complete as long as relevant items continue to be published. Like a manuscript, a single copy of any printed bibliography or catalogue can be updated by adding new items and revisions in manuscript at the end or in the margins, but how to retrieve and update *every* copy printed and widely distributed? This is accomplished only by recompiling and printing anew or by publishing a supplement. The latter compromises the unity of the list and makes it awkward to consult in its several physically separate sequences.

The computer did not make the closed file obsolete. The file on a CD-ROM is only the newest form to limit its updating possibilities to supplements or reissues because internal cumulation is impossible. The majority of closed monographic bibliographies and sets of citations never do get updated or supplemented, whether because of lack of adequate financing, the compiler's unwillingness or inability to continue, or users' disinterest in the product. Yet academic and national libraries do not routinely discard old bibliographies on any topic. It is always important to be able to discover what corpus of sources seemed integral to a topic at any given time in the past. After the Second World War, some large library card catalogues were photographed and issued in book format as working tools in interlibrary loan services elsewhere; few were ever kept up-to-date with published supplements.

Nevertheless, few bibliographic files frustrate their intended users as much as a catalogue of a growing library showing what was in it six months ago or a national or trade bibliography or A&I publication whose latest available issue indexes what was published a year ago. Such tools must be kept up-to-date. In the closed-file system which dominated library catalogues until a century ago and A&I services until the advent of computerization a generation ago, it remained a continuing challenge to determine how best to balance the economics of production with the convenience of users in issuing cumulations, interim supplements, etc.

The manual file in which each record occupies a physically separate piece—one or more cards—shares one important characteristic with the digital file as described later in this chapter. To either of them, a new record can be added at any time without changing any file characteristic (except its size) or any method of searching it. With the industrial revolution and compulsory education began an increase in publication unlike any since Gutenberg or until today's computer revolution. The sudden growth of, and attention to, library services in the mid-nineteenth century caused a much higher priority to be assigned than previously to the currency of bibliographic information.

A card system caught on quickly, especially in North America, as a means of updating a catalogue immediately as new acquisitions were processed. (This was the theory; months might elapse before the card found its way out of processing and typing procedures and into the catalogue.) Yet by the late nineteenth century, card stock of 7.5-by-12.5-cm. size became a standard medium for the storage and display of bibliographic data. This medium dominated the library world for a century both in a multiple-access search system described as the dictionary catalogue (see below) and as the perfect manual method of exchanging catalogue records among libraries and for union catalogues (see chapter 5).

The first record was put onto a catalogue card by hand using a pen. The use of cards continued well into the era of automation with xerography and laser printers producing the image. Omitting consideration of the initial cost of creating a record, essentially the same regardless of file structure and technology, the cost of the manual file is far greater in its expandable than in its closed form largely because of the continual maintenance cost of manual filing and revision. For all this expense, a library got one complete copy of a catalogue (the cost of a duplicate was normally prohibitive) which could not be transported or even consulted off the premises.

However superior it seemed to other forms in its heyday, it is the least permanently significant of all the types of file discussed in this chapter. Few of any size will remain by the turn of the next century except in the most economically depressed areas of the world. During their manual period, the A&I services used a mechanized (not computerized) variation of the card technique, keeping each record on a separate linotype slug or photographic negative to be shuffled about and interfiled for cumulations.

Access in Manual Files

A group of records, randomly assembled, becomes a file of useable information when the records are either arranged or indexed so that all, and only, those sharing a specified characteristic can be isolated by the access point assigned to that characteristic for display as a group. A manual file of bibliographic records arranged by the surnames of the documents' authors is very useful. So is one arranged by dates. A digital file arranged by barcode numbers is essential for automated processing. An *index*, generically defined, is also an arrangement, usually alphanumeric, of selected data. What differentiates an index from any other purposeful arrangement is that it consists only of access points, separated from the rest of the data in the file, each accompanied by one or more *locators* pointing to the location within the part of the file where the relevant full record or text may be found.

The manual version of this access device in its technically purest form is known and used by everyone: a name or subject index to its contents appearing at the back of a book. An index is most easily used if each locator is a sequential number with no meaning but a locational one: something one can remember or jot down accurately, then locate directly and confidently in the complete file. People are accustomed to looking for a page number in a book, a track number on a compact-disc sound recording, a file or box number in an archival repository, a range-and-shelf number in a compact-shelving unit, a serial number of a single citation in an A&I publication. Among manual files, it is possible for an index to include more data than just access points with their related locators. For example, a title index may include the name of the author in conjunction with each title access point. This partial merging of the pure index function with the informational function of the complete file enables some simple inquiries to be answered using only the index.

Limiting access in bibliographic files to a single intellectually significant access point per record (that is, not merely a serial locational number) is discussed above. Such a limitation is rare in manual files and inconceivable in computer-based searching, so this chapter treats only multiple access; that is, the ability to locate the same record or text no matter which of many access points assigned to it is searched. The file structure of choice to provide multiple access in a manual bibliographic file has traditionally been a combination of arrangement of full records and indexing of access points. The full records are displayed arranged according to whichever type of access point the compiler considered most significant or most frequently used in the context of the purpose of the listing. In the case of a bibliographic file, this is often but not necessarily an author's name. One or more appended indices display the other chosen types of access point.

Figure 14 shows a section of the full data in a hypothetical manual file along with two relevant sections of its name index. In the former, editions issued by a publisher are arranged chronologically. The latter contains nothing but names and locators, not even the equivalence links discussed in chapter 3. One locator at each of the index access points **Clemens** and **Twain** leads to the same description of *Huckleberry Finn* by its serial number in the file of descriptions. Might this

---

```
 .   .   .   .   .

2506   The Letters of Edward Gibbon. London: Special Editions Club,
       1974.

2507   Huckleberry Finn, by Mark Twain (S.L. Clemens). London: Special
       Editions Club, 1974.

2508   On the Origin of Species, by Charles Darwin. London: Special
       Editions Club, 1975.

 .   .   .   .   .

- - - - - - - - - - - -

 .   .   .   .   .
Clemens, Richard: 278
Clemens, Samuel Langhorne: 532, 675, 1893, 2507, 3855, 4580
Clement, H. Albert: 2638, 5993
 .   .   .   .   .
Tuohy, Adrian C.: 1083, 1084
Twain, Mark: 532, 675, 1893, 2507, 3855, 4580
Twistleton, Frederick: 559
 .   .   .   .   .
```

FIGURE 14.   Links to the same description from two different, but equivalent, access points in the name index.

leave a searcher unfamiliar with American literature in some doubt that Mr. Clemens and Mr. Twain are the same person? But then, is it a proper function of the bibliographic tool to clarify this? Its purpose is only to ensure that a search under either name leads directly to relevant documents. Finding one or more access points in an index, then having to transfer to a different sequence to find the record(s) related to each, adds a step to many searches. After all, having found relevant bibliographic records, one is still not finished: there remains the job of locating and retrieving the actual documents. Yet most manual bibliographic files have always been organized thus.

A *register* is a sequence to which additions are appended as events occur. The full records in a bibliographic register are arranged in the order in which the documents were received or the records added to the listing. Such an arrangement in itself provides no intellectually significant access point, the only expression of the arrangement being each record's serial number in the sequence. Every search must therefore begin in an index, but it is common to include just enough additional bibliographic information with each access point in an index that a large proportion of searchers are satisfied by what is found at the index and need not refer to the complete record.

This has come to be the file structure of choice for large ongoing bibliographies, including many national bibliographies, when they are distributed as *computer-output microform* (COM): microform produced directly from a digital file. This hybrid format continues to serve users unable to gain access via electronic communication to the original digital form of the file, whatever the reason. The potential eyestrain of using microform is no more (or less) a problem than seeing data on a monitor screen in brief nonconsecutive searches. This obsolescent manual format may remain useful for quite a while. Miniaturization makes it conveniently portable and remarkably economical both initially and in storage cost. The greatest saving of any register file over other manual formats is not its physical form but its file structure: the serial-number sequence of complete records, the largest part of the file, need never be replaced as new records are continually added at the end. Only the index sequences are recompiled and reissued regularly, each time incorporating all additions and changes.

Library Card Catalogues; Dictionary Arrangement

The only multiple-access file in which users came to expect the convenience of one-stop retrieval with the full record visible at each access point was the library card catalogue (and its later printed derivatives). Using cards and displaying only one record on each was an answer to the problem of easy updating (new cards can be interfiled among existing ones). It also permitted mechanical reproduction of copies of the same record, reducing the cost of maintaining this degree of redundancy. In this *unit-card method,* a copy of the full record is filed under each of several different access points in a user-friendly but costly file format.

During the hundred-year period (roughly 1870 to 1970) when this was the technology used almost exclusively in libraries to record their own holdings, the library card catalogue was unusual also in the arrangement of its access points. Instead of separating them by type into several sequences, a single alphanumeric sequence incorporating authors, titles, and subject terms was considered more user-friendly. This single-sequence *dictionary arrangement* was championed by Charles Ammi Cutter and adopted in most North American libraries of all types. When it became the arrangement of the internal catalogues at the Library of Congress, its consequences were also incorporated into all the cataloguing rules developed in conjunction with that library, including those in current use. The popular (as distinguished from academic) printed A&I publications were also structured this way. Libraries began abandoning the dictionary arrangement in the 1960s to separate at least topical-subject access points from the others.

The development of theories of information retrieval in the previous decade led to a realization that it is better to separate author and title access for document identification from subject access for information retrieval. Before librarians could standardize one of a variety of ways of dividing a manual catalogue into separate sequences, automation rendered it obsolete. Their thoughts on dividing a file were realized in the way indices to digital files are now separated for searching.

DATA MANAGEMENT FOR COMPUTER-BASED SEARCHING

A *database management system* (DBMS) is software to organize data so that the existence of any specified content (for example, Smith, John) of any specified type of data element (for example, a primary author) appearing in any record can be determined in a search and so that data thus retrieved in one part of a search process can be compared with data retrieved in another part (for example, **CHEMISTRY** as a subject access point) related to the same record. (A later section of this chapter is devoted to this important process of comparing, called *coordination.*) In this simplified definition, a librarian's rather than a programmer's, *specified* signifies that (1) the person constructing the file defines each data-element type to be separated from others in a search or comparison and (2) the searcher defines, ad hoc, which data element(s) the program should search and which specific characters (words, numbers, etc.) it should look for there.

The type of basic file structure almost invariably used by a DBMS for bibliographic purposes is the *inverted file*. Its most familiar analogy, if an oversimplified one, is in back-of-the-book indexing. In this analogy, the text of the book is a sequence of bibliographic records. Access points derived from, or established on the basis of analyzing, the content of the records are arranged in a searchable order in one or more separate files (name index, subject index, etc.). In each index, the access point is followed by one or more *locators* (*pointers* is a synonymous term also found). The searcher brings the access point together with the relevant record(s) by following the locators to their source (page numbers or item numbers). (*Relational file* structure has some advantages in searching complex files and is gaining favour for small-file applications in special libraries. However, it also has limitations and no major vendor to libraries is yet marketing a relational-database system, so it is ignored here.)

Discussion of the technical details of DBMS programming are not pursued further here. Few librarians need become familiar with them. The remainder of this chapter is devoted to the description of applications of the simple inverted file structure to bibliographic search procedures and the display of results of a search.

Every cataloguing rule in history has had two purposes:

1) to *format* bibliographic data for display in an intelligible manner as complete records and
2) to *index* some of those data by making them searchable in the form of access points.

Before automation, the verb *to format* was little used, and these two functions were considered separate (they are still separated in the two parts of AACR). Within a DBMS, they are the *same* function, the basis of both searching and display being the same differentiation of data elements according to their potential use for either purpose.

Whether for manual or computer-based searching and display, formatting requires human judgement in the application of rules which allow some latitude for interpreting particular bibliographic circumstances. With data elements, their expected locations, and the context of their usual occurrence defined precisely enough, programs to recognize specific elements when a title page or a body of text is optically scanned exist, but are not yet operationally satisfactory. Cataloguing and indexing without human intervention are applications of artificial intelligence still in the experimental stage.

Bibliographic formats are the focus of chapter 8, but the one most obvious difference between formatting for manual and automated searching transcends the formats discussed there. In addition to the data elements described in chapter 2, it is now usual for those who define bibliographic data elements to a DBMS to specify each single word (anything immediately preceded and followed by either a space or a mark of punctuation) as a separate searchable data element at least within some types of data. In figure 14, a locator consisting of a page or serial number suffices to link an isolated access point to other data identifying the concept, document, etc. Links in a DBMS are such locators: the otherwise meaningless *control numbers.* This is how a DBMS keeps track of what data are associated with one record, one access point, one data element. Each unit of data is inseparable from the unique and automatically assigned control number which associates it with related data.

One writes or purchases a DBMS as an integrated package of many separate programs, but it is only useable in conjunction with an operating system, communication links, and a user interface. Awareness of the first two is assumed here; the latter, programs to transmit requests from user to DBMS and convey results back, is discussed in the final section of this chapter.

The search capacity of a DBMS serves not only in information retrieval. It is put to use in every library operation requiring the identification of physical objects owned by the institution: selection, acquisitions, cataloguing, bindery preparation, serials control, circulation, preservation, etc. The DBMS is a necessary component of application programs to accomplish all of these operations.

A DBMS written for bibliographic uses has always seemed highly specialized to those familiar with what comes as part of software for word processing, accounting etc. Early ones were written to the specific demands of one library's operation, sometimes even by programmers on that library's staff, and could not easily, or at all, be applied to another set of circumstances. A DBMS is now so complex and expensive to develop that no single library is likely ever again to devise a wholly new one. Those developed within institutions or for single purposes a generation ago have almost all been bought by, or evolved into, private companies.

The maintenance, upgrading, and sale of a DBMS is now a major, and the most competitive, part of the international business of bibliography described in chapter 5. A commercial DBMS must be flexible enough to be modified, within limits, to local demands, both at the time of installation and later. The merits and drawbacks of how it meets requirements in local application are argued for months by librarians in any institution intending to buy a new one. Exactly how any one DBMS is programmed is unlikely to be revealed by its vendor in full technical detail in order to protect its features against software piracy.

In some ways, what a DBMS and its associated programs now do routinely would astound librarians who, like Rip van Winkle, have been unaware of developments over just the past twenty years. Memory, processing capacity, and speed of communication links are no longer serious problems. However, the early success of computer-based searching quickly raised user expectations beyond what many libraries could satisfy within short-term budget potential to upgrade systems and equipment. Few libraries have been able to keep pace with the state of the art in practice.

   Incompatibility and poor response time are the most common complaints as ever more users attempt simultaneous searching via one of many communication links a generous library provides to its DBMS. Networking, still the technical plague of all automation, is much in the mind of anyone trying to maintain and extend trouble-free "transparent" access to a library's database to users regardless of where they are or what hardware and software they use.

   On the other hand, basic search technique has changed remarkably little over the past twenty years. Rip van Winkle would still feel quite at home in front of the keyboard and monitor of his local academic or public library. Developments in the user interface have been directed more toward the technical issues of networking than toward changing the basic keying and display functions. The revolutionary changes from card-catalogue methods of searching were all the result of the earliest developments in automation, even before the application of electronic computers. The next revolution, the full application of fuzzy logic to searching, is in the earliest stages of application, more in A&I services than in library catalogues. Other long-promised breakthroughs in the application of artificial intelligence to information retrieval, like the automated data formatting mentioned above, are still experimental.

Finding, Browsing, Truncation

The most efficient method of information retrieval is to *FIND* something by anticipating its proper location in a file and going there directly. To do this confidently requires knowledge of both the vocabulary of the access points and the structure of the file. Without confidence, doubt sets in, followed by redundant and inefficient retracing of steps. In a manual file, every search is, to a degree, a *BROWSE* because one cannot help but see as much of a sequence of access points or of complete records as one has interest in or the patience to assimilate. Having starting at **WATER—POLLUTION**, a glance back as far as **WATER LEVELS** and ahead as far as **WATER RESOURCES** could hardly help but sharpen the focus of the search, with very little waste of time even if the starting point turned out in the end to be the best one. It was always considered a *dis*advantage of the card format that the need for a physical action to see the next or previous record inhibits this almost unconscious browsing.

In contrast, nothing in a digital file can be seen by the human eye until the data retrieved in a search are presented on a monitor screen, a printer, or some other visible output medium. To *FIND* a given access point is to ask the DBMS to compare, byte by byte, what is keyed in the search to what appears in the specified field(s) of the access-point index invoked. Having made the comparison, only two responses are possible: (1) here are the exact matches; (2) nothing can be found. Doubt is highly likely when a DBMS responds "Nothing found" in a split second; the searcher suspects that what is wanted is there, and very close. If only one could do what every manual search takes for granted and see what is hidden in the mysterious digital file in order to judge where the query went wrong! Developments in programming *fuzzy logic* into the user-interface part of a DBMS promise what is needed. If there is no exact match, the DBMS searches for and displays what seems *nearest* to the keyed request, following programmed parameters. Some bibliographic search systems are already applying this refinement.

Every DBMS can exactly mirror the act of manual browsing by displaying a sequence of access points, forwards or backwards from a starting point, until the searcher calls a halt to the browse. Once a search is refined into a command to locate and assemble a group of whole records, those records can also be browsed.

Truncation is technically used in a *FIND,* not in a *BROWSE,* command, but to the searcher it looks like a refinement of browsing because its effect is to specify boundaries for a browse. If one is unsure whether **EMPLOYABLE . . . , EMPLOYEE . . . , EMPLOYER . . . ,** or **EMPLOYMENT . . .** is the best place to look, one browses a manual index beginning at **EMPLOY** but stops on reaching the title *Emplumada* because nothing relevant can follow. The same result is achieved by using a truncation code allowed by the DBMS, as in *FIND* **EMPLOY?.** The actual truncation command, the so-called wild card, is not standard: it is most often the question mark (?), as in this example, or the octothorp (#). It replaces one or more characters; repetition may be used if the DBMS permits differentiation based on how many characters it replaces.

Truncation is a trap for the unwary. Keying *FIND* **PSYCH?** in either a subject or a title index almost certainly results in more items retrieved than one cares to scan for individual relevance since many will be irrelevant. Truncation is most useful when the resultant group is to be compared, or coordinated, with some other intermediate search result before a final display of results. It is also more efficient when applied to controlled-vocabulary access points because of the careful consideration given to their form and wording when they are established. However, inexperienced users commonly truncate any words of natural language in the hope of expanding a search as it stumbles toward a dead end.

The end-truncation (loosely called suffix-truncation) technique illustrated above is not expensive to program or to run and is the most widely used. The wild-card symbol typically stands for anything following the keyed characters preceding it, up to and including the next space. Allowing the search term to be truncated at the beginning (prefix) as well as the end is more costly in computer processing resources and therefore response time. It is not widely available as an option except in files of chemical data where the highly structured agglutinative nomenclature makes it valuable; for example, a request for ?GLYCER? retrieves **MONOGLYCERIDE, NITROGLYCERIN,** etc. Middle truncation, as in **ORGANI?ATION** to retrieve both *organisation* and *organization,* is possible but also costly. Using it, one can retrieve both *psychologist(s)* and *psychiatrist(s)* with *FIND* **PSYCH????IST?** (where each truncation symbol stands for one missing character). Programming for a single mark of truncation to take the place of a variable number of characters (*labor; labour*) is possible but the most costly variant to implement; fewer search systems are programmed to handle it. The problem of variant spellings is complex enough that vocabulary control, where this is possible, is a better method of dealing with it. Boolean operators (see below) offer another method of getting around it, since they permit keying alternatives, each of which is to be searched.

Interactive Searching

The previous section shows how the first bibliographic retrieval techniques programmed into a DBMS were direct transfers from manual search processes. It would be simple to say that the DBMS replaced the filing clerk in the card-catalogue system. It certainly did that. It also did much more. Even if a DBMS accomplished no more than the basic processes of a card search, it does so with speed and accuracy defying any comparison. These increase the motivation to continue a search which a person might lack the patience to bring to a satisfactory conclusion in a manual file. In addition, the speed, memory capacity, and accuracy of operation make practicable some highly productive search strategies described in the remainder of this chapter which are difficult or impossible in a manual process.

A reference librarian offered much help to users of manual files but was as constrained as the most inexperienced user by access limitations inevitable in any manual system. Policy decisions described in chapter 3 to control the size of the file for reasons of user convenience and cost are minor external features of an inherent and fundamental limitation. The user of a manual file cannot hold a "dialogue" with a file but can only receive what it has to offer, passively. Although each of its access points is linked to one or more records, no two access points are linked to each other except by cross-references or in the very restricted manner described later in this chapter as pre-coordination. A person may search a manual index whose access points have been separated from the material to which they point, and from other access points, then match the chosen access points with each other and with the pages or complete records referred to. However, no filing clerk stands next to the searcher at the manual catalogue, ready to reorganize the cards to bring together different relevant groupings as a search progresses and new search tactics come to mind.

A DBMS does not act on a file or files of complete records (called *logical records*) as such. It controls files (in a more restricted meaning of that word than hitherto) of data elements from those records, a separate file for each element type as defined by the formatting described earlier in this chapter. Each single data element is identified by a control number which relates it to the logical record of which it is a part. A programmer specifies, for a particular DBMS, which data-element files are searchable and which are not. There is general agreement among librarians about which natural-language data elements should be made searchable in addition to controlled-vocabulary ones, the very purpose of whose existence is to be searched. However, searchability comes at a cost, and libraries differ in details of how the search and display capabilities of a DBMS should be tailored to their specifications.

Thoughtful, accurate, and detailed formatting is therefore even more essential when an "invisible" digital file is searched using a DBMS than in a manual search of a visible file, where a searcher routinely scans results while simultaneously proceeding with the search. When a searcher keys a *FIND* command, an access-point type, and a particular access point of that type to look for, the DBMS searches the appropriate file and isolates each matching data element as a *hit*. Output programs within the DBMS (described in the section on the user interface at the end of this chapter) determine how much of the complete (logical) record of which each hit is a part is displayed to the searcher. The DBMS assembles the specified additional data elements from the logical record by matching the control numbers mentioned above. What is displayed is called a *hit list*.

The isolation and assemblage of search results occur only at the moment, and for the explicit purpose, of that individual search. The contents of all files remain unchanged, ready to be searched again according to some other parameters. However, the results of a search are held in random-access memory (RAM) by the DBMS so that they can be used as the basis for further commands to advance or modify the same search without starting entirely afresh. The fact that one can modify a search on the basis of results already obtained is what most specifically makes the process "interactive." Only when the searcher declares the particular search finished by keying a command such as SO (start over) or by signing off the system is the RAM cleared of all search results to that point.

While searching a digital database using a DBMS, the searcher is not merely a passive recipient of pre-determined information but is, to a considerable degree, a co-determinant with the original compiler of what the file can reveal. Not only can each searcher thus choose to make use of various capabilities of the same DBMS within a search, the same formatted records may be loaded into a different DBMS to be searched according to its different programming. Thus the operation of the DBMS is what differentiates an interactively searchable file (or, for short, *interactive file*) from a merely automated, or digital, file. If an interactive search result is transferred to a paper or fiche product for later consultation, it becomes, in that form, only a manual file.

Online, a term chosen in the earliest days of automation, evokes the wire (later, any other type of communication link) connecting the user's workstation with a computer's central processing unit to permit, among other things, interactive searching. In those days, before multiple ports to a computer and timesharing, and long before full networking, interactive searching was an expensive luxury and considered revolutionary, especially when the database could only be searched via a computer in a distant city. Although it is technically immaterial whether the connection be across a room or across a continent, the connotation of geographic distance adhered to the term when reference librarians adopted it to describe their linkage with a database service provider as *online searching.*

The opposite of online processing is *batch processing* or *offline processing*. In this mode, a request is submitted to the computer (originally on punched cards, later over that same wire or other communication link), but the processing is done out of immediate contact with the searcher (not interactively) and the response is returned at some later time. Batch processing remains cheaper but is less and less acceptable to those grown accustomed to the benefits of interacting with a database. Only the few administrative operations in which real-time processing is not an issue, such as the preparation of overdue notices, are still done in batch mode.

Online has a second connotation: putting the searcher in contact with a constantly changing database in its most up-to-the-minute form. Thus a library's circulation information is said to be online if the very second an item is charged out, every user of the system has immediate access to that fact. One can search interactively a database on the hard drive of, or on a disk in, a desktop computer; is that "online"? Is it when the database on that disk is a year out-of-date? It seems redundant to speak of a client computer being "online" with a server computer over the Internet. Although the term is still used, it has become more confusing than clarifying now that almost all searching is done interactively on the most current data conveniently available. In this book, *interactive* is used in preference to *online*.

COORDINATION, PRE- AND POST-

A searcher of any manual catalogue or index is often looking not for just one data element (a concept, name, date, etc.) in isolation but, for example, for two or more concepts treated in conjunction with each other, or for the name of an author in conjunction with the name of a work (a title), or for either of these in conjunction with a term expressing a subject, or for a subject in relation to a range of dates. This means comparing (coordinating) items sharing one data element with those sharing another to find which have both (or all) data elements in common. A major method of accomplishing this in a manual file is by using access points in which two or more characteristics have been juxtaposed by the cataloguer/indexer. However, if each requested data element has been isolated in an access point, the searcher can still compare the groups of records under each relevant access point. If only one requested characteristic can be identified through an access point, the searcher must look for the other desired characteristic among the descriptive elements contained in each record found at that access point. Either method is tedious; one only has the patience to do it manually when the number of records found at each access point is relatively small. Even then, it is not hard to lose track of the connections needed when going from one part of the file to another.

The previous two sections show that a DBMS can compare any data elements of any records quickly and accurately and—what is more important—interactively as the searcher defines and modifies the request. There is therefore less need for the cataloguer/indexer to have anticipated a request for a particular combination of characteristics. The manual and the automated techniques of coordination now co-exist in practice; searchers still need to understand both. They are therefore called by different terms to distinguish them.

Because the manual technique was integral with the history of cataloguing and indexing, nobody thought to give it a special name until the automated technique came along. Now, *pre-coordination* is used to imply that *before* any searcher approaches the index, an indexer has either linked two (or more) data elements (concepts, names, etc.) with each other in a single access point or arranged records in the file to juxtapose selected data elements, because that indexer judged it likely that a searcher would wish to find those data elements in conjunction. Conversely, *post-coordination* indicates that an indexer chooses, as access points, single-concept terms, single names, etc., which may come to mind to any later searcher, so that they may be linked for the specific purposes of any one search in whatever combination that searcher thinks effective.

When name elements are pre-coordinated in a manual file, it is generally by file arrangement (see the section below on names). The simplest example of this is so obvious that it is invariably taken for granted. A personal name is separated into given- and surname elements, but these are invariably pre-coordinated for filing as [surname] -comma-[given name].

The coordination of subject concepts is always more troublesome. Its theoretical foundation is not well formulated. Its essential problem is how to determine what constitutes one, and only one, concept. For example, "microwave optics" is a single well-defined topic. Yet this term combines two other topics, certainly not inseparable from one another: microwaves also heat foods, and optics is also the study of large wavelengths. Anyone who establishes controlled-vocabulary subject access terms is charged with deciding when any single subject access point expresses more than one separable concept. The practical application of coordination to subject headings, thesaurus descriptors, and index strings forms a significant part of chapter 7.

Thus one speaks of *pre-coordinate index(ing)* (both the activity and the resulting file of access points). To speak of *post-coordinate search-(ing)* is also correct. After reading the following more detailed description, one might ponder what *post-coordinate index(ing)* and *pre-coordinate search(ing)* mean, if anything, but these terms are also encountered. The key to the differentiation is that the indexer, not the searcher, pre-coordinates, while the searcher, not the indexer, post-coordinates! Pre-coordination might seem to imply that the indexer claims to have better knowledge of what a searcher *should* look for than the searcher has. However, modest indexers of the past were probably not claiming wisdom as much as making a virtue of necessity.

Post-coordinate indexing and the interactive searching which makes best use of it were conceived, but not satisfactorily realizable, in the context of the manual file. It took the arrival of the digital file and its computer-based searching to make them fully practicable. IBM had staff working on the problem of information retrieval using pre-computer electromechanical methods. Hans Peter Luhn's pioneering conceptual work resulted in the practice of selective dissemination of information (SDI), originally using punched-card technology. IBM in Germany later developed a DBMS applicable to bibliographic work, but it generally pursued hardware, rather than software, advances throughout the early period of library automation.

Among librarians, C. Dake Gull, Calvin Mooers, Ralph Shaw, Mortimer Taube, and other innovative special librarians in the applied sciences made the conceptual breakthrough of replacing pre-coordinate indexing with the post-coordination of desired concepts at the time of each search. They had inherited the cataloguing and A&I traditions appropriate to the monographic and journal literature of science. However, the flood of specialized documents acquired by their libraries after the war, the result of new interdisciplinary scientific advances, was not being well indexed in either of the old traditions.

The scientists these librarians served were exploring new, not rehashing old, discoveries and inventions. They sought concepts within documents in combinations not necessarily predicted by an indexer. Before mixing x and y experimentally in the laboratory, they came to the library to discover whether any of the literature on x mentioned y, however casually, or vice-versa. Unless the combination of the two was already a recognized topic of investigation, existing indexing techniques were of little or no help.

However, pre-computer electromechanical sorting devices such as those shown in figure 15, now primitive, were being widely adopted in accounting and other business practices to match separate pieces of data stored on punched cards as holes in specific columns or notched in fixed positions on the edges (in other words, formatted for automatic recognition). Huge piles of such cards served specialized information-retrieval needs in libraries (although never a full catalogue) and were issued as A&I tools during the 1950s and 1960s until computer technology and memory-capacity could replace them.

Coordination of Subject Concepts

Post-coordination was at first of interest only in subject searching, illustrated in the following example. In a group of thousands of documents to be indexed, one hundred deal with nitrogen, others with silver, salt, etc. Fifty concern the process of ionization; others concern electrolysis, etc. Among all of these, ten concern the ionization of nitrogen directly; others deal with the electrolysis of silver, etc. Indexing which respects the integrity of the intellectual content of the *documents* leans toward the view that if a document is about the ionization of nitrogen, it is most relevant to the user who sees that as

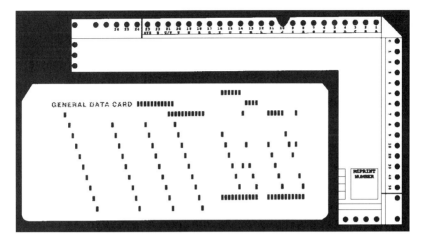

Figure 15. Two early methods permitting the physical sorting of a group of cards bearing access points coded within extremely limited parameters. The order in which the cards are kept before a search is not a factor. The punched "Hollerith" card (lower left) is processed by the passage of electric current through one or more holes simultaneously. This triggers one of a number of gates, directing the chosen card to a selected pile. The edge-notched "McBee Keysort" card is mechanically sorted when a modified knitting needle is passed through a hole. At a shake, any card notched at that hole drops out; two or three needles can be used simultaneously to coordinate characteristics.

one single topic and wants information about it. The indexing system should therefore make that user's path to that document as direct as possible, even at the expense of making it harder for others to find the document for their more peripheral information needs to which it might be partially relevant. This document-centered view is the one generally taken in indexing for manual searching (perhaps making a virtue of necessity as mentioned above).

For a manually searched file, therefore, an indexer might decide that each of the ten documents warrants the pre-coordinated access point NITROGEN—IONIZATION.[1] An equivalence link, IONIZATION OF NITROGEN see NITROGEN—IONIZATION, would ensure access under both the process and the substance (I and N), while preserving the unity of the pre-coordination as a single topic. (The words could be reversed in both access point and link without affecting either the search process or the argument advanced here.) Acting on the same principle for each of the hundred documents to be indexed means that the fifty dealing with the topic of ionization cannot all receive the same access point; that is, they will not all appear in an index at the single word IONIZATION. A searcher can follow up every equivalence link incorporating the root ion–. In a manual search, that is a cumbersome process; in an interactive one, it requires fussing with truncation and browse commands. In any case, it is unreliable in theory because of linguistic considerations: the morphology of a word may change depending on its position in an access point, for example, *United States* becomes *American* as an adjective. Finally, many an indexer would choose a blanket reference over a large number of specific ones: ION-IZATION *see also the name of the element ionized, followed by the subdivision*—IONIZATION. These are typical limitations of manual indexing in addition to those mentioned earlier.

In order to avoid the frustration caused searchers by cross-references, some indices with pre-coordinated terms display the pre-coordination as many times as necessary to locate it at *each* of its significant terms. This adds **IONIZATION OF NITROGEN** to the index every time **NITROGEN—IONIZATION** is called for, always with the same locators or attached citations. This is a common technique in back-of-the-book indexing, but it multiplies, not merely adds to, the number of access points required, still without isolating a separate and distinct access point for each concept (ionization, etc.). It further complicates the process if more than one word is required to express any one of the concepts involved, for example, *sales tax.*

This lengthy example has been restricted to two concepts in a coordination. If the desired coordination of concepts involves more separate concepts (say, **ELECTROLYSIS** and **HIGH TEMPERATURE** in addition), the limitations of pre-coordination in practice are even clearer. This is evident, for example, in the large and cumbersome permuted index portion of the ISI *Citation Index* series in its print version. Theoretically, twenty-four separate access points are required for the pre-coordinated display of the interrelationship of only four terms, shown as **A, B, C,** and **D** in the following table.

A B C D	B A C D	C A B D	D A B C
A B D C	B A D C	C A D B	D A C B
A C B D	B C A D	C B A D	D B A C
B C D B	B C D A	C B D A	D B C A
A D B C	B D A C	C D A B	D C A B
A D C B	B D C A	C D B A	D C B A

That six of these possible access points begin with each of the four terms introduces significant problems of meaningful word order. Some of these twenty-four combinations, when expressed in words, would make no sense in relation to the real topic, but how does one decide which—and would every indexer agree on which are valid and which are not?

The solution adopted by Taube, Shaw, and their colleagues was to stop pre-coordinating concepts within an index and to require the searcher to isolate each separate relevant concept to be combined at the time of a search (that is, post-coordinated). However, the several consequences of this were revolutionary in the 1950s:

1) a much larger average number of separate subject access points must be applied to each document or unit of text indexed; as a result,

2) some mechanical (later, electronic) method of sorting and comparing access points during searching is necessary: human memory and patience are generally insufficient to cope with post-coordination on the scale needed for any but the simplest searches; finally,

3) both the indexer and the searcher must bring to their respective processes a much clearer formulation of the intellectual organization inherent in the concepts at issue.

The first consequence is beneficial in that it eliminates, for both indexer and searcher, many of the technical annoyances of the existing practice of pre-coordination described earlier. Thirty years of the application of computer-based techniques by librarians and library users have neutralized the second consequence by making the technical process of post-coordination transparent to users. Even children now use the computer routinely for this purpose without recognizing the method. The third consequence remains the troublesome one. If anything, successful, speedy application of automated searching has lured lay users into thinking that careful prior formulation of a search strategy is unimportant: the computer will do it all! Pre-coordinate indexing/search techniques are more user-friendly in that the searcher has to follow the process in detail and think a bit about it. No searcher is as lost as one who has lost track of where a post-coordination swung away from a direct path to the desired result. Post-coordination has not totally replaced pre-coordination in computer-based information retrieval systems, although it has proceeded farther in the A&I services than in library practice. It is used the least in the preparation of monographic bibliographies and back-of-the-book indices because these types of retrieval tools are designed for manual searching.

One cannot predict when the last manual index will be produced to be searched on the pages or cards of a paper-based medium. Perhaps never. Pre-coordination will remain the method of choice for such manual media, so librarians must still study and apply it. In interactive searching too, post-coordination overlies pre-coordination rather than having supplanted it, not just because of inertia but because the latter is more efficient for simple predictable searches and requires less user preparation. If the lures of automated post-coordination seem irresistible, one need only remember that it is possible to post-coordinate pre-coordinated access points!

Coordination Involving Names

Post-coordination was not applied in its pre-computer days to searches involving names or titles as such (a title is the name of a work or a document). In fact, early computer applications to bibliographic work were typically restricted to sorting name and title elements for printout on cards or pages and had nothing to do with interactive searching. The names used as access points for a document are, on the average, few in number and predictable in form and type. The open-ended scope of possible concept-identification needs is not generally a problem with names even when the latter are used to designate the subjects of documents. Furthermore, the filing sequence determined by cataloguing codes for a manual file satisfactorily embodies any normally expected coordination of elements within a single name, whether personal or corporate.

An example of a search based on names asks for the text of a single work (*Henry VI*) by an author (William Shakespeare) as edited by a particular critic (G. B. Harrison). Three names must be coordinated because any one of them alone is an access point for a number of documents with a variety of content:

1) Shakespeare wrote a score of extant plays held in any library in numerous editions
2) *Henry VI* is the title of some (but not all) editions of one of his three-part plays; it is also the title of some writings *about* this play by other people and even of books unrelated to Shakespeare but about the historical king on whom the play was based
3) Harrison is an author or editor of editions of many Shakespeare plays and of many other books and articles.

A cataloguing or citation rule (for determining the order of elements within a record) or a filing rule (for determining the sequence of records presented under an access point) both typically require that items by the same author be subarranged by their titles or vice-versa. This ensures that the *work*—in this case, the particular Shakespeare play—becomes the searchable unit. The result is an alphanumeric arrangement of a series of subfiles; the whole sequence under the access point **Shakespeare, William** comprises a subfile for the work *Hamlet*, another for *Henry VI*, etc.

Nothing prevents the same complete Shakespeare sequence from being subarranged instead by the names of editors. In that case, the subfiles would consist of the editions by Bradley, by Harrison, by Kittredge, etc., and each of these subfiles would contain a number of different Shakespeare plays. However, that arrangement is not found in manual library catalogues because they reflect librarians' decision that to keep all editions of a work together by author-plus-title co-ordination is generally more important than any other coordination involving names. In a multiple-access catalogue, all Harrison editions of dramatic classics will be found together under the access point for Harrison. There, they are subfiled by the work in question, that is, by the inseparable pre-coordination of two elements: Shakespeare's name plus *Henry VI*, and not by a single element alone (the title of the document in question). In a manual file, economics and file size preclude parallel sets of different pre-coordinations: one cannot expect the records filed under the access point for Shakespeare to be subfiled by title, and (repeated a second time) by editor, and (a third time) by language, etc. Nor can one expect the Harrison file to appear in a subarrangement by title as well as in a subarrangement by the plays' authors (Shakespeare, etc.).

The pre-coordination of author-plus-title in order to identify a work is also valid in a subject search. A request for a book *about* Shakespeare's play *Henry VI* is not properly satisfied in a subject listing under H (for Henry) because the fourteenth-century king, not the play about him, is identified there. The play is properly identified by a pre-coordinated author-title access point for the work, SHAKESPEARE, WILLIAM, 1564–1616. HENRY VI, found in a manual list only under S. In an interactive search, it may be less easy to remember that the two elements should be post-coordinated for surest results in the subject file.

Coordinating Various Data Elements

In addition to coordinating subject concepts and coordinating names/titles, one must sometimes coordinate one of these types with the other or with a date, a form, a language, a location, or some other characteristic. The following are all reasonable user requests:

> Something issued by the Board of Trade on sulphur exports.
>
> Results of opinion polls on nuclear testing taken during 1993.
>
> A video on laboratory techniques in chemistry.
>
> A score of Handel's *Messiah* with the words in French.
>
> The text placed on reserve for the course CHEM251.

Several methods were made available in manual systems to make such coordinations at least possible without a record-by-record search through a single huge haystack to find a few needles. A library's manual catalogue was rarely only one file. Many libraries maintained separate location files (all course reserves in one file arranged by course number) and separate medium files (all videos in that catalogue over there).

Translations of works are so designated using a uniform title so that all translations of a work into the same language file in one group. A pre-coordinated subject access point may include a subdivision designating a form of presentation, permitting, for example, the isolation of public opinion on a topic in the subject file (presumably from expert opinion on that topic). The type of term most commonly pre-coordinated with a subject concept is a place name. In many academic libraries, the cards in a separate card catalogue of subjects were subarranged by the date of publication of each item. Much useful coordination has been done without a DBMS.

When an interactive search using a DBMS has effortlessly made a complex coordination in response to a search request, the results must still be presented to the searcher on a monitor screen or on paper, where they suddenly become a manual file in one fixed sequential order. What should that order be? Because each record's control number is what the DBMS uses to assemble the complete record for display, the easiest output order to program is that of the records' control numbers, that is, the order in which records were added to the database. In an A&I service used primarily for subject searching, this order (presented in reverse) is likely to be as useful as any other: it suffices to bring the latest information first. It can be useful for the same reason in the catalogue of a library, especially when subject access points are involved, but even for that purpose, coordinating with the date shown in each record is preferable because a library does not acquire items in the order of their publication date. The problem in libraries is that their users bring information requests of very diverse types, making flexibility desirable in how the results of an interactive search are presented. The development of such flexible user-friendly interfaces has been slow. It is discussed further in the last section of this chapter.

File Structure for Automated Post-Coordination

A file structure to permit automated post-coordination is shown in figure 14 on page 128. Since that example involves only names and is in the context of a manual file-with-index, figure 16 shows a subject-based example in the context of a fully automated system using authority files for controlled-vocabulary access points. Files including single significant words of titles, dates, or any other data element could be substituted in the example without affecting an understanding of the technique. The figure shows how the DBMS locates each of two requested subject access points in an authority file. (Their control numbers begin with S (*subject*) to distinguish them from control numbers beginning B, which identify bibliographic records.) Subject S10254 is located regardless of whether the searcher attempts access via **CHILD** or via **PSYCHOLOGY**. Bibliographic record

```
Child Psychology  (subject access point)
   S10254   (number identifying this access point in the authority file)

   B17389,  B35241,  B68172, [etc.] (numbers identifying the
             bibliographic records given this subject access point)
 .  .  .  .  .
Psychology, Child  (subject access point)
   S10254   (number identifying this access point in the authority file:
             the same number as above because it is identified as an
             equivalent term on the same authority record; bibliographic
             records need therefore not be separately posted to this form)
 .  .  .  .  .
School Environment  (subject access point)
   S02718   (number identifying this access point in the authority file)

   B06121,  B25713,  B35241, [etc.] (numbers identifying the
             bibliographic records given this subject access point)
```

FIGURE 16.   Parts of a subject authority file including links to a bibliographic file to permit automated post-coordinate searching.

B35241 (underlined in the figure) is common to subject S10254 and subject S02718 and so is retrieved when the DBMS matches the two access points. Its title, *School Stress and Anxiety,* its author, date, and any other programmed data element(s) are displayed to the searcher in a specified format.

TECHNIQUES OF POST-COORDINATION

The remainder of this chapter deals with the ways post-coordination is used to retrieve useful information from bibliographic files. For many years after computers were first applied to these processes, processing time, response time for multiple users, and RAM storage capacity were still significant problems even in systems using large mainframe computers. To offer searches involving truncation and coordination risked system overload because of the amount of memory and processing these techniques require. Libraries must still upgrade hardware and software regularly to avoid problems of this kind. However, a complex DBMS can now be applied to a very large file on a desktop computer and users have come to expect speedy response to questions requiring coordination such as:

1) Do both the word *law* and the word *family* occur in any title element in a record?
2) Does the word **Shakespeare** occur in any author access point and **fre** in any language code in the same record?
3) Does the word **SULPHUR** occur in any subject access point and the code for a state or provincial government publication occur as a type-of-document code in the same record?

Boolean Logic

To answer such questions, the librarians who mechanized coordination in the early 1950s replaced filing rules and manual scanning with principles already a century old. George Boole, a nineteenth-century English mathematician, left his name behind in boolean algebra, boolean logic, and boolean operators. The three boolean operators are *AND, OR,* and *NOT.* Each invokes a different type of coordination. In Boole's own time and even in the 1950s, no computer was involved. Now it is; only mathematicians know Boole in any context other than computer-based information retrieval.

The *OR* Operator

Figure 17 is a *Venn diagram,* a graphic representation of coordination. It shows the primary application of the *OR* operator. The searcher asks for documents about both Siamese and Burmese cats; that is, anything concerning *either* of these two breeds but not information specifically on any other breed. It is presupposed that some access point, in either natural language or a controlled vocabulary, exists to isolate the information relevant to each term searched. When everything accessible by the term searched first has been retrieved, this operator broadens, or expands, the result by adding to it everything accessible by the second term. This is an efficient way of retrieving information on a small number of separate topics which do not, when taken together, form a substantial part of a somewhat more general definable

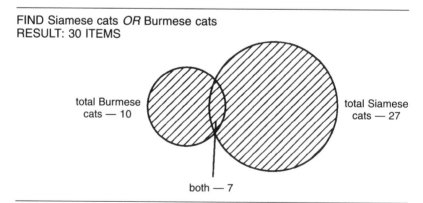

FIND Siamese cats *OR* Burmese cats
RESULT: 30 ITEMS

total Burmese cats — 10

total Siamese cats — 27

both — 7

FIGURE 17.   The *OR* operator retrieves everything shaded in the diagram: the twenty-seven records indexed under **SIAMESE CATS** plus the ten indexed under **BURMESE CATS**. The number of *different* records is thirty, not thirty-seven, because seven are indexed under *both* breed names (twenty relate only to Siamese cats, three only to Burmese). In most systems, each of the seven records indexed under both requested terms is counted and displayed only once.

group. Thus, in this case, one should not initially ask for everything about cats because (1) the latter is much too general a group in relation to the request, and (2) it is not practicable to exclude information on every breed other than Siamese and Burmese from the group "cats" using the *NOT* operator described below.

OR has a second useful function: to locate a single topic or name among access points expressed in natural language, that is, in an index not subject to authority control. One might therefore search for titles including either *Ceylon OR Sri Lanka* to retrieve books written before and after independence; either *streetcar OR tram* to get articles written in both North America and the U.K. Truncation, described earlier, may be a useful adjunct to this or any other boolean operator, for example, in a search for **Twain, Mark** *OR* **Clemens, S?** or for **LIBRAR?** *OR* **ARCHIV?**.

The *NOT* Operator

The least frequently used of the three operators is illustrated in figure 18. Its limited usefulness and difficulty of programming caused it to be ignored in many an early DBMS. *NOT* is the converse of *OR*. It limits or narrows a search by excluding some of what has already been retrieved through the term searched first, usually something in the same hierarchy of concepts. This makes it appropriate when a large part, but not quite all, of a more generic whole is wanted, but only if the part *not* wanted can be clearly defined and identified in one or a small number of access points. This can be a dangerous operator. One risks eliminating something relevant from a search if one forgets that some concept is encompassed within another when excluding the latter. Using *NOT* is particularly risky in a natural-language search of

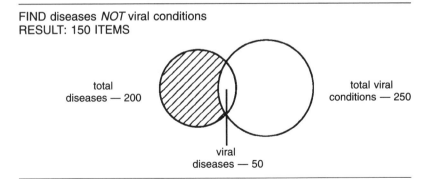

FIND diseases *NOT* viral conditions
RESULT: 150 ITEMS

total diseases — 200

total viral conditions — 250

viral diseases — 50

Figure 18. The *NOT* operator excludes the fifty records indexed under viral conditions (which must be specified in the search) from the two hundred retrieved as relevant to all diseases, so that only the hundred and fifty relevant to nonviral diseases are displayed.

a full-text database. A single occurrence in the entire text of the word declared to be "not" wanted will kill any relevance the rest of the search might have had.

The *AND* Operator

This operator, illustrated in figure 19, is the most frequently used of the three. When automated post-coordinate searching was first studied, it captured almost all the attention because most searches begin too generally and do not need further broadening with an *OR*. They need to be narrowed but usually not through the specific exclusions achieved with a *NOT*. This is a limiting operator whose action is more controlled. Its greatest value is in coordinating a concept with one or more others not hierarchically part of it. For example, a searcher does not want *all* the information available on Canada's external trade, only what is *also* relevant to another topic: taxation. Like *OR*, this operator is totally reciprocal. The same user wants not all the available information on taxation, but only what is also relevant to Canada's external trade. As with any post-coordinate search, manual or automated, it is more efficient to initiate the search at the access point likely to have the fewest records attached to it.

Especially if the file incorporates any natural-language access points, this operator should be brought into play only after *OR* has been invoked, in its second usage described above, to comprehend the whole of each desired category within the scope of the search. Thus one might use *OR* to link a title word *taxation* with synonyms such as *assessment* and *levy* before using *AND* to combine the result

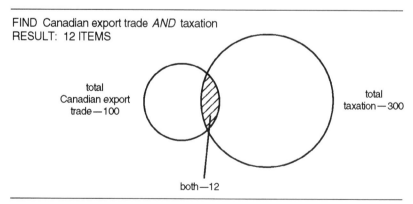

FIND Canadian export trade *AND* taxation
RESULT: 12 ITEMS

total Canadian export trade — 100

total taxation — 300

both — 12

FIGURE 19.   The *AND* operator retrieves only those records whose indexing shares the specified characteristic(s): in this case, only twelve documents from among the hundred indexed under an access point for Canadian export trade and three hundred under an access point for taxation.

with another term or combination of terms. The ability to use this operator is welcomed particularly in circumstances such as:

1) coordinating categories extensive in numbers of records but which overlap each other in only a small number of documents in the particular file
2) searching for information in an emerging field whose terminology is not yet stable but where particular words or terms can be expected to occur in conjunction in titles
3) coordinating more than two concept terms in a single search.

The **A B C D** illustration on page 142 shows why few manual systems have ever made any attempt to facilitate the coordination of more than two or three names or concepts at a time. Traditional subject headings may add to these one or more form or audience elements as part of a pre-coordination, for example, **MATHEMATICS—POETRY** and **CHEMISTRY—JUVENILE LITERATURE**. By using boolean operators and truncation, one can express a quite complex request in a single statement, for example, *FIND* **CANAD?** *AND* **TRAD?** *AND* **TAX?** *AND* **COUNTERVAIL?**.

Using *AND* to combine concepts offers potential for retrieving unexpected material from different disciplines. It can even start a train of thinking along new paths when the particular combination of concepts does not yet represent a recognized independent field of investigation. This is precisely when no pre-coordinate access point encompassing those concepts could yet exist. New knowledge, occasionally with startling and far-reaching implications, is often generated when new links are made between ideas never previously combined. The first combining of **COMPUTER** with **INFORMATION** might have been one of this century's most significant uses of *AND*!

Nesting Operators

The above discussion of *AND* includes an example in which four searches are applied successively; each uses that operator and therefore further limits the result. Each successive application of *NOT* would also further limit an initial result; successive applications of *OR* would each expand it. Most software permitting the use of boolean operators also permits more than one operator to be invoked during a single search. It is vital to understand how the search operations specified in the command must be nested in order to get the desired result from this procedure. The searcher must also know the DBMS well enough to know what is the default sequence programmed into it.

The two results shown in figure 20 are very different, although each is expressed as **A** *AND* **B** *OR* **C**. In the upper diagram, the program

FIND A *AND* B *OR* C
RESULT: 22 ITEMS

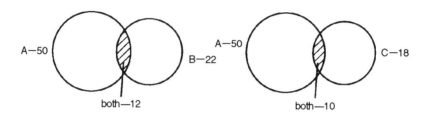

12+10 = 22

FIND A *AND* B *OR* C
RESULT: 30 ITEMS

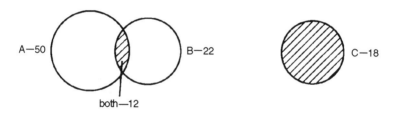

12+18 = 30

FIGURE 20.   The upper search retrieves a total of twenty-two items; the lower one retrieves thirty. The files, terms searched, and operators are identical; only the nesting differs.

in one DBMS first combines **B** with **C** (producing forty hits) before using that result to limit **A**. In the lower diagram, the program in a different DBMS first limits **A** by **B** (producing twelve hits), then adds all of **C** to that. Both results assume no overlap between what is retrieved as **B** and what is retrieved as **C**; if there is some overlap, the results would vary from what is shown. If the searcher does not want the result produced by the program's default sequence (or does not know what that default is), it is conventional to indicate the desired operation by enclosing within parentheses what is to be processed as a single unit. Thus the upper search is fully expressed as **A** *AND* (**B** *OR* **C**) and the lower one as (**A** *AND* **B**) *OR* **C**.

Proximity and Relational Searching

Searching for subject information among natural-language elements such as titles is particularly hazardous. Ambiguity is possible both in the meaning of any single word and in the context implied by any combination of words. Not to analyze the possibility of ambiguity before beginning the search is to risk retrieving *false drops* (irrelevant items), lowering the precision of the result, and perhaps even requiring a new start. On the other hand, word order is not as rigid a determinant of meaning in English as in many languages, and it is unwise to exclude combinations which may prove fruitful. The success rate can be improved through thoughtful application of *proximity searching*. As with defaults and commands for nesting, not every DBMS processes proximity searching in the same way.

As an example, a search for information about family law might request any title whose wording includes *family law* as a single two-word term. This retrieves both *Family Law in Canada* and *Introduction to Canadian Family Law* but does not retrieve either *The Canadian Law of the Family* or *Law and Family Rights in Canada*. To retrieve these as well, one might use boolean *AND* to retrieve any title which includes both words wherever they occur: *FIND family AND law*. This latter operation, however, also retrieves an unwanted hit: *The Effect of Family Poverty on Canadian Social Law*. To avoid that false drop, one can require that the words *family* and *law* occur within two words of each other. That would still retrieve the earlier titles and may suffice to exclude others in which the intellectual connection between the words is too tenuous to be relevant. In many systems, it is possible to request proximity of the desired words within any specified number of words of each other, from two to a dozen or more. Much experience of the vocabulary of the subject in question is needed to make a skilful user of this technique. If a controlled vocabulary is available for the search, it is always preferable.

The relational operators *greater than* and *less than* are represented graphically as > and <. Outside a numeric context, these characters are sometimes programmed to scroll monitor-screen output forwards and backwards, an operation linked with browsing. Their significance in coordinate searching is related to their use preceding any date formatted for searching. They permit the frequently desired chronological limitation of a result—not to a single year but to a range of years, either beginning or ending with the year specified (limitation by a month and day is also possible but little used). (This meaning of *relational* is entirely different from that in *relational file structure* on page 131.)

TOO MUCH ACCESS?

Among the consequences of automation is a notable increase in the amount of indexing of all kinds being done. It has also increased the ease and lowered the cost of searching all this indexing. Even in printed output, indices especially to reference books appear to take up a higher proportion of the books' pages every year. That this is an era of information overload is partly due to the fact that more of the information that was always there is being made a little more visible through an expansion of access possibilities. Does this represent the attainment, or even a closer approach, to the long-sought goal of perfect information retrieval? Full-text access to digital copy is now commonplace and the reference librarian is bemused by the possibility of locating every instance of any single word in an entire encyclopaedia within seconds. Sometimes this is the only way to answer a query; sometimes it is merely a game of which one tires easily. How useful is it to be able to ascertain which twenty items out of the million described on a single CD-ROM disk contain exactly 93 pages?

Today's access practices are Janus-like: they try to look forward to the most effective use of interactive search techniques but are still bound by the need of most users to continue to search some manual files as well. Although the potential in all the refinements of interactive searching is clearly greater than in manual searching, it may still be useful to draw comparisons between these methods without prejudice that the former must be able to overcome every psychological, technical, intellectual, and economic drawback of manual searching. It does not. Manual and interactive files are equally prone to good or bad content (that is, choice of appropriate terms for subject access, appropriate authority control, etc.). Where they differ is in structure and searching methods. In manual searching, the file's designer bears the responsibility for making it easy, difficult, or almost impossible to retrieve certain coordinations of access points or data elements (almost never are single words as such retrievable in a manual file).

Automated searching thrusts the responsibility for good search technique much more heavily on the searcher, since a DBMS is commonly designed to offer more access points (including single words) and searching methods. One can call few interactive files badly constructed, but their added flexibility is potentially confusing because more paths in them lead to dead ends. A manual file is therefore not necessarily a poorer search tool and need not throw up barriers to a successful search despite its more limited paths. The one sure gain in automated searching is speed (provided the system is not down or overloaded). The charm of this advantage should not blind one to ways in which a complex interactive system is more cumbersome than a simple manual one. The nature of the query and the intellectual acuity of the searcher are always closer determinants of the success of a search than whether the search is manual or interactive. What is more of a mystery is that it is not uncommon for the same person, searching for the same information, to get somewhat different—and not necessarily poorer—results when searching the same database in a manual (printed) form than when searching it interactively.

Administrators faced with staff cuts are increasingly hopeful that interactive searching leads, at least after initial training, to more end-user searching and less dependence on the costly interpretive services of a professional librarian. After all, the new generation is more accustomed to searching the Internet than the old generation ever was to searching reference books. However, when a naive end-user gropes blindly without adequately defining either the precise need or the most appropriate access strategy, there is a cost. In the use of manual catalogues and indices, that cost is typically the waste of the end-user's own time: a currency invisible to the library administrator. In an interactive search, it is more likely to be real library dollars if more equipment is needed or if a commercial database is consulted online. It is no wonder that such considerations are pressed in defense of user-fees for interactive searching.

THE USER INTERFACE

The user may want only one bibliographic record but has to search for it in a book, a card file, or a database full of them. The focus of this chapter thus far has been how the structure and search mechanisms of a manual file or a DBMS help the searcher find the needle in the haystack. During the process, however, the searcher must be able to determine what is happening in order to make decisions about how to proceed. At its conclusion, the record(s) finally selected must be displayed in some way either to be sensed (seen, heard) by the searcher or to be transferred to some other medium (disk file, paper). The system's *user interface* consists of the structures every DBMS must incorporate to deal with these functions, no matter how simple or complex.

In a manual system, the file and its user interface are the same thing. It is common for a reviewer of a printed bibliography to comment on its user-friendliness in terms of size of type, amount of data included in each index (as distinguished from what is in the full record), etc. In the 1960s, there was considerable discussion among librarians about whether a library's card catalogue should be in dictionary format (one sequence) or divided (subject access points in a separate sequence). However, the visual format and arrangement of a manual file are invariably constrained by the physical and economic bounds of feasibility. Therefore, any option in how a manual search process and its result might appear to a user has already been decided by the file's compiler on less than optimum grounds from the point of view of the user. The latter has no choice but to use the file in that predetermined manner.

An interactive file has no fixed state with respect to any searcher; each separate search process reassembles its records and their data elements. This makes it possible, even desirable, to offer a variety of options within the same DBMS to govern how both the process of searching a file and its result "look" to different searchers, each of whom has chosen to activate different options. It also makes it possible for the same file, mounted in each of two different systems, to be searched and seen in different ways. User reaction to the display of computer-processed information in large quantity is therefore a new and interdisciplinary field of investigation of which better designed interfaces for bibliographic files are only one product. Those who engage in it study the logic and psychology involved as much as the computer programming, all in the context of the intellectual content of the field in question—here, bibliographic information. That user interfaces exist in such diversity is partly due to experimentation in this early stage of their development. Moreover, the diversity is intentional because each user and each file bring individual characteristics to be accommodated. Their diversity is both benefit and bane: it can be confusing.

User Reactions to the Invisible File

The size of a file is closely related to the goal of any search of it, which is low-quantity recall along with high precision in the relevance to the query of each item retrieved. This goal is hardest to achieve in the context of subject searching. The size of a digital file is not the initial discouragement it often is in the case of a large manual file because it is not constantly obvious to the searcher. A digital file is essentially invisible until the process of searching makes some part of it visible, one screenful at a time. This is the most seriously detrimental feature of interactive searching for anyone but an experienced professional. The searcher cannot readily see (and therefore mentally grasp) the full scope of any component of a search and risks missing what might be right around the corner by terminating a search too early. It takes a skilful searcher not to get more irrelevant "noise" (false drops, etc.) when searching a larger file than when searching a smaller one. The earlier discussion of the browsing function touched on these points. Inexperienced searchers tend to forget, or ignore in their haste, the consequent necessity to plan more than one step of a search strategy *before* beginning. When the innocent request *FIND SUBJECT* **BIBLIOGRAPHY** gets the response "There are 2,579 items. Do you want to see them?" most searchers will ask to see the first few on the screen, as they once thumbed the first few cards in a subject group in a card file, then flee to the comfort of human contact at the information desk in the hope of getting a more comprehensible answer. A large manual file may have just as many records accessible via that term but at least seeing the actual records makes it easier to grasp their organization and their relevance to the search.

To the enthusiast, any interactive file can be similar to the Internet as an invitation to experiment. The more flexible its search strategies and display of results, the more complex becomes the task of identifying the relevant: finding, rather than muddling (a discouraging task) or playing (a happy one). At a point different for each searcher, the complexity leads to psychological hesitation to continue. Persistence is a function of motivation. This varies not only with the person and the purpose but also with file size and structure and with the feedback of satisfactory intermediate results. A look at an older card file tells much about motivation. In any larger group under a given access point, the first dozen or so cards are almost invariably more noticeably worn than the last ones in the group; both the fingers and the brain have tired. There is no doubt that the interactive searcher also is often mentally exhausted before the supply of relevant information in the file is.

User studies of manual searching helped define and apply the few interface options available then. These studies are being renewed in the context of interactive searching. Searching has changed radically, and there are many more feasible options whose effects can be examined. The simple phenomenon mentioned in the previous paragraph cannot be quantified in the same dramatic way in an interactive file as in a card file, but the time or the number of steps occupied in any given search is easily measured and averaged if users' searches are logged for later analysis. This is one of the techniques permitting a study of user reaction to an interface. However, the use of log files has ethical consequences, since identification of individual users intrudes on privacy. In any case, it is difficult, but worthwhile, to separate a study of the *process* of using a file from the type of catalogue-use study much more frequently undertaken: a study of the value of particular access points and access-point types in leading to satisfactory retrieval from a file.

The way interactive post-coordination quickly produces at least some superficially relevant hits from a search demystifies the technique of the search, perhaps too much. An end-user is not well served by the librarian who implies that information can be found "on the computer" as if the machine did all, or at least most of, the work. An extremely common failing among inexperienced searchers stems from this psychology: they do not see the forest for the trees, and therefore abort a search as soon as a single tree of interest comes into view. Anything that discourages continuation of a search until there is a *positive* reason to stop is not ideal. That "the computer" either has produced some result or has failed to indicate clearly what to do next is not such a reason.

Output of Results

A search is initially composed at a keyboard and verified on a monitor screen before sending. The result is returned to the same screen, the closest thing to the "face" of the interface. An interface can allow the searcher to edit the retrieved records, download the edited result to disk or paper, or even transmit it elsewhere electronically.

To date, the monitor screen has not been very expressive. It reveals relatively little of the result of a search compared with its manual counterparts, the card, book page, and fiche enlargement. Even the latter of these, also displayed on a screen with the user typically in an uncomfortable position for reading, shows more than some thirty lines of about eighty characters each. The tens of thousands of monitors in use for bibliographic display are of hundreds of different models from dozens of different designers and manufacturers and were made at any time over the past thirty years (they last a long time). Minimal standards of compatibility sufficed because bibliographic information was input only in the basic and extended ASCII character set for roman characters in text mode for many years. Even the use of character sets for nonroman characters did not initially require display in graphic mode.

Colour, pictures, and mouse-clicking operation did not become part of bibliographic display until the popularity of offering library catalogues on the World Wide Web (which can support graphics) began to replace telnet transmission (which does not). The visual shock of the switch from a library's colourful Web graphic "welcome" page to its dull bibliographic-file display is considerable. Suddenly, text-only VT-100-type terminals are vanishing from libraries, and for the first time since the beginning of bibliographic automation, librarians can seriously consider things commonplace in printed bibliographies for centuries: italic and bold characters! A century ago, the American bibliographer Henry Stevens suggested that a complete bibliographic record of a book should include a miniature photograph of its title page. Optical digitization of title pages is a necessary part of converting whole books to this format in the National Digital Library Project (NDLP) of the Library of Congress launched in October 1994. There is no reason a digitized title page cannot be made part of a record. There are library catalogues in children's rooms showing which shelf the retrieved item is on. A loudspeaker-equipped interface that speaks the result of a search to visually handicapped users is available, and voice recognition to input a search request is in experimental stages. The greatest advance of all for ease of searching will be the universal use of hypertext links along with a graphical interface so that one can click on an access point of any type in one record and be instantly connected with other records associated with that access point. This would automate something librarians have done mentally and in manual searching for centuries, but hitherto painfully slowly. It would also open another time-wasting and confusing trap for searchers not prepared with a sound search strategy.

The size limitation of the typical OPAC monitor is mentioned above. One or two average-length records can fill it. What is worse, they disappear from the screen to make room for more and therefore dim in consciousness before the search is complete unless they are printed out immediately. To many people who did not grow up using a terminal, scanning a large number of records on a screen seems more tedious and potentially confusing than scanning any kind of manual file. Libraries have been slow to invest in the larger screens now available and in the programming required for the better, and probably nonlinear, simultaneous display of multiple records. The increasing use of operating systems based on a graphical user interface (GUI) such as Microsoft Windows or the operating system of an Apple Macintosh makes it inevitable that the experimentation already taking place because of the World Wide Web will be extended to in-house uses.

At present, information about enough records to facilitate the comparisons needed for selection is typically first presented on a single page of a screen display in one of two methods: (1) showing access points only, or (2) showing only a few selected data elements of a record. Limiting this initial display to one access point or record per line is not unusual, although it requires truncation to fewer than eighty characters. This way, a score or more of either access points or records are visible simultaneously, each identified by an *occurrence number* in sequence so that it can be easily recalled later by that number alone. It is usual for only access points to be displayed in response to a *BROWSE* command, and records in response to either a *FIND* command or a command to show the records linked with an access point seen in a browse. The line-per-item display rarely supplies what the searcher needs to proceed directly, such as a call number. On the other hand, the complete record with all its formatting codes is expected to be needed only occasionally by library staff and never by lay users. Between the two, user interfaces are typically programmed to display records of at least two different degrees of completeness, at the option of the searcher. In screen displays intended for the general public, labelling the data fields as shown in the appendix has returned to fashion. However, this occupies more of the screen, leaving even less space for additional records.

Knowing how many records are retrieved at each step of a search is a major factor in the searcher's motivation and the consequent determination of how to modify the search if the immediate result is not satisfactory. It is normal for this count to be displayed at the beginning of a hit list. In some systems, if the number exceeds a programmed limit, it is assumed that the searcher should modify the search to lower the number of hits, so there is no record-by-record display until the searcher specifically requests it. A casual user delving into an unfamiliar topic has little basis for establishing a search strategy before examining at least some of the retrieved records.

Since a monitor screen can accommodate only a limited number of access points or records simultaneously, the sequence in which the items of a hit list are displayed is a particularly important factor in determining how the searcher interprets the result and decides how to proceed. In programming terms, the simplest display sequence is the one determined by the control numbers by which the DBMS has assembled the various data elements related to each single retrieved record. These numbers were randomly assigned to the logical records when they were entered into the DBMS, so a display in this order is merely a register as described early in this chapter. A sorting program must be invoked if the records are to be displayed in any other sequence. Although a filing rule is a part of every set of interface programs, it does not necessarily incorporate all the complexities of the standard ones described in chapter 9. In any case, how output is, or can be, sequenced for display by interface subroutines is rarely documented adequately for searchers, who are expected to deduce it from what appears on the screen.

Input of Commands

A search is initiated either by a direct command such as *FIND* . . . or through a selection of a choice from among several in a menu presented automatically as a search arrives at a predetermined point. The menu may be an entire screen or only a line at the bottom of some search results. It gives the searcher a limited number of options to choose from, whenever a decision is needed in order to advance the search another step. This is like having a librarian watch every move and give instructions: comforting and helpful to the beginner but frustrating and unnecessary for the person who knows how to proceed. Programmers like menus in general because they fix an invariable sequence of operations. Experienced users do not like them, particularly simple ones designed, as so many are, as if each user has never seen the system before.

Menu-based user interfaces are common regardless of the input/output devices used. A menu is essential if the hardware is a touch terminal lacking a keyboard where the user's finger at a displayed line or box on the screen activates the choice displayed there. Touch terminals went quickly out of favour in alphabet-based searching because breaking up an entire alphabet on a touch screen is simply inefficient and, in the age of the home computer, few except the very elderly totally lack the minimum typing skill needed to deal with keyboard-based searching. However, the use of a sequence of alphabetic segments to narrow a search is returning to fashion in graphic user interfaces where clicking with a mouse simulates touching a screen, and replaces input keying to transfer a user to the desired location.

In command mode, the user, not the program, decides what to do next. The blinking cursor or a single-character prompt symbol indicates that the program is ready to take keyed instruction. A good interface activates a command when a few mnemonic characters of it have been keyed, for example *B* or *BR* instead of the full *BROWSE*. At any time, the user can specifically invoke the verbal instruction of a *Help screen*, generally a prose form of menu instructions with a little more explanation, by pressing a function key (commonly F1) or some other, alas, nonstandardized key (a question mark, *H*, etc.).

Most current systems offer a choice of menu-mode or command-mode operation. Many offer both a simpler command mode and a more advanced one, the latter providing shortcuts in keying to accommodate searchers who have taken the trouble to familiarize themselves with command combinations and how to set global parameters. Every advance in the flexibility offered in commands is welcomed by the experienced searcher but increases the potential complexity of the system for both inexperienced users and programmers.

The actual words appearing on the screen in menus or which must be keyed to initiate an action in command mode constitute the *command language* of an interface, its most visible feature and therefore the chief magnet for either praises or curses on the entire system to which the interface belongs. Learning to use a search system is, essentially, learning its command language. Does one search for a direct match by keying *FIND* or *SEARCH*? Is a browse continued by pressing PAGE DOWN, ENTER, the space bar, or Y (for "yes") when prompted whether or not to continue? Does more than one of these serve equally in the same interface?

That interfaces differ in respect to these and a score of similar questions is the greatest annoyance to anyone who uses different systems frequently. That they tend to differ between interfaces designed for A&I databases and those designed for library processing systems is an enduring scandal. Differences in linguistic usage even among English-speaking peoples ensure that there will continue to be heated disagreement based on entrenched positions about which term should be keyed to initiate a function. An international standard exists for a command language acceptable to speakers of all languages, but it is being pointedly avoided at present among the established agencies and systems.[2] If it comes to be accepted, it will no doubt be taught in schools along with other aspects of computer operation and information access.

A search of a manual file retrieves *bibliography* only if it is the first word of a title or of a controlled-vocabulary access point. That it must be one of these two is obvious when access points are visible headings on records and when every manual library catalogue and most other bibliographies are constructed according to the same pattern. In an interactive search, there are many more options. The searcher must explicitly key the type(s) of data element to be searched and specify whether in any-word, first-word-only, or phrase mode (the latter searches a fixed combination of words anywhere they occur in the field searched). What is retrieved may be any single word within a controlled-vocabulary access point (possibly even as a subdivision: **CHEMISTRY—BIBLIOGRAPHY**) or in natural language anywhere in a record, including cataloguers' notes. Once the search has progressed a few stages in various files and indices, it is all too easy to forget what those choices were and therefore how to interpret what was subsequently retrieved.

Which access-point index should be searched for a particular data element is also not necessarily self-evident. For example, a series title requires vocabulary control and may therefore be included in a controlled-name index rather than in a natural-language title index. Any name may appear in a subject index. The searcher can hardly be unaware of which file is being actively searched, but it is helpful if the index being searched is stated on the screen for as long as that is the index being currently searched. The search process may appear linear to the searcher, but to the DBMS, it is much more complex as links are pursued in various authority and bibliographic files and their indices. The term *tree structure* is usually used to describe an interactive search. The most helpful interface is the one which can, at any stage of the search, retrace the steps already taken in a search as explicitly as the searcher requests. It is now common for the interface to store both the commands keyed and the resulting hit lists for later review at a simple command.

User Instruction

Users are not born knowing how to use bibliographic files. Almost every monographic bibliography and A&I publication in printed, and increasingly in digital, format has a prefatory explanation of its use and special features. The searcher "lost" in an interactive file because of either excessive recall with little precision or no recall at all is still usually stranded with less help about what to do next than any manual file offers. Merely seeing a manual file as a whole with its guide cards and other signposts to its organization is a considerable help. To compound the problem, any interactive system offers far more options than any manual one ever did. This is the primary factor in the confusion felt when the search is not going well. Through most of the first generation of OPACs, programmers concentrated on improving file structures and making search capabilities more flexible. Explaining the consequences of each option in practical terms in clearly written documentation or help screens seemed a secondary consideration. To design and write programs is always more fun than explaining them for the programmer whose specialized skill does not include expository prose.

Instruction in bibliographic technique begins in elementary education with drills in documenting and citing sources and using library catalogues and the A&I publications which index general popular magazines. It became more formalized in separate job descriptions, especially in the new college libraries of the 1960s, under the name *bibliographic instruction* (BI). Library tours for users at every stage emphasize signs and handouts explaining filing rules, the difference between name and subject searching, and the use of a subject authority file as an aid in planning a search strategy, whether the printed *Library of Congress Subject Headings* or an online thesaurus (see chapter 7). As databases become available in CD-ROM format and downloading via the Internet, each with potentially different search software and user interface, their networking becomes a technical nightmare, and many libraries resort to workstations each dedicated to searching one CD-ROM or a group with similar characteristics. The burden this places on librarians and technicians for instruction is great, particularly in colleges where each year brings a fresh group of students new to the particular databases they must search for citations for their term papers.

Human instruction in the technical use of a system cannot be divorced from instruction on how to refine a search strategy for a particular query, choose the best access points, and interpret the results. These have all been essential parts of bibliographic instruction, but in their first generation, help screens have generally been written only as technical guidance to the search system. Now, more attention is being paid to offering programmed instruction on the problems of content organization typically encountered by an inexperienced searcher and providing this instruction, as a search progresses, at the most opportune stage for each particular need. To recognize the basic difference of such instruction from the former purely technical help offered, the term *online tutorials* is being applied to this new form of assistance.

SEARCHING BY END-USERS VERSUS INTERMEDIARIES

A librarian is the last-resort feature of every good user interface, functioning even as typist and hardware technician in the early period of interactive searching. In addition to offering individual help in both the process and the substance of individual searches, librarians continue to spend time compiling short and highly relevant manual lists of citations from their own interactive searches in anticipation of predictable users' interests. An early benefit of automation to direct user-service is *selective dissemination of information* (SDI): the regular automated matching of an individual's interest profile against additions to a file. Notification of hits is generated and delivered automatically, now often by e-mail. Its success depends on the care with which the user defines the profile with the help of a professional thoroughly familiar with the system and competent to judge the effectiveness of particular access points in the context of the user's needs. Any serious end-user is now familiar with at least the basic techniques of interactive searching and is doing it confidently from a home workstation as well as at workstations in libraries, archives, etc. An increasing number primarily of self-employed professionals pay directly for access to A&I databases in their respective fields and rarely use an institutional library as intermediary. As they require training and ad hoc assistance beyond what their contract with the database vendor allows, they contract for it individually. Some librarians make part or all of their living by selling such services outside the context of any particular library's clientele.

The stable cooperative practices described in the next chapter ensured that, for almost a century before automation, an end-user saw library catalogues as essentially the same in their access techniques and data display. A&I publications were a different matter, each using its own display and index formats. When these were "reference books" physically separate from the library's catalogue and from each other, users did not question the differences. Now, however, an OPAC incorporates A&I files and links with catalogues of other libraries. In the process of automation, different libraries have selected different interface software from among the wide variety available, making their visual displays and search commands as incompatible as those of the various A&I services. As a result, the searcher at a workstation has hitherto been expected to key different commands to achieve the same result, depending on the database searched, and to interpret the results of searches appearing in different visual formats.

If an interface can be separated from the data it accesses and displays, surely the *same* interface can be the filter through which one can search files of different systems, provided the formatting of the data elements is standard. Bibliographic formatting *is* standardized among libraries, and that of A&I services is at least mutually compatible. A title index in any database, identified as such in its DBMS, can be transferred into a searcher's local interface. Writing programs to do this awaited the finalization of the standard communication protocol published as ANSI/NISO Z39.50.[3] A Z39.50 interface is now a standard feature of library processing systems. With it, a user is able to search every bibliographic file available at that OPAC with the same search, display, and download commands, and see the results in a uniform format. Programs of this type are also available for use at a home workstation when accessing catalogues via the Internet.

Librarians are aware that few of their institutions have easily or quickly met the budgetary requirements of the rapid expansion of demand for interactive search capacity. It is embarrassing, for example, when a library cannot afford, in sufficient quantity, the up-to-date workstation hardware many of its users have at home. Although librarians do not generally consider that end-users are deserting them, they worry that users who have less and less personal contact with a librarian may fail to recognize situations when they could profit from the intellectual help of a trained information professional.

There is also a financial aspect to independent end-user searching through a library's OPAC. The library must pay for the use of commercial remote search systems and their databases. Allowing an end-user total discretion over this use removes control over expenditures. This was the original basis both for user fees attached to online search services and for the requirement that a library staff member, not the end-user, do the actual search (assuming the greater efficiency of the former). These arguments are vanishing as more databases are held in-house, like reference books, and therefore do not incur per-use charges, and as end-users improve their own searching efficiency.

A PERFECT SYSTEM?

No professional in any field can ever claim that the status quo is perfect. Yet few librarians in the first half of this century saw any way of improving upon the book and card file as methods of storing and searching bibliographic data. So long a period of stability in the use of these techniques led to unwarranted complacency concerning the details of their application and therefore the entrenchment of a limited number of particular filing rules, catalogue formats, access-point structures, etc. in a field which might have remained more flexible. Independently of, and prior to, the impact of the computer, there was significant challenge to this stability in the early 1950s, particularly in the area of access points. At the Library of Congress, while Seymour Lubetzky was challenging long-standing rules for the authority control of name access points as discussed in chapter 6, Judson Haykin in an adjoining department was overseeing a less visible but just as revolutionary revision of controlled-vocabulary subject heading practice as discussed in chapter 7. Outside the Library of Congress (and, alas, therefore beyond the ken of many librarians), the new breed of information scientists were experimenting with access methods described earlier in this chapter: natural-language indexing and post-coordination.

By the 1970s, it was clear that the modal bibliographic file of any significant size would soon be the interactive file. The technology which brought this about was commercial and competitive: probably a blessing because it made the pace of change breathtakingly and mercifully rapid. Yet the transition to the fullest possible use of this technology was long and costly for libraries with their huge investment in existing databases, equipment, administrative organization, and staff expertise in obsolescent methods of searching. It will never be practicable to convert every old database entirely for interactive searching, an unfortunate situation particularly for those in the humanities still dependent on information in older sources. In the late 1990s, what can be expected of bibliographic control is astounding to those who recall what was and was not possible in the early 1960s. However, to hold that the Perfect System now exists is either an ego trip or an advertising ploy. If not, why does every operational system still regularly announce or promise yet further enhancements? Just when librarians felt that a period of stability had arrived in automation, they were called upon to mount their own Web home pages!

Both the technology and the intellectual foundations for the most beneficial applications remain in developmental stages.

The system as a whole will not be perfect until it is composed of compatible components as judged by a single acceptable standard. How will the Perfect System be recognized when and if it does arrive? There is agreement on its features, if only in general terms. Hardware and software developers will long argue over how individual pieces of equipment, systems and applications programs, communication protocols, command languages and menus, and data formats can most efficiently achieve—and librarians will continue to worry over the cost of—the following technical goals:

1) adherence to a standard format for all data of bibliographic significance, and standard protocols for file transfer, which transcend hardware and operating-system incompatibilities
2) ability to maintain files containing both name and subject authority records linked to multiple files of bibliographic records
3) ability to search interactively for authority-controlled access points and to activate links among them
4) ability to search for single words or terms individually or in stated proximity to others
5) ability to apply boolean or other appropriate operators at any stage of any search
6) ability to accommodate the demands of simultaneous users, both for internal processing (updating, correcting, etc.) and for public searching without serious deterioration of response time and
7) a user-friendly interface familiar to the individual searcher which can be used as the command and display mode with any interactive bibliographic database to which the searcher has rights of access.

As noted before, legal and social issues surrounding access to information of any type are beyond the scope of this book, but these technical characteristics of a Perfect System are completely realizable. Millennium Approaches!

5

■ · ■

The Business of Bibliography

Bibliographic records and their contents are intellectual property created by people paid for their work by salary, by contract, or by claiming copyright personally and receiving royalties for the use of their work. A small proportion of these people are freelancers who "write" the citations and monographic bibliographies already described as one of the three basic types of published bibliographic work. They depend on publishers—commercial, professional, academic, and author-based—to make their work available in print or digital formats, whether as separate publications or as bibliographic apparatus in the work of others. Many bibliographic indexers are employed or contracted by A&I services, an increasing number owned privately but many still owned by professional or nonprofit organizations capable of finding the money to subsidize this work. Finally, there are the many professionals on the staffs of the public and private libraries, archives, galleries, and museums.

A majority of the cost of creating a bibliographic record is payment for the time these people take to make professional judgements, not to input data to pile up pages or disks full of results. The slim product of their day's work is relatively intangible and invariably undervalued by anyone not involved in the information professions. (It is a common complaint of cataloguers that their own library administrators whose background was in other specialties also undervalue bibliographic work.)

The work of original bibliographic listing and indexing can rarely be made to pay for itself by any commercial measure. Most of it is highly subsidized. Today, governments pay, in one way or another, the lion's share of the cost of the original creation of bibliographic records. Much of it is done in national public-sector institutions. In less rich countries, the government is virtually the only possible source of money for the nation's entire bibliographic enterprise. Library users around the world have been spoiled by the generosity of American taxpayers who throughout this century have paid librarians at the Library of Congress to catalogue publications from almost everywhere on earth and then have virtually given away the resulting products. Only recently has some of the cost of the intellectual work by that Library's professional staff been made subject to cost-recovery.

A claim to copyright protection was rarely specified in the case of a local manual library catalogue because it could hardly be used anywhere else and few were ever copied as a whole. Now that interactive library catalogues are typically accessible by anyone with a home computer and modem, attention to legal issues of ownership is necessary, if not because of any immediate commercial value of the database, then at least to enable the originator to protect its integrity and ensure proper use. As a federal agency, the Library of Congress can only use U.S. copyright legislation to protect its records outside the country. This limitation has in the past led to near-fraudulent and intellectually inferior uses of its records in American publications.

It is difficult clearly to distinguish professional functions (whose per-unit cost will continue to increase) from clerical ones (which are more likely to be automated and become less costly per unit). To create an original bibliographic record is largely a professional job, and the Library of Congress gives its current average cost to produce one as something over a hundred dollars, a figure which has not risen substantially in many years because of the increasing use of cost-effective automated techniques.[1] Where records copied from outside sources form a large part of the input, it is harder for administrators to average their costs among different libraries because of the number of variables involved, often based in local circumstances rather than of general application.

The "cataloguing" function in a library is the one whose visible product is the OPAC. It is only part of the institution's total bibliographic function. Other professionals within and outside the library work with its cataloguers to fulfil this broader function, all of which involves bibliographic searching, record creation or copying, file and system maintenance, and periodic updating of software—all more complex and interrelated than in the days of the manual catalogue. Reference librarians have always listed and indexed useful sources in their own files, once kept in their own divisions. Now, such files are routinely incorporated into the library's OPAC along with files originating in the formal cataloguing operation and those purchased from outside. This is one symptom of a trend, now increasingly reflected in library organization and job descriptions, to merge cataloguing and reference functions.

The output of a cataloguing department can be measured more quantitatively than that of a reference department, so administrators have always subjected the former to closer accounting and applied more rigorous demands for efficiency to it. This chapter describes a long history of centralization and cooperation through which the local cataloguing function is shared between staff of the local institution and outside contractors. Administrators have always tried to enlarge the proportion of what is, to use the current term, "outsourced," but it is impossible to remove all of a library's cataloguing function from the hands of local staff.

SHARED AND CENTRALIZED RECORD CREATION

Bibliography was an object of commerce long before automation, but automation greatly enlarged and transformed it into a more entrepreneurial activity. This development closely parallels the three stages of library automation described below: the stage of individual-library automation, the stage of the consortium, and the present stage of widely distributed record creation and sharing combined with in-house integrated processing systems and OPACs with network connections.

To do the same work twice is not profitable in anyone's terms, whether in the private or the public sector. Since the document is itself the primary source of its own bibliographic description, it is surely redundant for hundreds of bibliographers, cataloguers, and indexers each to begin afresh in creating its own record for a different copy of the same document in isolation from one another. This was recognized within a hundred years of the European invention of printing multiple copies. The sixteenth-century bibliographer Conrad Gesner compiled a bibliography purporting to list all printed books then known, and "suggested that his work . . . should be used by librarians instead of compiling author catalogues themselves."[2] Librarians and others ever since have been annotating the margins of monographic bibliographies to show which of the listed items they hold.

Many reasons are advanced for duplicating bibliographic work, among them the following:

1) access points for subject-information retrieval must meet local users' needs and cannot be as standardized as descriptive elements and access points for document identification
2) cooperation entails its own overhead expenses and increases the time needed to produce the product; working in isolation is quicker and often cheaper when the product is smaller in scope and demands
3) although its uses in catalogues are fairly standardized, the bibliographic record is also vital to administrative functions from selection and acquisition to circulation and bindery control, all of which are more institution-specific and vary greatly in detail
4) it is in the nature of administrators to build separate local empires and resist giving up control over the tiniest operational detail and
5) professionals in all fields like to demonstrate creativity by reinventing the wheel.

Yet the overriding factor limiting the sharing of bibliographic work before the arrival of the computer was probably none of the above but the sheer practical difficulty of communicating a record cheaply and speedily from its creator to the many places where it might be used.

Uniquely among information professionals, librarians deal with documents of which copies exist in many institutions. This gives them the greatest interest in standardizing practices of document identification (cataloguing) so that copies of a common record created for a document can be shared wherever the document is held or listed. In the light of all the problems raised by standardization, it is a sign of librarians' insight and tenacity that sharing/centralizing record creation has been a major concern of theirs at least since the 1850s. The goal they developed is twofold: (1) to gather and format bibliographic data elements for every document as soon as it is published, or even before when it is announced, then (2) to store the result in such a place and manner that any bibliographer, library cataloguer, or indexer can retrieve, select from, adjust, and use the data in any local file, for any type of administrative or information-retrieval purpose, in any form of output.

Librarians approached the goal with remarkable success during the hundred years when only manual techniques were available, and they subsequently became innovators in developing automated techniques to fulfil it. While automation has removed most of the technical barriers, it has been less effective in removing human and institutional barriers. It has even reinforced some, particularly those based on cost and on social and institutional policy. The following are among the overlapping nontechnical questions the goal raises.

1) Is the provision of basic bibliographic information more a public-sector or a private-sector responsibility?
2) Who should create the model record?
3) Who should be responsible for transmitting it to different categories of potential users?
4) What is the most effective communication path from the agency which creates the record to the one using it?
5) How should the cost of each resulting bibliographic service or product be apportioned?
6) To what degree should any of these costs be subsidized, the remainder being charged equitably to users?
7) How can agencies which contribute more than they draw from shared databases be recompensed?
8) Can differential value be assigned to different records and uses?
9) How can quality control be administered if responsibility for record creation is dispersed among different agencies?
10) What priority should be assigned to pursuing standardization where it conflicts with local service and administrative considerations?

Many of these questions antedate automation, and none has a single or permanently valid answer. This chapter can only explain the history leading to present practice and explore trends.

Since the late nineteenth century at least, and particularly in the Anglo-American world, librarians have espoused trouble-free and cost-free access to information as a principle. In justifying budgets, they stress the virtues of sharing what their institutions have paid for with other libraries on a two-way basis. In this spirit, they have shared bibliographic records even to the extent of bearing some of the cost of their reproduction and distribution to others who request them.

Around 1850, two American librarians were addressing the issue almost simultaneously in practical ways. Their initiatives led directly to today's flourishing systems of (1) centralized journal-article indexing in the A&I services and (2) decentralized but cooperative library cataloguing.

While a student at Yale in 1847, William Frederick Poole worked in a student-society library. He started a list of articles he encountered in its little-used journal collection which he thought would help classmates working on papers and debates. When he published this first index of journal articles as the 154-page *An Alphabetical Index to Subjects Treated in the Reviews and Other Periodicals to Which No Indexes Have Been Published,* college librarians elsewhere were happy to buy it for their students to use. This was despite the fact that their libraries might not contain all the same journals.

Within five years, Poole produced a second edition six times larger and put the work on a continuing basis. Not able to do all the indexing himself in addition to administering the filing, printing, distributing, etc., he opted for the model of cooperative decentralization for creating new records. He sought British volunteers to select, cite, and index articles in British journals, as well as American volunteers to do the same for American journals. When the supply and the timely work of volunteers dwindled, the project finally had to be put on a commercial basis as a company with its own paid staff independent of any library. When the H. W. Wilson Company, formed in 1898, took it over, the twentieth century's explosion of independent A&I services was under way. The volunteer efforts of nonprofit societies, some of which antedate Poole, although not by much, continued in parallel, but automation eventually caused their merger into businesses with the necessary technical and commercial expertise.

Within five years of when Poole began his index, Charles Coffin Jewett of the Smithsonian Institution proposed that a book be catalogued only once, the resulting bibliographic record to be mechanically reproduced, using thin embossed printing plates, on *unit cards* (each card bearing one record for one book). Any library owning a copy of the book could obtain one or more copies of the matching card to file directly into its catalogue at access points appropriate to the book, after adding local information such as branch-location and copy-specific facts.

However, postal transmission of the request and the cards was still unsatisfactorily slow, cataloguing standards not yet widely enough adopted, and the Smithsonian could not bear the full cost. Jewett's concept lay fallow for over four decades, but sprang to life in 1901 when the Library of Congress simply offered for sale copies of the unit cards it was printing for its own newly established card catalogues, at a price which included neither a share of the cost of the original cataloguing nor even all of the distribution cost.

In this form, Jewett's idea became an instant success. At the manual catalogue's zenith in the early 1970s, the Library of Congress alone was shipping a hundred million printed cards a year to libraries all around the world by mail, each one picked by hand from a vast stock constantly replenished by new additions and reprintings of old records. This model was widely imitated also by commercial vendors, some of which created their own records while others adapted or merely copied those from the Library of Congress. The first uses of computers in library cataloguing were to produce yet more cards, albeit more efficiently and to specific order, for shipment from central agencies to libraries around the world.

In the 1930s, the Library of Congress began to send a free copy of each bibliographic record it produced to large libraries in various localities around North America. From 1947, it published all its records in a printed version in book format, including retrospective printing of everything issued previously. That most larger libraries subscribed meant that individual records were available to be reproduced locally instead having to be ordered from afar.

From the middle of the century, therefore, *derived cataloguing*—cataloguing an item by adapting a record obtained from an outside source—was a major factor in containing the cost of the cataloguing operations of all but the smallest and most specialized libraries.

The preferred record has always been one created at the Library of Congress or another national agency, whose records are known as *source records* to distinguish them from presumably less reliable records copied from other libraries, commercial sources, etc. Every administrator's goal is to maximize the use of derived (preferably source) records and to minimize *original cataloguing*, the vastly more expensive in-house creation of a record from scratch. The current digital file at the Library of Congress was started in 1968, and every record created or later converted for it, as well as records from many other institutions, can now be seen virtually without direct cost via Internet communication. Automated downloading of such records into a local system is another matter, however. The technical, commercial, and legal implications of this are just beginning to be explored.

In summary, both Poole and Jewett originally proposed that bibliographic work should be shared among those who would use the product. Poole concentrated on the work of what we now call the A&I services; Jewett on library cataloguing. Poole succeeded in implementing this model for a short time. However, their common vision came to a common fruition neither had proposed: centralization rather than cooperation. Business firms and some nonprofit organizations took over the production and distribution of A&I tools to be sold primarily to libraries. The Library of Congress took over the production and distribution of catalogue records to be sold to other libraries. Centralization was the predominant model of bibliographic control from roughly 1900 until the computer-communication revolution.

Cataloguing-in-Publication

Until the 1970s, the greatest barrier to using derived records remained the difficulty of locating and obtaining a particular one when it is most needed, which is as soon as the library acquires the book it represents. National (source) agencies have always given high priority to the quick cataloguing of new materials, but when their records had to be printed in national and trade bibliographies, reviewing tools, etc., many libraries had the book long before a derived record was available for it. Once located, that record still had to be matched with the book.

In a pilot "Cataloging-in-Source" project of the late 1950s in the United States, the Library of Congress and selected publishers agreed on a procedure whereby the Library could get selected cataloguing data to the publisher in time for it to be printed within the book, thereby overcoming the problems of time and matching. However, a library still normally had to transfer the data into its own catalogue by manual transcription into the catalogue-card format. This was the major problem leading to the project's temporary abandonment as a great idea whose time, like Jewett's in the 1850s, had not yet come.

By the early 1970s, automated communication of bibliographic data, discussed in the next section, was functional. Cataloguing-in-Publication (CIP), as it was renamed, is now operational in many countries with the cooperation of high proportions of their publishers. Some publishers refuse to cooperate; in some countries, the CIP managers prefer not to undertake government publications because of their numbers and complexity.

CIP puts some burden on the publisher, who must submit to a designated library galley proofs and other data for every forthcoming publication. The library guarantees speedy cataloguing (usually in one or two days) and communicates the result to the book's publisher in time to be printed within the book. (An example appears on the verso of this book's title leaf.) A particular benefit of the Anglo-American version of CIP is that it includes controlled-vocabulary access points, including classification designations, along with some formatted descriptive data elements.

A complete bibliographic record is not feasible in a pre-publication record: the publisher cannot be committed at that stage to such things as number of pages and exact size. The details significant for access, however, such as the author and subject, are unlikely to change. Nevertheless, misrepresentation (presumably unintentional) by the publisher and misunderstanding by the cataloguer (who may see quite limited information) do occur. A small proportion of CIP records must be substantially revised when the item is finally published, so it is a mistake for a library not to check for such revisions as it incorporates CIP data into its public catalogues. (As an amusing sidelight, some items for which CIP records become part of bibliographic systems are cancelled and never get published, leaving bibliographic CIP ghosts to haunt searchers forever!)

A CIP record is immediately incorporated into bibliographic databases and reviewing services designed to appear before the book's publication. Some publishers now merely declare in the book that a

CIP record is available from a given source rather than printing it, because these external appearances of CIP are of greater benefit to library selection and cataloguing than its actual appearance within the book. Certainly by the time the book arrives in the cataloguing department, and often at the time it is selected and ordered, a record for it can be located and incorporated into the local bibliographic system for both administrative and public use. Thus many OPACs now list what the library intends to receive as well as what it has.

In the United States, CIP is centralized at the Library of Congress. In some other places, including Canada, the work is shared by a different library in each region, but central coordination by the national library ensures consistency of practice and of such important elements as controlled-vocabulary access points.

Union Catalogues

The Librarian of Congress adopted the card format for the new catalogue in 1898 because it had become the format of choice in North America. Then, as later, everyone recognized that no matter what its resources, the Library of Congress could no more acquire every publication ever wanted anywhere in the country than could any other single library. A *union catalogue* lists the contents of many libraries in order to facilitate resource sharing. The idea of such a catalogue is almost a thousand years old, although many, like the thirteenth-century *Registrum Librorum Angliae,* a listing of all the manuscripts housed in British monasteries, remain incomplete.

In 1902, the Library of Congress started the most extensive union catalogue ever attempted by asking major American and Canadian libraries to send to Washington a copy of each new catalogue card they made. Various regional union-catalogue projects were also implemented. Most remained card files in a single location available to answer reference or interlibrary loan requests by telephone or post. The great catalogue in Washington also remained on cards until it was transferred to printed-book format beginning in the 1950s. At that time, it also merged with the aforementioned printed-book publication of Library of Congress records as they were created, to become the ongoing printed (later microfiche, then digital) *National Union Catalog.* The eight-hundred-plus volumes of its retrospective part cover pre-1953 imprints and constitute the largest single bibliographic file ever committed to print.

A very high proportion of all the records in the ongoing *National Union Catalog* originate at the Library of Congress, but many of them indicate other libraries which hold the items. Other records not only show holdings in several libraries but originate in those other libraries.

To the degree that a library uses records from this source for its derived cataloguing, the union catalogue also serves Jewett's ideal function of shared cataloguing, not merely centralized cataloguing by the Library of Congress. However, as long as the published union catalogue was limited to a manual format, it could do this only imperfectly.

The Private Sector

Creating bibliographic records as a private-sector enterprise outside the context of a library is no longer as unusual as it was before Poole's time. He established the first modern corporation to do this when he put his journal-indexing service on a commercial footing. In effect, he founded a private-sector A&I industry to take over what was previously done, if at all, in libraries by their own cataloguing staffs or, in a few early cases, by professional societies wishing to index their publications and related ones in detail.

Librarians did not value Poole's work or that of his successor, H. W. Wilson, any the less because they were commercial entrepreneurs. The latter's company has been, in the words of their motto, "the librarian's friend," donating to librarians' causes some of the profit from the sale of a respected product.

More to the point, from the beginning Wilson's pricing structure respected the nature of a large-scale bibliographic product, which is not used like a pair of shoes in that any one person (or library) never uses all of it but only a part. Wilson charged libraries for printed A&I publications not by physical unit but by the amount of their potential use to the subscribing library. A library holding fewer of the journals indexed paid less than one holding more of them. Per-use pricing is commonplace now that a computer keeps track of individual searches of a centralized database, but to sell a printed reference book to a library on this basis was innovative in the early twentieth century.

Private companies have since shared most of the market for abstracting and indexing with nonprofit societies. Once Poole, Wilson, the Chemical Abstracts Service, and others showed that their product was reliable in quality and the service viable, the resources of library cataloguing departments were diverted to other tasks and the budget for such indexing went to the acquisitions funds of reference departments to buy A&I products.

Private enterprise extended to another part of the work previously done in individual library cataloguing departments in 1937, when Wilson's company became the first of many to produce catalogue cards to sell to libraries, "competing" with in-house cataloguing and typing staffs and with the Library of Congress. In the 1950s, jobbers who previously sold only books to libraries began to compete with each other on the basis of which could provide better add-on services at lower cost. The most widely advertised add-on was to ship each book shelf-ready (with spine label, circulation record inserted, etc.) and catalogue-ready (with its relevant catalogue record on cards—later, on tape—tailored to the particular library's requirements). For a jobber to do this for every item shipped, it needed a cataloguing staff to create an original record for anything for which no derived record was available. These are problematic and costly exceptions in a business designed to use records from the Library of Congress, shared cataloguing from a union catalogue, or CIP. The latter was a major boon because the very book in hand provides its own derived copy for easy clerical processing.

A few private companies have existed for some decades doing essentially the same work as the jobbers just discussed except that they supply only the cataloguing service, not the books as well. Their customers communicate basic bibliographic details, now electronically and perhaps including a title-page reproduction via facsimile transmission. Many of their customers are special libraries in private-sector companies. Contracting for professional services is common practice in this sector. Now, administrators of institutions throughout the public sector are under increasing pressure to lower internal professional labour costs by outsourcing operations to the private sector. This can hardly be done for the day-to-day operation of libraries' public services, but librarians have long accepted the sharing of bibliographic records. The current question is not whether libraries have achieved the maximum efficiency attainable after a hundred and fifty years of purposeful interinstitutional sharing. Rather, it is whether an individual library's technical-services staff can be further reduced by contracting with an entrepreneurial private-sector business for services not yet encompassed in the history of library cooperation.

ELECTRONIC COMMUNICATION

The use of the computer as the basic tool for data communication brought as great a revolution to buying, selling, and sharing bibliographic information as the revolution wrought by the DBMS as a search tool. What was previously done using the postal service for print and the telephone *viva voce* can now be done using satellite transmission, if still normally combined with various wire- and fibre-optic-based methods at the ends of the communication.

In a manual communication mode, a given package of data (a request or a response) moves physically at any one time from one originator to one destination, making it easy to apportion the communication cost on a per-unit, per-transaction basis. Distance is the principal factor in both time and cost of nonelectrical communication; in telephonic communication, it is not a time factor but remained until recently a factor in long-distance fee structures.

Digitized electronic transmission has acquired very different characteristics, some by its nature, others through the business-based choices of the many companies now competing in the field. Both query and response are communicated from one source to many destinations simultaneously. Transmission speeds continue to increase and the real cost per unit transmitted, to decrease. That per-unit cost, moreover, is now largely hidden in the accounting books of the common carriers and is increasingly being charged to users in bulk rather than on a per-use and per-unit-of-time basis. For example, most people communicating via the Internet have no idea whatever what is the real-dollar cost of the communication portion of this activity. Institutions are able to negotiate communication fees to cover all uses over a given period and are likely to make only spot checks of the level of individual uses and types of use.

When a union catalogue existed only in some distant place, using it via post or telephone, and an intermediary searcher at the catalogue, was awkward at best. The barriers to using such a catalogue manually as a source of shared (not just centralized) records for derived cataloguing are even greater. The printed and fiche forms of the *National Union Catalog* are more convenient because they exist in many places (at considerable expense). Until recently, a record originating at the Library of Congress or one of the commercial services mentioned above could be acquired as a set of cards ready to file into the local catalogue. Any other record located in a union catalogue had to be manually copied for input into the local system. Electronic communication is the key to merging the reference function of a union catalogue for resource sharing with its new potential for shared cataloguing. This led to a wholly new type of bibliographic service.

Electronic Processing Services

By 1969, Frederick Kilgour grasped the implications of the computer-communication revolution for libraries. Within two years, he made it operational in the Ohio College Library Center (the original full name of OCLC), an agency cooperatively organized by a group of post-secondary institutions in that state and administratively separate from them. Kilgour boasted of having applied economic concepts to librarianship. For the age of automation, that he invented "the business of bibliography" is more than a half-truth.

OCLC operated a computer, a DBMS, and a dedicated telecommunication link to collect into a single organized database all records created by the Library of Congress (source records) plus records created (or adapted from source records) by member libraries if no satisfactory source record was available when needed. The system organized these records so that they could be (1) searched interactively directly from any member's terminal and (2) returned to the member library to be incorporated into its catalogue.

The grip of the card catalogue on both the habits of searchers and the economics of library administration was such that, for nearly twenty years, OCLC and others used computer technology to print cards to be interfiled manually into existing catalogues. Whenever a member library was ready to give up its card catalogue, however, its records, created and stored in digital form, needed no alteration to become the basis of its OPAC.

OCLC is the original automated version of Jewett's vision of shared cataloguing. It is a union catalogue for locating material for all resource-sharing purposes, a continuing repository of all Library of Congress records, and the working catalogue of each of many separate libraries. It needed a new name: *cataloguing support system* was an awkward first choice reflecting the limited purpose of OCLC and similar agencies at their start in the early 1970s. Soon, *bibliographic utility* was coined to express the much larger scope of activities they all undertook.

Electronic communication enabled searching and the creation and processing of records to be done simultaneously in real time by many libraries. The earlier model of centralized cataloguing was replaced remarkably quickly with one, along OCLC lines, called *distributed cataloguing*.

The Library of Congress was happy to make all its records available as the foundation of any bibliographic database supporting, or resulting from, distributed cataloguing. It did not, however, allow its own database to be used interactively or cooperatively by outside persons, libraries, or agencies for fear the high standards of quality control in that database would be weakened. It was 1976 before it allowed even another national library (the National Library of Canada) to add records to it (but only authority records for Canadian names). A decade later, the Library of Congress had started the National Coordinated Cataloging Program (NCCP), now a series of projects under the name Program for Cooperative Cataloging (PCC). In this program, a score of United States libraries contribute jointly to the Library of Congress database, but the selection of the libraries and the quality control exercised centrally are still stringent, making this a project unlike others in distributed cataloguing in that it has remained focused solely on database creation. Much significant history is omitted in this outline organized by concept rather than event. As the Library of Congress constantly encouraged moves away from pure centralization toward sharing the record-creation function with other institutions, it maintained its primary responsibility to ensure quality control over the content of the national bibliographic database in its care.

OCLC demonstrated, perhaps better than the H. W. Wilson Company, that the real "business" of bibliography does not consist of creating a database of bibliographic and authority records. That involves rigorous adherence to standards and high financial outlay per unit. Furthermore, the potential for commercial profit is low because it is hard to make the product proprietary when a government agency is the chief supplier (in the case of the United States, one unable to claim local copyright in its product).

The commercial potential lies in processing, storing, searching for, and communicating records created by others. As in every business, the potential is maximized by diversification, by vertical integration of functions within the same company, and primarily by performing a high volume of repetitive operations which can be individually charged to the maximum number of customers. The business flourished the more it found ways to use its only tangible product, the bibliographic record, not only in a customer's catalogue but also in its every other operation dependent on document and item identification: acquisitions, circulation, bindery control, resource sharing, etc.

Before workstations with megabytes of RAM and networked client-server communication among computers, a large "mainframe" computer was required to store even a modest bibliographic database and process the increasingly complex functions demanded by individual libraries. In the first stage of library automation, that of the single-library system based on records from just a few sources, a library typically shared computer hardware and software with a parent agency such as a city government or a university computing centre.

The second stage was that of the consortium, an organizational structure tailored for distributed cataloguing and other types of resource sharing using computer facilities. Including the word *network* in the name of a consortium meant cooperative use, and initially ownership, of computer hardware and software. The capital cost and long-term financial commitment involved in automation made it necessary for consortium members to sign complex formal contracts. The wise chief librarian did not do this hastily. Who could trust the judgement of others in a group of equally innocent beginners? The greater complexity of any project when many institutions are involved provides more opportunity for disagreement. The lack of operational models to imitate meant that early solutions to problems were invariably ad hoc; there was always concern that a poor decision would become entrenched. The early history of library automation had already been littered with failures and even some firings! Nevertheless, many groups of libraries with common characteristics or purposes coalesced into networks: public libraries of a province or state, school libraries of a district, the largest academic libraries of the country, etc.

The capital cost and operating overhead of a functioning bibliographic utility meant that not every consortium could have its very own. OCLC would never have many imitators or competitors. In the 1970s, however, public money to develop computer applications seemed plentiful, and the library and education fields were blessed with quite a lot of it. Although a private institution, Stanford University tapped into this source and programmed a general DBMS it named SPIRES (Stanford Public Information Retrieval System). Stanford's library adapted this into BALLOTS (Bibliographic Automation of Large Library Operations using Time Sharing) for its own uses. At the University of Toronto, the library was responsible for both the DBMS and the rest of the system, naming it UTLAS (University of Toronto Library Automation Systems). Even though public money funded capital development cost, both universities sought opportunities to recover some of it, if only to sustain the viability of expensive operation.

Both universities set out to market the use of their DBMS and database to other libraries as a basis for individual bibliographic services in each library and as a distributed cataloguing system. In effect, this gave rise to consortia of their customers, the reverse of OCLC history in which the consortium was responsible for the bibliographic utility.

To complete this sketch of the second stage of automation, which resulted in the four big North American bibliographic utilities, the Washington State Library funded both the adaptation of Boeing Aircraft Corporation's DBMS to library purposes and the compilation of a union catalogue of the holdings of libraries in the state, under the name Washington Library Network.

The development of these utilities over twenty years reveals the organizational variety of the current business of bibliography. The last has changed the least, except for extending its geographic scope to other parts of the Pacific coast and Northwest under a new name (but same initials), Western Library Network. Its importance in the more general history of automation stems from acknowledgement of its original DBMS, developed later than the other three, as superior. It also attempted an unusual degree of centralized quality control over the records contributed. It was the earliest utility to market its database on CD-ROM disks. It is the only one of them to license its

DBMS, independently of its database, to be implemented on the computers of other institutions.

The University of Toronto eventually sold its system, still known as UTLAS, to a private company and it has changed hands again since then. Because of the high proportion of Canadian libraries which had contributed records, the database constitutes a de facto national union catalogue. The ever-present possibility that, in private hands, control over it might leave the country has alarmed Canadian librarians. Legally, each contributing library always retained ownership of its own records in UTLAS, but the situation reveals the legal complexities of record versus database ownership.

OCLC's activities expanded around the world. Although its legal links are no longer those of the original consortium, its users together retain a measure of control through seats on its governing board. It remains the generalist in the field of library cooperation. Under the name OCLC Online Computer Library Center, Inc., its enlargement and diversification have been undertaken in an aggressively commercial manner. Among its major divisions and wholly owned subsidiaries is OCLC Forest Press, now the copyright owner of the Dewey Decimal Classification. The records in a few of its databases are now centrally created. Its original DBMS, limited in some capabilities, has been wholly replaced.

The Research Libraries Group (RLG) began with Harvard, Yale, and the New York Public Library, and its membership still reflects the interests of the specialist academic. It includes archival repositories, museums, and galleries which contribute records to the database for types of material not traditionally represented in library databases. RLG selected Stanford's BALLOTS as the software with which to manage its database, RLIN (Research Libraries Information Network). The needs of its members caused it to lead the search for technical solutions to problems of storing and displaying nonroman scripts.

This sketch shows that the four organizations offer very similar services, but their differing histories, governance, administrative structures, and commercial interests now give each a quite different niche in the history and the increasingly international business of bibliography. Electronic communication has made the location of a utility's headquarters or computers immaterial.

Ownership of Records

Questions of ownership of individual records never arose in librarians' use of manual union catalogues. A library bought and owned its copy of a print or microfiche catalogue and copied records from it at will. A distant catalogue on cards was consulted only for item locations. The records in the database of a consortium are stored and maintained as a pool jointly created for the common good. The costs are recovered from membership dues, regularly adjusted by mutual agreement in order to reflect the value of the service to each individual member. If a nonmember is allowed access to the database, it is as a courtesy.

The cost of computerization, the detailed accounting possible when using it, and the psychology of an increasingly privatized and commercial world of information management all brought ownership and equity issues to the fore. Behind many of these issues lies the permanent problem of distributed, as against centralized, record creation. Everyone wants access to the fullest and highest-quality record possible; nobody (other than a national agency, whose mandate this is) really wants to bear the largely unrecoverable expense of creating it.

It has already been mentioned that within the United States, nobody "owns" a Library of Congress record and anyone may use it. Whether each library owns a record it creates or turns ownership over to the consortium, which then owns the entire database, is no longer an academic issue. It must be addressed in the contract between a utility (or any other manager of a joint database) and each contributor of records. Internet access is creating renewed interest in licensing arrangements and password control for both cooperative and single-library databases.

What makes a single- or multiple-library database valuable is the same thing that has always given value to a commercially marketed bibliography in book format: its size, scope, and organization. A database may be considered like an anthology of poetry in that each single record (poem) has value, but the database (anthology) has its own value as a whole. A commercial organization (whether for-profit or nonprofit) seeks to own or license a bibliographic database in order to make money with it. Information professionals may remain idealists but cannot remain naive.

Local Processing and Integrated Systems

The third and present stage of the business of library automation is dominated by the *integrated library system* based on librarians' original goals: (1) within a library, one database of its bibliographic records should suffice for use in every local function requiring bibliographic data and (2) the local functioning and the chosen or available hardware should determine the system, not vice-versa. The major factor distinguishing this phase from the consortium movement of the second stage is the separation of database assemblage, for which cooperation and sharing are absolute necessities, from local processing and searching. Libraries need no longer pool resources to operate the latter cost-effectively. In-house microcomputers now have sufficient capacity to operate a DBMS of the required complexity and the database can be "served" to the client workstation from any distance. Only the largest libraries need the storage capacity of a mainframe.

It was both an advantage and a drawback that a utility once provided a single processing system for all users. A library can now return from indentured connection to a consortium/utility to its original freedom and flexibility to design its own services. The development of the common interface standard Z39.50, described at the end of the previous chapter, permits a library's locally programmed output format to override that of another system from which records are received during an individual search.

More and more libraries are using one or more utilities only as they once used national agencies: as sources of records to be downloaded into a locally maintained integrated system. The utilities are not disappearing, but like any competitive enterprise, each survives by constantly redefining its services and adjusting its pricing to appeal to whatever market(s) it can reach. Consortia and utilities are still needed for services such as resource sharing which transcend local or bilateral policies and communication. A utility will now negotiate a package of bibliographic services tailored to any library's request-for-proposal. Many of these agreements are for one-time upgrading rather than continuing services.

Developments in local processing led the utilities to adapt their systems for greater flexibility in local uses. Some even bought or developed local-processing systems as products they could sell to their members. However, most integrated systems originated in a different group of entrepreneurs not concerned with database content as such. Three prominent names in this area show different points of departure of this development. Gaylord Bros., a nationwide supplier of blank catalogue cards one hundred years ago, now supplies an electronic version: everything but the bibliographic data. GEAC started by computerizing banking operations, still the largest component of its business. NOTIS began as the in-house DBMS of a single library, Northwestern University, which opted (unlike Stanford and Toronto) to recover some of its capital cost by licensing its DBMS to others without becoming involved in the construction of a cooperative database.

An integrated system is often called a *turnkey system* because it is the purchasing library's responsibility only to fill its tank with whatever bibliographic records it wishes, then "turn" the system on. More than a utility or consortium, the supplier (*vendor*) is expected to relieve the library staff: regular program upgrades and staff training, emergency troubleshooting, etc. are part of a normal contract. Integrated processing systems now constitute the largest and most competitive area of the business of bibliography as it affects libraries.

Libraries differ from one another greatly in what their staff (and users, if asked) value. They also differ in the single most fundamental issue in computer programming. Many larger libraries still lack control over what computer hardware is available to them and therefore which operating system or *platform* all their applications must be designed for, although UNIX appears to be in the ascendancy. All these differences enable a score of companies to compete in offering what might seem to be a fairly standardizable product. Each offers a model which it hopes might match the budget and stated requirements of client libraries, or can be modified to do so. The absolute requirements of any reputable integrated system with regard to the bibliographic record are few: (1) the capability to receive records in a MARC format (see chapter 8 and the appendix) and (2) interactive searching from multiple terminals in time-shared mode using all the techniques—including authority control—discussed in chapters 3 and 4.

The professional ethos of librarians has always made them offer the free use of at least their own catalogues to anyone. When users had to come into the building to use the card catalogue, there was no additional cost to the library no matter now many searchers used it simultaneously. Now that users search OPACs from outside the library at the low cost (to them) of Internet access, they may not be aware of the library's rising budget to maintain system capacity, multiple ports, and communication lines for multiuser simultaneous searching. However, making the library's databases available in the homes and offices of users without seriously compromising response time is among a library's best possible public-relations moves.

Libraries whose budgets simply cannot keep up with the demand have several options. Some only make their catalogues, but no other databases, searchable through the services of a consortium; some adopt a form of password control to restrict use to formal, and perhaps paying, subscribers; and some allow internal users to jump the queue for quicker response at busy times, relegating those whose contact is through an external port to lower priority. New features available, system upgrades for added capacity, and competitive pricing are all reasons why a library is unlikely to maintain the same integrated system for more than a few years. The rule of thumb is still that if five years have passed since its initial installation, it is time to consider replacement or major upgrading.

A&I Services and Their Database Vendors

Library cataloguers share the work of bibliographic control with compilers of monographic bibliographies and indexers for the A&I services. These three types of bibliographic lists are intellectually and financially interdependent. For two centuries after Gutenberg, the monographic bibliography dominated the field. Today, the combined A&I publications far outstrip library catalogues in the number of new separate records added annually. In some areas, they also dominate in meeting current searchers' needs for bibliographic information.

Monographic bibliographies and A&I publications in printed form come from outside the library and are part of "reference" collections. The administrative organization of most libraries distances them in many ways from the library's catalogue despite the essential identity of the content of all three types of bibliographic tools. However, the essentially integrative effect of all automation on the functioning of a library is most strongly in evidence in the bibliographic area. Major bibliographies formerly published only in print are now finding their way into libraries' databases for end-user searching on the OPAC, along with some encyclopaedias and dictionaries. The online selective-dissemination-of-information service *Current Cites* is an example.

Similarly, A&I databases now form part of many a library's OPAC. This only recognizes more clearly the two roles they have always played in the functioning of a library's catalogue: (1) enhancing data in the library's in-house database concerning its own holdings of serials, anthologies, proceedings, etc. and (2) serving part of the function of a union catalogue by providing a searcher enough bibliographic data to initiate a request for interlibrary loan if the library does not own the journal sought.

Unlike a bibliographic utility, an A&I service can be viewed as monopolistic and self-contained as a business. It has no purpose but to index a definable group of journals not otherwise indexed. Each therefore creates its own database. A little direct competition has crept recently into the indexing of the most popular magazines, but in general, if two or more different services choose to index the same journal, it is usually because each intends to do so from the point of view of a different discipline and will therefore apply different subject access points to the same article. This illustrates how closely an A&I service adheres to its focus based on the needs of a defined group of users.

Well into the twentieth century, a routine part of a cataloguer's work in every library was to create *analytic records* for articles in otherwise unindexed journals, for papers in conference proceedings, for literary works in anthologies, etc. (the techniques are discussed at the end of chapter 8). This was often done selectively, based on a reference librarian's judgement of what would be particularly difficult to locate if it remained unanalyzed because the bibliographic record for the book or serial as a whole was insufficiently revealing. Some analysis will always be done locally, but as A&I services covered more and more of the ground, journal indexing unfortunately came to be almost ignored by cataloguers and cataloguing teachers and has diverged from cataloguing in details of its rules and practices.

This divergence is most noticeable in the techniques and administration of automation in the A&I industry which, in the industrialized world, took place virtually without reference to what was going on in libraries. Almost none of the specific standards or practices of librarians discussed in part II of this book, or even basic citation style, is applied uniformly by the A&I services. This causes problems, possible to overcome but still annoying, in searching an OPAC containing files of both library and A&I records. The National Federation of Abstracting and Indexing Services (NFAIS) in the United States, with hundreds of members, has also failed to foster much practical cooperation among these many separate and essentially private organizations. While some small ones still use the computer for little more than word processing, and many still produce products on paper, the largest ones not only developed integrated computerized systems for in-house operations but encouraged subscribers to contract for direct online searching. Examples are WilsonLine, CAS, and MEDLARS/MEDLINE, operated respectively by the H. W. Wilson Co., Chemical Abstracts Service, and the U.S. National Library of Medicine. (The latter's automation project, started in 1958, antedates all others.)

Most A&I services still prefer not to get involved with issues of computer operation, electronic communication, or even direct contact with searchers. These are contracted out, as production and distribution of a manual product was always contracted out by the smaller firms. The database vendor, sometimes still called an *online search service* or *online information service,* arose as an intermediary between A&I publishers and those who search their databases interactively. Another name, *database service provider,* emphasizes the similarity between this entity and a bibliographic utility. Like a utility, it acquires records from a variety of sources without creating any itself. It receives some exclusively but others in common with competing vendors. Statistical, financial, directory, and full-text files accompany bibliographic files in the databases of most vendors. Their primary customers were originally libraries, but the larger ones have extended their scope in order to target additional niche markets, including government agencies, businesses, and professionals in many fields: indeed, anyone with a microcomputer, modem, and credit rating.

A database vendor is much like a bibliographic utility. Its distinguishing property is its DBMS and user interface, which support all the automated search techniques described in chapter 4. It imposes a common command language with which to search all its files. Its value to its customers lies in the features supported by its DBMS and the size and scope of the databases under its management. It operates a capacious, reliable, and flexible service of searching, and communicating the results, incorporating all reasonable options. Its operational headquarters and computer can be anywhere. Charges to online users are based on usage but no longer as specifically or in as itemized detail as was at first normal. Charging for connect-time or the number of records displayed is giving way to negotiated long-term subscription fees. Some still offer batch products on CD-ROM, some offer the results of an individual search produced in batch mode on paper, but these formats are in decline.

A database vendor differs from a utility in one major respect: it makes no attempt to standardize the records in the files it serves. Each originating A&I service, not the vendor, determines the formatting of its own records, types of access points, and whether and what kind of vocabulary control is applied to each type of access point. The originating service also determines its own usage fees and any conditions of access to its files which the vendor must enforce.

The command language is determined by the vendor and is the same for every file under its control. The different vendors have made little effort to standardize this language among themselves. Since most searchers are happiest when they can search a database using a familiar command language, its language may be the feature garnering for a vendor the greatest degree of user loyalty.

Originally, some of the largest A&I services with their own search systems, including the H. W. Wilson Co. and the National Library of Medicine, refused to license their databases to any other vendor. All have now succumbed to the realization that searchers prefer to become familiar with fewer command languages, passwords, and invoices. In the increasingly privatized world of the vendors and utilities who service databases and market processing systems, the tendency toward multinational operation is pronounced, and licenses and whole companies are subject to sale and purchase by others.

For their part, vendors have proved unable to enforce total exclusivity in their contracts with the suppliers of their databases, the A&I services. It is common for a database to be available through more than one vendor. Furthermore, just as some functions of utilities are being bypassed by locally operated integrated systems, so are some database vendor functions being taken over from within the library market. Some A&I services now license files or whole databases directly to be mounted for searching on the local OPAC of a library or on a consortium's network. It will only do this if the library or consortium agrees to restrict searching of its file(s) to a specified group of registered users, for example, students, faculty, and staff in the case of an academic library. Most libraries have never restricted searching of the files they create themselves, so this means establishing a two-tier database in the OPAC, one password-controlled and one not.

The developments of client-server communication and a common interface standard will have significant impact on access to A&I databases, as they have already revolutionized access to library databases. The only reason for the lag is that the A&I services require a secure method of collecting fees before they will make their databases available via the Internet.

COMPATIBILITY

Communication is the essence of the business of bibliography. Its purposes are (1) to convey the content of a message unchanged from sender to receiver and (2) to facilitate the latter's interpretation of the content as the former intended it. The prime requirement for both may be summarized as compatibility: technical standards for the process and formatting standards for the content. Libraries communicate bibliographic data along routes involving both themselves and their users interactively: either might be the sender at one moment and the receiver at another.

A common goal of librarians is complete freedom of the exchange of publicly available information. It is not surprising that they participate through organizations and individually to prevent or circumvent, or at least minimize, all technical, legal, and commercial barriers to that goal. Standards they have designed specifically to support bibliographic functions are the focus of part II and the appendix of this book. The rest of this chapter deals with issues of direct interest in bibliography but which transcend the intellectual content of any particular record.

Libraries once chose individually what size of card to use in their manual catalogues. Some chose 4-by-6-inch ones, others 5-by-8 or 3-by-5. Even 2-by-5-inch cards for abbreviated shelf-list records were common! Eventually, the 7.5-by-12.5-cm. card became a de facto standard. Which size a library chose mattered little in a stand-alone operation, but it made sharing cards impossible. That cards and cabinetry had to be manufactured in smaller quantities in each of many sizes brought many disadvantages, even if card or cabinetry manufacturers might enjoy extra profit because variety offers greater potential for cornering a market in one size.

Automation encourages integration, but not necessarily standardization. Inter-computer transfer of data was not at first foreseen or planned, but librarians took their interest in standardization from manual operations into automated ones. Sharing is their very reason for existence. Like the old card manufacturers, however, today's hardware manufacturers and software designers compete and therefore find it commercially disadvantageous if their products are too easily interchangeable. The computer has become the primary communication device. Companies whose very business is electronic communication are like libraries in their need to adopt technical standards on an industry-wide basis. This explains why each different hardware and software firm must now assure prospective buyers that its equipment and programs can not only do any given job better than anyone else's, but can still communicate via common communication standards.

Character Sets

Like a letter of the alphabet, a byte has no inherent meaning. Meaning is assigned to it in context and by convention. The *character set* is therefore the most fundamental standard of computer-based communication. When the key labelled *A* was struck on a terminal in Vancouver in 1981 and the result stored on tape, it could be expected that a phototypesetter activated in Chicago in 1996 by state-of-the-art equipment would still display the same letter *A* when reading any input device capable of conveying the 1981 original as eight bits, or one byte, of unformatted digital information.

The character set known as basic ASCII (American Standard Code for Information Interchange) consists of 128 characters, all those available in the seven-bit systems of the time. Although it has never become an internationally recognized standard, a version of it is the most widely adopted de facto standard for encoding roman-alphabet and arabic-digit characters in digital form, particularly in in English-speaking world.

The position of English as an international language and its requirement of only fifty-two different characters (twenty-six in each of two cases) made this degree of standardization relatively easy even when early users demanded some diacritics, special characters, etc. Agreement among manufacturers, programmers, and users on character sets including diacritics, nonroman scripts, symbols, etc.—even on an ASCII extension to the other 128 characters of an eight-bit system—is still not a foregone conclusion despite much progress toward internationally recognized standards. It is natural that if a language and script are native to only one country, that country's interests are likely to prevail within the country, at least, even if they are incompatible with standards adopted elsewhere for other reasons. A

Unicode governing character sets for all the world's scripts therefore remains a published proposal more than a de facto standard.[3]

Standardizing character sets and conventions for dealing with the nonalphabetic scripts of Chinese, Japanese, and Korean continues to be fraught with problems. Not the least of these is how to input thousands of different characters using a manageable keyboard. One system uses an extended keyboard for the segment-by-segment composition of such a character and for combining the Korean phonetic elements into graphic syllables. Another, now obsolescent, uses a numeric code for each different character. The one favoured for bibliographic work calls for keying in a romanized form, whereupon a program displays all the possible original-script characters for that romanization and asks the operator to choose the intended one for input. The adoption of operating systems with a graphical user interface in bibliographic processing is making the option involving digitization of a drawn character more practicable. These methods all rely on complex software associated with the input workstation. Different scripts are still something of a socio-economic barrier to automated bibliographic control, but are now only a minor technical one.

Interconnection

Most of the integrated systems described above use a *local area network* (LAN) consisting of linked *workstations* (intelligent terminals) within a single institution or among those of a geographic region or even a national or international consortium. *Local* refers to the system; the number of, and distance between, its processing nodes, terminals, printers, etc. are irrelevant. The communication software linking parts of the LAN is a very simple type of *communication protocol,* a package of programs designed to ensure that hardware and software recognize and display the content of every message with as little degradation as possible. Some loss or change of data may be inevitable, but even then, a sophisticated protocol will attempt to reconstruct the original.

Librarians' use of utilities, consortia, and database vendors is being reassessed as electronic communication develops. Hardware and software incompatibilities preventing reliable direct computer-to-computer communication have finally been overcome, and the Internet is now a means of sharing databases and computer programs virtually without limit. The most widely used protocol for Internet communication, incorporating telnet, is TCP/IP (Transport Control Protocol/Interface Program or, according to another dictionary, Transmission Control Protocol/Internet Protocol). This allows for the transfer of any kind of data (programs or data files) from one system to another.[4] *File transfer protocols* (FTP) lag in their practical application to transferring complex formatted bibliographic data, so to date reference librarians have explored the Internet as a source of bibliographic (and much other!) information more than have cataloguers. Any more detail of librarians' Internet use will be out-of-date before this book is published. For example, the establishment of a second internet restricted to "academic" uses now that the original one has become clogged by commerce immediately raises the question of whether various types of libraries can remain as easily interconnected as at present.

QUALITY CONTROL

Error is inevitable when humans create, code, and input so many separate data elements for each of so many items. A generation ago, anyone in private business would have envied the high standard of quality control prevalent in the typical bibliographic file created by librarians. People tended to remain at the same job for many years, making a long in-service training process worthwhile, and became thoroughly familiar with rules and routines.

Records from national agencies and the major A&I services are still expected to be of higher intellectual quality than others because of the professional and academic expertise of their cataloguers and indexers and because these agencies accept responsibility for preparing definitive records for a broad spectrum of users. They also traditionally revise and proofread more stringently to eliminate clerical error. While the quality of work done in local libraries and in smaller A&I services was not necessarily suspect, the background experience and knowledge on which the isolated professional can draw is inevitably more limited than what is brought to bear among a team in a larger operation. Alas, cost-control has caused the gradual disappearance of the proofreader and the diminution of most checks once made manually during file construction.

Sharing and distributing the work make it even harder to maintain as high a level of quality control over a database whose very size militates against it. Who guarantees the quality of investigation, rule application, subject knowledge, or simply judgement? These are too important to be left entirely to goodwill but often are. Reducing costs, the primary purpose of sharing, only fosters a psychology of corner-cutting.

It is impracticable for the actual documents catalogued ever to be seen by staff at a consortium headquarters: the work of that office is system maintenance and administration, and perhaps clerical input, but not bibliographic judgement. Nor does that office have the reference tools every cataloguer needs to do quality work. Most consortia consider that it would be too costly (and a step back toward centralization) to assign trained cataloguers to oversee quality control. Did the record not originate in professional work in the library which owns the document? Peer pressure plays a part in keeping every cataloguer vigilant.

The first step in incorporating a new record into a centrally maintained database is to see if the database already has a record for the document in question. On finding a matching record, one needs only add copy and location data to customize it. However, every shared bibliographic database accumulates multiple records for the same document. These come about when the initial search fails to retrieve a record which is in fact there but not where expected, or when a new record differs from an existing one in any way a DBMS has been programmed to consider significant when it compares them.

Clerical input errors are a major cause of unintended duplication. Even if authority control is applied, errors can slip past it. An existing record may also be missed because it was added so recently that the file's access-point indices were not yet updated when the search was done. Index maintenance is such a drain on computing power that it is best done in batch mode overnight when the computer is not busy with interactive operations. In bibliographically complex situations, a cataloguer might not immediately recognize an existing record as pertinent. For example, it should be no surprise if each of the two different records in figure 1 on page 45 finds its way into a file when cataloguers from different institutions see the book and each checks the database under only one access point. Variant imprints and monographs within serials, the former discussed in chapter 2 and the latter in chapter 8, are other situations in which this problem is rampant.

Whatever the reason for these "duplicate" records, once they creep into a file, each one has the potential to attract and compound other errors. Searchers finding only one of the records are not notified of all the libraries which actually own the item. Identifying and removing duplicates, or *deduping* a database, is impracticable manually when it consists of records from many sources. It can only be done automatically by programmable comparisons based, for example, on an ISBN, a Library of Congress record-identifier number, or to a degree by a compression code. Instant secure identification by a computer program is why numeric strings and codes are applied to documents to begin with, but most of those devised cannot distinguish every possible edition or state a cataloguer might choose to. They are an imperfect tool for deduping a file, but better than nothing. Furthermore, any large file contains many older records for material to which no such number or code was ever applied.

The importance of authority control over the access points in a bibliographic file is stressed in chapters 3 and 4. Authority control is the type of quality control most difficult to maintain in a cooperatively produced database. Yet failure to examine every new controlled-vocabulary access point added to the database to ensure that it meets the required standard of vocabulary control almost ensures a very high proportion of duplicate records, as well as more fundamental access problems for searchers. This explains the stringent quality control exercised by national agencies over such projects as CIP and the Program for Cooperative Cataloging, mentioned earlier, and CONSER, mentioned below. The owner of a bibliographic file whose authority control is substandard may contract to have its access points "walked through" (compared with) an external authority file to see which do not match and might therefore need review. A good authority file being a rare and costly jewel, the sale or "rental" of one has become part of the business of bibliography.

Maintaining quality control over textual content in a human language is hard enough. It is even harder to ensure, during input, the accuracy of digital formatting codes such as MARC tags, indicators, and subfield codes (see the appendix). The first and last records in almost any unrevised machine-sorted file got there, whereas they clearly belong somewhere else, not because of miskeyed access points but because of errors in these codes, which are suppressed in the visual display but are major determinants of how and where data elements are displayed. Coding errors are a significant problem in the largely unrevised A&I databases. At worst, a coding error can cause a program to abort a computer process and damage the file.

Automated Error Detection

The final stage of manual filing into a card catalogue always constituted a fruitful exercise in error detection because the filer has at least the opportunity to review the entire record, not just the access point being filed. Filing is now universally done by computer programs, removing this effective method of error detection. Administrators long for the day when automated formatting and input processes involving digital scanning and optical character recognition are sufficiently reliable to be operationally effective. This would reduce both the cost of routine input and the incidence of clerical input error but would further reduce the likelihood of human checks involving

judgement. Many human error-detection processes have been eliminated through changed administrative policies and automated techniques. It is now common to wait for an error to be (sometimes)
noticed by a searcher and then (perhaps) to correct it, rather than pay
the price of constant vigilance to prevent its occurrence.

Automated error-detection techniques are the preferred solution. A
good proofreader knows where in a given kind of text particular types
of error are most likely to occur. Clerical errors of tangibly definable
types can also be detected and sometimes even corrected by a computer program, perhaps with the help of a little additional input. Numeric transcription is particularly prone to error, for example, keying
12435 instead of the correct 12345, so a *check digit* is now part of most
standard numbers such as the ISBN and ISSN. The digit is calculated
and appended to the number automatically at the time the number is
assigned. It is an arithmetic function of the number's other digits. To
ensure that the right record is retrieved for acquisitions, downloading
of source records, deduping, etc. in a bibliographic system, an error-
detection subroutine of the search program routinely reproduces the
original arithmetic calculation on the ISBN or other such number. If
the result matches the check digit, one has about ninety-five percent
assurance that the number was correctly transcribed. Another type of
error-detection program checks that all the required areas, elements,
and codes of a record are present in the record even though it cannot
ensure that the content of any of these is correct.

Automated authority control is the single most important form of
error detection in any bibliographic system. It prevents an access
point from being applied to a record if that access point cannot be
exactly matched in the authority file. This comparison check can be
overridden; that is, a cataloguer can err deliberately, if inadvertently,
by inserting into the authority-control system an incorrect or improp-
erly linked access point. It is also possible to err by applying an authorized access point to an item for which that access point is
irrelevant or a poor choice. Automated authority control does not
make judgements. However, at least it ensures that any attempt to key
in an access point not already accounted for by the system results in
a message to the cataloguer to recheck that access point. The name
Twaim, Mark or the topic **HISTROY** are unlikely to appear in a file
with automated authority control; they are all too likely to appear in
a file without it.

Errors of this kind are less serious in a manual search, where the
user sees many records at a glance and almost inevitably browses a bit,
than in those types of automated search where browsing is not an option
and one must rely on what can be retrieved in a *FIND* command, for
example, when using boolean operators (see chapter 4). Cataloguers

are not the only people who make mistakes; users make them too. Neither a person nor a computer can adequately deal with a user's totally mistaken notion of a name, title, or subject term. Every reference librarian has a stock of users' bloopers, such as the patron who asked for Norman Ward's book of humour as *My Sin, the Beer* (its actual title: *Mice in the Beer*). One cannot clutter error-detection programs or authority files with possible goofs, only with probable ones.

Automated Revision

After all the automated systems have had their chance, it remains necessary for trained, perceptive, and experienced librarians to judge when something is going wrong and to correct and revise files constantly. Not only are there inaccuracies in every bibliographic file; a record of impeccable quality when it was created may fail to be adequate in the future because of the discovery of further facts about the item or a change of cataloguing rules. The most labour-intensive clerical operations of the pre-computer era were devoted to changing and correcting existing records. This is never faced with much enthusiasm. It adds nothing to output statistics except those which leave an uncomfortable feeling that the work was not done properly the first time. The cost and practical difficulty of changing individual records in a large manual catalogue were long considered insuperable barriers to accepting some rule changes even when it was acknowledged that they were very desirable. It is no wonder that older cataloguing codes were deliberately written more with a view to creating a "permanent" record than with a view to the changing needs and perceptions of users.

Automation has drastically reduced the cost of the clerical operations involved in correcting and revising. With an editing program, one can find and simultaneously change every instance of a character string wherever it occurs in an entire file. Keeping controlled-vocabulary access points only in an authority file reduces revision of an access point relevant to thousands of individual records in the bibliographic file to a change of only one record in the authority file. Few changes ever require rekeying an entire record. A change in processing systems is the most drastic revision ever undertaken in a library's bibliographic service. It requires years of planning and is rarely trouble-free, but the entire old database is reloaded into a different DBMS without rekeying much if any of the original data.

By about 1975, the automated methods of file maintenance briefly sketched here were available in most larger libraries. Until then, the larger the library, the greater was its resistance to much needed changes in cataloguing rules, subject heading practice, display techniques, etc.

Outright hostility to rule changes now appears only among librarians who choose not to differentiate between a failing (an error to be corrected) and an improvement (a new form of access point to make the file more user-friendly or more effective). That the quite radical changes in the library standards detailed in part II have largely been implemented during the past twenty years is not a coincidence but a direct result of automation. Very few A&I services ever update, or even correct, previous work, since their focus is on providing access to the most current material. A significant exception is the National Library of Medicine, which feels it must keep access points for all citations relevant to the current terminology of searchers.

Levels of Cataloguing

Level is used in this section to refer only to the degree of completeness of a record, a meaning totally distinct from the different levels of identity within a publication discussed at the end of chapter 8. It is unfortunate that the same word is used for both. When each library created separate records tailored to the supposed needs of its own users, the issue of how many data elements the model record should include was a matter of lively debate. Over a century ago, Charles Cutter recognized the validity of short, medium, and full levels of cataloguing. He was not being whimsical when he cautioned "that the Short Family are not all of the same size, that there is more than one Medium, and that Full may be Fuller and Fullest."[5] The current successor to Cutter's code, AACR2R, permits the same kind of latitude, both in rule 1.0D and by making it a matter of option whether to include specified data elements such as a second imprint, most notes, and multilingual repetitions of information on a title page. Within the bounds of cataloguing codes and local policies, the professional cataloguer has always had to decide what bibliographic information is or is not essential in the case of an individual document, considering its bibliographic nature. Two records for the same item need not be identical for both to be applications of the same standard.

The mode of distributed cataloguing has ensured that few records are any longer created for use in only a single library. A source record is distributed nationally and internationally; a record in a shared database is searched by the patrons of many libraries, usually of varied types and sizes. In this context, the bibliographic record of highest quality is necessarily the most complete one: the one incorporating the highest proportion of the data elements relevant to the document and access points useful for a searcher with any particular interest to find it. Ideally, it contains more information than any one user or any one library requires at any one time. What data are selected from the complete record for display to a searcher at a local OPAC is governed by the local processing system and its user interface (see the end of chapter 4).

Early in the days of automation, smaller libraries objected to maintaining fuller records in their systems than seemed required by their local users' needs, but the overhead cost to store a more complete record is no longer significant. It is, however, always more costly to compose. Control over the quality and completeness of records contributed to shared databases has always been uncertain. Peer pressure among participants in a consortium to uphold agreed standards of completeness has some effect, but local economic pressure to cut corners is always present. Most utilities and consortia publish formal guidelines for input to a common database specifying whether a code or data element is (1) absolutely required, (2) required if it applies to the particular item, or (3) entirely at the option of the record creator.

The pace-setter in this, as in almost every bibliographic practice, is the Library of Congress, the level of completeness in whose records is rarely described in relative terms but is simply taken for granted. In fact, what it does in practice has closely influenced the writing of all the Anglo-American cataloguing rules of the twentieth century. Nevertheless, at various times since 1948 the Library of Congress has maintained at least two different standards of completeness for single-item description. What it once called *Limited Cataloging* is much the same as what it now calls *Minimal Level Cataloging,* although since 1981 it has been applied to different categories of material than previously. In addition, the Library now creates more records at what it calls *Collection Level Cataloging* in which a single record is made for a group of related items.[6] It still appears typical for libraries contributing to a shared database to agree to imitate the standard, rather than the minimal, Library of Congress record in completeness. Any record not meeting the norm for the file should be coded as such.

For local purposes, however, it is becoming more and more common to accept whatever record can be derived or composed easily at the moment of selection or acquisition as a de facto permanent record, even when it is official policy to replace it with a fuller one "as soon as possible." Much corner-cutting involves nothing more serious than ignoring descriptive data elements generally considered of minor significance. In practice, however, it more often means restriction of data elements to the barest minimum and of access points to natural-language ones; that is, restriction of search capability to keywords in a brief record unless a CIP or other derived record happens to be available very early to provide some controlled-vocabulary name and subject access. The detriment to searching is far more serious in the case of subjects than of names. The highest aim seems no longer to be completeness but merely compatibility with the requirements of the DBMS.

No convincing argument other than an economic one can be advanced for keeping too brief a record in a catalogue for long. However, a very strong one is valid for putting nonstandard (never substandard!) records there in the first place. In the days when each process from selection to circulation had its own separate files, there was a separate standard for each file. Only records meeting the highest cataloguing standard went into the catalogue consulted by the library's end-users. Today's integrated multipurpose database rightly includes records of every level of completeness pertinent to any purpose, all accessible by every searcher through the same DBMS.

This blurs the notion of a cataloguing backlog. What was once considered an inherent evil is now only a briefer or lengthier holding pattern during which items are accessible through at least some access points, albeit often only natural-language ones. A laxer attitude to backlogs increases the likelihood that incorporation of a complete record will be postponed in the hope that one can eventually be derived and the expensive horror of original cataloguing can be forever avoided. However, distributed cataloguing is only effective if every participant does not wait endlessly for someone else to act. A consortium's fee structure is typically used as an incentive for each participant to accept a reasonable share of costly original work, for example, by offering a credit for each record newly input according to the accepted standard. If everyone waits for someone else to create the perfect record, there will never be any!

One argument frequently advanced for brevity is that fewer data elements suffice in records for material considered ephemeral and to be held only temporarily or immediately placed into some storage facility. On the contrary, anything in storage which can therefore no longer be browsed easily needs more and better, not fewer and uncontrolled, access points in catalogues. As for temporary or ephemeral material, why keep it even briefly if it cannot be located by all who need it while it is around? When arguments for brief-listing such material are examined, they usually come down to the fact that it is sought not by the individual item but by the group of items. In other words, something closer to archival than to library retrieval practice should be applied both in bibliographic listing and in reference help to locate it, and the issue of complete item-by-item description is simply irrelevant.

Another argument for cutting corners relates to local modification of records available for downloading from a remote database. The entire history of centralization and the shared creation of databases is one of increasing standardization and decreasing library-specific idiosyncrasy or tailoring to local needs. The consequence of this is not all good. There remain valid reasons why a special collection or special user requests should occasion special bibliographic treatment, but its cost increasingly militates against it. It should be a matter of great concern outside the United States that increasingly homogenized bibliographic, and particularly subject-retrieval, usage is modelled so closely on the American context and perspective.

NATIONAL DATABASES

Each year there are additions to the alphabet soup of named cooperative arrangements. Each of these increases librarians' awareness that financial resources for bibliographic control are not best deployed as single-institution budget items but as a common, yet finite, fund with which to establish and use a group of databases as a single resource. Both public-sector and private-sector organizations play their part in creating and communicating this resource. Libraries and archival repositories, whether as individual institutions or in consortia, are important channels, but not the only ones, through which end-users approach the resource. The proportion of end-users who make direct connection with bibliographic databases, not via a library, is increasing. Even when a library remains the intermediary, the proportion who visit the physical place or consult a librarian by telephone diminishes as more users access the library's database and even the content of its collections via a modem. A library's bibliographic service is no longer circumscribed by its walls.

It is therefore not impractical to consider the many existing databases as together constituting a single national bibliographic database. National borders are not yet transparent to the transfer of library and information services, so it may be unwise to proclaim the universal database which Paul Otlet envisioned earlier this century, but an international infrastructure, of which the Internet is only a part, exists. The world's national libraries act in some ways as a grand bibliographic consortium, their directors meeting regularly under IFLA auspices. Those of Australia, Canada, the United Kingdom, and the United States accept so many of the same standards and practices that their relationship is particularly close. In 1996, the British Library and the Library of Congress signed the Cataloguing Policy Convergence Agreement (CPCA) to build a joint name authority file, only the latest of a series of their contractual cooperative arrangements as they work toward a joint database.

Bibliographic sharing among libraries is now firmly based on digitizing records according to the MARC family of formats (see chapter 8 and the appendix). In contrast, the major A&I services of the industrialized world neither contribute to, nor use, each other's databases and therefore never adopted a common format as each automated along its own path. In the developing world, however, automation is initially too costly not only for private A&I services but also for any redundancy in designing and operating systems. There, centralization remains the only economically feasible mode and a single national, normally governmental, agency is responsible for all bibliographic control functions, joining traditional library services with traditional A&I services.

While committees of IFLA and Unesco have helped set international standards acceptable to both richer and poorer nations, the technical practices of libraries and associations in the wealthier countries, particularly the United States, naturally predominate. This is gradually resulting in adherence to standards sufficiently compatible to permit the easy use of records worldwide, regardless of where they originate, again, with the Internet as a strong impetus. Librarians in developing countries are poised to jump from card catalogues to the World Wide Web, bypassing the developmental trials and errors of their colleagues in richer countries. Centralization and cooperation thus look increasingly like two faces of the same coin. Poole's and Jewett's proposals are coming to fruition jointly and in reasonable harmony with one another.

Data Conversion

Considering not the single library but the collective of North American libraries, the transition from manual catalogue to OPAC has occupied the entire generation of the 1960s and since. The version of the cataloguing code AACR in current use is still phrased largely in terms of manual input and output of bibliographic data. Only in late 1995 did the Library of Congress feel it could abandon reference to the image of the record on a 3-by-5-inch card when describing its rule-interpretation and implementation policies to the library community at large in its *Cataloging Service Bulletin.*

During the generation of the transition, converting the data on cards to digital form was a major concern and a significant part of the business of bibliography. Lucky the library whose conversion project was (nearly) finished while money for it was still available, even if it resulted in many partial records, inadequate matching of access points against a high-quality authority file, and a residue of snags and records not yet (or never to be) converted for one reason or another. Cleaning up the errors of the past is usually the most costly and time-consuming part of an automation project. For the shorter or longer period that a library's database must exist partly in manual form and partly as an interactive file, end-users are annoyed because one cannot always tell which part to consult. A record for a hundred-year-old item might well be the latest added to the catalogue. For processing functions, however, notably circulation, a divided database is simply not an option. Most conversion projects began with circulation records with too little bibliographic data to be useful for any other purpose, just to make it possible to finish conversion quickly.

Conversion necessarily began with the manual rekeying of data from cards and the addition of the necessary formatting codes. Gradually, the databases primarily of the bibliographic utilities incorporated enough converted records that it became worthwhile to search them for derived copy to be downloaded. Eventually, utilities and others offered the service of automated matching of an entire shelf list in card form against the database(s) likely to generate the largest number of hits on records already converted. The Library of Congress shelf list from 1898 through 1967 was converted and formed a major tool for converting those of other libraries. To make such sizeable projects economically feasible, the keying had to be done with the least expensive clerical help or with optical character recognition and even automated format recognition. These methods are inherently prone to a high error rate, and quality control over the result was minimal. These great converted databases speeded many local conversion projects but left a residue of strange records in local files to which they were copied.

The ongoing CONSER (Cooperative ONline SERials) Program in which the cataloguing of serials is shared began twenty years ago as a project to convert manual records, under the name CONSER (CONversion of SERials) project. Because of the complexities of serial records, a high degree of quality control was deemed essential, and it was agreed that either the Library of Congress or the National Library of Canada would authenticate every record input by any other cooperating library before it was identified as up-to-standard and added to the national CONSER database maintained at OCLC.

The A&I services were never as concerned to convert what had previously been listed only manually. Chronology has a different significance in a search of journal literature, particularly in the sciences where total cumulation is more a hindrance to quick searching than a boon. Even in their digital versions, many A&I databases are searchable as segments, each containing a few years of indexing. Constant updating of subject access points is a major concern of an A&I service because changes in terminology and concepts make their first appearance in most fields in journals. For all these reasons, journal indexing of the past is likely forever to remain in its original manual form while library catalogues are largely converted.

PART

II

■ ■ ■

Library Standards

Part I of this book deals with principles, not rules, although they are elucidated as specifically as possible in the context of present practice. Having reached this point, therefore, the reader may feel frustrated that there is not one instruction in the whole part about which keys to press on a keyboard to create or to search for a single real record in a single real file. Deliberate avoidance of such instruction stems largely from the fact that part I deals with records in all three types of bibliographic file: the A&I publication, the monographic bibliography, and the library catalogue. While the basic principles are the same for all, their specific implementation differs, from very little to considerably, among the three types.

The least degree of standardization is to be found among monographic bibliographies. Internal consistency is still the basic principle, but the compiler of one of these feels no compelling need to adhere to specific pre-existing standards for selecting and arranging data elements, for formulating individual access points, for dividing the database into subfiles, or even for alphanumeric arrangement. The full records in one of these bibliographies are most often arranged according to a classification scheme, but it is most often one created anew for the purpose and not an existing one.

This does not mean that monographic bibliographies are make-work projects of amateurs, poorly constructed, or hard to use. They are specialized topic-specific, medium-specific, or user-specific tools.

They exist precisely so that the intellectual requirements of the topic, medium, or user can determine what arrangement, access, and level of description best meet their purpose. They supplement general bibliographic tools like library catalogues in which the same items are identified and organized in a different way. In consequence, however, a searcher cannot unthinkingly transfer the same searching procedures and expectations from one to another.

There is somewhat greater uniformity of practice among the A&I services, particularly among products of the same firm and those covering the same subject areas. As described in chapter 5, database vendors also impose common search commands and output formats on the different databases they service, so the pattern of an interactive search of an A&I database is likely to seem familiar even when manual searching differs among the print versions of the databases.

It is in the construction and use of library catalogues that adherence to national and international standards has been pursued the most purposefully and for the longest time, now over two centuries. For the past century, this has been largely for the reasons of cooperation discussed in greatest detail in chapter 5. For the past thirty years, automation has exercised a significant integrating influence, felt more practically among libraries already willing to cooperate than among independent A&I services.

The factor which most differentiates libraries from all other bibliographic agencies, however, is the more general nature of the typical library collection. It includes material in all formats on all subject areas and, in all but the so-called special library, is used by a very diverse clientele. To say that librarians wrote standards at the lowest common denominator for their cataloguing and classification would be unfair: one does not approach the catalogue of a general library for certain levels or types of bibliographic data or organization. Librarians devised their standards so that their own primary searching tools could be of the broadest value to the largest number of people. Librarians are the generalists among information professionals.

A notable peaking of interest in standardization among North American librarians of the last quarter of the nineteenth century resulted in their adoption of a common technology (unit records on cards); a common basic arrangement and filing system (the dictionary catalogue arranged according to Charles Ammi Cutter's principles); discipline-based classification (realized in practice by both Cutter and Melvil Dewey); verbal subject access points expressed directly and specifically, again according to Cutter's rules; and a common philosophy of bibliographic service. Within a year of each other in 1876–1877, national library associations were established on both sides of the Atlantic, and their primary focus of activity for the remainder of the century was the cataloguing function, broadly interpreted. By the end of the century, the Library of Congress had adopted most of the emerging standards and practices mentioned here, entrenching them and spreading them around the Anglo-American world.

The four chapters of part II and the appendix explore the standards and practices of librarians working in this tradition, in their late-twentieth-century automated context. These deal with controlled-vocabulary name access points (chapter 6), access points for subject retrieval, using both words and classification symbols (chapter 7), description and formatting (chapter 8), and the alphanumeric arrangement, or filing, of access points (chapter 9). The brief description of the MARC format in the appendix arises out of all the above, since that format is the basis for automating the entire record. These chapters embody the realization in librarians' practice of the principles analyzed in part I with as little repetition and rephrasing as possible. Compilers of bibliographic tools other than library catalogues are also intelligent enough not to reinvent the whole wheel if only a new spoke design is wanted. Many are in fact educated as librarians. They copy or adapt the model of the library catalogue in whole or in part as they find it relevant and affordable.

WHAT IS A BIBLIOGRAPHIC STANDARD?

Human nature being what it is, there is never only one accepted way of doing anything that can involve different purposes, processes, costs, or historical antecedents. Bibliographic standards do not have the compelling force of, say, an electrical standard: without 60-cycle alternating current of 110 volts (more or less), a North American home grinds to a halt. Using a bibliographic file not based on one particular standard occasions neither physical disaster nor, in a stable person, emotional trauma. It is not hard to recognize the title of a series regardless of whether it precedes or follows the imprint in a citation.

There are several basic ways of programming a computer to search for access points. However, bibliographic standards facilitate cost-efficiency in sharing data and give searchers a sense of familiarity with any library catalogue. Lacking any compelling reason why one way of doing something is necessarily better than another, reasonable people are still persuaded that the advantages of standardization outweigh disadvantages, and eventually, one way preponderates while the others wither from disuse. Once this type of consensus is well enough advanced, the prevailing practice is usually codified formally by a representative committee of practitioners who ensure that it is stated as clearly and comprehensively as possible. At that point, the codification is a standard. If formally ratified by an officially recognized body, it is a de jure standard of that body; if only widely implemented in practice, it is still a de facto standard.

A standard, of whichever type, provides (1) a unified structure, (2) a statement of minimum expectations, and (3) guidelines to determine when absolute uniformity in execution is essential and when it is not. A standard is ignored when it comes to be perceived as either unnecessary or as too difficult or costly to implement. To be adopted, particularly at the international level, it must be as flexible as its purposes permit. Larger and smaller, richer and poorer, general and specialized, institutions everywhere can then at least aspire to adhere to it and lay any necessary groundwork for its eventual implementation instead of simply ignoring it. The purpose of most bibliographic standards is not the absolute uniformity without which, say, a computer program fails to function, but rather compatibility ensuring mutual understanding.

The stated purpose of the joint British-American cataloguing code of 1908 was to address "the requirements of larger libraries of a scholarly character" (American edition, p. viii: this and other codes are cited in note 1 to chapter 6). The 1967 Anglo-American code, a de facto standard until 1980, was "drawn up primarily to respond to the need of general research libraries" (North American edition, p. 1). In effect, the most influential codes published until very recently limited the field of their own operation even within the library community. Yet because they were the basis of cataloguing instruction in recognized library schools, librarians were led to feel they *should* be adopting them in practice in other types and sizes of library. A standard was at odds with itself.

The current code, AACR2R, more closely matches the characteristics of a good standard. It was "designed for use in the construction of catalogues and other lists in general libraries of all sizes" (rule 0.1), in part by authorizing variant practices as long as these result in the creation of compatible records. For example, it permits the use of any of three levels of descriptive detail (rule 1.0D) and allows the access point for a given name to appear in differing language forms and romanizations (cf. rules 22.3C2, 24.1A, and 24.3A). Similarly, not every library using the MARC format for digital bibliographic data provides every possible processing or searching code. The resultant record may not be as complete, but different database management systems can accept and process it satisfactorily.

Most bibliographic operations are relatively free of controversial political, linguistic, racial, and cultural implications. In the area of subject analysis treated in chapter 7, this is not possible. There can be no totally objective view of the subject of any document because every topic is perceived differently in different cultures, in different contexts, and when approached for different purposes or even for the same purpose by different people. All the natural problems of intelligent communication interfere with the unambiguous expression of subject content, whether through words as subject access points or through the logical juxtapositions of a classification scheme.

It is possible to analyze the working of internally consistent systems for subject indexing (see chapter 7). However, it is not possible, or necessarily desirable, to ensure that two different indexers will approach the content of a particular document from the same point of view and therefore come up with the same subject-indexing terms for it. This ultimate impossibility of uniform subject analysis for all purposes is reason enough for the same item to be indexed over and over again in different ways in different subject-oriented lists. It is also the reason why those who access bibliographic records solely for document identification, and in any international context, rely on name-title, code, and numeric access points in preference to subject-word and classification-symbol access points. Applying the former is objective; applying the latter is highly subjective.

Standards Agencies

Variations in bibliographic practices in different countries or among quite separate groups of users (for example, school librarians in Indonesia and medical-journal editors in London) are tolerable to the degree that their worlds remain separate. Every field has its formal standards applicable only within a particular country or countries or otherwise of limited enforcement. Had no other force for standardization existed before, the integrating computer would still have made the entire world of information communication a practical unity in economics and technology.

Only socio-political differences still divide the world of information. Although these are not insignificant, librarians always try to rise above them. In every field in which they operate, computer programmers demand an answer to the question "Why is *this* done differently from *that*?" Idiosyncratic variants tend not to get into the program when the answer is "I don't know." Fixing international standards for manual library catalogues took about a hundred years; for computerized ones, it took about ten.

Librarians throughout the English-speaking world have long cooperated. Their language and their library and reading traditions are shared. Their budgetary problems are small compared with those of librarians almost anywhere else, so they can devote more professional staff time to the formal codification of bibliographic practices. Active

Anglo-American cooperation is almost a century old, although interrupted by periods of apathy and by inactivity during two world wars. After the Second World War, it remained the basis for new projects in bibliographic control, notably under Unesco aegis.

Unesco has supported three major programmes in bibliographic control: using their current names, they are the General Information Programme (PGI), the Universal Bibliographic Control and International MARC Programme (UBC), and the Universal Availability of Publications Programme (UAP). It also operates the United Nations Information System in Science and Technology (UNISIST), the original home of the ISSN Network. It tries to ensure that these programmes are as relevant to the work of the A&I services as they are to that of libraries, a particular concern in poorer countries where the two are rarely organizationally separate.

IFLA, twenty years older than Unesco, was founded on American initiative, but until the Second World War had a basically European focus of activity. Following the war, and often with Unesco financial subsidy, it became a significant agency in developing international bibliographic standards, carrying the message of standardization particularly to developing countries. Approval of a project or standard by one or another of these international bodies is more effective there than mere presentation of the practice in richer countries.

Bibliographic data are now communicated electronically, whether using a local area network in a single room or the Internet. The standards for this communication are necessarily as detailed and highly technical as those in any other field of engineering. As with bibliographic standards originating in the practice of, say, the Library of Congress, these standards originate with the staffs of individual companies in the worldwide telecommunication industry. Each change in hardware or software involves the risk of some incompatibility to be resolved in first instance by intra-industry bodies such as the International Telecommunications Union. The interests of librarians are represented in the deliberations of these bodies, although they are not always high among their priorities.

The ultimate international standard-approving organization is the International Organization for Standardization (ISO). Both the original initiative for a new standard and the ultimate responsibility for promulgating it and persuading people to implement it rest with ISO's component national bodies; for example, the British Standards Institute (BSI), the Canadian Standards Association (CSA), and the American National Standards Institute (ANSI). Technical committees in each national body ensure that the best professional expertise is brought to bear on each particular issue, be it the pitch of a screw thread or how to cite the publication facts of a book.

When the scope of ANSI's subcommittee "Z39, Library and Information Sciences and Related Publishing Practices" broadened into into electronic communication generally, it was renamed the National Information Standards Organization (NISO) in 1985 (Z39 remains the prefix of its standards numbering). Since NISO has no direct counterpart in CSA, Canadians act on NISO working groups for particular standards along with Americans, representing various library associations, library consortia, the association of A&I services, the database vendors, the bibliographic utilities, etc. No national bibliographic standard could be effective without involving the major players in both the public and the private sector.

NISO and its counterparts in other countries have taken a number of prevailing bibliographic practices through the long process of adoption by ISO Technical Committee 46 (Information and Documentation) or Joint Technical Committee 1 (Information Processing Systems) and to eventual publication as ISO standards with the highest level of recognition possible. Many bibliographic practices will never be subjected to ISO scrutiny and yet will remain standards in a very practical sense. The following chapters are based on existing ISO standards and on Anglo-American, sometimes only North American, de facto standards; in other words, on what tends to be done in libraries by librarians. The author's nationality is the only justification for the frequent choice of Canadian examples.

DE-STANDARDIZATION

For a hundred years, every informed user of a manual library catalogue came with a clear mental image of its individual record and knew almost instinctively which few of its data elements could be accessed directly. The revolution of interactive searching described in chapter 4 could not immediately impose a new standard; its (perhaps temporary) effect has been the opposite.

Libraries are still in a period of experimentation to determine what techniques and displays are sufficient, user-friendly, and economically practicable. Almost every access possibility is being tested somewhere. For example, while there was instant agreement on word-by-word access to titles (other than words such as articles, on a stoplist), does this also mean words in parallel titles, titles included in notes, etc.? When a date is made searchable, should it only be to qualify a term from another field or fields using a boolean or relational operator? All fields? Which fields? Access to *every* word in the record is possible. Is this desirable? Does it benefit a user to be able to determine which items are written by persons who use the given name

John? Need every word in a general unstructured cataloguer's note be accessible? Does it matter if they are but few users take advantage of the possibility? Most of the former conventions of designating only certain data elements as accessibile were carried over into interactive library catalogues because, for a long while, they continued to be output in batch mode onto cards, microform, or the printed page. Is it time to reassess these decisions now that virtually all library-catalogue searching is interactive?

The first stage of the revolution is over, and inertia is reinstating itself. Having spent a great deal of time and money installing the system which most pleases (or least offends) library staff and users, any administrator finds that commitment to its features sets in. One might have expected that after some twenty years, a very few integrated systems and user interfaces would now constitute the new standard, pushing aside all others as Library of Congress catalogue cards pushed aside other means of display a hundred years ago. Two things have prevented so quick a return to a period of stability: (1) the highly competitive nature of what is now a commercial, and for many profitable, business of supplying processing systems and user interfaces to libraries and (2) librarians' enthusiastic espousal of the Internet, particularly its graphical facility, the World Wide Web, for bibliographic communication.

In summary, automation de-standardized both the appearance of, and methods of access to, bibliographic records in databases. Written documentation for puzzled searchers lags notoriously behind rapid developments. While there is no compelling need to return to the same degree of uniformity once familiar in manual catalogues and some very good reason to rejoice in today's more flexible technology, users have a right to *some* greater degree of common expectations in the not too far distant future. If there is not one *right* way, there are surely some *better* ways.

6

■ ■ ■

Controlled-Vocabulary
Name Access Points

A name uniquely identifies

1) a person
2) a corporate body; for example, a society, an institution, a business, a government, or a government agency
3) a place: a definable geographic location or feature or a jurisdiction known by a place name
4) a work or
5) a publication or document.

This chapter deals with librarians' standards of authority control in establishing access points for single entities in any of the first four categories: *persons, bodies, places,* and *works.* The fifth category, the name of a publication or document per se, is *not* subject to authority control. The implications of this are raised in the following paragraphs and are then taken for granted in the remainder of the chapter where document titles are not an issue.

The difference between a work and any particular document (publication) embodying it, and the practical importance of observing the distinction, are raised in the first pages of this book and taken up in several subsequent passages. Its title proper is the name of a document, not a work. The author(s) of the work in question may suggest a title, but an editor or publisher feels free to impose a different title on the work as originally published or on any later edition, version, translation, etc. If a document itself lacks a title, and one cannot be associated with it from another source, its cataloguer must make up a title to include in its bibliographic record. It simply has to have some name!

The primary usefulness of the title proper is therefore to identify an existing document so that someone who wants it can locate it. If that person remembers or sees the title cited accurately, the most obvious search procedure is to look under its first word (other than an article), because the identifier is the sequence of words, not just one or a few of the words out of context. Searching under the first word is the only possible method in a manual file whose access limitations are discussed in chapters 3 and 4. A person who only remembers one or a few of a title's words, but not necessarily the first, is grateful to be able to find the title in a keyword-indexed interactive file by scanning what has been indexed under *any* significant word in the title, perhaps combining more than one remembered word in a boolean search to increase precision. In either case, however, if the title wording is tampered with, it is of no value in identifying the document.

To the surprise of many, an author is usually denied the final say in titling if a publisher's sales staff or editor disputes the choice. Nevertheless, a work's author, and probably a majority of users, feel that the title identifies the *work* and conveys something of its content. If the work never appears but once (as is true in a vast majority of cases), the distinction between work and document is academic and irrelevant in any practical terms. However, the same work may be embodied in publications with different titles: *Matthew's Good News* and *The Life of Christ as Told by Matthew* are differently titled editions of Saint Matthew's Gospel. Someone looking for this Gospel seeks only the work; any version (in a familiar language) satisfies. Another person, however, requires the screenplay adaptation for Pasolini's film *Il Vangelo secondo Matteo*. That Matthew's Gospel is also part of yet another work, the Bible, merely expands this work-of-many-titles example, admittedly an extreme one and used for the sake of its familiarity and the large number of its versions, editions, and adaptations.

The user who needs to find all, or at least many, different publications of the same work—or critiques, etc. by others *about* it—cannot be expected to remember or look up all its possible publication titles. What is necessary for this purpose is a single authority-controlled index term or search key naming the work, constructed according to cataloguers' rules and linked to the titles naming its various publications. This is the work's *uniform title*: **Bible. New Testament. Gospels. Matthew** for the above work according to current rules.

Any name may be a subject access point as well as an access point of some other type; that is, a work may have as its *subject* any person, corporate body, place, work, or particular publication of a work. Someone may write a book about John Lennon, the Sony Corporation, the United States presidency, the Loire Valley, Homer's *Odyssey*, or even about a single copy of the Gutenberg Bible. When a name is used as a subject access point, it is reasonable to expect to find it in a subject index in the same form as when it is used in a name or author index, at least in the same database. It would make no sense, for example, to use **Twain** as the authorized access point for books *by* the writer of *Tom Sawyer* but **Clemens** for books *about* the same person, regardless of whether authors' names are interfiled with subjects in a single index or appear in separate ones. This chapter therefore deals also with the establishment of names as subject access points.

Even before the modern OPAC with its multiplicity of files searchable in combination, users were clearly better served if whenever a person, body, place, or work was named in any catalogue, bibliography, or A&I publication, its name appeared in the same form. Yet variant forms of name for the same person or entity were then, and remain, more than an annoyance. They are barriers to locating desired information and documents. Librarians have had some, but limited, success in extending the use of the rules for name standardization analyzed in this chapter to other segments of the greater bibliographic enterprise.

A name is as objective as a number. References to Bill Clinton, to William Jefferson Clinton, to the 42nd President of the United States, or to the Governor of Arkansas in 1990 all point to the same man. However, if one gets a detail wrong and says Jeff Clinton, or the 41st President, or the Governor of Tennessee, the message is garbled. A user may or may not know whether the surname of a particular person is spelled Smith, Smythe, Smithe, or Smyth. One may not recall whether the corporate body wanted is the Department of Education, the Ministry of Education, or the Education Department. However, like a publication with its explicit and fixed title, so a person, body, or place does not have some vague name whose form may be this or that depending on the user's whim. Even if there is more than one name, each is as precise and objectively determinable as the title on a title page. These objective forms must be respected when access points are established, even if it is desirable also to include some additional forms as cross-reference links.

NAME AUTHORITY WORK

Name authority work involves the processes introduced in chapter 3, based on the principle that a searcher is entitled to find everything related to a particular person, body, place, or work regardless of which (reasonable) name-form is used as the search key. To accomplish this, the cataloguer must:

1) determine all the names, including all their variant forms, found in any document or other usage to identify the individual person, body, place, or work at issue
2) choose one of these (if more than one exists) as a preferred name or form to act as the primary identifier of the person, body, etc.
3) present the preferred name or form in such a way that it can be most readily located in an alphanumeric file and most surely distinguished from all other names in the same file and
4) either
   a) in a manual file, link all other names or forms under which a user might reasonably look for the person, body, etc. to the preferred form by means of visible cross-references or
   b) in an interactive file, link each form of name for a given person, body, etc. which is likely to be sought as an access point directly to each relevant bibliographic record as shown in figure 14 on page 128.

All but the first of these processes require the application of cataloguing rules, but they cannot be started until the first one is complete. It is that first one, not the others, which is costly and time-consuming. The search for relevant facts, although theoretically exhaustive, is necessarily limited in practice. The reasonable cataloguer searches for any clue to the existence of a problem with the name in question in biographies, directories, gazetteers, etc., but must sense when to give up if no problem surfaces. If the name appears in an existing authority record compiled according to the same rules, it is accepted and copied (downloaded) into the local authority file just as derived bibliographic records are downloaded into the local bibliographic file.

Not surprisingly, the Library of Congress and other national agencies do most of the world's authority work and are valued even more as sources of high-quality authority records than as sources of bibliographic records. At one time, printed lists of authorized name forms for corporate bodies of troublesome types (especially religious or governmental) were published by library associations as aids in individual cataloguing departments. Electronic communication of the authority files of the national agencies has made these redundant.

Scope of the Problem

Some investigation must be done on every name encountered, but any significant problem is expected in only a small percentage of cases. Counts of random samples have consistently shown that more than sixty percent of the persons whose names appear in a library catalogue as authors are so represented for only one work each; there is hardly much latitude here for name variation. In fact, the vast majority of all published works have appeared only once. Therefore, only one work-title/publication-title ever exists, and only clerical error at input or a searcher's faulty recollection (neither predictable) can occasion a problem in the work's bibliographic identification. No amount of vocabulary control can guarantee against confusion if the user asks for *Mice in the Beer* as "My Sin, the Beer" or if the typist has absent-mindedly keyed *The History of England in the Middle Ages* when the title page reads *The Story of England in the Middle Ages* and the error remained undetected. As discussed below at some length, however, corporate bodies and works translated or frequently republished provide abundant possibilities for confusion and are magnets for bibliographic problems. Special precautions are wisely taken when dealing with any instance of one of their names or titles.

On encountering the name of a given person, body, place, or work, a cataloguer can investigate other names or name forms by which that person, etc. is known now or has become known in the past. Some A&I services also do this much in their authority control. Library practice also keeps an eye on the future, acknowledging that changed circumstances regarding a name may cause a review and perhaps a change of an existing access point and/or its links. Few other bibliographic agencies accept any such concern for the future. That library records are created cooperatively over an indefinite time period by many different cataloguers in different libraries also exacerbates problems of maintaining, as well as initially creating, an authority record.

VOCABULARY CONTROL AND COMPUTER SEARCHING

Librarians were not the inventors of authority control over personal names. Western surnames arose centuries ago out of the lack of specificity of such naming as Eric, John's son (Johnson), or Ralph [the] Shoemaker. Although he knew the surnames of those authors who bore them, Gesner still arranged his mid-sixteenth-century universal bibliography according to their given names. Yet it was not long before any searcher looked for Hector Smith among the Smiths rather than among the Hectors, however much more distinctive and easily searchable *Hector* might be than *Smith*. Chinese, Hungarians, Japanese, and some others also speak and write their names beginning with the family or clan name, having used the latter for a much longer time than Western Europeans.

Interactive files and post-coordinate access have not changed this linking of name structure with access and are unlikely to do so even when telephone and other name directories no longer exist in print form. It is simply not efficient to require either the user or the computer programmer to conceive of the process as one of post-coordinating **Cooper** with **Richard**, locating a few hundred Coopers in the file, and some thousands of Richards, to find the two or three different Richard Coopers there. A controlled-vocabulary personal-name access point is intended to be used as a pre-coordinate unit.

The structure of a corporate name is neither so predictable nor so solidly entrenched in people's consciousness. To be able to search for any significant word in it, singly or in combination, is almost essential when:

1) the name is long and the order of its words not self-evident
2) the most distinctive access element for the name of a subordinate body is the name of its parent body or
3) a corporate name begins with a term so frequently used in the file that browsing, or even understanding the filing sequence, under that term is difficult; for example, **United States**.

A combination of truncation and post-coordination enables the user to search, for example, for any access point including both **Canad?** *AND* **Environ?**, retrieving access points for the (hypothetical) government agencies **Canada. Department of the Environment** and **Canadian Environmental Pollution Study Group** and for the nongovernmental body **Canadian Association for the Protection of the Environment**. Retrieving a conference name is simplified if one can, for example, *FIND* (**Confer?** *OR* **Sympos?** *OR* **Workshop?**) *AND* (**Astronom?** *OR* **Astrophys?**) *AND* > 1985.

Despite all these benefits of keyword access to corporate names, satisfactory results from a search of this type are much more likely when the terms being post-coordinated are themselves part of controlled-vocabulary access points than when they are only part of the natural language of titles, abstracts, text, etc. This is because invoking any part of a controlled vocabulary also brings into play its cross-reference links, which are absent from natural-language searching. Vocabulary control is therefore the key to efficient name retrieval from any file. Its application is taken for granted in the rest of this chapter. What follows may at first glance seem to apply more to the manual catalogue (where the user finds item descriptions attached only to the preferred form of a name) than to the interactive catalogue (where a description is linked with all relevant access points, whether in the preferred form or not). Nevertheless, a "preferred" form is still required in an interactive system as a basis for the required links in the authority file.

CATALOGUING RULES FOR
NAME ACCESS POINTS

Charles Ammi Cutter's 1876 *Rules for a Dictionary Catalog* were the basis for the first international cataloguing code, the so-called "Joint Code of 1908." It was adopted by the British and American national library associations. More important for its widespread adoption, it was ratified (indeed, largely sponsored) by the Library of Congress and put into practice in that library's influential centralized cataloguing projects described in chapter 5.

Through this code and its revisions, Cutter's influence spanned a century and is embedded in older published bibliographies and library catalogues. Reference librarians must still know how the rules based on Cutter differ from current ones. Such information is therefore given throughout the remainder of this chapter in generalized form, along with more detailed analysis of current practice.

Although they were adjusted and added to regularly, the 1908 rules were not radically challenged until Seymour Lubetzky attacked many of their principles in his 1953 *Cataloging Rules and Principles, a Critique of the A.L.A. Rules for Entry and a Proposed Design for Their Revision*, a report commissioned and published by the Library of Congress. The resulting review led to the appearance and initial implementation of the *Anglo-American Cataloguing Rules* in 1967. Lubetzky based his challenge on altered views of the purposes of the library catalogue and changing conventions in how people, corporate bodies, and governments choose to name themselves. Automation was not originally a factor, but it soon dominated the application and the further development of AACR. The current version of AACR is a 1988 revision of its second (1978) edition (AACR2R). In it, the inevitable loose ends discovered in twenty years of applying the new rules in the context of the development of automation are tidied up. The changing conditions of bibliography ensure that no code can ever remain static.[1]

Although Cutter's own rules were considerably modified after his death in 1903, they remained the basis of Anglo-American practice until 1967. His surname is used throughout the remainder of this chapter to designate almost a century of the evolution of his rules. Similarly, "AACR" is used as shorthand for the new, and current, practice imperfectly effected with the first (1967) edition of AACR but only fulfilled with the widespread implementation of the second in

1981. Where no mention is made of either Cutter or AACR in the detailed discussions following, the practice described is essentially the same under both types of rule.

The transitional period from 1967 through 1980 was one of confused practice in which developments in automation were at times a hindrance but became the ultimate solution. A policy of the simultaneous application of both Cutter-type and AACR-type rules dominated this period. This misguided policy, called *superimposition,* was considered necessary by the largest North American libraries, including the Library of Congress, until the application of automated authority control was well enough advanced to permit access points to be changed for many records at a time rather than on a one-by-one basis. The only alternative, which these libraries considered unacceptable, seemed to them to be the maintenance of two catalogues, one of "old" records and another of "new" ones. Many academic libraries did just that, if for a different reason, mummifying an existing card catalogue while an interactive one was being built. The hope that all records on cards might be converted to digital form and all their access points to the new-rule forms is now largely, but not wholly, fulfilled.

AACR is of international, not just Anglo-American or English-speaking, significance because it is the fullest expression of the twelve so-called "Paris Principles," promulgated in October 1961 by the International Conference on Cataloguing Principles (ICCP). This conference successfully reconciled many of the previous differences among the Anglo-American, the French, the German, and other cataloguing traditions inasmuch as they affect name and title access to records in library catalogues. Among the rules to appear in languages other than English based on the Paris Principles, some, such as *Regeln für die alphabetischen Katalogisierung* (RAK), were independently written, but the majority are direct translations or adaptations of AACR. Conformity with the Paris Principles and particularly with AACR has become the cornerstone of the standardization of name access points in the world's major libraries and national bibliographies; AACR is the closest thing we have to a universal cataloguing code.

In the remainder of this chapter, each of the four categories of controlled-vocabulary name—of a person, a body, a place, and a work —is treated separately. In discussing the principles and rules involved,

1) a problem is identified
2) examples are provided to show something of the range of situations encountered
3) valid criteria on which to base a solution are evaluated and

4) the relevant AACR-type rules are briefly summarized and, as useful, contrasted with Cutter-type rules.

PERSONAL NAMES

Personal naming is simultaneously varied and changeable. A person may be identified by one or more of the following types of name:

1) the complete personal name given by the parents and legally registered in an office of vital statistics: Mary Roberta Smith
2) any title bestowed upon Mary by a monarch or the state or inherited: Marchioness of Bucktooth; Prime Minister of Lower Slobbovia
3) any kind of abbreviation of any of the above: Mary R. Smith; M. Roberta Smith; M. R. Smith; Lady Bucktooth; The P. M.
4) any nickname, known to many or to few: Bobbie; Buckie; Cuddles
5) any pseudonym (a name designed to conceal identity): Agent 009; M. R. S.; Jane Doe; ——————D
6) any name which represents a formal change from a previous name or title: Mrs. John Young; Duchess of Worcester.

Mary's experience also shows that a woman is still likely to, and some are legally required to, take a different surname at marriage; that people acquire and renounce titles; that pseudonyms serve various temporary purposes; and that many people are quite casual about when they use a full given name or just an initial letter. Spiritual conviction, fad, and obfuscation have always been reasons for seemingly whimsical legal and extra-legal changes of name. There is a time and an occasion for each.

This busy, if hypothetical, person is also entitled to various terms of address: in addition to *Lady* and *Mrs.* attached above to their appropriate names, these might include *the Right Honourable, Her Grace,* etc. A term of address is not a title (such as Duchess of Worcester) nor an occupation (such as Prime Minister). The most common terms of address are the gender-based *Mr.* and *Ms* and their equivalents in other languages. These honorific trappings of class, rank, and status may be increasingly disparaged in some societies but have far from disappeared, especially in the more formal presentation in reference sources. Most are ignored in the formulation of access points, but a few, such as the British use of *Sir,* are included as virtually integral to the name.

Choice of Name

Not all of this is a bibliographic problem, but many people are referred to in works for which they are responsible, and in reference sources, by more than one name or name form. In determining which should be preferred for alphabetic searching, the cataloguer may follow either of two available principles, both equally reasonable. Which is better depends on the purpose of the file in question, cost factors, etc.

Cutter's principle was that the access point should be based on the full official personal name as it would appear on the person's birth certificate or most recent passport (preferring the latter if there has been any formal change of name), along with the latest of any legally conferred titles. The primary advantage of adopting this principle is administrative convenience. This form of name is both objective and relatively stable: there can be no doubt as to what the full official name is once it has been found; its change requires formal action and is therefore rare. The chief disadvantages are that (1) it may not be easy to discover the full official name of Dr. X. or J. L. Smith, and (2) the average searcher may not instantly recognize a person by his or her full name, for example, Thomas Edward Lawrence, George Herman Ruth, Friedrich Hardenberg, and Hilda Doolittle. However, where legal identification and stability of naming are prime requirements, as they are in archival finding aids, this principle serves the requirements of searchers as well as convenience in administration.

The ICCP adopted a contrary, but equally reasonable, principle now embodied in AACR. It requires the access point to be based on the name encountered commonly or most frequently, be it a name given at birth or acquired later, a title, a pseudonym, etc. Formal statements of responsibility in publications of an author's work issued in the author's own language are accepted as principal evidence of such common usage. For persons not known as authors, what prevails is the cumulative evidence of how the person is referred to in other publications in the person's language or place of residence. AACR better serves the user who approaches a name index from a footnote citation, from a title page of a publication, or from a newspaper article or magazine story. The name form found in these places is also the one most likely to reflect the preferences of the person in question and therefore to be perpetuated on title pages, in reference books, and in general usage; for example, T. E. Lawrence, Babe Ruth, Novalis, and H. D. for the four persons named by their official names at the end of the previous paragraph.

The chief disadvantage of AACR is the instability of the resultant access points in the case of living persons, who are notoriously fickle in their use of different name-forms at different times of their lives.

Consider the following not improbable situation: The title page of a person's first work shows the form John L. Smith, but in his next two works he uses J. L. Smith. He reverts to John L. Smith on the title pages of his fourth and fifth works. After his death, a publisher re-issues the second work using his full name, John Llewellyn Smith. If a library acquires each of these publications in the order in which they are published and follows the AACR rule literally, the preferred access point for Mr. Smith's name must be successively reformulated three times! The first book generates the preferred form **Smith, John L.** After the third has arrived, the preferred form becomes **Smith, J. L.,** but **Smith, John L.** is once again the correct form on the arrival of the fifth. The library may not acquire all six but is still required by the rule to determine what name-form(s) appear on all of them. This seems an administrative nightmare compared to applying the Cutter principle. Is it not simpler to learn the author's full legal name, at whatever cost but only once, and use **Smith, John Llewellyn** from the beginning? Yet this form is not sanctioned by AACR at any time in the sequence described.

AACR is actually preferable from the point of view of cost-effectiveness as well as user convenience because this example illustrates an exceptional, not a normal, situation. As mentioned earlier, most persons identified in library catalogues are obscure and not readily found in biographical sources. Most authors are represented by only a single work published in only a single edition. To use the name-form on its title page and not have to search for full official names is a great economy as well as matching most user needs more adequately. However, sufficient investigation is always needed to satisfy that no pseudonym or other variant name-form is involved.

Public and school libraries long urged that a person clearly identified differently for different writings should be permitted to have more than one preferred access point; for example, **Carroll, Lewis** for fantasy writings and **Dodgson, Charles L.** for the same person's mathematical writings. AACR now specifies this if in the cataloguer's judgement the person intends to hold two different identities simultaneously, even though this breaks the principle of only one preferred form for each person.

Notwithstanding the above, the preferred access point is changed immediately on a deliberate formal change of name or acquisition of a title. The formality of the change makes it clear that its owner intends the new name and will promulgate it. Rules have always left the cataloguer some latitude for judgement, providing for the retention of an earlier name if it appears to continue as the person's intended identification. Thus John Buchan's title, Baron Tweedsmuir, is not the basis for the preferred access point because he continued to write under his personal name. The problem with exercising this judgement is that it is not made with confidence until long after the formal name change.

Language

When the community of European writers was more international, a personal name might appear on title pages and in commentaries in any of several language forms. The seventeenth-century Flemish scripture commentator Cornelius van den Steen published principally under the Latin name Cornelius a Lapide, but is also known by the Greek form Cornelius Petros and the French one, Corneille de la Pierre. Cutter allowed no translation of any element of a personal name, preferring the use of the person's vernacular; for example, Juan de la Cruz; Quintus Horatius Flaccus.

AACR makes an exception for (1) Romans of classical times and (2) persons not identified by a surname. If a name in one of these two categories commonly appears in English-language reference tools in an English-language form, that is preferred: **John, of the Cross**; **Horace**. The language-related problem of romanization, or transliteration, which may occur in any kind of name access point, is discussed at the end of chapter 9.

Choice of Access Element

By almost universal convention, a name of modern times appears in an alphanumeric list arranged under the surname or family name regardless of where that appears when the name is written in direct order. Any given names and initials follow after a comma: **Rogers, J. Eliot**; **Deng, Xiao-ping**. However,

1) a compounded or prefixed surname consists of more than one unit, perhaps leaving uncertainty as to which should serve as the access element; for example, Richard Dennis Hilton Smith, Karel ten Hoope
2) the preferred name chosen according to the above criteria may not contain a surname at all; for example, Crazy Horse.

If no surname exists, the preferred form begins with the first element as the name is spoken (**Crazy Horse**), although it may be subtly structured with punctuation appropriate to a two-part name (**Leonardo, da Vinci**).

In the case of a compound surname or a surname involving a prefix, the access element is that under which the surname normally appears in alphanumeric lists in the person's own language: **De la Mare**,

Walter; **Gaulle, Charles de**; **La Fontaine, Jean de**. When a title of nobility is part of the chosen name, the proper word in the title is the access element, and the personal name is given between it and the rank: **Devonshire, Spencer Compton Cavendish, Duke of**. The acquaintance with different linguistic and national usages needed to apply this principle is offered in a number of reference sources.[2]

Qualifiers

A searcher would be rightly confused if any one access point encountered serves to identify more than one individual person, body, etc. A qualifier of some kind is therefore needed if the access points for two different entities would otherwise be identical, for example, two authors both named John L. Smith on their title pages. Qualifiers available to distinguish persons include birth/death dates, occupation, place of residence, and academic degrees. Dates, the most objective and stable qualifier, have always been preferred in cataloguing rules, but when it is known what the initials in a name stand for, AACR encourages the addition of a qualifier consisting of the full name or names; for example, if two persons are both commonly known as T. S. Eliot and their full names can be determined, the appropriate access points are **Eliot, T. S. (Terence Stephen)** and **Eliot, T. S. (Thomas Stearnes)**. This not only separates the two in a file, it also ensures that each is located in the alphanumeric sequence under the best-known form (the one containing initials) and is identifiable at a glance as the person sought. Names which lack a surname are very likely to be common to many people, so a qualifier stating an office, epithet, rank, status, etc. is always added to the access element: **John, King of England**; **John Paul I, Pope**; **John, the Baptist**.

CORPORATE BODIES AND THEIR NAMING

A corporate body is a person or group of persons choosing to act as an entity under a name other than that of any one person. Thus John Smith is a person but The John Smith Corporation is a corporate body. A legally recognized modern nongovernment body is easily recognizable and distinguishable from others because a government registrar has officially authorized an unambiguous and distinctive name for it, after comparing its proposed name with its stated purposes and with a list of existing authorized names in the jurisdiction.

In bibliographic files, one cannot restrict the notion of a corporate name to one thus legally authorized in at least two areas. The first of these is widespread and pervasive in corporate naming because corporate bodies breed separately identifiable, but not legally separate, subordinate units. If everything published by the American Library Association were subarranged by title without grouping what emanates from each of its separate component associations, sections, committees, discussion groups, etc., a searcher who identifies a topic or report with one of these subunits could not easily locate it. In other words, even if the association's Subject Analysis Committee is not a separate legal entity, it must be separately identifiable in an access point. Similarly, in referring to a publication by or about the Library of Vancouver Community College, the *library*, a functional but not legally incorporated entity, requires its own access point separate from that of its legal entity (the college as a whole) and from that of any hierarchically superior body (the provincial government's Ministry of Advanced Education).

In addition to legally separate and otherwise subordinate bodies, a catalogue must also provide access points for ad hoc events such as conferences, fairs, projects, etc. The legal or organizational status of any of these is usually unclear and irrelevant to a searcher. Their temporary nature ensures that few become widely referred to anywhere except in documents produced for the event itself. For example, most people wanting information about Expo 67, a world's fair held in Montreal, are not much interested in seeing reports of the Canadian Corporation for the 1967 World Exhibition, the legal corporate governing entity for the fair. The fair itself is something different. By the early 1960s, cataloguing rules were treating any such event as if it were a corporate body in itself, provided it had a recognizable name.

Isolating any corporate name as such from the rest of the wording on a title page, etc. is a matter of interpreting both graphic and linguistic style and intent, much like isolating a title as such as illustrated in figure 1 on page 45. Names of corporate bodies commonly consist of a mixture of subject words, generic terms, proper words (that is, personal or geographic name elements), grammatical links, articles, etc.:

> College of Physicians and Surgeons of British Columbia
> 5th Annual Symposium on the Effects of Air Pollution in Coastal Areas
> National Council for Educational Technology.

The casual searcher is probably unaware of the specific point of beginning and ending of a corporate name embedded in prose text, particularly when it contains no proper words as in the last two examples above. Formal presentation in grammatical or typographic isolation from other data, as is usually the case on a title page, is an aid to identifying a name as such. However, title-page presentations are also not always unequivocal in this age of corporate logos with graphic imagery to obscure the identity or parts of a formal name.

To constitute a useful access point, a name must be a specifying appellation, not merely a generic reference to the existence of something. Clues to this are the use of full or initial upper-case letters, definite articles, etc. Just as *Mary Smith* is a name but "the girl who lives next door" is not, so *Bureau of the Budget* is a name but "the office that looks after budget preparation" is not. The dividing line becomes very subtle in the case of ad hoc events. The formally presented wording "Conference on the Analysis of Brain Waves" is accepted by AACR as a name, but the wording "a conference on the analysis of brain waves" is not (especially if presented only in grammatical connection with other text). An individual corporate body may be identified by one or more of the following types of name (again, the example is hypothetical):

1) the name under which it is officially incorporated by letters patent or other legal means: The Canadian-American Railway Corporation
2) any abbreviation thereof including any acronym however fanciful: CanAmRail; CANARY—some of these have legal or quasi-legal status while others are only used informally
3) any translation of one of the above types of name whether the other-language form has legal status (as is true if the body is officially bilingual) or is merely used for convenience in referring to the body in foreign places: the Frankfurt sales agency may use Kanadisch-amerikanisch Bahnlinie (KAB) in local advertisements
4) any name which represents a formal change from a previous name (as distinct from one of several variant forms used simultaneously): North American Railways, Inc.; Interail.

Choice of Name

The same criteria generally apply whether the name identifies a corporate body or a person. Thus Cutter requires the access point **European Atomic Energy Community** (the full official form), while **Euratom** (the form common in the body's publications and reference sources) is the AACR choice. The form commonly found is more and more frequently an initialism or acronym: many bodies, such as the Association of Special Libraries and Information Bureaux, changed their names officially to a long-recognized acronym form (Aslib). The perception that an acronym or initialism must represent a fuller form of name which should be the basis for the access point greatly complicated older filing (not cataloguing) rules. For example, the abbreviation *U.S.* in an access point was filed as if it were spelled out as *United States,* regardless of whether or not the abbreviation is an official part of the name in question. It took several stages of revision of both cataloguing and filing rules to overcome this habit. Now AACR treats any initialism, acronym, etc. as an acceptable preferred access point provided it predominates in the body's own usage. However, librarians still have occasion to wish that the use of catchy acronyms had not gone quite out of control, confusing both the identification and the file location of many corporate bodies.

Language

Two or more different language forms of the same corporate name, each equally official, exist in the case of a bilingual or multilingual body. What should be the language of the preferred access point? Should it be the language of the form of name occurring first, or most frequently, in the body's publications or in other sources? Should it be the language of the jurisdiction where the body is incorporated or that of the cataloguing agency (unless these are also bilingual)? What of a body's name in a language largely unknown to those likely to consult the catalogue?

Here Cutter and AACR both betray their origins in an English-speaking environment and give preference to naming in English provided (1) the body itself officially uses an English name as well as others or (2) the body is old and international (for example, the Catholic Church) and an English name for it commonly appears in English-language reference sources. In addition, AACR permits translation (for example, German Federal Railway instead of what is found in the body's publications, Deutsche Bundesbahn)—but only as clearly needed to serve users in nonscholarly unilingual situations such as school and small public libraries. In all other cases, the vernacular form as determined from the body's publications is preferred, and links are provided with any other language form likely to be sought by users of the catalogue—but not from every other possible one.

Change of Name

Corporate name changes, which are increasingly frequent, present a very different problem from personal name changes and require different solutions. While sometimes a change reflects nothing more than a desire to project a different image, many corporate name changes result from a change of purpose or constitution or from a merger with or a split from another body. When a name change results from one of the latter more radical reorientations, Cutter still attempted to preserve the continuity of the body's identification using the original access point with cross-references from later names. This practice broke down long before AACR. Pragmatically, there is no objective manner of determining when a change comes to affect the essence, rather than just some accident, of the nature of the body. AACR therefore dictates arbitrarily that, upon any deliberate change in a body's name, a different corporate body has come into existence. Both the old and the new names are established as preferred access points linked to each other in an associative, not an equivalence, relationship; that is, in a manual catalogue, by *see also* . . . (not *see* . . .) references. Thus although the name of Long Beach State College was changed to California State University, Long Beach, the former remains valid as an access point for all documents relating to the institution before the name change. The latter is used as an access point only for materials pertaining to the institution following the name change.

This leaves a significant practical problem. What *subject* access point best applies to a work describing a body's history both before and after a name change? Cataloguing rules are silent on this point. The solution usually adopted is to use only the latest name borne by the body during the period covered by the work being catalogued. In practice, this means that a search for material about a body should begin with its latest name, and the links with earlier names should only be pursued if noncurrent information is specifically wanted.

Choice of Access Element

Choosing an access element for a corporate name is either much simpler or much more complex than choosing one for a personal name. Cutter veered early toward complexity by beginning a search for some obvious element in corporate naming to correspond to the personal surname: a distinctive—that is, not generic—element everyone could agree upon as significant, yet one which could be defined in a cataloguing rule. The simple solution is to accept the body's name as a whole and let it be sought in a manual file like a title, under its first word other than an article. When automation made searching by any keyword feasible, AACR could finally adopt this simple solution as the basic principle, yet even then one major exception for subordinate bodies (described below separately for nongovernmental and for governmental bodies) was deemed necessary.

In the context of manual searching, it was not unreasonable of Cutter to dislike the simple solution: the first word (other than an article) of many a corporate body's name is generic (University of . . . or Department of . . .) or a personal given name (John Smith, Inc.); that is, a word whose location in a manual file causes problems. In retrospect, it might have been as well to let each cataloguer decide, ad hoc, which word in a given corporate name would be most useful for access, but this is not a "rule"! For example, it might be thought quite reasonable to find the National Education Association under E: as with titles, to seek a word with some subject connotation comes naturally. Yet defining what is a subject-oriented word, or which of two should take precedence, is impossible. In a manual one-sequence dictionary catalogue, such naming would also become confused with access under a true subject access point. As an objective finding device, a corporate name, like a title, must be treated as a name, not like a topic.

Cutter's diversion toward the complex solution led to a hundred years of making more exceptions than rules. Later rule makers did not quickly perceive how the ground was actually shifting under them as they looked at it because the patterns of corporate naming were themselves changing. One illustration of this is the development of names consisting only of acronyms and initialisms as described above. Another is the naming of a subordinate body in such a way as to hide its relationship with the parent body rather than celebrating it as had typically been the case before. Thus the part of the American Library Association concerned with public libraries was once the Public Libraries Division but opted to rename itself the Public Library Association.

Nongovernment Corporate Bodies

When Cutter did not want to locate a name in a file in its direct word-order, he opted to make the name a *subheading* to be filed after either (1) the name of a hierarchically superior body or (2) a place name. The rationales for direct, subordinate, and place-name access to corporate names are next described briefly. The amount of detail and the small number of examples given here can only provide background for a close look at the quite complex rules in the cataloguing codes from Cutter through AACR2R. This is exactly the area where a century of tampering led to the greatest morass of exceptions to principle along the route Cutter took. Furthermore, this is where rules for nongovernment bodies have always diverged the most from those for government agencies. Governments and their agencies are discussed following a section on place names as such, because the latter are the basis for access to their names.

Direct Access

Cutter and AACR differ in the proportion of corporate names, whether related to governments or not, they accept as access points with no change. In Cutter it is smaller; in AACR, much greater because AACR opts for this as the overriding principle. Even Cutter treats the names of most independent private-sector bodies in this direct way, whether or not the first word of the name is distinctive (in the first example it is a proper adjective, in the second it is a generic term):

> **American Association for the Advancement of Science**
> **Council on Library Resources.**

Cutter (but not AACR) arbitrarily excludes an initialism or a personal given name from consideration as the access element. A single example illustrates both: Cutter's access point for the R. J. Young Tractor Company is in inverted word-order: **Young (R. J.) Tractor Company**, as if the personal surname were also a true surname of the body. Cutter's distaste for initialisms results from well-known problems of filing and finding these in an alphanumeric sequence. Any telephone directory will illustrate the problem. The largest number of clerical filing errors in a manual file is almost always to be found among initialisms beginning with a letter by itself, as any library's old card catalogue shows.

Subordinate Access

As noted previously, a hierarchically subordinate body must be allowed its own access point; its identity cannot simply be merged with that of its superior body. An ever increasing proportion of subordinate-level bodies have entirely distinctive names, such as the Bodleian Library (a part of the University of Oxford) or the Library and Information Technology Association (LITA: a part of the American Library Association). Is it desirable for all subordinate units of a parent body to be found together with the latter in a sequentially searched alphanumeric file? Whether the file is manual or interactive is not a primary concern in this question because, in the latter, a searcher also typically begins by browsing a sequential list of access points.

Cutter leans toward a positive answer, and today's reference librarian must still be prepared to search older bibliographies and catalogues at access points such as **Smithsonian Institution. Renwick Gallery**. More value was attached in Cutter's day than now to using file arrangement to classify, or "bring together" like things. A searcher was expected to approach a catalogue armed with the knowledge that the Bodleian is part of Oxford, that LITA is a division of ALA, etc. or be prepared to be shunted by cross-reference links to the "correct" access point. Yet how is the searcher who has encountered the Newberry Library, a totally independent institution, to suspect that the Bodleian Library is a subordinate one? Names of this type offer no hint within themselves of any hierarchic relationship with a parent body.

This is where Cutter and AACR diverge most significantly: AACR looks only at the name, not the relationship. If the name can stand alone, so does the access point. An equivalence link may direct someone who first approaches the name of the hierarchically superior body:

> **American Library Association. Library and Information Technology Association**
> *see* **Library and Information Technology Association.**

Alternatively, an associative or hierarchic link may suggest the names of related or subordinate bodies to be found elsewhere in the file:

> **American Library Association**
> *see also* **Library and Information Technology Association Public Library Association**
> [etc.]

For a subordinate body to have a distinctive name not explicitly denoting its place in a hierarchy was once rare. It is now the norm for any body allowed to act under quasi-independent direction, which is ever more common in both business and government. In the private sector, the trend toward conglomerates and mergers almost ensures that each subsidiary, whether partially or wholly owned, has a distinctive name, although in very tiny print one may also find words like "a Division of . . ." after the name. The Bodleian Library is a very old example of another category of subordinate bodies with independent naming. As public institutions seek private donors, it is becoming very common to name a subordinate unit after some eminent person or a donor, for example, Harvard University's John F. Kennedy School of Government.

Buildings have long been so named. While a building might not issue publications, others write about it so it must be possible to name a building in a subject index. The same rules discussed here are the ones applied.

A majority of subordinate bodies are not named after donors, etc., and do not claim the degree of independence on which the type of naming discussed above is based. Their names consist of only a string of generic (or at least nondistinctive) words such as

> The Library (a unit of many a college, private business, etc.)
> Nominating Committee (a unit of almost any association or society)

There are also bodies so closely related that their names and functions are inseparable, and one of them, although not subordinate, can be named only by inferring the other. Board of Trustees, for example, is the name of many a governing body. Nondistinctive naming of this kind implies either dependence or close relationship; it characterizes single-purpose and very close control or linkage. The very identity of the subordinate or related body is defined by the more distinctive name of the related or higher-level body. Nondistinctive names are typically shared by many different bodies. The University of British Columbia has a subordinate body named Department of Finance, but so does General Motors. The immediate reaction to nondistinctive naming is therefore, "*Whose* Department of Finance?" and the searcher heads directly to the name of the superior or related body. This may be the result of a hundred years of training people in bibliographic searching. Nevertheless, how would a searcher who has located a Department of [anything] under **D** know that it is the one wanted? The name of the higher body is a necessary adjunct for identification. The preferred access point therefore consists of a *main heading* (the name of the superior or related body) followed by a *subheading* (the name of the body for which the entire access point is established): **Queen's University. Faculty of Law.** (*Main heading* is not to be confused with the term *main entry heading,* an obsolescent synonym for the principal access point for a publication or work, for which see the end of this chapter.)

The corporate names Yale University Library and Bibliothèque de l'Université de Montréal are distinctive. According to the above criteria, they should appear as access points without change or inversion, under **Y** and **B** respectively. However, such names often occur both within prose text and in more formal presentation in a way that visually or grammatically separates the name of the higher body; for example, by eliminating the preposition and placing *Library* or *Bibliothèque* on a different line than the name of the university so that the searcher cannot be expected to know whether or not the university's name is also part of the library's. For this reason, AACR continues Cutter's requirement that the lower body be named in a subheading following the name of the higher body and a period:

> **Yale University. Library**
> **Université de Montréal. Bibliothèque**

Cutter and AACR are written from the point of view of English-language usage where a subordinate body is normally named following, not before, its superior body and without an intermediate preposition. This makes the hairsplitting in the Yale example seem particularly silly. What possible difference does the presence or absence of a period make? Why not just **Yale University Library**? Furthermore, if sub-ordination is the issue, why is the access point not **Yale University. Yale University Library**? Redundancy in an access point has always been avoided unless objectionable distortion of the name would result. As to the period, some (but not all) filing rules *do* make a distinction based on whether or not a period exists in an access point (see chapter 9).

More than one level of hierarchic subordination may be involved. For example, the School of Library, Archival and Information Studies is a part of the Faculty of Arts of The University of British Columbia. AACR prefers the access point

> **University of British Columbia. School of Library, Archival and Information Studies**

omitting the middle element. The faculty's name (under **F**) cannot be the access element anyway, and it is not needed to help distinguish this school from others of the same name within the university. In the following example, however, all three parts of the hierarchy must appear in the access point because there are many Admissions Committees within the same university:

> **Queen's University. Faculty of Law. Admissions Committee**

Place-Name Access

Some corporate bodies are closely identified with permanent structures in a locality whose populace provides their core of supporters or users. Cutter calls such a body an *institution* to distinguish it from a society, a business firm, or an association. The activities of any the latter are not so closely linked with a geographic location or edifices. Schools, colleges, universities, galleries, theatres, museums, churches, hospitals, prisons, and libraries are typical institutions. In English, the name of the place served is often the first word of an institution's name. Even if not, it may still be the only proper word in the name and therefore the one element either best remembered or considered most significant in searching. Public libraries provide good examples of this; the following alphabetic list shows names of some public libraries as they are predominantly given in their own publications:

> The Borough of Etobicoke Public Library
> Carnegie Library of Pittsburgh
> The Fraser-Hickson Institute
> The Free Library of Philadelphia
> Greenwich Library
> Indianapolis-Marion County Public Library
> Kirn Memorial Library

The Library Association of Portland
Portage La Prairie City Library
Prairie Crocus Regional Library
War Memorial Library

Only three of these names begin with the geographic name of a jurisdiction (Greenwich, Indianapolis, and Portage La Prairie). Another implies a geographic area (Prairie Crocus Region). Three name people, not places (Carnegie, Fraser, and Kirn). The last consists solely of generic words. The third does not even designate the function of the body.

Someone who knows enough about a particular public library to seek its name in a directory or other list probably knows where it is but may not remember, and may never have consciously known, its precise name. Does the average searcher consciously consider whether the name of a particular gallery takes the form [Place] Art Gallery (Vancouver Art Gallery), or Art Gallery of [Place] (Art Gallery of Ontario), or even [Name] Art Gallery of [Place] (The Norman Rockwell Museum at Stockbridge)? As with the naming of subordinate units, linguistic patterns strongly influence the structuring of such a name but do not ensure a uniform sequence of elements. For example, the word sequence in the first art gallery example above is more common in English, while the second would be more common in French.

With some significant exceptions, Cutter opts to treat a name of this type of institution as a subheading following the name of the place (municipality) in which it operates, whether that place name appears in the name of the body or is only implied:

London, Ont. University of Western Ontario
Paris. Musée nationale du Louvre
Akron, Ohio. Public Library[3]

His principal exception (there are many) is that if the name of the body *begins* with a proper word other than a place name, it is accepted as an access point directly:

Victoria University (the one in Toronto, named for the Queen)
Mendel Art Gallery
Enoch Pratt Free Library (another exception: *not* Pratt, Enoch, Public Library!)

When Cutter distinguished a society from an institution and established place-name access as the basic rule for the latter, it made good sense. The boundaries of a municipality's jurisdiction were clear both geographically and functionally; an institution was likely to be known and named by its municipal location even if its functions were broader; in general, only one institution of a particular type existed in any one municipality. Using a municipal place name as access element became largely irrelevant by the middle of this century. Many growing institutions drifted to suburbs; some dispersed their activities among several locations. Their naming has also changed: they are now much less likely to adopt a name with the simple structure of [Place]-[Function] or [Function]-of-[Place].

A single set of examples illustrates the incomprehensible morass which resulted from a century of exceptions to match Cutter's basic rule of access under a place name to changing reality. The University of Oxford's name was established as a subheading using the name of the city (Oxford) as the access element. The University of Michigan's was established using the name of the state (Michigan), not the city (Ann Arbor), as the access element. The university in, and named after, British Columbia's capital city is similarly treated: **British Columbia. University of Victoria**, and to provide an access point for its art gallery, **Maltwood Gallery** was added to the end of that!

The long-standing and increasingly complex practice of using a place name as the access element, or main heading, for the name of an institution affected access points on a huge number of individual records in the catalogues of larger libraries. The principles of AACR could only be implemented in these libraries painfully slowly as old authority records were gradually revised. The AACR forms of the Cutter-type access points used as examples in this subsection follow:

> **University of Western Ontario**
> **Musée nationale du Louvre**
> **Akron Public Library**
> **University of Victoria**
> **Maltwood Gallery**

Under AACR, only the name of a government agency (see below) may be given as a subheading after the name of a place.

Qualifiers

It is less frequent that two or more corporate bodies bear the same name than that two or more persons do, but when this happens, they must also be distinguished from each other using qualifiers. The most typical qualifiers name either a superior body or a place, resulting in something close to an inversion of the Cutter-type access points in many such cases:

> Newman Club (University of British Columbia)
> Newman Club (York University)
> National Portrait Gallery (Great Britain)
> National Portrait Gallery (U.S.)

A qualifier may also be useful to help identify the body or simply to clarify that an otherwise ambiguous name does represent a corporate body: **Guess Who (Musical group)**.

Conferences

In the case of a conference name, a qualifier is always required. That a conference name will remain unique cannot be predicted: a successful Symposium on [Topic] is quite likely to be followed by a Second Symposium on [Same topic]. In addition, a searcher is as likely to recognize a conference by its number, venue, or date as by its name alone. These are therefore useful parts of the access point:

> **Ferring Symposium on Brain and Pituitary Peptides
> (3rd : 1979 : Munich)
> Bibliographical Society. Annual Meeting (93rd : 1987 :
> University College, London)**

Cutter uses commas instead of the colons shown here and gives the date after, rather than before, the place name. In the second example, *Annual Meeting* is the actual name of the conference. It appears as a subheading following the name of the society because it is a subordinate body without a distinctive name, a situation discussed above.

PLACES

A place name as an access point in its own right serves to identify a geographic location as a subject. It also has a major function in a name index because of its conventional use to name a political jurisdiction; that is, the government exercising authority over the geographic territory so named. Finally, by naming a government, it also serves as the main heading (access element) in access points for many (not all) government agencies, the agency's name being a subheading. A place may be identified by one or more of the following types of name:

1) the name assigned to it by tradition or by an official agency in the jurisdiction in which it is located; for example, by the Canadian Permanent Committee on Geographic Names in the case of a Canadian place

2) any name assigned to it by an official agency in some other jurisdiction, for example, by the Board on Geographic Names in the United States, which prescribes geographic names for locations the world over for use in the United States civil service
3) any translation of an official or traditional name as found in a gazetteer or other reference source in any language: Londres (London), Munich (München)
4) any name resulting from a formal change: Hò Chí Minh Thành (formerly Saigon).

Using any name in translation rather than in the vernacular (the third case in the above list) poses a significant problem for international standardization. In library catalogues, the practice has always existed but only under rigidly restricted circumstances—except in the case of geographic names, where it is commonplace. People tend to treat place names very differently from names of persons or bodies. English speakers who would never dream of translating the name Mr. Schneider into Mr. Tailor (or Taylor), or even the name NHK into Japanese Broadcasting Corporation, have no qualms about translating the name Huanghe (a romanization of 黄河) into Yellow River or the name Venezia into Venice or the name Svizzera/Schweiz/Suisse/Confoederatio Helvetica (take your choice: they are all official) into Switzerland.

A place of little significance beyond its immediate region is unlikely to be identified anywhere except by its vernacular name. However, conquest, colonization, travel, and trade have fixed many a place name so firmly in the minds of people everywhere that it has become part of many local languages. Bombay is only a war of occupation away from the Portuguese city Bom Bahía (Beautiful Bay) and has now reverted to a more indigenous name, Mumbai. Looking at it from the point of view of speakers of other languages, who is to say that Atlantisches Meer names space outside national jurisdiction less legitimately than Océan atlantique, Mar atlantico, or 大西洋? Increased travel and familiarity with foreign place names mean that more geographic names are now widely used in their local language-form than in the past, but this is an area where international uniformity of access points can never be achieved and where equivalence links in large numbers will always be necessary in internationally maintained databases. In all English-language cataloguing rules, a predominant English form of a place name, as found in English-language gazetteers, is the preferred access point.

It may seem redundant to use a qualifier when one London is so much better known than any other; for the most famous place of any name, Cutter did not. However, many geographic names are used over and over around the world, expecially where a language like

English is common to many countries. Computer-based filing was also made more complex when a qualifier might or might not follow a place name. Eventually, AACR had to remove options based on judgement and made it standard practice to include a qualifier in the access point for any name of a place below the national, federated state, or provincial level. The (sometimes abbreviated) name of the next larger jurisdiction in which the place is located is the usual, if not entirely trouble-free, qualifier: **Victoria (Tex.)**. Changes of geographic name and changes of the jurisdiction in which a locality exists are treated generally the same as the changes of corporate names discussed above.

GOVERNMENTS

The official name of a government is usually found in its constitution, etc.:

> République française
> State of Rhode Island and Providence Plantations
> City of El Paso de Robles
> Corporation of the Municipal District of West Vancouver

It is rare to find this official form as an access point in a name index. Instead, the geographic name of the territory governed is normally used. In library usage, this means following the principles outlined in the section immediately above. The access points for the governments just named are therefore **France**; **Rhode Island**; **Paso Robles (Calif.)**; and **West Vancouver (B.C.)**.

International wars change boundaries; civil wars change governmental forms as well as individual regimes. Even within peaceful states, the geographic extent and the naming of local jurisdictions are not as stable as they once were. In the United States, counties and municipalities are constitutionally autonomous, and over two centuries only a few changes have radically affected their naming. The need for regional and other larger-base services has been answered there generally by single-purpose corporate bodies responsible to two or more jurisdictions, for example, the Twin Cities Metropolitan Planning Commission composed of members from St. Paul and from Minneapolis. Such an agency is not an independent jurisdiction, and its name is treated the same as the name of a nongovernment corporate body.

In most jurisdictions, however, municipalities are the creatures of a higher level of government. The United Kingdom and several Canadian provinces have in recent years radically revised municipal naming, boundaries, and functions. For example, the county Dyfed in Wales covers much but not all the territory of the former Cardigan-shire, plus some territory formerly in other counties. The pattern in Canada has been to impose an additional supra-municipal level of government on the existing levels. In some instances all the previous jurisdictions have remained intact (although with changed powers) within the new framework; the Municipality of Metropolitan Toronto is a political entity additional to its component parts, the City of Toronto and several surrounding municipalities, all of which retain their old names and (as of 1996) political existence. On the other hand, the creation of the neighbouring City of Mississauga obliterated the political existence of several former villages, including Malton and Streetsville. The names of the latter remain in older memories but no longer appear on many maps.

Places have been named for millennia using words to describe or recollect a natural feature or in honour of an explorer, the home locale of immigrants, etc. Hot Springs, Long Island, America, New Dundee, are all typical. As new jurisdictions come into existence today, not all are assigned a name of this type. "Metropolitan Toronto" names the precisely defined area governed by the municipal jurisdiction mentioned in the previous paragraph. However, particularly in the United States, *metropolitan* connotes only a vaguely defined market- or population-area. Gazetteers have typically been lists of geographic names, not jurisdictional ones as such. One now finds Metropolitan Toronto under **M** in the Ontario volume of the *Gazetteer of Canada,* and Capital Regional District (a political jurisdiction in another province) is to be found under **C** in the British Columbia volume.

Government Agencies

Most governments list and describe their agencies in a directory called a government organization manual—for state governments in the United States, this is the "blue book." If carefully edited and frequently revised, such a directory is an indispensable guide to anyone who indexes or searches for government agencies. Hierarchy in a bureaucracy is the basic principle of government, but autonomous and arm's-length public agencies greatly complicate the organization of modern democratic governments. So do increasingly frequent name and function changes within the civil service, the executive arm of any government. The primary difficulty in establishing the access point for the name of any government agency is to decide whether or not it should be a subheading following the (geographic) name of the jurisdiction in question. Should the name of the Smithsonian Institution, a government-owned museum, be left as it is or made a subheading after **United States**? Differences in attitudes toward this issue can be expected as between free-enterprise societies and more social-ized systems, but a deep penetration of government into areas of cor-porate activity is a fact of modern life everywhere.

The principles involved in subordinate access and outlined above apply in general to government agencies as well. Cutter preferred to group, that is, to ensure that a person who browses an alphabetic sequence at the name of a jurisdiction finds the largest possible range of its agencies there. He therefore made an agency's *function* the pri-mary determinant of whether or not the access element is the name of the jurisdiction. Names of agencies exercising direct executive functions of government therefore appear as subheadings:

> **United States. Federal Bureau of Investigation**
> **United States. Southern Forest Experiment Station**
> **Canada. Royal Canadian Mounted Police**

The principle espoused in AACR is that the broadest possible range of government agencies should be treated like any other body. Sub-ordinate access is only appropriate if the *name* (not only the function) of the agency explicitly denotes this subordination. Added to the rea-sons given earlier for this principle is the fact that it is unrealistic to think a lengthy grouping of subheadings following the name of a jurisdiction will be systematically examined by most users; in any case, it duplicates what can be found in the government's organiza-tion manual.

However, there are two areas of agreement between Cutter and AACR. Government involvement is ignored in establishing the access point of an arm's-length agency such as a government-owned but commercial business (crown corporation), a public-sector educational or cultural institution, a quasi-commercial board, or a government-regulated but not government-owned company. In the case of institu-tions (universities, museums, etc.), this means that the Smithsonian Institution has always appeared in a library catalogue under S.

AACR also continues Cutter in another, but very limited, way. It specifies the few most basic government functions and requires that agencies carrying out these functions are always to appear as sub-headings following the name of the jurisdiction. These functions are now only the legislative, judicial, military, and highest-level executive functions, and in these cases, it does not matter how distinctive the name of the agency is:

> **Israel. Knesset**
> **Canada. Royal Canadian Air Force**
> **Alberta. Alberta Culture** (a major cabinet-level agency)

(Here, the redundancy of two Albertas is required because **Alberta. Culture** would be ambiguous.)

For the general run of executive agencies of government, nondistinctive naming incorporating a term which denotes subordination prevailed for centuries: Department of Cultural Affairs; Real Estate Commission; Home Office. It was, and remains, natural to search for any of these under the name of the jurisdiction just as any private-sector body named nondistinctively is best located under the name of its parent body. However, there is now a very strong trend toward giving government agencies distinctive names, usually made unique by the incorporation of the name of the government in question as an adjective or noun: Canadian Wildlife Service; Telecommunication Authority of Singapore. An intent to obscure the organizational hierarchy is probably a deliberate part of this trend; for example, first the Dominion Bureau of Statistics became Statistics Canada, then that agency's Health Division became the Canadian Health Information Centre.

Such name changes, taking place in more and more jurisdictions, are having a profound influence on the way the average person identifies what is in fact a government agency and where it is most naturally sought in an alphabetic file. During the thirty-year period of AACR implementation, the proportion of names of government agencies for which the name of the jurisdiction is the preferred access element has been considerably reduced by both additional rule changes and changed naming practices among governments themselves. Now, the name of a government agency stands alone as an access point except when (1) the agency exercises a basic function identified in the previous paragraph or (2) its name fails to meet the test of independent identification and distinctiveness.

> **Royal Canadian Mounted Police**
> **Southern Forest and Range Experiment Station**
>   **(New Orleans, La.)**
> **Telecommunication Authority of Singapore**
> **Canadian Health Information Centre**

Logically, but perhaps surprisingly, the exceptions mean that the full name of the FBI remains a subheading of **United States** because *Bureau* implies subordination. In another example above, *Station* does not.

One more issue remains to be discussed. It affects nongovernment bodies as well but was not treated above because its impact is much greater in access points for government agencies. It is the degree to which the several levels of a hierarchy should be explicit in the access point for a subordinate agency when that access point begins with the name of a higher or related body. In the following hypothetical hierarchy, the name of no intermediate agency can stand alone, so the main heading is inevitably **Canada** and the last element of the access point is necessarily **Egg Unit** if that is the agency for which the access point is intended. Does **Canada. Egg Unit** suffice?

Canada
Agriculture Canada
Production and Marketing Branch
Poultry Division
Turkey Section
Egg Unit

If it does not, how many and which intermediate levels of the hierarchy are either necessary or useful? Again, this is an issue of grouping within a sequence. Whether the search is a manual one among
cards or on the page of a printed index or is a browse of access points
on a terminal screen, not every combination of hierarchic levels is
displayed as a group. If the Egg Unit is not shown with other subdivisions of the Turkey Section or of the Poultry Division, it appears
necessarily between the Duck Section and the Farm Implements Division. The only situation in which it does not matter is when a *FIND*
command is possible using a keyword in the body's name. Although
now favoured, this technique is prone to many false hits when the
keyword is common to many bodies as is likely among the names of
government agencies. As with nongovernment subordinate bodies,
Cutter preferred to include more elements of a hierarchy in an access
point than AACR: **United States. Dept. of Agriculture. Dairy Division.** AACR eliminates the intermediary body but only after it is as-
certained that there is only one body named Dairy Division in the
United States federal government.

The complexity of the considerations raised in this section helps
explain why in most telephone directories, government agencies are
now segregated into their own separate section(s), often on coloured
paper. This may seem exactly opposite to the trend in library catalogues but in fact serves the same purpose: to define that group of
government agencies which users expect to find grouped in one file
location. The actual agencies grouped in the two types of list differ
because users of library catalogues tend to focus on names as found
in citations, etc. whereas users of telephone directories are primarily
concerned with administrative functions.

WORKS

As illustrated with the Saint Matthew's Gospel example at the beginning of this chapter, one cannot rely on the words of the title proper
of any one document or publication to retrieve all the manifestations
containing, or concerning, a particular *work*. As a corollary to this
statement, any title borne by a particular publication does not necessarily correspond to a particular user's approach by a title to the

sought work. The many works published only once, in only one form, and under only one title are of no concern here. Major problems for their users are presented by the reissues, adaptations, translations, critiques of, and commentaries on the very small number of very important works in the history of the transmission of knowledge and culture. Such a work may be known to someone searching for it by one or more of the following types of title, all of which identify the same work by Agatha Christie:

1) the title proper assigned to the work on its first publication: *Ten Little Niggers*
2) any title given to any subsequent publication of the complete work, whether in the original or in any other language: *And Then There Were None; Dix petits nègres; . . . e poi non rimase nessuno; Letztes Weekend*
3) any title given to an adaptation or other modification of the work: *Ten Little Indians* (the title of a dramatization)
4) any wording in reference sources specifying the work but not necessarily by the title proper of any particular publication of it—this is more likely to be an issue in the case of works originating before the advent of printing and formal titling.

A work may later be re-created or otherwise modified by someone other than its original creator: such an adaptation often bears a different title proper than the original as in the third case above, of a dramatization. Jonathan Larson's *Rent* is Puccini's *La Bohème* in an adapted version whose title page does not betray its origin. Puccini's is itself an operatic version of a novelette, *Scènes de la vie de bohème* by Henri Murger. The title proper of a translation almost always differs from that of the original. A work created separately and still known by its own title may also come to be thought of as part of a larger work; Saint Matthew's Gospel later became part of the canon of the Bible; a poem or an article with its own title often appears only as part of an anthology or in a periodical. Like a corporate body, a work may have parts (arias, chapters, sections) known by or separately published under their own titles, such as *Nessun dorma*, every tenor's encore.

Uniform Titles

Using one preferred title as a controlled-vocabulary identifier of a work is the same as using one preferred form of name as a controlled-vocabulary identifier of a person, corporate body, or place. This *uniform title* (prior to 1967, it was called a conventional title), used in association with the name of the work's author if one can be identified, ensures that there is one location in a file, or one search key, where everything both containing and concerning a specific work can be located. It is usually the title proper of the original published version of the work, but it may be a title commonly adopted by later critics and commentators.

A uniform title is an essential access point for a work with no definable author but issued with different titles proper. In the case of various editions of the *Chanson de Roland,* these titles are scattered throughout a file, including *Song of Roland* and *Rolandslied,* and there is no author's name to provide a common file location. Uniform titles have been used for such anonymous classics since the dawn of library cataloguing. Ninth-century monastic library catalogues show **Biblia** as an access point for all versions of the whole or part of the Bible. Through equivalence links in an authority file or a manual catalogue/index, a searcher can be led to the uniform title from any number of variant forms:

> **Song of Roland**
> *for editions of this work, search under* **Chanson de Roland**

Titles proper of the several different publications are also appropriate access points, but each identifies only one publication.

Uniform Title Together with an Author Access Point

When an author's name is available as an access point for a work, it may seem less, or not at all, important to use a uniform title as a grouping device. Agatha Christie's mystery cited as an example above is, after all, accessible under her name no matter which title appears on the edition the library happens to own—but does a particular user who wants this work know which title proper the library's copy bears? Does the user who looks for *And Then There Were None* (whether by that title or under Christie's name) go away unsatisfied when the library actually has the book only in its original publication with the unfortunate title? Christie is not a one-book author: a search under her surname reveals the titles of her many other mysteries interspersed alphabetically among those borne by *this* one. The only solution to this problem of both identification and searching is to use the author's name followed by the uniform title of the work as a *name-title access point.* This linkage of two elements within one access point identifies one work uniquely and provides a single predictable file location for all its editions, translations, adaptations, etc.

This technique has been used the most consistently and for the longest time in the cataloguing of scores and recordings of serious music. It is a rare composer who publishes only one piece of music.

Music publishing is international in scope and not essentially dependent on the use of any particular language. A Chinese pianist performs from the same musical notation as a French one. Labels on many recordings are multilingual. An individual concert goer, score reader, or listener may best know the same Mozart opera as *The Marriage of Figaro, Le Nozze di Figaro,* or *Figaros Hochzeit.* A recording of the same Shostakovich quartet may bear a label reading *Quatuor no 1, Erste Streichkvartett,* or *String Quartet no. 1.* Without organization by their uniform titles, the lengthy list of Mozart's compositions subarranged under his name, or even the more modest list under Shostakovich's, would be a disorganized grab-bag.

The organization made possible by the name-plus-uniform-title access point is best effected through the use of the authority file with its equivalence links. A typical format of such a link as expressed in a manual index is:

> **Mozart, Wolfgang Amadeus. Marriage of Figaro**
> *for editions of this work, search under* **Mozart, Wolfgang**
> **Amadeus. Nozze di Figaro**

The uniform title established for this work is *Nozze di Figaro.* Like the composer's name, this title has been composed according to a cataloguing rule: a uniform title, unlike a title proper, is subject to authority control. In manual catalogues, it was not common to file an equivalence link (*see* reference) also at a title. There might be many of these and in any case, one or another would show up in the file as the title proper of a single edition in the library's collection. In the case of music particularly, it was also assumed that an informed searcher would always begin a search at the composer's name rather than at any title. The next section, on principal access points, helps explain this: it is the best technique for confident searching for *any* work. The elements of the equivalence link are, however, all usually separately coded for interactive searching, so a search of the title word *Nozze* also retrieves the link, and therefore all the records for the work in question regardless of which title is on the document(s) containing it.

In manual catalogues, it was common to restrict the consistent use of uniform titles to anonymous classics, music, and primary legal materials such as treaties. Only for these did they appear on Library of Congress printed cards because smaller libraries containing material in only one language found the general use of the uniform title intrusive and confusing to end-users. Larger libraries would pencil them onto catalogue cards as *filing titles* to serve for file organization as needed. For example, an academic librarian would thus ensure that records for original-language editions of literary works and editions in the working language of most users would be found in the catalogue adjacent to each other.

Where a personal or corporate name is assigned as principal access point, the use of a following uniform title remains theoretically optional in AACR. However, it is now routinely added by national bibliographic agencies in any case of possible confusion in identifying a work because its editions, versions, etc. bear different titles proper. Whether and how it forms part of the display at any library's OPAC is left to the programming of the local interface.

The Access Point for a Work

Chapter 3 describes many types of both natural-language and controlled-vocabulary access points in addition to the names and titles discussed in this chapter. All modern cataloguing codes acknowledge the need to provide access to a work or a document at any of several types of access point. As a carry-over from the context of the manual catalogue (in which the number of retrievable data elements was necessarily limited), but also to ensure consistency in the context of distributed cataloguing, AACR2R still specifies individually which nonsubject access points are required. These required access points, except for most types of title, are subject to vocabulary control as described throughout this chapter.

While it integrated so much else in bibliographic control, automation *dis*integrated the formerly unitary bibliographic record. It made virtually every data element, vocabulary-controlled or not, retrievable, whether from bibliographic records or from authority records, including all the cross-reference links in the latter. In addition to any single data element or single word or group of words, any combination of either is retrievable via boolean operators. The user interface, not the cataloguing code, is now the primary determinant of how a record is accessed and displayed at an OPAC. It is a reasonable, if erroneous, conclusion that no one access point has greater value than any other in searching an OPAC.

Yet cataloguing codes continue to prioritize access points. Every English-language code from Cutter's in 1876 to the current AACR2R calls one display version of a item's record its *main entry*. Cutter and the 1908 Joint Code define this as "the full or principal entry; usually the author entry." The first clause, the mention of fullness, arose from an economic concern. When each record to be filed at each access point had to be handwritten, typed, or typeset individually, it was a luxury for each to be complete; all but one was typically made a briefer index reference to the main, or full, one. That the full record should be the one filed at the author's name (provided a useable one is available) accords with the standard citation practice described in chapter 3, a practice whose purpose is to identify the work more than the document.

The printing of unit records made the economic concern irrelevant a long time ago. Automation led to more focus on individual data elements than on the whole record or work. Any descriptive data element—that is, one recorded according to ISBD and part I of AACR —is easily made retrievable by a DBMS. All such elements exist, however, primarily to identify the *document*. The access points specified in part II of AACR, as well as the subject access points discussed in the next chapter, exist primarily to identify the *work* it embodies (see AACR2, rule 20.1). If one is looking for a government publication, or an edition prior to 1900, or a two-volume format, the focus is the document, whose retrieval can be facilitated by a search among its descriptive elements, singly or in boolean combination.

Attention is now returning to methods of identifying a work as such. AACR defines *main entry* as "the complete catalogue record of an item, presented in the form by which the entity is to be uniformly identified and cited." That this entity is the work, more than the document, is the reason for rule 0.5 in AACR2: "the concept of main entry is considered to be useful in assigning uniform titles and in promoting the standardization of bibliographic citation." In other words, the main entry is the standardized access point to a work, involving a uniform title.

A work is not the same entity as the work's author. It is retrieved most surely by searching for *two* data elements in combination (provided both are relevant: authorship is sometimes unknown or, for cataloguing purposes, irrelevant). These are (1) the work's title and (2) its (predominating) author's name. Why neither of these two elements alone can be counted upon to isolate one work unambiguously, and why the author's name takes precedence in citation and must be vocabulary-controlled, are discussed in chapters 2 and 3. The examples above in the section on uniform titles show that vocabulary control (standardization) is, in principle, just as essential for a work's title as for its author's name. As with authors' names, the proportion of real "problem" cases, those involving titles with many variants, is small. If a work only ever appears once under one title, that title is also the work's uniform title. That this is the usual case does not undermine the principle that using uniform titles is a necessary precondition for the confident retrieval of works in a bibliographic file.

In the manual record format specified by AACR and its predecessors, and in both the manual and the computer-based filing rules designed to match these codes, a title proper (or, wherever relevant, a uniform title) always immediately follows the name of the predominating author: the pre-coordination is regulated as a whole. This is the "main entry heading" of cataloguing lore (the term is not used in the codes). It is the access point of the main entry. Only if there is no useable author's name does a title stand alone in this function. However, the title must be a *uniform* title wherever one is relevant, whether or not an author's name precedes it (cf. AACR2 rules 20.4, 21.0C, 21.1C, 25.1).

By making each data element separately searchable, automation encouraged the view that all searches involving more than one data element should be post-coordinate searches. That a pre-coordinate pair is the most efficient identifier of a work tended to be forgotten, but in two situations involving the identification of works, the pre-coordination is as explicit a part of search vocabularies for interactive retrieval as it ever was for manual retrieval: (1) a subject access point for a work which is the subject of another work and (2) a reference to a work related to another. Retrieval in either of these cases is *not* most efficiently achieved, even in an OPAC, by searching either an index of authors' names alone or an index of titles alone.

What is retrieved in a subject index at the controlled-vocabulary personal-name access point **SHAKESPEARE, WILLIAM** is something about the person, not about any of his individual works. A subject search at *Henry V* can be expected to retrieve much with no relevance to Shakespeare's play. When a screenful of hardly a score of access points is visible at a time (often in full capitals and unpunctuated), all but the expert searcher is confused before puzzling out which are the wanted items. This is why a name-title access point (in this case, **SHAKESPEARE, WILLIAM. HENRY V**) is the appropriate controlled-vocabulary subject access point for a work. This work-identifier, its *main entry heading* (in the preferred terminology of this book, *principal access point*) thus serves also as an added or subject access point.

In referring to a related work, the careful reference librarian therefore does not tell the inquirer, for example, that Tom Stoppard's play *Rosenkrantz and Gildenstern Are Dead* is "based on an incident in *Hamlet*," but rather that it is based on "Shakespeare's *Hamlet*." The fuller reference might inspire the inquirer to search for the related work in the most appropriate manner, combining both the author's name (or part of it) along with the title (or part of it), perhaps with a boolean *AND* coordination at an OPAC.

The typical subject authority file has always included such pre-coordinate access points to identify works which are the subjects of other works. However, the typical name authority file, even if it includes names of all persons, corporate bodies, and places appearing in the catalogue, includes this pre-coordinated name of a *work* (author plus title) only in the relatively few cases when an "added" non-subject access point for the work is needed in the catalogue. Figure

21 shows examples. This is a continuation of the practice in manual systems, where it was common for a name authority file not to be complete; that is, not to include records for access points requiring no cross-reference linkage, scope note, or other interpretive comment. The bibliographic file itself served as sufficient record of the

---

```
DESCARIE
DESCARTES RENE 1596
DESCARTES RENE 1596 CORRESPONDENCE FRENCH SELECTIONS 1988
DESCARTES RENE 1596 GEOMETRY
DESCARTES RENE 1596 MEDITATIONES DE PRIMA PHILOSOPHIA
DESCARTES RENE 1596 MEDITATIONES DE PRIMA PHILOSOPHIA
        ENGLISH 1989
DESCARY THERESE
DESCAVES LUCETTE
DESCAVES LUCIEN 1861
DESCENDANT 1786
DESCENDIT DE CAELIS
DESCENT DAVID 1955
DESCENT OF INANNA TO THE UNDERWORLD
DESCENT OF INANNA TO THE UNDERWORLD ENGLISH 1992
DESCH H E HAROLD ERNEST
DESCH H E HAROLD ERNEST TIMBER ITS STRUCTURE PROPERTIES
        AND UTILISATION
HEADING: Descent of Inanna to the underworld
USE FOR: Descent of Inanna
USE FOR: Inanna's descent to the nether world
FOUND IN: Meador, B. De S. Uncursing the dark, c1992,
        p. 19 (The descent of Inanna to the underworld)
FOUND IN: Wolkstein, D. Inanna, queen of heaven and earth,
        c1983, p. xvi (The descent of Inanna) p. xiii
        (Sumerian literary document)
FOUND IN: Kramer, S.N. From the poetry of Sumer, c1979,
        p. 82 (Inanna's descent to the nether world)
```

FIGURE 21.   A typical name authority file contains records for *some* works along with access points for persons (and, although not shown in this short segment of the file, for corporate bodies and places). The authority record for a single one of H. E. Desch's works is an "added" access point for the record for a later edition of this work, which happens to bear a different title proper. *Descent of Inanna to the underworld* is a uniform title for an anonymous Sumerian literary work. Its full authority record is shown in the lower part of the figure. Since user interfaces vary greatly in what is displayed initially in response to a search command, both this figure and the commentary in the text should be taken as an exploration of principles rather than as a literal description of what a searcher would see at any given OPAC; for example, the figure's quick and cheap one-line, truncated display in full-caps and without diacritics is the authority record's access point, displayed only as its filing key.

existence and form of these access points. After all, most authors named in a bibliographic file are responsible for only one work each, and offer no problems of identification. In the case of works, most exist in only one edition, again offering no problem to occasion an authority record separate from the bibliographic record.

The very function of an authority file is an entirely different matter in an OPAC, described first at the end of chapter 3 and illustrated in figure 16 on page 147. The operation of a DBMS and its user interface means that the display of any "browse" for a name or subject is not a sequence of bibliographic records, but a sequence of only the access points of name or subject authority records, respectively. Only when the searcher keys the occurrence numbers of those deemed relevant does the interface retrieve the relevant bibliographic records for partial or full display. In other words, authority files including *every* controlled-vocabulary access point used in the system are essential to the very search-and-display process. The issue raised here is that a name-plus-uniform-title combination is the appropriate controlled-vocabulary access point for a work. However, present practice is to include this type of access point routinely in subject authority files, but only in special cases in name authority files. In most OPAC interfaces, a "browse" command calls for the display of access points on successive authority records, sometimes in full capitals and without punctuation to distinguish data elements except for the period separating the two elements of a name-title access point. No wonder searchers are confused when they find name-title access points routinely in a browse of the subject authority file and sometimes in a browse of the name authority file, but cannot determine why there is a difference. That a one-line-per-record initial display format does not provide space for both an author and a title is not a satisfactory explanation. Nor is the response that more users search for personal names alone than for individual works.

The ability to post-coordinate when searching an OPAC therefore has not eliminated the desirability of including both elements of a principal access point in an efficient search for a work. It has, however, improved retrieval by allowing each of these, like any other data element, to be searched in whole or in part and without necessary regard for the filing sequence. Assuming that any word is searchable and that vocabulary control has been applied as the rules require to both author's name and titling, the command FIND **dream** [in the title index] *AND* **Shakespeare** [in the name index] is an understandable and effective method of retrieving the record for every representation of the text of that play.

Since access to a work traditionally begins with the work's author or principal author, library cataloguing codes for three centuries were often called "author-title" cataloguing codes. What theory underlay them focused on defining the functions of authorship and establishing an order of priority among these functions so that a principal author can be identified when a work has more than one author or more than one authorial function. As an extension of this theory, Charles Jewett began the extension of the concept of authorship to include corporate bodies as authors. However, a century of developing this essentially fictitious concept resulted in rules so complex and hard to apply that they became counterproductive. With AACR2, corporate authorship was abandoned as a principle, to be replaced with pragmatic rules defining limited circumstances in which the name of a corporate body is a useful first element of a principal access point.

The terminology "principal access point," which does not appear in the cataloguing code, must be taken to mean access point for a work, not a document. This can be made clear in OPAC indexing and display in a way which simply did not occur in manual filing and display, where all descriptive and access elements were visible together in predetermined sequence on a record whose overall focus had to be the document. Distinguishing between the work and the document, an issue raised so often in this book, is a help to understanding this important point. It is the reason for the proposed replacement of *main entry* (which can only focus attention on the document and its whole record) with *principal access point* (which has some chance of focusing attention on the work). Welcome attention will be drawn to this issue by the recent proposal of an ISO working group for a standard numbering system for works to parallel the existing system of standard document-numbering schemes. Finally, as more of the "documents" sought are screens of data with little physical tangibility downloaded from Internet sites, the concept of an access point such as a URL almost replaces that of a record.

7

■ ■ ■

Subject Access

The names discussed in chapter 6 form a large proportion of the access points in most subject indices and subject-classified arrangements. When one thinks of access by *subject,* however, what comes first to mind is more likely to be a non-name concept or topic: psychiatry rather than Carl Jung; dog-training rather than Barbara Woodhouse. This chapter deals with the access points for indexing and searching such concepts. Its titling differs from that of the previous one, however, because it is about a process as much as it is about the resultant access *points.*

Furthermore, the title of the previous chapter indicates its restriction to controlled-vocabulary access points—except for a brief treatment of titles proper as uncontrolled name access points because any word of its title, used as a search key, may serve to locate a document. In the case of creative works (fiction, drama, feature films, video games, etc.), this is the only purpose of searching title words. In the case of nonfiction, however, any word or combination of words in the natural language of titles, abstracts, and especially the full text of a document serves the additional purpose of identifying something in the file relevant to the word(s).

Controlled vocabularies of the several types discussed later in this chapter have been devised for subject searching. As in the case of name access for identification, a well-prepared search for subject information is almost certain to be more efficient and to produce more satisfactory results if pursued via controlled-vocabulary access points. However, beginners, people in a hurry, and those without sufficient prior information or experience to formulate a good search strategy in advance make much use (some make exclusive use) of words and terms of natural language in subject searching. A search of this kind is not necessarily poor, ineffective, or nonproductive, although it is highly likely to be less efficient unless the query is a very simple one. Controlled and natural language are often mingled during a single search.

A philosopher distinguishes, defines, names, and categorizes each separate concept as an abstraction. A librarian—whether as indexer or as searcher—must be more pragmatic and thinks of any concept as something a creator has chosen to write (paint, compose, etc.) about or something an inquirer searches for. For example, sound is a subject. The means of producing sound is a subject. The electronic production of sound is a subject. Music is a subject. Contemporary music is a subject. Popular music is a subject. Rock music is a subject. The use of electronic mixing boards in rock music recording is a subject. The music of John Lennon is a subject. The relationship of rock music to serious music is a subject. The influence of Lennon's music is a subject. There is almost no end to the proliferation of the separate subjects which consist of levels of, ramifications of, or combinations of other subjects.

It is actually hard to conceive of a work so intellectually shallow that the whole of it deals with only one subject. It may have one *focus,* which is a quite different thing, but its *internal* index typically isolates dozens, if not hundreds, of the topics it treats, some more directly and fully, others in passing and more peripherally and superficially. The subject-oriented component of a library catalogue, an A&I publication, or a monographic bibliography does not attempt to duplicate that internal back-of-the-book index. It only directs the searcher to the topical focus or focuses of the *whole* work (in fact, of the whole publication described in a bibliographic record, which may be an entire run of a serial publication). It normally makes no attempt to isolate the subject of any one volume, issue, part, section, chapter, paragraph, etc. of that whole.

Typical subject indexing done by an A&I service also has the work as its focus, but in the A&I context, the work is the single article, the paper at a conference, etc., not the published unit (the journal issue, the whole volume of conference proceedings, etc.). Subject analysis at more detailed levels, once the domain of the back-of-the-book index, is gradually being incorporated into library-based searching as keyword searching of the full text of documents more and more often accompanies the searching of their bibliographic data.

Knowing the principles discussed in chapter 6 gives a searcher some confidence in locating an access point for an individual person, body, place, or work in an index. There is an objectivity about the process not present in a typical subject search. *Subjective,* from the same linguistic root, better expresses the latter. It is fraught with all the ambiguities, inconsistencies, and problems of definition inherent in communicating ideas.

Despite some overlap in their problem areas, the following are ways in which establishing or searching for a name differs from establishing or searching for a concept.

1) A person or corporate body can undergo a change of name, giving rise to a new (or additional) access point. However, there is no ambiguity about what the new name is or when it takes effect. Is it ever as clear precisely when a subject term (for example, **MOVING PICTURES**) is no longer effective for its purpose and another should be used, or precisely what new term should replace it? This is a problem of defining equivalency.

2) A controlled-vocabulary name access point identifies one, and one only, person, body, place, or work. One subject access point may identify more than one topic; for example, *libraries* and *automation* are separate topics explicitly identified in the single access point **LIBRARY AUTOMATION** whether it is expressed that way or as **AUTOMATION OF LIBRARIES** or as **LIBRARIES—AUTOMATION.** How many topics belong in one subject access point or search key, whether controlled or uncontrolled? This is a problem of coordination.

3) Except in fields such as genealogy or organizational studies, it is not a common concern of an alphanumerically arranged name index to link related persons, bodies, etc.; for example, most people searching a biographical index do not expect the names of Judy Garland and her daughter Liza Minnelli to be linked with each other as access points. In contrast, only a very incomplete and less than useful subject index fails to relate **MOTORCYCLE** somehow with **MOPED**, whether by

   a) using a hierarchic or associative link to display the other term as a suggestion during a search of a bibliographic file

   b) showing the relationship of indexing terms to each other in a separately maintained authority file so that the conscientious searcher can, *before* consulting the actual catalogue, plot a search strategy on how to use the best ones in the best sequence or

   c) collocating the access points for related concepts in a subject-classified arrangement. This is a problem of linking.

Cutter described a catalogue incorporating hierarchic and associative links as *syndetic,* that is,

> connective, applied to that kind of dictionary catalog which binds its records together by means of cross-references so as to form a whole, the references being made from the most comprehensive subject to those of the next lower degree of comprehensiveness, and from each of those to their subordinate subjects, and vice versa. These cross-references correspond to and are a good substitute for the arrangement in a systematic [that is, classified] catalog. References are also made in the syndetic catalog to illustrative and coördinate subjects, and, if it is perfect, from specific to general subjects.[1]

The process described in point 3b above introduces a preliminary step into a subject search. This does not appeal to the user who lunges at an index expecting instant results. It is, however, increasingly necessary in searching an interactive file because the contents of that file are essentially invisible to the searcher, as described in chapter 4. Interactive searching begins in this way whenever only index terms, and not complete bibliographic records, are displayed as the first response to a query.

The equivalency problem briefly stated in point 1 above challenges everyone's definition of what constitutes any given topic as potentially ambiguous. It is always clear what constitutes an individual person and fairly clear what constitutes an individual corporate body, place, or work. Despite his use of a pseudonym, Woody Allen lives and acts in particular time and space regardless of the perceptions of others or any external circumstance. He cannot be mistaken for any other person. The geographic boundaries clearly drawn on a map of the area of Geneva, Switzerland, make it impossible to mistake this city for its namesake in New York State or for Carouge, its adjacent suburb in Switzerland. Linkages among various forms of name for the same person, etc., therefore express only an equivalence relationship; for example, *Clemens* equals *Twain* and *Twain* equals *Clemens.*

What constitutes any particular concept is not definable objectively but only in relation to how someone wishes to use it for a given purpose: every communicator of topical information has an agenda and posits a context which any particular recipient may not hear, wish to hear, or understand. What that recipient understands as the scope and focus of the topic is affected by the "baggage" it carries: fashions of time and place and particularly any emotional charge surrounding the term(s) in which it is expressed and any topical juxtapositions. In what context is the topic **HANDICAPPED PERSONS** defined and named? Is the topic so named the equivalent of **INVA-LIDS**? If not, can they be objectively distinguished, and which type of link between these terms—hierarchic or associative—is the more appropriate? Subject identification is a messy and often indeterminate business. After everything else in bibliographic control has been programmed into a computer, this area will remain in the domain of human judgement.

CONCEPT VERSUS WORD(S)

When a topic is expressed in words, it is tempting to equate one word with one topic for purposes of indexing. In English, the single noun (architecture) and gerund (fishing) are ideal parts of speech with which to express topics in an indexable fashion. They predominate in every topical index. But a topic as the equivalent of a single word in a dictionary is the philosopher's abstraction mentioned in the fourth paragraph of this chapter, not what an indexer or a searcher deals with in practice. Their first task is to define the scope and boundaries of the topic in two possibly different but equally concrete contexts: (1) the documents in which it is treated and (2) the purpose of any given searcher. The first context is known and fixed; the second is well known by the searcher, but for the indexer it is hypothetical, and for the librarian who assists with searching it is variable from one client to another.

Every context affects the value of each potentially relevant word. Nevertheless, computer-based searching, more than manual, focuses attention on single words because a word—anything with a space or a mark of punctuation immediately before and after it—is the easiest thing to input cheaply into, and to retrieve automatically from, a database. A single word often suffices to identify a topic (**COSMETICS**; **USURY**). In English and most other languages, there is a natural tendency for a new topic to become defined in a single word (needlework is work done with needles; xenophobia is the fear of foreigners), but this is not always the case.

When more than one word is needed to express a concept, each word may or may not carry its original context(s) and meaning(s) into the combination. Each of the two words in **PRESSURE BROAD-ENING** is used in the same sense it has as an independent word, but only in combination, and only in this order, do the words identify a single topic in the discipline of astrophysics. In isolation, *pressure* connotes mechanics to most people. *Broadening* might relate to anything from subject analysis to tailoring.

Whether or not a nonastrophysicist knows the meaning of pressure broadening is irrelevant. What matters is that anyone who speaks English and is informed about the topic knows it best by that term. It also matters very much to those using an index that if *pressure* appears outside this context, the average searcher legitimately assumes a different context: that of physics or engineering or social interaction. *Black hole* also has a specialized meaning in astrophysics, but here each word in the pair has been totally and very obviously divorced from any but allusive connection with its original meaning. Since one subject often cannot be equated with one word, any system relying on single words (**PRESSURE** or **HOLE**) as search keys in a topical index must be used with great caution because the integrity of subjects cannot be guaranteed in single-word searching.

NATURAL LANGUAGE

Despite the issues of meaning in multiword combinations raised in the previous paragraph, the use of computers in searching has focussed attention on single words as search keys. No previous technology for searching made it easy to isolate each word for ad hoc post-coordination in whatever combination, as described in chapter 4, a technique with enormous potential for speedier and more user-friendly searching.

A word from the natural language of a title, cataloguer's note, abstract, or text of a document and considered useful for subject access is often called a *keyword* or *derived keyword*—derived, that is, from the document or its record rather than from a controlled vocabulary. In the title *Should America Go to War?* there can hardly be any disagreement that *America* and *War* are keywords but that *Should, Go,* and *to* are not. However, it is neither uncommon nor necessarily unwise to include in a search a single word from a multiword term of a *controlled* vocabulary. This is also usually called a keyword. The term is therefore avoided in the remainder of this chapter in order to clarify a vital distinction; the more awkward *natural-language access point* is used as in chapter 3 to mean a word used as an access point but not because it comes from a controlled vocabulary.

The use of natural language for subject indexing is sometimes thought to have originated in the *keyword-in-context* (KWIC, intentionally recalling *quick*) and *keyword-out-of-context* (KWOC) indexing techniques which inaugurated the automated (but not yet interactive) bibliographic file just after the Second World War (see figure 12 on page 105). In fact, it is much older. Books and articles were indexed using the natural language of their texts long before

Poole and Cutter developed modern controlled-vocabulary subject indexing. Multiple access points in a subject index looked exactly like those in a KWIC index; they consisted of the significant words of a sentence (for a back-of-the-book index) or of a title (for an index to periodical articles or books), permuted to bring each significant word into position as a filing element:

> Federal Policymaking, How the Press Affects
> Policymaking, How the Press Affects Federal
> Press Affects Federal Policymaking, How the

To preserve the sense of a juxtaposition involving a qualifier, the word order might be adjusted:

> Names, transformation of, for use as catalogue headings
> Cross-references, system of, in the British Museum catalogue

The second example above shows how the whole natural-language string was typically preserved even when part of it (here the part between commas) could easily be eliminated. This manner of indexing gave rise to the terms *rotated index* and *permuted keyword index* seen in the modern literature of subject analysis.

Applying this quasi-mechanical technique to natural language requires no new indexing vocabulary but was labour-intensive when a human had to make each decision as to (1) whether or not any word should be a filing element and (2) how to place the other words in the resulting access point for manual transcription or typing into the index. This was not a notably cheap process until it could be mechanized in the mid-twentieth century, although it is essentially clerical and therefore not costly in professional time.

Cutter, Dewey, and others successfully focused the attention of professionals a hundred years ago on controlled vocabularies for subject access: classification schemes and lists of subject headings. That their application resulted in indexing and searching on a sounder intellectual basis was so quickly recognized that for generations to follow, librarians shunned natural-language access points for subject retrieval. Among the access points for *Should America Go to War?* (used as an example above), the title word *America* became a controlled-vocabulary subject access point beginning with **UNITED STATES**, and the cataloguer determined whether the *War* of the title is war in general or a particular war; if the latter, the cataloguer chose its name, **WORLD WAR I**, as a subject access point. Finally, the cataloguer decided on the need for any cross-reference links, perhaps an equivalence link with **EUROPEAN WAR**. As the first word of the title, *Should* continued to be an access point for known-item identification but not as a term intended for subject retrieval per se. It does serve an indirect purpose in subject *analysis* because it is a clue to the indexer that the book is not about proposed American military action but about American social opinion and political and diplomatic stances.

Its development during and after the Second World War made automation a necessary solution, not just a chosen one, to the problem of greatly increased information demand coinciding with a general shortage of professionally trained staff to deal with it. The practice of using natural-language access points for subject searching was both revived and greatly expanded by automation, at first more for journal indexing in subject-specialized A&I publications. A library's card catalogue was too cumbersome a format in which to make single title words accessible, but during the short period when library catalogues were produced on microfiche, a few made for public libraries indexed them. However, the documents of scientific investigation and technical application were the most receptive to the new treatment of natural-language retrieval; the precision required of the terminology, writing, and abstracting in these fields gives to their expression many of the characteristics of a controlled vocabulary. It is no surprise, therefore, that special libraries were the first to produce title-word indexing, originally in the KWIC/KWOC formats.

The effect became a cause: authors, editors, and publishers in other disciplines came to appreciate the advantages of retrieving their books and articles using natural-language access points in computer-based information retrieval systems. That natural-language subject searching is now considered indispensable is a great incentive for authors and publishers to choose title wording carefully and for those who write abstracts to give consistency in wording from abstract to abstract the highest priority. Still, until the 1960s, it was not common for an A&I service to develop a formal controlled vocabulary of its own, largely because the links of a controlled vocabulary are its most costly part to devise and to maintain. Without links, responsibility for identifying a need and matching it with the available terminology of natural language is divided between the creators of the document and its abstract and the searcher. In a search using a controlled vocabulary, a bridge between writer and searcher is provided by two additional intelligent participants in the process: the creator of the vocabulary and the indexer who uses it when indexing the document.

Automated Natural-Language Indexing

Automated indexing and searching had a slow start when pre-existing text had to be rekeyed into digital format. The entire content of most current bibliographic tools produced by libraries and A&I services is now originally in digital form. So is everything in the newest academic medium, the electronic journal. Current issues of ever more newspapers and periodicals can be seen on the Internet or in the databases of commercial vendors of online searching, such as DIA-LOG, before the printed issues can appear on the racks of the street vendor. The text, at least, of most books is now produced from digital copy; the first (1982) edition of this book was the earliest one so produced by its publisher from a tape sent by the author.

The only significant remaining barrier to automated natural-language indexing of almost anything is now ownership/copyright clearance to use the full text of a document in an information-retrieval system. Format-translation problems and common transmission protocols have overcome barriers to compatible communication. (For simple word indexing, little or no special formatting is needed.) Techniques range from simple-minded to quite sophisticated. The ultimate goal is to make automated indexing indistinguishable from human indexing; that is, to program a computer to recognize meaning and context and to adjust the indexing accordingly, incorporating all the processes of vocabulary control. *Artificial intelligence* is the clearest way of expressing this goal because it embodies everything encompassed by human thought. It is as far in the distance as clear thinking often seems.

What is operational now is at the simpler end of the spectrum. Programming a DBMS to treat each word as a searchable term except those placed on a stoplist is a one-time cost to the indexing operation. The stoplist may consist of specified words (most articles, words devoid of determinative meaning in the given context) and/or of words which a program can identify automatically (words of one or two characters are often deemed not to convey enough significant information to repay the cost of dealing with each individually). In a specialized field, a stoplist can be something like a controlled vocabulary in reverse, tailored to make accessible only words highly significant for retrieval purposes.

More sophisticated indexing or retrieval programs count the frequency with which a word or word-group is used in the natural language of the material to be indexed or searched. At a certain threshold of its use, perhaps even considering a specified context, sentence pattern, etc., the program determines that the word or group is significant enough to index or retrieve. A program can be written to *stem,* that is, to analyze the morphological patterns of a language and determine what truncations leave only the meaningful roots of words to be searched.

In any human search, an occasional pause is needed to review progress and determine whether the search is still proceeding along the best path. Programs providing for interaction with the searcher, feedback based on the degree of satisfaction with results to that point, and resultant modification while a search is in progress represent the most advanced experimentation to date. At the moment, these are still a bit distant from the practice of searching the average library catalogue or A&I database.

Natural-Language Access Points and Coordination

Natural-language retrieval relies heavily on the techniques of post-coordination described in chapter 4 and therefore on the common sense and terminological awareness of the searcher. The title *The Reign of the Theatrical Director: French Theatre, 1887–1924* contains three nouns. *Reign* might be useful in accessing material about political history, but not about theatre. The other two are also less than useful when isolated from one another, but in combination, *Director* and *Theatre* pinpoint the conceptual focus of the book well. If the geographic context is also wanted, the searcher must always be aware of the need to use both the substantive and the adjectival forms (France/French) if the same truncation will not do for both as *Canad?* will for Canada/Canadian. Truncation involves a form of boolean *OR* logic.

The social worker wants some current data on marriage breakdown (not divorce); the interior designer knows that the venetian blind is something to consider for a particular job. Like pressure broadening and black hole, neither of these topics can be expressed in a single word. Post-coordination using proximity searching can retrieve any record containing *blind* provided that word immediately follows *venetian* (neither a blind Venetian nor a Venetian bas-relief in a hospice for the blind is the desired topic). Since proximity searching involves a form of boolean *AND* logic, its use is essential in the searching of natural-language full text, which is likely to contain almost any two significant words somewhere.

Post-coordination using boolean *AND* retrieves any text in which both *marriage* and *breakdown* occur, thereby catching phrases such as "breakdown and dissolution of a marriage." To use post-coordination effectively with natural language, the searcher must be aware of whether a group of words denotes a single topic or more than one topic. This can usually be determined easily, but it takes a moment's thought, since meaning is not always revealed by the mere forms of words. For example, press law is a combination of the topic *press* (or its synonym, *journalism*) with the topic *law*, but a press release, despite its connection with journalism, is neither *about* journalism nor about most meanings of the verb *to release*. Experienced indexers may disagree whether a pre-coordination of separate topics or a single multiword topic is at issue. For example, whether the juvenile press is closely associated with journalism probably depends on the indexing context. As another example, a pressure group is a group (of people) which exerts pressure (on politicians, etc.), and a pressure gauge is a type of instrument for measuring pressure. Both might seem to be post-coordinations of separate topics, but it is probably better to consider the first (pressure group) to be a two-word single concept, since neither *pressure* nor *group* is used in its most unambiguous sense in this combination: both are used allusively. Allusion is the very spirit of language but the deadliest enemy of natural-language indexing and searching; it adds context and meaning outside the bounds of vocabulary control.

The topic of life on other planets illustrates limitations of the available techniques of post-coordination when used with natural language. *Life* (in the broadest biological sense) and *planets* (we think we know precisely how many there are in this solar system) are unambiguous terms; yet their post-coordination to retrieve the above topic can produce only poor results. Other planets can be expressed negatively (*FIND* [planet] but *NOT earth*) or positively (*FIND mercury AND venus AND mars AND . . .*). Yet post-coordination using *NOT* will not produce a satisfactory result because Earth is virtually always implicit, not explicit, in writings on the subject. Using *AND* works no better because individual planets (except perhaps Mars) are rarely named explicitly in the literature on this topic. Using a pre-coordination in a controlled vocabulary is the only sure way to index this concept.

Natural-Language Access Points and the Larger Database

As mentioned earlier, it is possible for natural language in a limited technical field to approach the characteristics of controlled vocabulary without links. This is especially the case with the language used in titles and abstracts, the language most commonly searched for its subject significance. Searching the full text of newspapers, journal articles, encyclopaedias, etc. is becoming more common, but a skilled searcher does this only with an expectation of retrieving something relevant because of the context. Concordances of single works of creative writing (myth, poetry, fiction, etc.) have been compiled for centuries to enable the student of that writing to identify any single word in the entire text. A DBMS in effect makes it possible to search a concordance of any digitized text, but the purpose of the classic concordance was always the critical, linguistic, and semantic examination of the writing, not *subject* retrieval.

The larger the files searched and the broader their subject coverage, the more skilful any natural-language search must be to avoid the false drops of homonyms and particularly irrelevant context, both detriments to the motivation to continue a search as well as problems in isolating what is relevant. Yet in general, users appear to appreciate

the ability to search many, rather than few, records or databases in a
single operation. Both libraries and database vendors once kept files
(both manual and digital) of distinct materials and for distinct purposes separate from one another. The trend is now toward combining, or at least permitting the searcher to combine ad hoc, many files
for simultaneous searching.

The necessary compromise considers the speed, ease, and extent of
a search and the quality and relevance of the result. There is no doubt
that natural-language access provides answers to some questions better than a controlled vocabulary can. It is, at first, even exciting to
discover in a fraction of a second at an OPAC that the truncation
environ? occurs 1,675 times in titles in the library's internal catalogue
file and 35,236 times in the texts of magazine articles published during the last calendar year.

Does the promise of so much more information than one could
previously discover also bring the motivation to pursue it all? When
a check of the result reveals titles such as *The Work Environment in the
Civil Service,* it dawns on the searcher that more unpleasant surprises
may be in store. That user is even more discouraged on discovering
that the most relevant item has eluded the search process: *Man and
Earth: Their Changing Relationship.* A contents note included in the
catalogue record is now almost always made searchable, and there
have been periodic suggestions that whole tables of contents for any
nonfiction work should also be indexed for retrieval, but this expansion of the data searched need not guarantee retrievability of *Man and
Earth . . .* via the search key *environ?.* What it does guarantee is a vast
increase in the number of irrelevant items retrieved. Does that serve
the searcher's needs?

The limitations of a natural-language access system are at first less
visible than its ease and copious results. At their present stage of
development, automated indexing and natural-language searching,
two faces of the same coin, are excellent tools for *document retrieval;*
they are still, in general, blunt tools to use for *information retrieval.*
Their primary virtues are low cost and a sense of immediacy in the
user's approach to the database.

TYPES OF CONTROLLED
SUBJECT VOCABULARY

A controlled subject vocabulary does not foster a sense of immediacy;
it places a mediator—some would say a barrier—between the searcher
and the database. It is of greater help to someone less well informed

about the subject under investigation than to one who knows the subject intimately. Paradoxically (and unfortunately) the former is the one more likely to be impatient with having to go through an intermediate and seemingly unproductive step in a search. Making a controlled vocabulary demands the conscious exercise of disciplined judgement about the nature, naming, and relationships of concepts in both the context of a particular need and the context of the documents available to meet that need. *Using* a controlled vocabulary in any search enforces the same mental discipline on the searcher. That may be its most important function.

Cataloguers can work independently of each other when they establish name access points using the rules and principles discussed in the previous chapter. Those rules call for decisions based on the examination of objective evidence. However, establishing access points for subject searching—not merely applying existing ones—eludes consistency when the very technique is, as its name implies, subjective. People will always disagree, for example, in making a choice between synonyms. In a pre-coordinate vocabulary, how many and what concepts to pre-coordinate are also very subjective. What kind of relationship suffices to establish an associative link is even more context-dependent and subjective.

Cutter's *Rules for a Dictionary Catalog* includes rules for establishing, as well as for applying, subject access points. These were adopted by the Library of Congress when it began its card catalogue in 1898. However, the subjective nature of the entire process means that subject access techniques *should* not aspire to the degree of uniformity expected of name access techniques which are common to all materials and all types of library. The evolving practice of the Library of Congress was therefore intended only to meet its own internal needs, yet it came to be applied worldwide through the published *Library of Congress Subject Headings* described later in this chapter. The dominance of this system of headings in library cataloguing meant that despite significant alterations in its very basis over the twentieth century and a paucity of written documentation on it until the 1980s, there was almost no attempt among libraries to codify rules for establishing subject access points from Cutter's day until the development of automated post-coordination and its associated use of the *descriptors* discussed more fully later in this chapter. Descriptors, the simplest type of subject access point to regulate in a theoretical way, now conform to the international standards cited in note 3 to chapter 3. Somewhat later, a set of rules for string indexing appeared as a guide to the system called *PRECIS*, also described below.

Most cataloguers and indexers therefor do not create new access points; they only *apply* the terms of an existing consistent, but pragmatically constructed, controlled vocabulary to the particular documents it is their job to catalogue or index. Even this work is subjective enough that the lack of consistency among different indexers of the same documents is a significant topic of investigation in the literature of information theory. The vocabularies they apply are minutely itemized classification schemes and term-by-term lists of approved access points with their links. Three such vocabularies are very well known, almost universally applied, and described in a little detail in later sections of this chapter: the classification systems devised by Melvil Dewey and at the Library of Congress and the *Library of Congress Subject Headings* already mentioned. An offshoot of Dewey's classification scheme, the Universal Decimal Classification (UDC), is better known outside North America. A very recent word-list, the *Art and Architecture Thesaurus*, is more broadly applicable than its title suggests and is becoming widely admired and applied. There are hundreds of others, broader or narrower in scope, more current or more obsolete in application, better or poorer in quality, devised by individuals or by committees, published only once or frequently revised. Many reflect the indexing and arrangement of a particular coherent group of materials within the limited context of their intellectual content and the perceived needs of their specialized users.

Classification

The oldest type of controlled subject vocabulary by far is a classification scheme. In Dewey's scheme, the subject access point for baseball is the number **796.357**, an access point familiar to tens of thousands of Americans who use public and school libraries and who head directly to that numeric location in the shelf arrangement every spring.

The three types of controlled subject vocabulary described in the following sections use words to name a topic and arrange those words alphabetically. Classification is the type of controlled subject vocabulary which arranges topics according to how they are logically related rather than how they are verbally named. It places the aardvark closer to the zebra (because both are animals) than to the abacus.

The resulting arrangement is expressed as a *notation,* a numeric, alphabetic, or alphanumeric coding which makes it possible to arrange the classified (logical, systematic) sequence as easily as (indeed, usually more easily than) one can file subject access points in word form. The pattern of the notation which expresses its concept-arrangement differs for each classification scheme. To use examples from some schemes used in libraries, the dog, classified as a biological species, is designated **K[5791]** in the Colon Classification, **TUS** in Rider's International Classification, **QL795.D6** in the Library of Congress Classification, and **599.74442** in the Dewey Decimal Classification.

Centuries before anyone retrieved a document using a subject index consisting of words, people were devising classification schemes both to arrange physical documents in collections and to arrange their listings in bibliographic files. In most printed monographic bibliographies and in the print versions of a significant proportion of A&I publications, classification remains the most prominent method of subject identification, and only at the filing position of a classification notation is the full bibliographic information printed. A user may become familiar with the intellectual organization of such a bibliography, but few pay much attention to the actual notation applied. A formal notation, rather than simply numbering the logically organized citations in a single numeric sequence beginning with 1, is more common in an A&I publication where it serves to identify the same topic to searchers in each of many issues and cumulations. The specialist in international trade who frequently consults the *Index of Economic Articles . . .* or its digital form, EconLit, gets to know that the relevant section is the 410s and looks for that section without needing to consult the alphabetic word-index first (see figure 22), just as the baseball fan heads directly

---

Classification System

400 International Economics
        4000 General
            Most articles pertaining to the New International Economic Order are classified here.
    410 International Trade Theory
      411 International Trade Theory
        4110 General
            For theory of international investment see 4410; for balance of payments theory see 4312.
        4112 Theory of International Trade
        4113 Theory of Protection
            For theory of protection in relation to development see also 4114; for commercial policy see 4220.
        4114 Theory of International Trade and Economic Development
            For agriculture and development see also 7100; for multinationals and development see 4420; for international aid see 4430; for international investment see 4410.

FIGURE 22.   A small part of the pre-1994 classification scheme and notation from *Index of Economic Articles in Journals and Collective Volumes* (Nashville: American Economic Association) showing both the classified arrangement itself (expressed by both indentation and a hierarchically expressive notation) and links (expressed by cross-references in italics).

to 796.357 in the public library. Although the earliest interactive files tended not to provide access to a classification notation (if indeed one is used), such indexing is now more common.

With their different interests, viewpoints, purposes, and linguistic usages, different people who use the same language often name the same subject in different ways. It is only natural that they should also differ about what logical grouping best encompasses a particular topic. There are at least as many different classification schemes as there are different word-indexing vocabularies. As is true of the latter, most classification schemes are not ones, like Dewey's, which comprehend all of knowledge; they are ones covering a limited subject field. New ones are constantly being invented. Merely to put ideas into prose is to invent a classification scheme, a scheme whose notation is the table of contents of the resulting book or the captions of the article. The hardest part of writing anything is the usually lengthy process of deciding what is the best possible order of concepts and the best notation for that order, the latter being the chapter, section, and subsection numbering and captioning which clarify the flow of thought to the reader.

A classification scheme and a controlled vocabulary using words are not as different as might at first appear; they are mirror images of one another. The primary sequence of a word-based vocabulary is the verbal index to the classification scheme; the secondary structure of a good word-based vocabulary, its system of cross-reference links, is the primary structure of a classification scheme. Thus a classification scheme puts baseball near football by making their access points appear near each other in the prescribed sequence; in Dewey, 796.357 and 796.33 respectively, both of them part of the sequence sports—games—ball games—. . . . A verbal controlled vocabulary collocates baseball and football by making them common links with the same terms: sports, games, ball games, etc.

The difference between a classification scheme and a controlled vocabulary of words is very small indeed if *all*, not only the most obvious, indexing techniques of classification and of words are considered. Both classificatory and verbal aspects are necessary in either type of controlled vocabulary: a classification is less than fully effective if it lacks a good word-index, and a word-vocabulary of subjects is less than fully effective if it lacks a good classification scheme evident through in its linkages.

A searcher does not always have to attempt both methods of subject retrieval to arrive at the needed documents or information. If either a verbal or a logical search answers a particular need, it would be redundant to retrace one's steps and try the other technique as well. However, each can best supply a different type of the needed insight into subject relationships, and the two ideally work as a pair in the formulation of a search. Why else do librarians devote resources to maintaining two parallel subject-retrieval systems? If librarians are wasteful in doing this, are the commercial producers of classified bibliographic files also wasteful? Many A&I services, particularly in scientific fields, include some kind of logical classified approach among their options for searching even if it consists only of separate subfiles for the different logical parts of the whole field.

When a library maintained its files manually, one file was invariably the *shelf list* of records arranged in the order of the library's classification scheme. It was the means of keeping track of the call numbers assigned to avoid their duplication and of taking inventory before automation provided different methods. Through most of the twentieth century in North American libraries, the verbal approach was the more valued one for subject retrieval, so the shelf list was rarely located where the public could consult it.

In Europe, where closed-stack libraries and multilingual users are more common, classification has always served a more fundamental subject-retrieval function within the library's catalogue system. A shelf list there is often the basis of a full *classified catalogue,* a subject catalogue in which each of the multiple subject access points for an item is a classification notation, rather than a verbal subject heading or descriptor. One of these notations is identified as its shelf location. The links proper to any controlled vocabulary are also provided in a classified catalogue. In this way, classification for information and subject retrieval becomes separate from classification for physical shelving and document retrieval. As North American librarians return to a realization of the value of classification for retrieval, not just for physical shelving, almost every OPAC now permits a browse of items in the library's collection sequentially by call number; that is, in a classified sequence. The use of classification notation in the other techniques of automated information retrieval are also being newly explored.

The classification of publications for their arrangement on library shelves is probably still the most important subject-analysis technique to the user of a public or school library, where browsing satisfies so many needs. Many end-users in every type of library consult a verbal subject index in the OPAC primarily to get some call numbers where they can browse the classification sequence on the shelves. In larger academic libraries, classification as a basis for physical location is in decline. These libraries use storage facilities to solve space problems and turn to temporary listing instead of full cataloguing (including subject analysis) to avoid the cost of original cataloguing when a derived record is not immediately available for a

newly acquired item. In reducing dependence on classification as a
shelving device, such policies tend also to cause it to be overlooked
as a means of retrieving information from databases.

DDC and LCC notation both appear on a high proportion of Library of Congress records. There is no reason why a user should not
be able to browse or search for subject classes in an OPAC using these
or any other classificatory code already included (and therefore cost-
free to the library) in a downloaded record. Yet programming the
DBMS to index these "unused" fields is rare and many libraries even
eliminate them entirely when downloading records into the local
DBMS.

Classification by Discipline

Classifying *concepts* rather than *documents* reveals all the tensions between the philosopher and the practitioner of subject analysis. Defining what constitutes a subject raises a major one. A general (that
is, all-subject) classification must be equally impartial to every viewpoint toward a subject, a theoretical impossibility. The practical solution is normally to force every treatment of a subject into the
context of a discipline, that grouping of subjects typified by their
organization into the academic departments of a university.

There are many more specialized classification schemes than general ones. Those oriented to a single discipline avoid this problem,
but in a general discipline-oriented scheme, there is no location for
"the cat" as one subject. There is a place for the cat primarily as the
focus of art works; as a symbol in religious ritual; as a pet; as an
inspirer of poetry; as an amount of living (or dead) tissue, bones, etc.;
as a controller of rodents and other pests; or even as bystander at an
historical event.

Discipline orientation therefore causes difficulties in practical application. When assigning a notation to a particular document, the
cataloguer is forced by the scheme to decide which of these predominates in its viewpoint; in theory, it cannot provide a specific place for
the very general document, the "cat" book covering *all* the above
viewpoints. In practice, one concept-location emerges from among
them as the best one for a document of comprehensive scope. This
explains why the classification schemes most widespread in library
use are more suited to publications in the traditional academic dis-
ciplinary framework than to those written from many popular viewpoints, to subject-oriented visual materials, to archival materials, etc.
Finally, it explains the considerable problems for both the revision
and the application of classification occasioned by the increasingly
inter- and multi-disciplinary approach of academic writing. One

modern general classification, Brown's *Subject Classification,* claims to focus in principle on the subject rather than the discipline. It is being re-edited but has never gained much notice in application.

Dewey, LC, et al.

Devising an ad hoc classification scheme by which to organize some prose writing or a subject-specialized bibliography is commonplace. Devising a general scheme which arranges all of knowledge is among the most intimidating possible tasks for either a philosopher or a librarian; few will ever undertake it. Only two such schemes are now in widespread use in English-language libraries:

1) the Dewey Decimal Classification (DDC), devised by Melvil Dewey in 1876 for a college library and
2) the Library of Congress Classification (LCC), originally adapted from the *Expansive Classification* on which Cutter was still working at his death.

The Universal Decimal Classification (UDC) is an authorized adaptation of Dewey's, devised and maintained in sections more as a collection of specialist schemes than a unified general scheme. It is used more to classify bibliographic files than for library shelving and more outside the English-speaking community than in it. It exists in versions published in several languages; that a classified arrangement transcends the problems of language in subject analysis is significant in its propagation and maintenance.

Any topic can be assigned a notation within a general classification such as DDC and LCC. A topic need not be specifically named in the words of the published scheme in order to have its own proper place there, among all the relationships of a given field in the scheme's organization of knowledge. This makes classification a much more flexible tool in accommodating new concepts in their formative stages. A new concept can have no place in a vocabulary of subject words until it is definable as a term with equally definable word-links.

Despite their age, LCC and DDC are not antiquated. They are subject to continuous revision in the light of their practical use, an advantage they share with few other classification schemes. LCC owes its worldwide application to the same economic factor that made all Library of Congress services de facto standards: LCC notation appears on Library of Congress source records for derived cataloguing. DDC owes its long-standing popularity everywhere to the simplicity and memorability of its decimal notation and its easy-to-grasp primary division into just nine disciplines following an initial category, *Generalities.* (To the average member of the lay public, "Dewey" stands for everything a librarian does to organize both documents and information!)

In view of the entrenchment of DDC among American public, school, and at that time also college libraries, the Library of Congress began to add DDC numbers to its records in 1930 and now does so for a high proportion of what it catalogues. This makes the Library of Congress one of the biggest users of DDC. It was therefore no surprise that when the ability of the DDC copyright owners to finance further revision was threatened in the mid-1950s, the editorial office of DDC was transferred to, and is still at, the Library of Congress. Editorial policy decision on LCC revision is the sole responsibility of the Library of Congress, although it heeds the suggestions of other users. In the case of DDC, an international committee continues to govern revision policy under its present owner, OCLC.

The Controlled Subject Vocabulary Using Words

The focus of the remainder of this chapter is word-indexing, not classification, so for brevity, particularly in this section, the single word *vocabulary* stands for the heading of this section. The four functions of such a vocabulary are:

1) to standardize which of two (or more) synonyms to prefer as the access point for a given topic: **COURTSHIP** or **WOOING**?
2) to determine the preferred lead term, or access element, when a single topic can only be expressed as a multiword combination: **VENETIAN BLINDS** or **BLINDS, VENETIAN**?
3) to provide explicit links both among equivalent terms (**WOOING** *see* **COURTSHIP**) and among hierarchically and associatively related terms (**MATE SELECTION** *see also* **COURTSHIP**) and
4) to determine whether and how two or more conceptually separate topics should be linked in a single pre-coordinated access point: **ZEN BUDDHISM AND SCIENCE**.

Not every vocabulary accomplishes or even undertakes all four functions. The first is the most obvious one. It illustrates the very fine line between natural-language indexing and the use of a vocabulary. When writing abstracts of material in the same or related subject fields, an experienced abstractor tends to exercise this function without conscious attention to vocabulary control, without making any permanent record of the decisions taken, and without thinking of any of the other three functions described here. To think of the second function comes as naturally as thinking about which element of a personal or corporate name should be its access element. The third and fourth functions, linking and coordination, deal with the processes of logical arrangement described in the previous section on classification. The third function produces the syndetic catalogue described in Cutter's words at the beginning of this chapter. This is usually the most time-consuming function and, perhaps because of that, the one least well fulfilled in a poorer vocabulary.

Vocabularies fall into two major groups depending on whether or not the fourth function is undertaken at all: a list of *subject headings* includes pre-coordinated access points; a *thesaurus* does not. There follows a brief history of the three types of access point resulting from the application of a vocabulary and of their underlying theory. The practical application of each is described a little more fully later in the chapter, following an analysis of the user's approach to subject access.

Subject Headings

Jewett and Cutter were instrumental in devising a type of pre-coordinate vocabulary to index libraries' bibliographic records

1) to replace the previous style of permuted natural-language phrases for subject retrieval (because it produces more relevant and consistent results) and

2) to supplement the only controlled-vocabulary subject approach then prevalent, the classified catalogue described above (because it is more direct and therefore quicker to search).

Throughout this book, *access point* is preferred to the now obsolescent term *heading*, but the general (all-subject) vocabulary most widely used in the library world remains the *Library of Congress Subject Headings* (LCSH). The older term is therefore used in this book with specific reference to an LCSH access point. What characterizes this and all other vocabularies of this Cutter-based tradition is pre-coordination, as defined in chapter 4. Prior to the 1960s, almost all vocabularies, both general and specialized, were of this tradition because it best met the technical requirements of manual searching. The techniques and actual terms of LCSH were adopted early in this century by the emerging A&I services to index journal articles. They have also strongly influenced back-of-the-book indexing practice and vocabularies.

It is unlikely that any major new pre-coordinate vocabulary will ever be constructed now that interactive searching has found its technical match in the descriptors discussed in the next section. Nevertheless, LCSH remains the predominant subject vocabulary in library cataloguing. The reason is partly economic: the verbal subject access

points on Library of Congress records consist only of those authorized by LCSH. However imperfect, illogical, or inconsistent LCSH
may be—and it is all of these—it survived the transition to the interactive catalogue. It remains a practical user-friendly tool for general indexing purposes and for quickly and easily locating at least
something relevant to almost any request.

This most extensive vocabulary ever devised covers every subject
area and represents some ninety years of thoughtful and continuous
development, revision, and updating by an army of subject specialists.
This, perhaps even more than its use on Library of Congress catalogue
copy, explains its adoption or adaptation everywhere in the library
world where English is the working language and even elsewhere in
translation. At what expense would one redesign, much less reinvent,
this wheel? It became the model for almost every special-purpose vocabulary until the development of the thesaurus. One of these still in
active use is *Sears List of Subject Headings,* tailored to the collections
and users of smaller libraries. Vocabularies of its type continue to be
used for the manual searching of files such as the yellow pages of a
telephone directory; this structure also underlies the arrangement and
display of much natural-language back-of-the-book indexing.

The value of a pre-coordinate vocabulary is not limited to its efficiency as a manual way of joining the concepts **ZEN BUDDHISM**
and **SCIENCE** in order to find the few documents in a file in which
these two separate concepts are treated in conjunction with one
another. A deeper issue is how to determine when someone thinking and writing about these same two concepts has, in the process,
merged them into a single new subject, arising out of but no longer
integral to the two others, so that as a single subject, it requires different links in a vocabulary than those appropriate to its separated
parts. The potential for confusing the form of a pre-coordinate access
point and the reality of a concept is illustrated by changes made to a
now obsolete pattern naming ethnic groups and places anywhere:
ITALIANS IN THE UNITED STATES. Among other changes aimed
at making the parts of a coordination more recognizable by punctuation and coding, this was changed to **ITALIANS—UNITED STATES,**
but almost immediately, the linguistic implication was recognized:
these Italians are not really Americans! The current form **ITALIAN
AMERICANS** is not a pre-coordination of two concepts but a two-
word single concept.

As the model pre-coordinate vocabulary, LCSH leans in favour of
creating a new pre-coordinate subject heading combining concepts
previously accessible only separately as soon as there is some *literary
warrant* for it, that is, evidence of writing treating the combination as
a unit of thought. If this appears more a pragmatic than a theoretical

basis for action, it only emphasizes that LCSH is essentially a pragmatic vocabulary.

LCSH has proved extremely flexible, evolving through many changes in the actual terms used, the amount of pre-coordination incorporated into any one access point, the choice of access element whenever two or more words are involved, the syndetic structure, and other features. These changes have been occasioned by sociolinguistic fashions, changes in how concepts are treated in the actual books catalogued, and periodic re-evaluations of its effectiveness as an indexing vocabulary. A history of it distinguishes four stages in its development prior to the current updating project described later in this chapter, each characterized by a markedly different policy toward the choice and structure of its headings.[2] In its present form, LCSH is not inconsistent with post-coordinate searching. One may find it useful to compare two different pre-coordinations, whether manually or interactively. Nor does LCSH limit the application of headings to one per document: the intellectual content of any document may warrant several headings, each a pre-coordination of more than one concept. The use of index strings (see below) is the best of the three methods discussed here if one wishes to avoid post-coordination.

Descriptors

Post-coordination, which permits single words or terms to be combined in a particular search, is most effective when each access point expresses a single concept. A vocabulary designed for post-coordinate searching therefore tends to keep concepts which *can be* intellectually separate also separate for searching regardless of the existence of individual documents in which they are merged as a single topic. It is more concept-dependent and less document-dependent than a pre-coordinate vocabulary.

This kind of vocabulary was given the name *thesaurus* to distinguish it from a list of subject headings, not only because of its superficial similarity to the work of Roget. For that same reason, its originators did not want to call its individual access points *headings*. Early in the history of post-coordinate indexing, *uniterm* was used, clearly denoting that one term equals one concept. It is a shame it has disappeared from use. An access point in a thesaurus is now usually called a *descriptor* or, more vaguely, just a *term*. A multiword (but not multiconcept) descriptor is called a *compound term*. Punctuation, a characteristic part of pre-coordinate vocabularies, is avoided in descriptors partly because of the problems it causes in the context in which descriptors are primarily used: computer-based filing and searching (see chapter 9).

The thesaurus is as natural to interactive searching as is the subject-headings list to manual searching. Virtually all new vocabularies since 1960 are thesauri. Interactive searching began to have its effect on LCSH by the early 1980s. Since then, most of its headings containing grammatically linked pre-coordination have been separated into a term-plus-subdivision format for easier recognition of the separate parts in automated, and potentially post-coordinate, searching; for example, **ELECTRICITY ON SHIPS** became **SHIPS—ELECTRIC EQUIPMENT**. Beginning with its 11th (1988) edition, LCSH incorporates many external features of a thesaurus while not abandoning pre-coordination. These changes are discussed more fully below.

Index Strings

A subject heading or descriptor is established and put into a vocabulary because the content of some document to be catalogued or indexed calls for it. In the resulting catalogue or index, however, even a subject heading identifies the concept(s), not the document. Either of these two types of access point posits a subject and asks, "What documents concern themselves with this?" In contrast, the older style of rotated- or permuted-word natural-language access point in an index, examples of which appear on page 259, focuses on the individual document, saying "Here is what *this* document is about." In this sense, it is more completely pre-coordinated than a subject heading can be: it places each concept used as an access element (the filing element in an access point) in the precise context of the document which generated it. The modern term for a complete access point of this type—search term plus context—is *index string*. Wherever it is filed in the index or occurs as a hit in a search, it is displayed in full. This does not preclude the possibility of a single word or term alone expressing the whole subject and context of a document, for example, the one word **CHEMISTRY** as the entire index string for a general textbook on that topic. It also does not preclude the possibility of a computer-based search for any single word in a string.

In the mid-1960s, Derek Austin, at that time responsible for the subject indexing of the *British National Bibliography,* proposed a technique to automate its indexing. He wished to preserve the technique of one index string per document to be filed at different access locations but to achieve more intellectually coherent and meaningful results than are possible by a merely clerical rotation of natural-language words. In his system, the cataloguer

    1) composes a statement of the topical focus of the document in context, unrestricted to a list of authorized terms, but never-

theless aware of the need to retain consistency in terminology and

2) codes the parts of that statement based on their syntactic and semantic functions.

From the cataloguer's choice of words and codes, which constitute the basic index string, a computer program generates the actual access points for the document, adjusting the display of the entire string at each access point according to meaning and context.

Austin called his version of string indexing *PREserved-Context Indexing System* (PRECIS). It is the most sophisticated of the more than two dozen variants on computer-assisted string-indexing.[3] A string indexing system is controlled in the structure more than in the words comprising its access points. PRECIS does, however, incorporate a full system of linkages.

What string indexing does, and a system based on subject headings or descriptors cannot do, is to supply context to subject terms used as access points. Its intellectual advantage is therefore most obvious in the indexing of interdisciplinary writing. In an interactive search, where post-coordination can serve much the same function of combining concepts meaningfully, it is not so clearly superior. It serves best as the format of a good manual index, particularly a back-of-the-book index, whether produced manually or with computer assistance. Much less is heard of it for other purposes than a decade ago, when it was still considered superior to a vocabulary of traditional subject headings for pre-coordinate bibliographic searching.

Comparisons

A single-concept term, whether a single word (**COLLECTIBLES**; **POLLUTION**) or more than one (**BLACK HOLES**; **CREDIT CARDS**) can be a subject heading, a descriptor, an unusually short index string, or only some natural language waiting to be searched. It is the use of terms with respect to linkages, coordination, and context that betrays their origin either in natural language or in one of the three types of vocabulary described above. Differences emerge among the three types of vocabulary and how they are searched when what needs to be indexed or searched is a combination of concepts (the credit card versus electronic account debiting as a method of payment), a special aspect (credit card security), a relationship among two or more concepts (the influence of credit cards on the family budget), or parts of a concept (the magnetic banding of the credit card). To emphasize their distinguishing characteristics, access points appropriate to each system are shown below for the same hypothetical book or article, entitled *Language Study, Reading, and the Computer Lab in the American School.*

Subject headings (following the LCSH model):

1. LANGUAGE ARTS—UNITED STATES—COMPUTER-ASSISTED INSTRUCTION
2. READING—UNITED STATES—COMPUTER-ASSISTED INSTRUCTION

Descriptors (following the model of the Educational Resources Information Center's *Thesaurus of ERIC Descriptors*):

1. COMPUTER ASSISTED INSTRUCTION
2. LANGUAGE LABORATORIES
3. READING INSTRUCTION

Index-string access points (following the PRECIS model):

1. COMPUTER SYSTEMS. Applications in teaching reading skills to students in schools in the United States
2. READING SKILLS. Students. Schools. United States. Teaching. Applications of computer systems
3. SCHOOLS. UNITED STATES. Students. Reading skills. Teaching. Applications of computer systems
4. STUDENTS. SCHOOLS. UNITED STATES. Reading skills. Teaching. Applications of computer systems
5. TEACHING. READING SKILLS. STUDENTS. SCHOOLS. UNITED STATES. Applications of computer systems

Here, full capitals and upper/lower case distinguish what appears on the two lines of a typical PRECIS access point. Not all string-indexing applications make such distinctions based on syntax-based coding. Simpler systems ignore semantic and syntactic implications in displaying all terms following the access element in simple alphabetic order, for example:

> READING SKILLS. Applications of computer systems. Schools. Students. Teaching. United States
>
> STUDENTS. Applications of computer systems. Reading skills. Schools. Teaching. United States

The links or cross-references which form part of each of the three systems add many additional words from which the user might arrive at one or another of the access points listed above. It is, however, typical that, as seen here, a string-indexing system makes more access points searchable directly (not via a link) than is true in the other pre-coordinate system, that of subject headings.

Each of the two pre-coordinate systems, subject headings and string indexing, is or has been applied to books in all subject fields within a single database. The application of LCSH as seen on records originating at the Library of Congress serves as the model for how libraries everywhere use this vocabulary. Librarians' views of how string indexing works in practice are based on the British Library's application of PRECIS in its national bibliography from 1969 through 1993.

There is no such centralized model for the application of the third type of vocabulary. Thesauri and their descriptors are associated with a high degree of subject specialization, or at least close orientation to a discipline, in the databases of many different A&I services and special libraries. Not all of these organizations have published their thesauri, many of which are seen only in their application. The two largest published thesauri to date are one of the earliest of them all, the 1967 thesaurus of the Engineers Joint Council Library, and one of the most recent, the *Art and Architecture Thesaurus*. The latter is already becoming known as a thesaurus to serve as a model in the way LCSH serves as a model subject headings list or PRECIS as a model string-indexing system.

The number of vocabularies operational among the many databases a librarian routinely works with renders the present state of word-index searching very untidy. A professional searcher must at least distinguish when natural language must be relied upon and what are the peculiar features of each controlled vocabulary encountered. Each has strengths and weaknesses in answering particular types of query. Will there ever again be a time when subject concepts are accessible in most major indices and library catalogues using essentially the same vocabulary and search techniques, as was the case for a few decades earlier in this century? The computer, so good at enforcing standardization, has not brought stability in this respect.

THE TOPIC AND THE SEARCHER

This section deals with how those who apply controlled vocabularies attempt to match the mental processes involved in searching.

Point of View

Different people, both writers and searchers, perceive the same field in different ways, and their views change as they encounter and are influenced by one another's arguments, whether they support or challenge those arguments. Anyone who writes about a topic after making some detailed study of the views of others advances the process of

constructing and redefining both its terminology and its perceived relationships with other topics. It would simplify subject access greatly if
the question of what information a particular user wants and that of
what information a particular document contains could be considered
separately. They cannot. It is unfortunate that the cataloguer/indexer
and the reference librarian are usually two different persons, but in
whichever capacity, the librarian must judge what choice of terms and
which point of view might best help each individual inquirer: there is
no such thing as a generic search. Figure 23 suggests the relationships
among these players in the information game, and between each of
them and the bibliographic record which links them all.

To the historian, Hugh Trevor-Roper's book *The European Witch-
Craze of the 16th and 17th Centuries* is a social history of early modern
Europe. To a psychologist, it is about mass psychology. To a theologian,
it is a study of the perception of Satan. To a philosopher, it is about the
misapplication of theories of good and evil. To a jurist, it is about the
validity of evidence and confessions. To a sociologist, it is about the difference between the establishment and the outcast. Everyone agrees
that this is *not* a book about witches nor about how to practice witch-
craft, but is it clear (or does it matter) which of the above was the
author's primary point of view?

Is any particular cataloguer's perception of its central focus preferable to that of either the author or any given end-user who might
profit from reading the book? This suggests that matching an indexing vocabulary with an actual document is a "mission: impossible."
Inter-indexer inconsistency may be seen in many records produced
by cataloguers at the British Library and the Library of Congress for
the same publication using the same vocabularies: LCSH, DDC, and
LCC. Here are two:

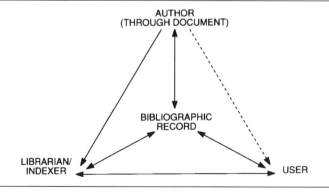

FIGURE 23.   The interrelationships among author, user, and librarian showing
the central importance of the bibliographic record.

Title: *Worlds of Reference*[4]

> LCSH applied by LC:
> 1. ENCYCLOPEDIAS AND DICTIONARIES—HISTORY
> 2. REFERENCE BOOKS—HISTORY

> LCSH applied by BL:
> INFORMATION STORAGE AND RETRIEVAL SYSTEMS
> DDC applied by LC: 030.9
> DDC applied by BL: 025.5209 (CIP, later revised to 001.5)
> LCC applied by LC: AE1
> LCC applied by BL: Z699

Title: *The Physical Environment at Work*

> LCSH applied by LC:
> 1. WORK ENVIRONMENT
> 2. HUMAN ENGINEERING

> LCSH applied by BL:
> 1. PSYCHOLOGY, INDUSTRIAL
> 2. INDUSTRIAL PRODUCTIVITY
> DDC applied by LC: 620.82
> DDC applied by BL: 658.314
> LCC applied by LC: T59.77
> LCC applied by BL: HF5548.8

In the case of differing LCSH applications, a user could in most cases get from an access point assigned by one cataloguer to that assigned by another through the linkages because the terms fall within the same more general discipline. However, points of view can be so radically different that no such linkage exists at any level.

To accept a subject request at face value is therefore rarely wise. A request for "information" about abortion is reasonable, but a request for "an article or a book" about all aspects of abortion is almost meaningless. Is there a single document covering any subject (even one less controversial than this) in all its ramifications and from all points of view? To the degree a subject request is less comprehensive in scope and context (physiological changes in hormone secretion following an abortion) the possibility is greater that something has been written with exactly the requested scope. Most documents deal with a topic each from a single point of view (techniques of, or the history of, abortion). The so-called textbook, such as this one, is the classic example of the attempt impartially to present all viewpoints. In a pre-coordinate vocabulary, it is common to use a subdivision to express a point of view: [TOPIC]—HISTORY; [TOPIC]—PSYCHOLOGICAL ASPECTS. Value judgements, however, are best left to the end-user to make: that a book favours or condemns abortion, or what a psychological aspect of abortion signifies, is not normally revealed in its subject access points.

Precision versus Recall

To the child taking a first conscious look up on a clear night outside, the whole of astronomy is the topic *the sky*—a children's book on the topic is both general and short. To the post-doctoral fellow investigating black holes, astronomy is a thousand separate topics so diverse that the general term is almost irrelevant except as the name of the department administering the fellowship. A general book on astronomy, however lengthy or excellent, is no longer of professional interest to this person. Between the two extremes, the lay adult of modest education may wish to find both a survey of the whole of astronomy and books with a detailed focus on a single astronomical phenomenon (eclipses), methodology for its study (spectrum analysis), or closely related topic (life on other planets).

The most desirable documents to retrieve in response to any request are those whose *primary* focus is the topic in question and which deal with that primary focus from a point of view relevant to the user's need: in Ranganathan's apt maxim, the right book for the right person at the right time. Does the right document exist? Yes: often. If the match is obvious, the end-user finds it in the bibliographic file or stacks without professional help. The person who wants *any* document (and preferably *only* one) about a topic also normally finds it unaided. This person is unlikely to be very critical about which one best suits the purpose and is best served by using a natural-language index if one is available, not wasting the effort to deal with a vocabulary.

At the other extreme, the user who wants *everything* bearing in any way on a topic is also rare. Every available technique of subject retrieval must be used in answering that type of request, because each uncovers something the others do not. What is intended (and probably never achieved) is an exhaustive subject bibliography compiled in a specific context and for a defined goal. That is the very purpose for which people compile monographic subject bibliographies.

The purpose of a library catalogue or A&I publication is different: they are expected to answer requests as yet undefined and even unpredictable. They analyze subject content more impartially. The person consulting a library catalogue or an A&I publication usually wants something between the quick fix and comprehensiveness: a high-quality selection of what is available within the scope of the collection or the bibliographic file consulted. It is precisely when nothing seems to meet this need exactly that professional help is called upon to identify a number of peripherally relevant documents, each of which answers part of the need. Phrasing this in technical terms, the user wants to recall as few documents as is consistent with a high degree of relevance in each of them.

To give someone investigating black holes a book on astronomy does *not* meet this criterion. It may represent low recall (one item), but it cannot be said to be highly relevant if only ten of its six hundred pages deal with black holes. Furthermore, a general book on astronomy is written at the level of a person wanting a survey of the field, not specialist information on any one part of it; thus its viewpoint also reduces its relevance for the black-hole specialist. If no documents are available whose primary focus is the black hole, the more general book represents the highest-recall/highest-relevance material available and may have to serve until interlibrary loan can come up with something more suitable. No-recall/no-relevance is probably not a concern as long as the collection has a general encyclopaedia, but each user establishes a minimum threshold of acceptability of what is offered.

Precision is a synonym for *relevance* in this context. The goal of every information-retrieval system is to be able to identify everything in the database *precisely* applicable to any given topic; that is, to maximize recall and precision (relevance) equally and not to enlarge or diminish either at the expense of the other. If documents are available which precisely match the request, the goal is to retrieve all of them. If no such document is available, the net must be cast more widely, but not so widely as to encompass much irrelevant information. In practice, higher recall (more documents retrieved) inevitably means lower precision (some of the retrieved documents are less than totally relevant). Conversely, higher precision (each retrieved document is central to the topic wanted) inevitably means lower recall. Concentrating on either is inevitably at the expense of the other, as acknowledged in the term *recall/precision balance*. Striking the best possible balance involves judgement, not measurement, as it is constantly adjusted in the course of a search. One of the chief objectives of a professional searcher is to determine, in a reference interview with the end-user, that precise compromise between recall and precision that suits the needs of a particular request.

What is closely relevant and what is only distantly relevant is for the individual searcher to determine. Satisfaction leads to termination of the search; dissatisfaction or a sense of incompletion should lead to a further attempt to improve the recall/precision balance through some adjustment of the search strategy. A user often becomes more aware of what is relevant only while engaged in discovering what exists, so expectations of a search expand or contract while it is in progress; not uncommonly the focus also shifts. The user cannot know, and even the librarian rarely finds out later, whether something better (or additional) exists but was completely missed in the search. When this happens, either the request-definition stage or the search stage of the retrieval system (or both) somehow failed.

It is much harder to determine and measure the failure rate than the satisfaction rate, but where this has been attempted, the failure rate is discouraging. Until it can be reduced, there is good reason to allow an inefficient redundancy in retrieval systems; for example, by letting both classification and word-indexing, both natural language and controlled vocabularies, and the personnel of different indexing services do what each can do best even with the same material.

Specificity

The quantity of the recall in a search is closely related to the size of the file consulted. The degree of precision possible is more closely affected by the choice of indexing terminology and its application to the particular documents indexed. So is ease of searching; no user wants to be shunted around a system of linkages. No matter how transparently a computer-based search can treat equivalents, direct access to the desired topic should be provided where the informed user first expects it. Precision is maximized when the scope of a document's intellectual content is exactly matched by the scope of the one or more subject access points assigned to it. Cutter took pains to distinguish his then novel system of word-indexing using specific, direct access points from the previous preference for contextualized index strings or classified indexing. As he put it, a book on the cat should be indexed under **CATS**, not under **MAMMALS** or **DOMESTIC ANIMALS**.

The specific approach requires many more distinctions than the beginner in subject retrieval might wish. Subtle differentiation of meaning is at the very core of intelligent communication, but what differentiation seems necessary is dependent on culture and context. The Inuktitut language has a score of different words for the various kinds of snow. If it lacks a generic word for the cold white stuff, no indexer should impose one on material written for these people as if their own distinctions were meaningless. Because English is an agglomeration of words from so many different cultural sources over so long a period, it may be the modern language richest in subtly different connotations, each separately indexable. A significant difference between **DECEPTION** and **FRAUD** may only be immediately evident to one trained in ethics or the law, but the layperson who happens upon one of these terms must be shown (by an associative link) that the other is also a valid access point for related material treated from another point of view.

Applying the principle of specificity is the key to controlling the recall/precision balance regardless of whether the index is to support general or specialist searching. The problem is to know how specific is specific enough for a given purpose. To stretch the astronomy example above to the breaking point, the child considers *sky* specific, but the specialist in black holes considers it so general as to be irrelevant.

To serve beginners in a field or those to whom the field is of only peripheral interest, a satisfactory indexing vocabulary for that field may contain, say, only a hundred terms other than names, each fairly broad. Provided they are well chosen, it should be possible to index any existing book, article, etc. in the field under one or another of the hundred. Thus music terms in a vocabulary designed for the retrieval of information about literature may be restricted to the level of **JAZZ** and **ROCK MUSIC**, allowing no more specific terms for the subgenres of either. Using this vocabulary, a book about the music of Jimi Hendrix shares the same access point as one about the music of Alanis Morissette. The average number of items listed under each of a smaller number of terms is higher, but this is no disadvantage if the collection as a whole is small and the anticipated requests are fairly general.

Precision is desirable in the abstract, but if the collection indexed contains little or nothing of a high degree of specificity or if its users typically ask more general questions, what has greater precision achieved? This is the reason why vocabularies containing only a fraction of the number in LCSH can still cover all of knowledge. The Sears List and the abridged version of Dewey's classification continue to be more useful vocabularies than LCSH and the full DDC in the smaller library because they serve adequate retrieval purposes with far less complexity and potential confusion to users and with lower cost of indexing. It is also the reason why a highly specific and detailed vocabulary for a specialized field includes some few very general access points for related fields in which the target collection and users will only have general material or questions.

The accepted method of increasing the precision of a word-indexing vocabulary is to add complete hierarchic levels of specificity. If **ROCK MUSIC** does not provide enough specificity for the content and the target users of what is to be indexed, then **ACID ROCK, CLASSIC ROCK, FOLK ROCK, RHYTHM AND BLUES, ALTERNATIVE ROCK**, etc. must be added consistently for an entire level of subgenres—not one at a time ad hoc. Books about the music of Hendrix and Morissette can then no longer be found near each other in the subject index. Cutter called this latter the *dictionary* approach because specific terms appear, as in a dictionary, with no intent to collocate those of related meaning. (In an only slightly different context, he used *dictionary catalogue* to describe a single alphabetic sequence of authors, titles, and subjects without regard to the differing functions of the three types of access point.) In the dictionary approach, it is up to the hierarchic links to group related terms at the beck of the searcher. The more levels of specificity are incorporated into a vocabulary, the more subtle the differences of meaning among its individual terms. It takes a more knowledgeable searcher to use a more specific vocabulary effectively.

A technique used in older manual subject indices to improve the recall/precision balance increases the specificity of an access point as a whole but is the verbal equivalent of classification. It groups the subparts of a broader topic together under a hierarchically superior term (**ROCK MUSIC—ACID ROCK; MINERALS—COAL**). An index with access points of this type is called *alphabetico-classified* and is an unabashed attempt to have one's cake and eat it too. It is not based on pre-coordination, since an access point of this type does not embody a relationship of two different topics. It names one concept in two of its hierarchic levels. The hierarchic links in a vocabulary now replace any advantage it ever had.

The most disputed issue in the history of indexing using words is whether a multiword single concept (compound term) is better filed under the specifying word or the classifying word, that is, **ELEC-TRONIC MUSIC** or **MUSIC, ELECTRONIC**. This is not the issue raised just above of alphabetico-classified indexing because it does not involve levels of a hierarchy explicitly. Classification underlies this issue but is only allowed to surface in practice when two (or more) words constitute the natural expression of the concept; in other words, **MUSIC, JAZZ** is not considered because almost nobody naturally calls it *jazz music*. When two words are the natural expression, making the second the access element looks rather like personal-name inversion to get the surname first. This is appealing when an adjective (the distinction) precedes a noun (the thing distinguished), as it usually does in English, because nouns are generally favoured as access points. It is even helpful to force the searcher to think a bit more about the intellectual organization of the topic, which is always desirable in principle.

In an interactive search, it is irrelevant whether the words of a single concept are keyed in direct or inverted order, provided the search is based on a controlled vocabulary and provided equivalence links effect an automatic switch to the preferred form. The issue of word-inversion is still, however, alive and disputed in back-of-the-book and other types of manual indices. There, the indexer should make an ad hoc judgement as to the degree to which a more classified approach in the index will help the searcher find what is dispersed in the text as a whole, or merely duplicate what can be found in a table of contents or the good systematic organization of the full work.

Because classification historically preceded specific-term indexing, an older word-index is much more likely to have evidences of it. For library cataloguing, Cutter began a century-long process of weaning alphabetic indexing away from the grouping function and toward the alphabetico-specific and direct-word-order approaches. He took into account the assumption that any desired grouping of related material is better accomplished by classification and the linkages built into a vocabulary. However, prior to the implementation of full automated authority control over the access points in a file, it remained awkward for users to take advantage of all the links provided, and occasional remnants of classification may still be found in LCSH. Removing the last of them is part of the current revision projects detailed more fully below.

Depth of Indexing

Subject headings in LCSH are based on the primary focuses of those documents-as-a-whole, typically monographic printed books, which the Library of Congress catalogues. A book's internal (back-of-the-book) index is expected to specify each concept, name, etc. treated significantly at the level of the book's separate paragraphs. The practical difference is clear: the same three-hundred-page book whose internal index identifies five hundred separate subjects is very likely to appear under only one or two subject headings in the subject index of a library's OPAC. The principle of specificity is adhered to in each case at the level of the defined unit of indexing. At one extreme, this level is the book as a whole; at the other, it is the individual paragraph or even sentence (automated keyword indexing of full text makes the level the single word). This does not mean that the same vocabulary cannot serve at both levels at which some measure of vocabulary control is exercised in the indexing, although parts of an additional level of specificity may occasionally have to be added when the basic terminology chosen is a bit too broad. LCSH is a very useful terminological aid even for essentially natural-language back-of-the-book indexing. What it does mean is that the required level of specificity must be consciously determined for, and consistently applied in, any indexing project be it ad hoc and single-purpose or as broad and timeless as the catalogue of a general library.

The typical A&I publication falls between the extremes of the library catalogue and the back-of-the-book index. It generally attempts subject indexing in greater depth than the former partly because journal articles and similar materials lack the equivalent of the book's internal index. The astrophysicist pursuing the topic of pressure broadening searches the A&I publication first because this topic is more likely to be the focus of a journal article than of an entire book. The internal index of a general astronomy text is a last resort because it is unlikely to reveal anything this person does not already know.

The indexing in some A&I publications, especially in the disciplines of science and technology, approaches the depth of back-of-the-book indexing, providing perhaps a dozen index terms for a brief but specialized article. This is generally because the many processes, materials, etc. named in articles in those disciplines must be individually retrievable, not because the A&I service tries to divide the concepts themselves as minutely as a back-of-the-book index would.

Names

Names of persons, corporate bodies, places, and works, established in the forms discussed in chapter 6, are the most highly specific of all index terms, since each names only one entity. With such names, neither recall, relevance, nor specificity is a major problem. Information retrieved about Alanis Morissette under her surname is of necessity totally relevant because *only* information about her as a person can appear there. This does not mean that her name should also be the index location for her musical style.

Because name indexing is so relatively simple and sure, indexers sometimes get carried away with it and index every available name whether it has any bearing on the topic in hand or is merely mentioned in passing as an example. Similarly, many a searcher seizes on a name in a query even when it is not at all representative of the conceptual focus needed. While names can be traps, they are an implicit or explicit part of every vocabulary.

APPLICATION OF DESCRIPTORS AND THESAURI

The thesaurus is historically the most recent type of vocabulary. Since it is composed primarily of single words, it appears superficially to be the most uncomplicated type of vocabulary; its use is also the easiest to describe. However, in the complexity of relationships it typically expresses, it is more sophisticated than any pre-coordinate vocabulary of the past. It is aptly named after Roget's eighteenth-century work whose primary purpose (in its original classified order) it imitates so closely. This purpose is to display relationships among single concepts. One therefore gets a clearer grasp of the conceptual relationships of the subject field covered from a thesaurus than from a pre-coordinate vocabulary, particularly if one can scan it in a printed form, not just a screenful at a time. Thesauri are generally constructed with the indexing of a particular collection of documents, and often the needs of a particular user group, in mind. However, the systematic analysis of concepts demanded by its rules of construction generally ensure that the thesaurus is somewhat more comprehensive than its immediate uses require.

A descriptor in a thesaurus may consist of one or more words, but it identifies only one concept. A qualifier may be necessary to specify a context for an inherently ambiguous term; for example, **DISTRACTORS (TESTS)**. This is not an attempt to impose or imply any context, point of view, or classificatory relationship. Nor does a descriptor imply any particular level or scope of treatment of that concept. The subject index at the back of a book is often composed of descriptors. If so, the access point **WOMEN—19, 74, 157** does not mean that the topic of women is treated generally, and reasonably completely, on each of the three cited pages. Far from it. The only implication is that there is *some* mention of the concept, in some depth or other, in some context or other, on each of those pages. It makes a difference to the user whether the reference is to the history of women's right to vote in the Netherlands, to women hippies in America in the 1960s, or to the incidence of throat cancer among Japanese women. Without a context, finding the isolated descriptor **WOMEN** can only result in frustratingly high recall and frustratingly low relevance, but in a back-of-the-book index, this context is normally provided by the very subject and point of view of the whole book, be it politics, sociology, or medicine. Furthermore, reference to the actual text of the book to ascertain the relevance of what is there is relatively easy, since the book and its internal index are a single physical unit. It requires no trip to the shelves, call-in from a storage facility, or interlibrary loan to see whether the index search is fruitful or not.

These are reasons why descriptors are useful in back-of-the-book indexing in specialized areas. However, their widespread use in the indexing of bibliographic files came only with the advent of the interactive file. Post-coordination is almost essential in a search to give a descriptor context and relevance. As many descriptors are applied to a document as are needed to encompass its principal focus, within any limits set by the indexing system. A document on the rehabilitation of patients with heart disease using massage therapy is indexed using separate descriptors for each of *rehabilitation, heart disease,* and *massage therapy.* It is probably undesirable to index the concept *patient* separately in this context since the more specific *rehabilitation* implies it.

Figure 24 illustrates the characteristic manner of displaying linkages in a thesaurus. The linkages consist of any scope notes (abbreviated *SN*) as well as what are traditionally called cross-references. The latter are indicated in the thesaurus using conventional codes. A term authorized for use as an access point is linked with one or more instances of:

1) a synonym; the code *Use for* (*UF* or, in an older convention, *x*) is followed by nonauthorized synonyms or other orthographic forms also in the thesaurus; at its own location in the alphabet, each of the latter is followed by the instruction *Use* (*U* or, in an older convention, *See*) and the authorized term(s)

2) a term in the same hierarchy of meaning but broader in extent and including the meaning of the starting-term, designated as *Broader Term* (*BT*)

3) a term in the same hierarchy of meaning, but narrower in extent and included in the meaning of the starting-term, designated *Narrower Term* (*NT* or, in an older convention, *See also*) and

4) a term closely related to the starting-term, but in a way which cannot be expressed hierarchically, designated as *Related Term* (*RT* or, in an older convention, *See also*).

LANGUAGE PLANNING   *Aug. 1969*

SN Planned language change directed toward improving the utility of a language or increasing its use in a given country or region

NT Language Standardization

BT Planning
    Sociolinguistics

RT Bilingual Education
    Bilingualism
    Educational Policy
    Immersion Programs
    Language
    Language Attitudes
    Language Maintenance
    Language of Instruction
    Language Usage
    Languages
    Multilingualism
    National Norms
    National Programs
    Official Languages
    Second Languages
    Sociolinguistics

Language planning *(May subd Geog)*
    [P40.5.L35]

Here are entered works on planned language change directed towards improving communication within a society. Works on government language policy are entered under Language policy.

UF Language and languages—Planning
    Planned language change

BT Sociolinguistics

NT Language policy
    Languages, Artificial
    Standard Language

FIGURE 24.   The same access point as shown in two vocabularies: on the left, *Thesaurus of ERIC Descriptors,* 13th ed. (Phoenix: Oryx, 1995); on the right, LCSH, 19th ed., 1996. The linkage structure and its display are the same, but the relationships of the concept are viewed somewhat differently, distinguishing the specialist's approach from that of the generalist. LCSH's adoption of thesaural display conventions is discussed in the section on that system below.

The first is the equivalence linkage; the second and third, the hierarchic; the last, the associative. Close attention to logical rules is required to create and display the syndetic structure described by Cutter at the beginning of this chapter. The enunciation of these rules in the form of standards is cited in note 3 to chapter 3. Using the terminology introduced there, the first linkage expresses the equivalence relationship; the second and third, the hierarchic relationship; and the fourth, the associative relationship. A scope note usually expresses one or more associative relationships in prose and with more explanation than a simple enumeration of terms allows. The hierarchic relationship is normally expressed at only one level higher, and one lower, than the starting (filing) term.

The two terms of an equivalence relationship need not have precisely the same meaning: **PERCUSSION BANDS** *Use* **RHYTHM BANDS AND ORCHESTRAS** only means that for practical purposes, the indexer has decided to locate everything connoted by either of the two terms under one access point. This may be because the material being indexed does not make the distinction clear or because the index is for a group of users to whom the distinction, although real, is irrelevant. These are called *quasi-synonyms*.

It has become common, although not universal, practice for a thesaurus to display its terms in at least two ways identified below, additional to the basic alphabetic display illustrated in figure 24.

1) Not every word of a multiword term forms part of the syndetic structure. To avoid cluttering the basic alphabetic display of terms with references such as **Relationship, Peer** *Use* **Peer Relationship**, many thesauri include a KWIC index, sometimes called a *Rotated Keyword Display,* to show every significant word in the thesaurus in a single alphabet.

2) Since the hierarchic relationships are shown minimally in the basic list (that is, at only one level higher and/or one level lower), a display of *all* the hierarchic links is useful. Cutter described this as a "synoptical table of subjects" but advised against it because of the "immense labor" involved.[5] The labour is no longer so immense because of the computer.

Two forms of what Cutter envisaged are now common in thesauri:

1) a list of *Descriptor Groups,* in which each term in the thesaurus is listed as part of a broader class of concepts, the latter arranged either alphabetically or in an explicitly classified order

2) a *Hierarchic Term Display,* in which the complete hierarchy of *BTs* and *NTs* associated with each term at every level is shown in association with that term; the term highest in the hierarchy is sometimes designed the *TT,* or Top Term.

In addition, one occasionally finds a thesaurus with a graphic, or nonlinear, display of the relationships among its terms.

APPLICATION OF INDEX STRINGS

An index string is called that because it can be a pre-coordination of all the major concepts in the content of a document: **POLLINATION. CROPS. BEES.** By convention, dashes are not used in the display of an index string because the succession of its parts does not necessarily represent subdivision of concepts, only their juxtaposition. A string is of particular value in manual display and searching because in giving the entire substantial context of the document, it can bypass a need to locate and look at the rest of the record in another part of a file. Since the string is intended to indicate the subject focus of a document precisely, the amount of pre-coordination is determined by the document indexed, not by an external vocabulary such as LCSH. The string is very user-friendly. Since it is displayed as a whole under each of its significant elements, the user is not much troubled with cross-references. This may be seen in the example on page 278, which gives two LCSH access points, but five derived from an index string for the same hypothetical document.

The larger number of access points typically generated from a string is one reason why string indexing can concentrate less on the control of single vocabulary terms than either a thesaurus or a list of subject headings. The focus of the indexer's judgement is rather the *structure* of the resulting access points. As with LCSH, there is only one "correct" sequence of the remaining elements in the string following each access element. In PRECIS, the most complex of the string-indexing systems, only the sequence whose syntax is the most meaningful is generated by the computer program's interpretation of the codes (called operators) input by the indexer. For example, the following access point is *not* produced for the hypothetical book in the above example because it does not make sense, a decision implicit in how the string was coded:

> STUDENTS. TEACHING. APPLICATIONS OF
> COMPUTER SYSTEMS. SCHOOLS. READING SKILLS.
> UNITED STATES

The full impact of this, perhaps more than of other examples in this chapter, is only evident when it is seen in the context of hundreds of other access points with the same lead term in an actual string index.

Since string indexing typically provides more access points for direct retrieval, rather than two-step retrieval using cross-references and coordinations, PRECIS was proposed more than once in the 1970s as a replacement for LCSH in manual library catalogues on cards or fiche. However, interactive searching using keywords and boolean logic overtook PRECIS: it is no longer used even in the BNB, where it originated. String indexing remains a prominent method primarily in back-of-the-book indexing. Its lasting benefit has been to introduce intellectual discipline into the linguistic analysis of subject statements and access points. Theories of indexing and classification have always paid attention to the differentiation of action, purpose, material, agent, etc. in the creation of access points. Derek Austin's successful programming of these relationships as codes for the computer manipulation of indexing terms has been an important part of the theory of subject retrieval.

APPLICATION OF SUBJECT HEADINGS (LCSH)

People who routinely use boolean logic and keywords in post-coordinate interactive searching are not only still familiar with the century-old pre-coordinate system of subject access represented by LCSH, they search its access points using those modern techniques as well as in the way it was originally intended to be searched. LCSH is the cumulation of currently authorized forms of all the subject headings applied to bibliographic records by or under the authorization of the Library of Congress since 1898 and all the currently valid links among them. Its continued importance, as well as the variety of access-point types and structures included in it, demand a rather lengthy description of its essential features. Even those which have been rendered irrelevant in interactive searching are still embodied in a great many past and present manual files and in the printed version of LCSH, widely consulted independently of or in conjunction with interactive searching.

That LCSH *permits* pre-coordination does not mean that every access point it authorizes actually combines several concepts; only some do. LCSH presents a pre-coordination in a number of ways, using:

1) an adjective-noun combination in either word-order: **PAPER WORK; ADVERTISING, MAGAZINE**
2) a compound: **LOCKS AND KEYS; CHRISTIANITY AND INTERNATIONAL AFFAIRS**
3) a phrase: **INCENTIVES IN INDUSTRY; EMPLOYEES, DISMISSAL OF**
4) a dash-subdivision: **WATER—FLUORIDATION; BIBLIOGRAPHY—DATABASES**

It cannot, however, be assumed that every access point incorporating both an adjective and a noun, a conjunction or preposition, a subdivision, etc. is a pre-coordination. Each of the following is a single indexable concept, not one that could be readily divided into separate concepts for post-coordination: **DELEGATED LEGISLATION; CEREALS, PREPARED; THOUGHT AND THINKING; DIVISION OF LABOR; OPERA—SOCIAL ASPECTS**. A parenthetical qualifier (**SEX (PSYCHOLOGY)**) should not represent a second topic any more than it does in a thesaurus, but in the manner in which LCSH is applied to particular documents, it sometimes seems to.

A dash (*never* a hyphen) is the most typical signal of pre-coordination. In addition to indicating the pre-coordination of separate topics (**LIBRARIES—AUTOMATION**), a dash may show that a topic is being pre-coordinated with:

1) a place: **ARCHITECTURE—CANADA; CANADA—ENGLISH-FRENCH RELATIONS**
2) an intended audience: **DOGS—JUVENILE LITERATURE** or
3) a form: **LITERATURE—BIBLIOGRAPHY; CHEMISTRY—CONGRESSES**

The use of place names in LCSH is discussed later in this section. Considerations of document-form and audience transcend types of vocabulary and are treated at the end of this chapter, but the mingling of form and audience terms with concept terms can cause ambiguity: does **CATALOGING—PERIODICALS** apply to a book about how to catalogue a periodical or to a periodical about cataloguing? The same access point cannot serve for both.

Creating New Subject Headings

The treatment of two separable concepts within the same work results in the application of two subject headings. When do two such concepts, treated in combination, merge into a single new concept? This is a basic problem of any pre-coordinate vocabulary and one faced daily by cataloguers at the Library of Congress. Neither pre-coordination nor literary warrant implies that one single subject heading must exist or be created precisely to fit the topical scope of each work catalogued; that remains a primary distinction between a pre-coordinate vocabulary and an index string. The book *The Ethnic Origins of Nations* was judged still to deal with two separate concepts in relationship to one another, and the separate subject headings **NATIONALISM** and **ETHNICITY** were assigned to it.

The source of a new pre-coordinate subject heading is that work which finally convinces the cataloguer that topics once written about only in relationship to one another have merged into a unity. The wording of a title or subtitle may provide the final evidence needed. For example, the access point **FRAIL ELDERLY** was created on August 11, 1989, for the book *Aging in Place: Supporting the Frail Elderly in Residential Environments* because that single new topic was deemed to have emerged from its origins in what would previously have been expressed in the two separate access points (1) **AGED** and (2) **HANDICAPPED**.

Pre-coordinating **COAL MINES AND MINING—DUST CONTROL—WATER INFUSION** may appear to go too far toward identifying a single document (or extremely few of them even in a highly specialized collection). In doing so, it hides some of its concepts in a welter of links which a user may not track down, not realizing they could reveal a useful result. The interdisciplinary nature of so much recent writing puts strain both on the process of creating new pre-coordinations and on the process of deciding how many separable topics a book treats. What may seem like hair-splitting and subjective judgements is nonetheless essential to the nature of a pre-coordinate vocabulary.

Building Blocks: Free-Floating Subdivisions and Multiples

If LCSH authorizes the pre-coordination of one topic with the subheading —ACCOUNTING or of one place with the subheading —FOREIGN RELATIONS, corresponding pre-coordinations in the same forms must obviously be permissible with many, if not all, other topics and places. The printed LCSH has never listed separately every such authorized pre-coordination. To do so would multiply the size of the print version, already ten thousand columns, and make it even more intimidating to end-users who profit most from consulting it in order to prepare a search strategy. It would also make the interactive version unnecessarily unwieldy by requiring many screens for the display of a single lead term with all its subdivisions, however predictable. This is already a considerable visual problem when users browse a library catalogue's subject index on an OPAC, particularly one which suppresses punctuation in browse lists.

A term authorized as a subheading with many lead terms is called a *free-floating subdivision;* its uses are closely controlled. A slightly more complex application of the building-block principle is shown in *multiples:* the pattern shown as **ARTS, AMERICAN [FRENCH, etc.] —IRANIAN [etc.] INFLUENCES** authorizes **ARTS, YUGOSLAV—JAPANESE INFLUENCES**. Instruction on the correct application of each different type of building-block is part of LCSH but perhaps not always where a cataloguer or searcher would first think to look for it.

A *see also . . . (SA)* note appears at some headings to establish and explain the pattern. All these instructions are detailed and regularly updated in the Library of Congress *Subject Cataloging Manual: Subject Headings;* a separate listing of free-floating subdivisions is now published annually.[6] Thus a new (that is, previously unused) access point may be created without an explicit change in LCSH and without reference to a Library of Congress record or cataloguer. Cataloguers elsewhere, however, often prefer to wait until evidence of what they wish to do appears on a Library of Congress record: there are pitfalls in creating a new access point solo from generalized instructions.

Place

The rules in AACR, discussed in chapter 6, for establishing place names do not adequately govern the naming of a geographic unit such as a metropolitan or suburban area, or a land or water feature, coastal area, etc. which crosses jurisdictional boundaries. Such an area may have legally defined boundaries but often does not; it is not itself a jurisdiction, and its extent and nature may be quite vague in the public mind. One does not find "Pacific Northwest" named in gazetteers and atlases, the basic reference sources for establishing place names as access points. Yet many works are *about* this rather vague territory, requiring subject access points. One author treats the Pacific Northwest as solely the states of Washington and Oregon; another includes Idaho and part of a different country: southwestern British Columbia. Yet another takes in Alaska. Should the same subject access point be applied to all three? No published vocabulary can cover every such area in its decisions. Cataloguers tend to use their own judgement in naming local areas but await Library of Congress decisions on others.

Geographic space is treated in documents as either (1) a topic whose focus is a jurisdiction or some vaguer location as in the previous paragraph or (2) a qualifier of a nongeographic topic. In LCSH, either of these uses of a place name calls for its pre-coordination with a topic, with another place name, with a form, with a corporate-name subdivision, or even with several of these. A place name is rarely used alone as an access point in a library catalogue governed by AACR and LCSH. It may seem self-evident that some such pre-coordinations are more likely to be approached by a searcher through the place element (JAPAN—SOCIAL LIFE AND CUSTOMS) while others are more likely to be sought under the topical element (BUDDHISM—JAPAN). Cutter found it so hard to define the dividing principle that he felt each such pre-coordination *should* be filed under *both* elements;

yet he admitted that in practice, a choice must be made between them as the one alphabetic location of the pre-coordinate access point.[7]

Equivalence cross-references are the obvious solution, but in any larger catalogue, impossible to maintain separately for the hundreds of localities in conjunction with which a single topic might be treated! Searchers had to be trained to perceive the difference between [PLACE]—[TOPIC] and [TOPIC]—[PLACE], however arbitrary it might seem at times, largely without cross-references. This remains a major problem in any manual file. A place name is so important in access that in the digital formats for both name and subject access points, it is coded so that it can be searched separately whenever it occurs along with other elements. Cutter's concern over the alphabetic file location of an access point involving a place name is therefore obsolete in respect of interactive searching in which elements selected by the searcher are post-coordinated using boolean operators. However, the searcher who is merely scanning a browse-list of subject access points, usually many screensful under the same main heading when place subdivisions are present, is at the mercy of an adequate supply of links.

A related issue in pre-coordination involving place names also defeated every attempt to resolve it for the manual file. It, too, is no longer a matter of any consequence when the separately coded place name is post-coordinated with the topic using a boolean operator in an interactive search. However, when a searcher scans a browse-list of subject access points in an LCSH-based subject index of a library catalogue, the order will still be that determined by the following discussion. Contrary to the situation in the previous paragraph, one cannot expect any links to help. This issue involves the use of a geographic name which is both (1) a *sub*division within an access point, following a dash, and (2) at a level of jurisdiction below the national level. It is illustrated in two different access points:

BULLFIGHTS—SPAIN—BURGOS
BULLFIGHTS—BURGOS (SPAIN)

The former pattern displays all material about bullfights in Spanish localities together, with a document about bullfights in all of Spain appearing at **BULLFIGHTS—SPAIN**, immediately followed by treatments in specific places in the country (alphabetically subdivided by the city or other local place name). All of this is kept separate from material about bullfights in France, Mexico, Portugal, etc. In LCSH this is called *indirect subdivision*. The latter pattern subarranges everything about bullfights strictly alphabetically according to

the direct name of the place involved, from the principality of An-
dorra through the city of Burgos, the province of Chihuahua, the
country France, and on to Z regardless of either geographic locality
or level of jurisdiction. This is called *direct subdivision*. If the current
ALA Filing Rules described in chapter 9 are the method of file arrangement, subdivisions other than geographic names also intrude
into this sequence, for example, BULLFIGHTS—BIBLIOGRAPHY.

In the basic [PLACE]—[TOPIC] issue raised first, the Library of
Congress adopted a stance early and applied it quite consistently
from then on. In this latter issue, the Library's policy was flip-flopped
several times over the century. At one time or another, every possible
variation short of applying the random whim of the individual cataloguer ad hoc was tried. The present policy of indirect geographic
subdivision has recently been strengthened with the dropping of a
long-standing major exception preserving direct subdivision for New
York City. The indirect subdivision begins with the name of the country when a lower-level place is to be specified *except* in the case of
provinces of Canada, states of the United States, and similar units of
a few other specified countries where the highest named unit in the
subdivision is not the country but the province, state, etc. If the city
of London, Connecticut, ever held a bullfight, its documentation
would be found at BULLFIGHTS—CONNECTICUT—LONDON.

Pre-Coordination and the Searcher

A common complaint of end-users about pre-coordinate subject access points is well illustrated by a very reasonable query: "Have you
a list of the Canadian colleges where a wheelchair-bound student can
be relatively mobile?" How does one arrive at the tortured but LCSH-
authorized UNIVERSITIES AND COLLEGES—CANADA—BUILD-
INGS—ACCESS FOR THE PHYSICALLY HANDICAPPED—
DIRECTORIES which precisely answers the query? This pre-
coordination consists of three concept-segments, one place-segment,
and one form-segment; two of the concept-segments are themselves
pre-coordinations. The answer is that nobody, end-user or librarian,
finds it unaided. In a manual file, one is led to it by following up more
than one LCSH link. Skilled use of the syndetic structure actually leads
to this access point from at least a dozen different starting-points,
although the route is often less than clear. Locating it in an interactive
search by using keywords and a boolean operator is at least faster for
most people; a librarian probably now finds this a very simple search.

When a user searches it by its single words, LCSH becomes in
effect a series of single-word descriptors devoid of the control exercised over access points as wholes. One can locate SCIENCE as a

one-word access point, as the first word in **SCIENCE MUSEUMS**, as a word other than the first in **WOMEN IN SCIENCE**, or as a word in a subdivision: **DEAF—EDUCATION—SCIENCE; CLASSIFICA-TION—BOOKS—SCIENCE FICTION.** Adding the truncation feature, probably unwisely, one can even retrieve **SOCIAL SCIENCES!** This is a misuse of pre-coordinate access points which have been carefully constructed within a context, not independently. The last two examples above do not even relate to the discipline of science. A single-word search done with care after analyzing the topic(s) to be searched and identifying the relevant LCSH building blocks can be both effective and efficient, but in principle, it is not an appropriate technique for high-recall, high-precision results using this kind of vocabulary.

On page 278 appears an example where two LCSH-authorized subject headings are applied to a hypothetical book:

1) **LANGUAGE ARTS—UNITED STATES—COMPUTER-ASSISTED INSTRUCTION** and
2) **READING—UNITED STATES—COMPUTER-ASSISTED INSTRUCTION**

Each happens to have three components, but among the six are only four *different* ones: the other two appear in each of the two subject headings. The pre-coordinate nature of LCSH makes such a situation not only possible but even probable when more than one heading is applied to the same item. When subject headings are searched interactively on a segment-by-segment or even word-by-word basis, the DBMS generally does not show multiple hits for the same item, but this is a further reminder that pre-coordinate subject headings were not invented with their separation into component parts in mind.

The cataloguer-librarian is also a user of LCSH, if from the opposite point of view from the end-user. Some problems encountered in using its free-floating subdivisions and multiples as building blocks are mentioned above. Links in a thesaurus need only relate the meanings of single-concept terms to one another. In a pre-coordinate vocabulary, they bear the additional burden of helping to indicate how the terms are to be correctly assembled as building blocks. The **A B C D** example on page 142 shows that the five separate segments of which the example on the previous page is composed can be assembled in no fewer than one hundred twenty different ways. If *college, handicapped,* or *physically handicapped* (none of which occurs at the beginning of a segment) was added, the number of possible permutations would multiply! Yet only *one* of these many possibilities is correct; any other is a misapplication of LCSH and would be of little or no use to a searcher because the whole syndetic structure of the list is designed to lead only to correctly assembled pre-coordinations.

Changes in LCSH

LCSH has been in a state of constant, even hourly, change since the day it was started almost a century ago. It did not arrive then from heaven fully formed; the ten millionth book to which it is applied has as much impact on it as the first book did. Every quarterly issue of *Cataloging Service Bulletin* details numerous additions and revisions. During the past decade, two different initiatives in its continuing development are resulting in what are probably the most radical changes in its history. The first has less outwardly noticeable effects. For most of its history, the Library of Congress treated LCSH as its own not only to make but to use. If other libraries wished to use it too, they must recognize that it was developed out of and for users of a national research collection of scholarly materials.

The Library of Congress now delegates some subject, as well as name, authority work to other members of the Program for Cooperative Cataloging mentioned in chapter 5. It also invites suggestions by others for additions and changes "in order to build a subject authority file that will be useful to other libraries receiving materials not acquired by LC or cataloging items at a depth not practiced by the Library of Congress."[8] Incorporating new headings for this purpose will make LCSH increasingly like most thesauri in being less closely linked to a particular collection. This initiative is not as new as its publicity suggests: since the early 1970s, Sanford Berman's ceaseless and sometimes intemperate prodding in favour of more socially acceptable terminology and the quicker inclusion of new popular terms has been instrumental in effecting many changes in the wording of headings.

The second initiative for change has the same ultimate goal but is a much more radical one. It began with a change in the very structure of the cross-reference links. Users of OPACs had long treated LCSH headings as if their separate words and subdivisions were descriptors in thesauri; that is, single-concept terms for post-coordination in an interactive search. LCSH now acknowledges and assists this type of use. The resulting changes had to await the ability of both the Library of Congress and other libraries to make changes in their files by computer; manual revision of a catalogue on this scale was never practicable. In 1985, linkages began to be established and coded according to the thesaurus conventions described earlier in this chapter in the most thorough and highly visible one-time restructuring of LCSH ever undertaken. The fact that the original links were not always logically developed left much clean-up to be done after the initial automated data conversion.

Following this, a re-examination of the system of subdivision was initiated in 1990. Its goal is simplification of the building-block technique of constructing headings. Some of the subtlety of meaning and distinction possible in the more complex headings and patterns of the past may be lost, but so will fewer searchers be lost as they pick their way through the new simpler structures. One visible result is an increase in the use of free-floating subdivisions; for example, **BASE-BALL MANAGERS** has become **BASEBALL—MANAGERS** and, with rather more changes of actual wording, **HISTORY, COMIC, SATIRICAL, ETC.** has become **WORLD HISTORY—HUMOR**.

WHICH SYSTEM?

Manual bibliographic files, especially large ones and ones designed to be kept current with additions, are vanishing but the techniques used to search them are not. Some have been adjusted to the needs of interactive searching; in any case, a librarian must still be familiar with how to search the remaining manual files most effectively. It is clearly impracticable to assign terms from all four types of controlled vocabulary (classification, subject headings, descriptors, and an index string) to each document even if in many cases these would be almost identical. Which of these is capable of providing the best indexing in a given situation is rarely obvious. The best use of natural language is much more obvious: it is usually most effective in locating material in a new or rapidly changing field because the leading edge of novelty is expressed in titles, and also because what the novelty is called may be unstable over the initial period of interest in it. Additions and changes in a controlled vocabulary are eventually necessary, but must be made cautiously because all the existing linkages are potentially affected. It is difficult to make good judgements for the long term when the relationships of a new topic to its own and other fields are just being developed by its investigators.

In North America, classification is often too readily dismissed from consideration, and keyword searching of anything that comes to mind, the words joined simply with boolean *AND*, is too easily accepted as a scientific search strategy just because it is necessarily computer-based. Each of the four types of controlled vocabulary described in this chapter should be able to deliver good recall with good relevance provided the person who applies it, whether to index or to search,

1) engages the vocabulary's complete syndetic (concept-linking) apparatus
2) is competent in the subject field(s) in question and
3) has enough technical skill to master the search system, whether manual or interactive.

Few have dared to test the effectiveness of the four systems as such in controlled experiments because of the subjectivity of the variables.

Each will probably remain entrenched in the areas where it currently dominates, although rather less is heard of string indexing now that the *British National Bibliography* no longer uses PRECIS.

End-users tend to be less skilled in search techniques, whether manual or automated, than librarians, while the latter tend to be less familiar with specialized subject areas than end-users. The pre-coordination built into subject headings, index strings, and classification schemes is extremely user-friendly to the searcher who finds it hard to define what is wanted in terms of isolated descriptors. It may be harder to locate a relevant pre-coordinate access point but once it is found, directly or through links, the searcher has a sense of success unmatched in a post-coordinate system where doubt lingers about the utility of additional term-matching. Post-coordination may be a valuable tool in an interactive search but is no panacea. Other things being equal, it takes more prior knowledge of the topic being searched and more technical skill to get good results from a search involving post-coordination than from one based on pre-coordinate access points.

SUBJECT, FORM, AUDIENCE

Thus far in this chapter, it has generally been assumed that a controlled subject vocabulary is only used to identify what a document is *about*. If a user wants a literary critique *about* nineteenth-century children's fantasy, the search involves a particular creative form written at a particular time for a particular audience. Someone who wants to read a nineteenth-century children's fantasy may or may not care what it is *about,* be it magic mushrooms, life on the moon, or dwarves. If the library has a fantasy involving mushrooms (perhaps by Lewis Carroll?), is **MUSHROOMS** a good subject access point for it? This example illustrates the difference between access points for concepts/subjects/topics and those for form/audience. It also illustrates that both are needed in an indexing vocabulary. In the convention of the library catalogue, the latter are part of a subject vocabulary because they are most often thought of in connection with a subject search: a dictionary of the French language; a collection of interviews on abortion directed at teenagers. Whole library collections are divided on the basis of audience (the children's, young people's, and popular reading collections) and on the basis of form (the periodicals and government publications collections). There is increasing recognition of the value of "subject" access to fiction.

In a pre-coordinate vocabulary, a form/audience term appears generally as a free-floating subdivision in a list of subject headings. In a classification scheme, it appears as a separate but secondary component of the notation. It is rarely the primary access element. However, it sometimes takes precedence: both DDC and LCC prefer the classification of all bibliographies together, subdivided by the topics of the individual ones, rather than vice-versa. For a nonverbal creative work such as a musical composition, a form may be the only possible access point: LCSH provides a form heading **SYMPHONIES** for scores and recordings of musical compositions of this genre as well as a subject heading **SYMPHONY** for works about this musical form.

CHANGE

Much appears in earlier sections of this chapter on changes in the structure of controlled vocabularies, particularly as occasioned by automation. Here, the focus is on changes in the way people, both cataloguers and searchers, view the concepts involved, not the changes in vocabularies through which they are indexed. Vocabularies change with fashions in language; changing from *moving pictures* to *motion pictures* involves little more than altering an equivalence link. To accommodate updated perceptions of existing topics may involve more. When *domestic economy* became *family and nutritional science* after pausing along the way under the guise of *home economics*, the field itself changed radically.

Since they deal with the most current material, indexers in the A&I services face additions, name changes, and shifts in meaning first; however, they are generally less concerned than the reference librarian about relating newer material to older. It is a major problem for librarians to decide how to deal with older material. Should what was written in the 1950s on information retrieval remain under the obsolescent access point **DOCUMENTATION** as a signal of the period and context in which it was written? Should older material on bibliographic automation remain classified with library administration? Is it reasonable to add to the existing grouping of material under **COMMUNISM** after the events of 1989–1990? Locating information in a classification scheme, but from newly emerging points of view, on topics such as political ideologies of the right and left, sexual mores, and environmental concerns is skewed by what many consider to be outdated juxtapositions embedded in the structure of existing schemes such as DDC and LCC. There is no simple answer to any of these concerns. The interests of users who want only a present-day perspective will always be in conflict with the interests of those interested in historical antecedents. Archivists do their subject indexing in the context of the period when the documents were generated, not in that of the period when they are presumably going to be used. There is much to be said for removing from a library's subject catalogue the records for any material more than a generation old and letting footnotes and other such citations guide readers to the older material in a more appropriate subject context. As for shelf classification, the academic library's practice of placing older materials into storage solves more than just the space problem.

In any discipline, the most significant investigators, writers, artists, etc. do not create new works about existing topics. They create new topics, even if these are at first perceived as merely extensions of existing ones. Marshall McLuhan's 1962 *Gutenberg Galaxy* reflected a decade of his thinking about the effects of mass communication. Most librarians at the time shelved it and listed it in their subject catalogues among works on the history of printing, a topic peripheral to both McLuhan's intent and the subsequent perception of the book by most of its readers.

Every type of change identified above is more difficult to accommodate in a cooperatively maintained database. It is hard to find consensus among contributing institutions as to when and how to effect a change even when all agree that the change is desirable. Most libraries wait for a national agency like the Library of Congress to take the lead, but there is as yet no practicable method of inserting its changes into every separate library's OPAC automatically and instantly. In particular, the North American view of classification more as a method of in-house physical location than of information retrieval tends to shunt classification changes to the bottom of almost everyone's priority list. Changing the relationships embedded in a classification scheme is more complex than merely providing new links in a word vocabulary. The former is, however, probably more important because the word-links between old and new are generally more quickly and widely assimilated by users.

8

■ ■ ■

Bibliographic Formats

$\mathbf{A}$ typical bibliographic record consists of

1) the data elements described in chapter 2 which a cataloguer considered relevant to a given *document*
2) controlled-vocabulary access points chosen and structured according to the principles described in chapters 3, 6, and 7 to represent significant facts about the *work(s)* represented in that document and
3) housekeeping data relating to the *record* itself such as a record-identifier number, the date it was last revised, and the name of the cataloguer.

In generic terms, a format is a container for information, not the intellectual content of that information. Language may be called a format for thought.

In the jargon of manual bibliographic files, a format is the arrangement of all the above pieces of information as a complete visible record on a physical medium (card, fiche, printed page) along with clerical details of their presentation such as punctuation and capitalization. Traditional cataloguing rules have always been the catalogue's "style manual," prescribing that format as closely as they govern the choice and structuring of each individual data element and access point. At the beginning of this century, the Catalog Rules

Committee of the American Library Association even prescribed sizes and styles of type for the various data fields on printed records, their recommendations being followed by the Library of Congress for as long as it printed cards. Before automation, this was important because the format controlled the consistent visual presentation of the record to the searcher. It did little else, having no role in searching.

In the digital storage and interactive search systems described in chapter 4, the role of the format is almost reversed. It plays a crucial role in the process of searching. However, it is not the final determinant of what the searcher sees when a record is displayed or printed. For that, it serves only as raw material to be customized by each particular user interface. In the jargon of digital files, a format is what identifies to the DBMS, by its type, each data element and each access point which might need to be separately sorted, searched, or output for a given defined use. Traditional cataloguing rules, including AACR2, do not prescribe a format in this sense at all. There is no reason for them not to do so, but in the history of automating the bibliographic record, a digital format was initially seen as a subsidiary adjunct to the cataloguing rule, not vice-versa as a systems librarian now treats it. It continues to be maintained and published separate from, although necessarily compatible with, the cataloguing rule.

If language is the generic format for thought, prose may be considered a specialized format for ideas expressed in words. Its phrases, clauses, sentences, paragraphs, sections, and chapters clarify the meaning of words by giving them a context. A bibliographic format does the same thing in roughly the same way. It is the grammatical structure, or syntax, of the bibliographic language referred to at the beginning of chapter 2. It serves to identify the function, and helps in comprehending the meaning, of each data element in isolation and in combination. In prose, what appears between parentheses is recognized as a qualifier or a brief digression. In a standard library-cataloguing format, it is recognized as a series title. In English-language usage, the name of a corporate body is recognized when embedded in a prose sentence by the capitalization of its individual words. In the standard digital format detailed in the appendix, it is recognized by a 1 as the second of three digits in its identifying tag. In English, the basic syntactic order is: subject / verb / object. In the language of bibliography, it is: author-access-point / title / edition / place / publisher / date.

The native speaker of any language reacts instinctively to most of the language's formatting, but to comprehend an unusual pattern causes a pause for reflection just as one must consider and perhaps look up the meaning of an unfamiliar word. Even a casual library user is unconscious of the formatting of basic bibliographic data elements, but it is easy to misinterpret a more unusual statement because bibliographic syntax is compressed and contains few redundancies to aid in its interpretation. The following statements imply quite different things; only by knowing the bibliographic format in which they are expressed can one clearly convey in (or understand from) a citation what are the true facts of the particular document:

> Terrorism, a bibliography. Supplement. Second edition. 1987.
> Terrorism, a bibliography. Second edition. 1987. Supplement.
> Terrorism, a bibliography. Second edition. Supplement. 1987.

Footnotes and short lists of references at the close of a chapter or book, and the style manuals used to govern them, typically ignore any problem of bibliographic identification that cannot be conveyed in the simplest of formats. Whether or not this greatly affects the quality of the file depends on the proportion of problematic or ambiguous records it contains. If each of the tens of thousands of records in an A&I database describes an article of personal authorship in one of a small number of journals, a quite simple format suffices because all the data elements are regular and predictable. A more complex format is required when

1) records for different ages and types of material appear in the same file and/or
2) bibliographic relationships of many kinds exist among the documents listed and among their access points.

Situations of such variety, encountered regularly in library cataloguing, provide troublesome formatting problems.

FORMAT STANDARDIZATION

A variety of dialects still exist in the language of bibliography. A group of citations looks strange if half of them are composed according to the format imposed by one style manual and the rest according to that of another. Humans who can interpret the differences understand most of the details, but unpredicted format variation is not tolerable to a computer program. Automation has been an effective prod toward a greater degree of standardization in bibliographic, as in all other, formatting.

A *style manual*, familiar to every writer of a term paper or thesis, includes a bibliographic format for citations as footnotes or in a list of sources. Most do not rule on bibliographic problems in any great detail. Since the scope of their application is largely restricted to the author-arranged listing of small numbers of documents, they devote little attention to the issue of access points. There are a great many such manuals whose rules vary considerably in detail but little in principle. Each standardizes practice for a group of users which may be as broadly based as those who follow the Chicago Manual of Style or as narrow as those who publish in one small professional journal.

The editors of academic and professional journals, often working with the A&I services which index them, are primarily responsible for a second category of bibliographic formatting standards called *reference manuals*, guides for making bibliographic references (citations). Most of these began as the in-house rules issued to potential authors of articles for a single journal. A&I services and database vendors have exercised effective pressure to standardize, or at least diminish the impact of variation among, these various styles. One result was the 1977 publication of the *American National Standard for Bibliographic References* (ANSBR), designed for manual records, as ANSI/NISO standard Z39.29. Another was the publication by Unesco of a combination of a style manual and digital format known as the UNISIST reference manual, used in the developing world more than in North America or Europe.[1]

Librarians' Cataloguing Codes

Librarians originally also developed rules for formatting their catalogue records independently in each major library. Union catalogues and the sale of Library of Congress cards, described in chapter 5, were the major incentives to librarians to reduce the number and the divergence of such independent cataloguing codes. When automation arrived, the period of format experimentation preceding almost universal standardization was a very brief one. Cutter's 1876 *Rules for a Dictionary Catalog,* whose significance for controlled-vocabulary access points and for file arrangement permeates these chapters, also contains a format for document description. This became the basis for Library of Congress practice and thereby spread throughout the English-speaking world with the 1908 cataloguing code as described at the beginning of chapter 6.

Modernizing Cutter's format for description began with a challenge to its complexity in the 1940s. The beginnings of automation and a move toward internationalization influenced the revision published in 1969 as the International Standard Bibliographic Description (ISBD). ISBD succeeded in standardizing the formatting of document description more internationally than has ever been possible for access points. AACR2R embodies ISBD in the context of the manual catalogue; the MAchine-Readable Cataloging (MARC) family of digital formats encodes it for applications involving a DBMS. MARC prescribes the formatting of everything in a digitized record, including the housekeeping data mentioned at the beginning of this chapter which are a concern of neither ISBD nor AACR nor any style manual.

Before AACR and automation, smaller and specialized libraries tended to apply very selectively the rules and formats devised by and for their larger and general counterparts. Automation and the business of bibliography have established the supremacy of AACR2R (including ISBD) and MARC. Whether these are imposed on or welcomed by an individual local institution is perhaps a matter of personal viewpoint; that they have been adopted is what makes the interchange of bibliographic data possible.

The final step of bibliographic format standardization is still in its early stages and may never be completed. A&I services do not implement the same rules as librarians do for the formatting of either descriptive data elements or access points. As already discussed in previous chapters, there is a high degree of compatibility between these two groups in some areas, little in others. As databases originating in both camps are now being searched together (if not simultaneously) at the same OPAC, the differences among them are annoying to users and even more to systems librarians maintaining the DBMS. Developments in user interfaces discussed at the end of chapter 4 can make many inconsistencies transparent to the end-user but only at the cost of complexity in the system.

MANUAL FORMATS FOR DESCRIPTIVE ELEMENTS

This section and the next one on the ISBD are not concerned with formatting access points.

Monographs

The first bibliographic format was established when European printers of the late fifteenth century implicitly agreed on what data elements should appear—and in what order—on the title pages they were just beginning to design. They placed the titling and authorship of the work there (in effect also inventing titles) and gave visual prominence to these two elements, which identify the work. Logically, information related to production of a manuscript, for example the name of its scribe and/or the date it was completed, had long been placed at the end, as a *colophon*. Continuing this practice, the earliest printers also placed their names and dates there. However, as printers (later booksellers, then publishers) began to realize they were business firms, the importance of advertising and product identification led to placing the firm's name and corporate symbol on the title page. It took a little longer to get onto the title page a statement of change or updating of the content; that is, an edition statement, which along with the dating helps establish the currency of the content.

The spine and half-title page may bear some of the same data, but these physical parts of the book are intended primarily for physical protection, and the former is removed in rebinding. The twentieth-century dust wrapper serves as advertising and therefore cannot be relied upon to present bibliographic data in their clearest and most sober form. How natural, then, for the standard bibliographic format still to be based on a transcription of the title page. This is very visibly the case in Cutter's rules for formatting the catalogue card: a separate paragraph, the *title paragraph,* comprises that transcription. Information expected, but not found, on the title page might be included in this paragraph if available elsewhere, but the fact that it is an intrusion from a different source is indicated by its enclosure within brackets. All other data (information on series, physical description, and relationships, etc.) are visibly separated from the title paragraph by typography as well as location. The close relationship between a title page and a Library of Congress record according to the rules followed there between 1898 and 1948 is shown in figure 25. The series title is a relative latecomer to bibliographic data and rarely appears on the title page. This is why its location in the bibliographic record varies wildly from style manual to style manual and among different cataloguing rules.

Even stricter adherence to title-page copying is still followed in the more detailed cataloguing of rare books, sometimes called *bibliographic cataloguing.* The capitalization, line-endings, styles of type, etc. of the title page are all recorded, the binding is described in detail, each leaf of the item is accounted for in the enumeration of the pagination, etc. Figure 26 shows a description of this kind for the same item.[2] For comparison with it and with the card in figure 25, there follow citations of the same item composed according to the current edition of the Chicago Manual of Style and ANSI Z39.29, respectively:

> Gill, Eric. Art and a Changing Civilisation. The Twentieth Century Library. London: J. Lane, 1934.

> Gill, Eric. Art and a Changing Civilisation. London: J. Lane, 1934. 158 p. The Twentieth Century Library.

Journal Articles, etc.

A typical record transcribed from one of the earliest A&I publications, Poole's mid-nineteenth-century index of journal articles, still presents familiar data elements intelligibly. However, it does not con-

The Twentieth Century Library
Edited by V. K. Krishna Menon

ART

A R T

and a changing civilisation

by

E R I C   G I L L

JOHN LANE THE BODLEY HEAD LTD.
LONDON

First published in 1934

Gill, Eric, 1882–
    Art and a changing civilisation, by Eric Gill. London,
John Lane ₁1934₎
    xi p., 1 l., 158 p. 19^{cm}. *(Half-title:* The twentieth century library,
ed. by V. K. Krishna Menon)
    "Appendices: ɪ. The question of anonymity (by Rayner Heppenstall)—
ɪɪ. The school of Baudelaire (by G. M. Turnell)": p. 141–151.
    Bibliography : p. 152.
    1. Art.   2. Esthetics.   ɪ. Heppenstall, Rayner.   ɪɪ. Turnell, G. M.
ɪɪɪ. Title.   ₁*Full name:* Arthur Eric Rowton Peter Joseph Gill₎
                                   35–4636
    Library of Congress   N70.G48
                    ₁5₎   701

PRINTED IN GREAT BRITAIN
BY WESTERN PRINTING SERVICES LTD., BRISTOL

FIGURE 25.   The half-title page, the title page, and the verso of the title leaf of a book, along with its Library of Congress catalogue card prepared according to pre-1949 rules for description.

form to the library-catalogue standard for monographs, either of his day or now:

Cabinet System, English. (G. Bradford) No. Am. **118**: 1.

29. ART AND A CHANGING CIVILISATION

TITLE-PAGE: ART | AND A CHANGING CIVILISATION | BY | ERIC GILL |
JOHN LANE THE BODLEY HEAD LTD. | LONDON

SIZE: 7¼ × 4¾. COLLATION: [A]⁸, B–L⁸.

PAGINATION AND CONTENTS: Pp. xiv + 162; [i] [ii] half-title to series worded:
THE TWENTIETH CENTURY LIBRARY | EDITED BY V. K. KRISHNA MENON | ART,
verso blank; [iii] [iv] list of other volumes in the *Twentieth Century Library*, verso blank;
[v] [vi] title-page, verso printers' imprint worded: FIRST PUBLISHED IN 1934 | and,
at foot: PRINTED IN GREAT BRITAIN | BY WESTERN PRINTING SERVICES LTD.,
BRISTOL; vii–x Preliminary; xi–[xii] Contents, verso blank; [xiii] [xiv] half-title worded
ART, verso quotations from Ecclesiasticus and A. K. Coomaraswamy; 1–138 text;
[139] [140] blank, verso author's and publishers' acknowledgements; 141–5 Appendix I
The Question of Anonymity by Rayner Heppenstall; 146–51 Appendix II *The School of Baudelaire* by G. M. Turnell; 152 Bibliography; 153–8 Index; [159] [160] publishers' announce-
ments concerning the *Twentieth Century Library*; [161] [162] blank.

ILLUSTRATIONS: None.

BINDING: Red cloth, lettered on front, at top, in black: THE TWENTIETH
CENTURY LIBRARY with a design ('Laocoon'), specially made for the series by
Eric Gill, blocked in black. Lettered in black on spine: TWENTIETH | CENTURY |
LIBRARY | ART | ERIC | GILL | and, at foot: THE | BODLEY HEAD All edges
cut.

DATE OF PUBLICATION: 1934. MS. dated 8 December 1933–6 January 1934.
PRICE: 2s 6d.

NOTES: The following note appears on the flap of the wrapper: "The design on the cover
and wrapper of this book has been specially made for *The Twentieth Century Library* by
Mr Eric Gill, who writes: 'I can think of nothing more appropriate for a symbol for
The Twentieth Century Library than a version of Laocoon, that is Man, fighting with the
twin snakes of War and Usury. These are the powers of evil with which man in the
twentieth century will have to settle, or perish.'"

REVIEWS: By Wyndham Lewis, *The Listener*, 26 September 1934. By Harold Nicolson,
Daily Telegraph, September 1934.

SUBSEQUENT EDITIONS: A new edition, entirely re-set in a smaller format, was
published by John Lane, The Bodley Head under the title ART, in 1946, and again in
1949. Price 5s.

FIGURE 26. A fuller description of the item illustrated in figure 25, reproduced
from Evan R. Gill, *Bibliography of Eric Gill* (London: Cassell, 1953).

Poole chose to make use of the format also as an aid to subject searching, so he tampered with word-order in titles to bring a word useful
for access into filing position. Considering the quantity of items to be
listed, he saved as much space and input time as possible, abbreviating and printing issue numbers and dates in appended tables of
journal titles rather than with each citation. He apologized for his
work as "crude and feeble on its bibliographical side,"[3] yet whether
consciously or not, he formulated principles still applied a century
later to describe many or all types of document, not merely journal
articles; for example,

1) a data element considered desirable is given whether found in the source document or not
2) data elements are arranged in an order based not on their appearance within the source document but on a fixed rule and
3) a larger unit of which the item described is a part is cited in an arbitrarily abbreviated form or in a linked record.

New Layouts, New Media: The Threat of Fragmentation

Basing bibliographic identification on exact transcription of a title page assumed a standardized title-page format. The modern fashion for a simpler title page chased some data elements to the verso of the title leaf and elsewhere, but the effects of this are not nearly so damaging to standardization as the present-day trend among typographers to make graphic design statements with the wording they are given, and even more among publishers' sales departments to choose wording more for advertising than for identification purposes. As desktop publishing flourishes, prominently in the case of conference proceedings but now also for many other types of material, both the words and the display of identifying data are more and more often delegated to a clerk who is not paid to know and apply either graphic design principles or bibliographic tradition. The results can challenge anyone trying to cite or catalogue the item because they ill match the expectations on which bibliographic formatting has been based.

Documents in the newer media could, with a little awkwardness, be made to fit the mould as long as a quasi-title page could be agreed on. From the label of a disc sound recording to the thin header at the top of a microfiche or the box containing the parts of a kit, documents in each medium have an expected location for titles, statements about their creation, publication details, etc. However, electronic documents are difficult to cite consistently, not only because their primary existence is nonphysical but more because their creators are not channelled by the bibliographic common sense of established publishers and distributors in choosing and presenting identifying data.

Establishing stability and agreement takes time and a sense of common purpose. For a long time, cataloguers were not leaders in promulgating this common sense for nonprint media. Their rules, designed for print media, seemed increasingly irrelevant to those who administered audiovisual departments, often independently of libraries and those educated as librarians. When libraries began to collect audiovisual material seriously after the Second World War, bibliographic standardization was seriously threatened as ad hoc rules were devised in individual situations with many reinventions of the wheel, each divorced from reference to another or to any previous standard.

Two parallel developments of the 1960s went a long way to stem the threat of fragmentation and to lay a basis for dealing with any new medium to come: the manual format known as ISBD and the digital format known as MARC. The time was ripe to pursue the goals of international standardization and automation.

In what was originally seen as only an economy measure, the Library of Congress decided in 1966 to accept bibliographic descriptions of current publications (but not access points) without editing from some two dozen national bibliographies despite minor inconsistencies among these. At the same time, the first digital formats covering all bibliographic data were being developed, notably at the Library of Congress. Bibliographic data had been represented as holes on a punched card for mechanized sorting and printing three decades earlier, but this technology could only accommodate the few data elements needed for brief listing or for a circulation-control system.

The move to digitize complete records made librarians realize that, although automation began with the in-house development of circulation control, it would inevitably extend to all the sharing of data they had been engaging in throughout the century. Even in the wealthy days of the 1960s, it was clear that developing software for processing and writing file definitions for automated systems involved costs which could not be duplicated from library to library and for a wide variety of formats which would probably differ in only minor detail anyway.

THE INTERNATIONAL STANDARD BIBLIOGRAPHIC DESCRIPTION

A sketch of the history of digital formats occupies the next section. In the late 1960s, most people outside the largest and richest libraries knew little of automation, and ISBD was conceived only in terms of the manual record. Goodwill prevailed at the 1969 International Meeting of Cataloguing Experts (IMCE) held under the aegis of IFLA. All agreed that the minor differences in data-element formatting which resulted from differing national cataloguing rules were of little or no practical significance but merely stemmed from historical accident. Few compromises were needed to achieve an internationally agreed format provided it did not stray into the much more controversial territory of controlled-vocabulary name or subject access points.

International standardization of subject access points is inconceivable and the 1961 International Conference on Cataloguing Principles had reached agreement on the twelve Paris Principles for name access points mentioned in chapter 6. The 1969 "Experts" therefore designed ISBD only as a parallel standard to the latter, for descriptive data elements. The first version of ISBD dealt only with data for printed monographs, but once agreement on the basic structure was achieved, committees were struck to extend the format to serials, audio-visual materials, etc. The automated future, then just on the horizon, and the need to interpret the structure of records independently of their language were also considerations. In almost every detail, ISBD is now the manual counterpart of the MARC digital format described below.

The decision to separate the function of describing from that of access was inevitable in the context of later computer-based systems, in which each data element can be, and is, searched and displayed as a separate building block within a complete record. In 1969, however, it represented an unpleasant change for cataloguers who followed the rules for description which the Library of Congress had adopted uni-laterally in 1949 as a simplification effort. The basis of those rules was the indivisibility of a record on a card, consisting of a description following a principal access point, a copy of the whole being filed at each other access point chosen. In the effort to eliminate all redundancy in this unit record, those rules allowed outright tampering with the most basic descriptive data element, the title. Thus if a person or corporate body is named in both a principal access point and in the following title proper, the name was simply omitted from the transcription of the title. The title *Bach's Greatest Hits* became the author access point **Bach, Johann Sebastian** followed by the title *Greatest Hits*.

This may seem inconsequential hairsplitting in the case of mono-graphs, but it was disastrous for the identification of serial publications. On a record produced between 1949 and 1980, a title in the very common form *Journal of the American Statistical Association* was reduced to the one word *Journal* following the principal access point **American Statistical Association**. Being common and not at all distinctive, that one-word title was not even accorded an access point. As a result, the searcher who came to a library catalogue looking for the journal by its full title, or who knew one of its common citation abbreviations (*JASA* or *Jl.Amer.Stat.Assoc.*), was offered no direct approach in that catalogue to any familiar identification of the journal. These distorted titles are prominent in every serials listing based on the rules followed for over thirty years (including all the early auto-mated ones), had an impact on the original version of ISBD for serials (revised in 1977), and still plague reference librarians.

Sources, Organization, and Display of Data

ISBD embodies the opposite of the principle of title-page transcription. It still acknowledges the title page of a book as the most important source of the data required for its adequate description, but the prescriptions of ISBD replace the title page as the format for both the choice and the arrangement of the data elements in the record. To recognize the existence of documents without title pages, ISBD identifies a *chief source of information* for material in each distinct medium. The title page is the chief source in the case of printed media in book form, but even then, a different chief source is specified in the case of a book without a title page. One cannot expect the data desirable in a record always to occur on the chief source, so additional *prescribed sources* of data are specified. These include locations such as the verso of the title leaf, cover, and external reference sources, and they vary depending on the type of data element involved. Any data included in the record but not transcribed from either the chief source or from a prescribed source for the type of data in question are enclosed within brackets.

ISBD specifies an *area* for each of eight types of data. It prescribes that when the record is displayed in full, the eight (or those applicable to the document in question) are to be arranged in the following sequence, separated by a period-space-dash-space as a unique four-character area separator.

> Area 1. Title and Statement of Responsibility Area
> Area 2. Edition Area
> Area 3. Material (or Type-of-Publication) Specific Data Area (used only for cartographic materials, printed music, computer files, and serials)
> Area 4. Publication, Distribution, etc. Area
> Area 5. Physical Description Area
> Area 6. Series Area (includes data for a second, etc. series if applicable)
> Area 7. Note(s) Area (repeatable, each note being a separate area)
> Area 8. Standard Number and Terms of Availability Area (another repeatable area)

Every published item has at least a title, even if it must be made up for identification purposes by the cataloguer (area 1), some facts concerning its origin (area 4), and a physical presence which can be quantified (area 5, although whether and how to use this area for documents in electronic but not in tangible physical form are debated). Area 3 is required for the media specified above and includes data specific to the medium; for example, the scale of a map; the numbering pattern of a serial. The existence of any other area in a given description is dependent on the availability of data for that area concerning the document being catalogued. Only a few books have an edition *statement*, for example, and the reasonable assumption that an item is a first edition does not suffice for mention in this area. An area for which there are no data relevant to the item is simply omitted.

Each area except the seventh (notes) comprises a formal structure for a number of the separate data elements described in chapter 2, usually derived from the document itself. Thus area 1 comprises one title proper plus the following as applicable: one general material designation (by convention, this is not specified for the commonest type of material, the printed text item), one or more parallel titles, one or more units of other title information (including any subtitle), and one or more statements of responsibility. Area 7 differs. This is where the cataloguer states in a relatively unstructured way whatever cannot be put into the form or context of any other area. Originally and logically, this was the final area in a record, but standard numbering, widely applied only after ISBD had been fixed, got tacked on after it. Many of the bibliographic relationships described in chapter 2 must be stated as notes, since other areas (2 and 6) carry information on only the two most frequently encountered types of relationship. Area 8 is sometimes used in practice, although not intended in theory, for standard numbers of related items such as a paperback version or an edition distributed by a different publisher, in addition to that of the item actually described in the record.

Amount of Detail

Cutter's view that the same rules could accommodate full, medium, and short records is quoted on page 198. When the Library of Congress printed card became the de facto standard, the post-Cutter rules it helped write were written to specify the degree of detail represented on its records. Technically, many libraries did not follow those rules. They produced shorter records, perhaps omitting place of publication or preliminary pagination sequences, or even an article at the beginning of a title. When ISBD became the basis for part I of the second edition of AACR, it brought with it the concept of data elements to be considered separately, some essential, others optional, in a given record depending on the item catalogued and the purpose and uses of the file. Rule 1.0D of AACR2, "Levels of detail in the description," specifies elements to be included at each of three different levels, making the code relevant and acceptable in all, not merely large academic and national, libraries. Another consequence, however, may be that this is more encouragement than libraries need to cut corners in cataloguing while waiting for someone else to supply the more complete record desirable as discussed in chapter 5. This use of the word *level* is unfortunate, although perhaps unavoidable. In ISBD and later in this chapter, the word is used in a very different sense related to the titling of different entities within the same publication, not levels of completeness of a record.

Area 1 and Problems of Access

The elements specified above for area 1 can be difficult to separate cleanly from one another. Ideally, titling should always be separable from, say, statements of responsibility, but this simply does not conform to the language of title pages, etc. Two examples are used above to show the consequences of tampering with that natural wording: *Bach's Greatest Hits* and *Journal of the American Statistical Association*. The format has important implications for interactive searching when, as often, the searcher is not conscious of the element in which the sought word occurs, or even if what is being searched is a description or a controlled-vocabulary access point. Three examples may illustrate this; all are equally likely title-page wording, given how conferences are named and how their proceedings are published. In the second, what follows the colon is a subtitle; in the third, what follows the slash is a statement of responsibility.

> *Proceedings of the Third International Conference on Security*
> *Password control : Proceedings of the Third International*
> *   Conference on Security*
> *Proceedings / Third International Conference on Security*

The name of the (hypothetical) conference is in the name authority file as **International Conference on Security (3rd : 1996 : Chicago)** and is therefore searchable in a name index by any of those significant words. In a controlled-vocabulary subject index, these proceedings are sure to be accessible directly or indirectly via the word SECURITY, although that may not be the only or first word of the appropriate access point. It is perhaps more likely that the average user will search for *security* in a title index hoping to find this or a similar work.

A smaller or older automated system programmed to index only the title proper and subtitle(s) for such a search will not retrieve the item in the third example. ISBD is not at fault in this; blame lies with the person who decided what words to put on the title page. With its greater processing and memory capacity, a DBMS now typically allows every (significant) word of area 1 to be included in a "title" search. This means that one can search for the second word of the title *Prester John* (not remembering the first) and retrieve every item whose author's Christian name *John* is in a statement of responsibility! It helps if the searcher is told exactly which data elements are searchable in each index. Libraries are often remiss in not sharing this information with their end-users, but the documentation of every

A&I database vendor specifies the indices available for each separate file and the elements indexed in each of these. It also specifies whether the indexing is by separate words or by phrases (combinations of words), and whether and how proximity searching (see chapter 4) is permitted. Most well-known A&I services have not adopted ISBD as such, but their indexing is governed by the same type of formatting standard as ISBD.

Punctuation

Formalized punctuation to indicate what kind of data are about to appear has always been a part of bibliographic formatting. Both long-standing British practice and that of the Chicago Manual of Style separate a place of publication from a publisher's name by a colon. Library cataloguing rules have long enclosed data elements relating to a series in parentheses. When ISBD was in draft, a suggestion was accepted that prescribed marks of punctuation should be used systematically, not only for some elements, in order to delimit each area and element unambiguously. The accepted pattern is shown in the following skeletal record along with the capitalization pattern prescribed by AACR.

> Title proper [general material designation] = Parallel title : other title information / first statement of responsibility ; second statement of responsibility. — Edition statement / statement of responsibility relating to the edition, Additional edition statement / statement of responsibility for the additional edition statement. — Material specific details. — First place of publication ; Second place of publication : Publisher, date (Place of manufacture : Manufacturer, date of manufacture). — *extent of item : other physical details ; dimensions + accompanying material. — (Series title proper = Parallel series title / statement of responsibility for the series, ISSN ; numbering within the series. Title of subseries ; numbering within the subseries) (Second series with elements arranged within its separate parentheses as was the first). — *Note. — *Note. — *ISBN : terms of availability (qualification).

> (*An asterisk indicates where it is permissible to begin a new paragraph, in keeping with the style of the old card format, instead of using the area separator.)

The value of the regularized punctuation in helping to interpret records across language boundaries may be evident in figure 27. A colon preceding "ein Handbuch" clearly tells the clerk who does not

ေဒၚ်ေဟၚာင်း ေဒၚ်သစ် စာကြည့်တိုက်ခရိုၚ်း, ၁၀၅၇-၁၉၇၉ / မေၚင်
ကောၚ်းမြင့်. — ရန်ကုန် : စာေပဗိမာန်, 1978.

261 p., [4] leaves of plates : ill. ; 20 cm. — (ပြည်သူ့လက်စွဲစာစဉ်)

ਭਾਈ ਵੀਰ ਸਿੰਘ, ਸੰਦਰਭ-ਕੋਸ਼ / ਸੰਪਾਦਕ ਵਿਸ਼ਵਾਨਾਥ ਤਿਵਾੜੀ, ਹਰਿੰਦਰ ਪੰਨੂੰ,
ਜਗਤਾਰ. — ਚੰਡੀਗੜ੍ਹ : ਪਬਲੀਕੇਸ਼ਨ ਬਿਓਰੋ, ਪੰਜਾਬ ਯੂਨੀਵਰਸਿਟੀ, 1974.

220 p. ; 23 cm.

Μιχαὴλ Περάνθης : εἰσαγωγή-βιβλιογραφίαχρίσεις / ᾽Ι. Μ.
Χατζηφώτη ; μὲ τὴ συνεργασία τῆς Νίκης Πολίτη. — ᾽Αθήνα :
᾽Εκδόσεις τῶν Κριτικῶν Φυλλῶν, 1976.

524 p. ; 21 cm.

FIGURE 27.   ISBD descriptions in nonroman scripts from Library of Congress records. The access points are not reproduced.

know German that *Handbuch* is not an author's surname. The bibliographic data shown in figure 25, above, become the following in ISBD format:

> Art and a changing civilisation / by Eric Gill. — London :
> J. Lane, 1934. — xi, 158 p. ; 19 cm. — (The Twentieth
> century library)

ISBD punctuation deliberately looks artificial, with its space preceding as well as following the actual character except in the case of the comma and period. Those two characters, still needed within names, titles, etc. are only prescribed in ISBD when the following element is unambiguous (a date, an ISSN, a new title): in other words, when the punctuation is not necessary to recognize the nature of the element. The same punctuation is never used for different purposes within the same area. The rather awkward four-character area separator with its dash (not a basic ASCII character and therefore normally displayed as one or two hyphens) is normally suppressed in OPAC output. In fact, ISBD punctuation, originally the format's most strikingly radical feature, has become largely a nonissue with respect to user interfaces because record display now typically consists of a selection of "labelled" data, each displayed field being identified by a brief verbal caption.

The Family of ISBDs in Relation to Cataloguing Codes

It is possible to catalogue simple items with only the guidance provided in the table of elements and the skeletal record reproduced above, but most cataloguers demand more interpretive guidance, specific rules for esoteric bibliographic situations, and enough examples to ensure inter-cataloguer consistency. In addition to the original ISBD for printed monographs, therefore, IFLA sponsored separately published ones show the application of the format to antiquarian (pre-1820) books, to cartographic materials, to machine-readable files, to audiovisual materials generally, to printed music, to serials, and to component parts (analytics). That these do not result in contradictory practices is ensured by the conformity of all to the basic principles and format structure enunciated in ISBD(G), the *General* ISBD. There is also an ISAD(G), a general International Standard Archival Description, to guide the work of archivists as they follow librarians in attempting standardization of their record-formatting practice. Once AACR and other cataloguing codes incorporated ISBD as their basic format for description, cataloguers who use these codes have little reason to refer directly to the ISBDs themselves.

MACHINE-READABLE (DIGITAL) FORMATS

A computer program is totally dependent on the formatting of the data with which it deals. Even for a keyword search, the program must be explicitly told what a "word" is, each and every time it occurs. This is the simplest format: a word is anything both preceded and followed by a space or a (specified) mark of punctuation—the qualification allows the programmer just a little flexibility. A human recognizes a title in a complete bibliographic record in any format used for the past four centuries because it is either the access point or the first thing after an access point. Still, this requires the person to know what an access point is. The computer is so stupid it even has to be told that a record is beginning (or ending) just as it has to be told that a word is beginning. The code which does this is called a *delimiter:* it starts or stops a search or process. Delimiters are of such general application that each must be a unique character: one which cannot occur in the content of the record or in any other conflicting context.

If each title (or other data element) occurs in certain specified character positions, the same ones in each record, which the computer locates by counting from a delimiter, one has a *fixed-field* format. This results in simple data input and programs and quick, cheap processing. However, a fixed number of characters must be allotted to each data element, resulting in truncation of the data or filling unused bytes with blank spaces. Codes are devised to reduce naming systems to fixed-length data elements in the fewest characters possible: a Universal Product Code (the ISBN is an early example of this) identifies a product, a social security number identifies a person, a telephone number identifies an access line. Printing one of these on a barcoded label permits its laser scanning as direct input to a program for processing, where it can also be matched with whatever words, graphics, etc. a human needs to identify the object. Many huge business operations require nothing more sophisticated than this because their statistical, currency, stock-market, or reservations data fit this kind of formatting, and most required displays are either single-item displays for online consultation or batch output for reporting.

Many bibliographically relevant facts can be expressed in code and assigned to fixed-length fields; for example, one byte suffices to show whether a document is a government publication or not: a predetermined code shows that it is not (perhaps a zero, or a blank: the code in the character set created by striking the space bar). Another code (perhaps x) shows that it is, but using the same single byte, one can even identify the type of agency responsible for the document (local, intergovernmental, etc.) by replacing that x with an appropriate predetermined code. To display most bibliographic data to users, however, fixed-field formatting is unsuitable, although it is cheap and there are still libraries which send an overdue notice for UNITED STATES. DEPAR/ ARGUMENTS PRESENTED TO THE COM, where twenty characters are the maximum available for an author's name and thirty for a title.

Variable-Field Formats

Librarians were largely responsible for developing the programs needed to process data in a variable-field format using *content designation* to indicate not only that a data element is beginning, but what kind of element it is.[4] A variable-field format is complex. It requires a different content designator for each type of data element so that the program can distinguish, say, a title proper from a series title. For practical reasons, many, if not all, content designators must consist of the same numbers, letters, and punctuation appearing in the bibliographic data. The format must therefore be capable of distinguishing a content designator from the data element to which it relates, so that the processing programs can identify which is which. A further problem is how to deal with the fact that one record contains many different data elements, another only a few.

A *repeatable field* (or subfield) is often required for bibliographic data. As examples, a record may contain no, one, or (theoretically) any number of different subject access points, each with no, one, or several subdivisions; one or more publishers and distributors may be named in publication data. A variable-field format which permits a field or subfield to be repeated an unpredictable number of times within the same record causes significant problems for programmers and for the efficient operation of processing software. This is a major reason why it took so long for microcomputer processing capacity to become adequate to the demands of processing complete bibliographic records. It is also a major reason why almost all, and certainly every large, bibliographic file is still, to its DBMS, an *inverted file*. *Relational file* structure, in which repeatability of fields is even more problematic, has yet to be adopted in most large or even medium-sized library systems, although many consider it more desirable for interactive searching.

The *address* (location) of any given data element within a complete logical record is the *character position* containing its first byte. The very first byte in the logical record is said to be in character position 0 (*not* 1). The byte in character position 1 is therefore the second byte, etc. Perhaps confusing at first, this facilitates the mathematical calculation of addresses because the address, or starting character position, of any field is the address of the previous field plus the number of characters in that previous field. Thus the title proper in one record might begin in character position 25 and end in position 59, while in the next record it begins in position 46 and ends in position 187. All processing is based on locating the data to be processed via an address. In a fixed-field format, the address of each defined data element is the same in every record, fixed by the format.

A variable-field format depends on a *record directory*, the part of the record which serves as an index to the record by showing the tag of each field used with the character position in which the field begins. When it creates this directory, the input program must be able to determine how many bytes there are in each field so a delimiter is the final byte of each field. In the MARC formats, a field generally corresponds to one access point or one ISBD area. Since ISBD divides most areas into elements and a name or subject access point may consist of more than one element, the MARC format also uses a third delimiter to indicate the beginning of each subfield within a field. None of these three delimiters can be a byte in the character set used for any other purpose, hence it is a character which can only be shown in program documentation in hexadecimal form. Finally, the record begins with a *label* or *leader*, containing "housekeeping" data primarily describing the record itself. A DBMS needs quantitative information about the record including how many bytes it contains and how many bytes are in the standard unit of the record directory; also qualitative information such as whether the record is for a monograph, a serial, etc. because this governs which of different possible sets of codes apply in a given field.

MARC and ISO2709

Punched-card equipment was well known in libraries for inventory and circulation purposes by the 1950s. Using this inherently fixed-field technology, librarians at first designed a unique format for each given application, circulation control and fund accounting among the early ones. Applications and perceived needs differed from library to library. By 1965, variable-field formatting to be applied to the catalogue record, not just to one application, was the subject of experimentation at the Library of Congress and other institutions. This raised the very real threat of format incompatibility which would inhibit record sharing. The Library of Congress used its powers of persuasion and subsidized development to convince the librarians of North America at least to accept records in its complex and comprehensive variable-field format even if each library had to use a different and simpler format for in-house record processing. In 1966 and 1967, tests of the first draft of MARC were undertaken to determine how it could support local cataloguing operations.

MARC and Cataloguing Codes

After significant revision, an operational version of MARC was published in 1968 and quickly became the model format for sharing, or exchanging, digitized bibliographic records worldwide. However, MARC was intended not to replace manual cataloguing rules or formats but only to accommodate their provisions to manipulation by a computer program. AACR had been published and adopted only the year before; the conference which led to ISBD was held a year later. Effective use of a manual catalogue is not greatly inhibited if its records do not all follow a common standard to the letter, and there was no prospect of changing existing records to conform with new rules before adding them to a digitized database. MARC therefore had to include formatting provisions for any practice of the past which might still be evident on records to which it would be applied.

Although the cataloguing rules used might have varied over the century, the catalogue card had become the virtually universal medium, at least in North American libraries. The interactive catalogue was foreseen in the late 1960s, but was not immediately practicable as a widespread replacement for cards.

MARC was therefore designed as much to automate the production of catalogue cards as to facilitate searching. This unfortunately stabilized its characteristics a little too early. It would have been better had MARC and the interactive file developed hand-in-hand. As with the original ISBD, MARC at first accommodated only the characteristics of printed monographs. Twenty years of additions and changes ensued to make provision for serials and nonprint media, for the successive revisions of AACR, for the increasing sophistication of OPAC software, and for assistance in increasingly specialized searching. Meanwhile, remnants of obsolete cataloguing practice remain visible in MARC code books, making them increasingly cumbersome and in some respects mysterious to those who do not know its history well.

With additions for most present and foreseeable types of material complete by the early 1990s, a significant rationalization of the basic structure was effected in a *format integration* project. Other possible, even desirable, changes have not been pursued to date. The cost of incorporating changes in basic file definition is always great. It explains why resistance to such change, whether in a cataloguing code or a digital format, has always delayed implementation of change until it is long past due in the view of theoreticians.

Many possible, even desirable, changes to MARC are not yet being actively pursued. It is of no consequence that while tag numbering follows the ISBD sequence generally, that of the final (eighth) area precedes that of the first. It is, however, of considerable practical consequence that a uniform title, which is always an access point or part of one, is often treated in MARC as if it were a descriptive data element, which it never is. This results from the fixing of the original MARC tagging in the context of the pre-coordinated elements on a unit catalogue card and prior to the rationalization of the uniform title as a general principle in AACR, as discussed at the end of chapter 6. It perpetuates serious problems of understanding, displaying, and arranging uniform titles.

It took two decades of hardware and software development before all the complexities of MARC could be accommodated for in-house applications in a library of any size on microcomputer workstations. Early in that period, using MARC normally meant *importing* (receiving, downloading) records from a national agency, utility, or consortium. This fostered the pattern of centralized cataloguing described in chapter 5 because only these large agencies could afford the computer capacity and software maintenance to handle the format fully. The individual library receiving a record for in-house applications of acquisitions, cataloguing, catalogue display and searching, circulation, etc. both reduced it to the fewer data elements and features essential to each service (at first with separate programs) and probably also (by a program) changed the format of what remained into a simpler one suited to the hardware and software it could afford or imposed on it by a parent body. Greater memory capacity, client-server network architecture, communication protocols such as those of the Internet, and interface developments represented by the Z39.50 standard, all noted in chapter 4, now make it both feasible and desirable for the fully formatted MARC record to be the local processing, as well as the exchange, format. This makes it possible for a library to *export* records widely, as well as importing them: another step in sharing.

ISO2709

Whether or not the design of MARC is ideal for the interactive file is immaterial. It works, and interlibrary bibliographic cooperation depends totally on it. Developing so complex a format and writing file definitions and processing programs for it were not about to be duplicated when the Library of Congress exercised little proprietary control over it but actively supported its worldwide imitation and spread. However, almost everywhere else MARC was adopted, the original version was changed a bit to accommodate local needs. It was also improved, especially when examined by librarians outside North America who were not so strongly influenced by either the Cutter tradition or the Library of Congress unit-card manual format. It took a "general" ISBD(G) to keep the ISBDs for various types of material in line instead of fragmenting into incompatibility. Similar agreement was soon sought on an internationally accepted digital format, perhaps a little more general and abstract than that of the Library of Congress and less attached to any one previous practice, so that records might be exchanged across the national variants. Whereas ISBD never reached the status of an ISO standard, a digital format did. It was defined in 1973 as ISO2709, "Documentation—Format for Bibliographic Information Interchange on Magnetic Tape," which must be used in conjunction with other ISO standards relating to character sets and tape labelling. This is essentially the same standard as the American ANSI/NISO Z39.2 and the British BS:4748. It regulates only the essential structural features of a variable-field format. Librarians use it for authority and holdings, as well as bibliographic, records. Archivists use it as the basis for MARC(AMC)—MARC for Archival and Manuscript Control. Other ISO2709-based formats are in use to process any kind of information requiring fields of variable length. A&I services around the world also use such formats, although they are generally not historically based on MARC.

ISO2709 is quite general and flexible. Only the following are regulated in absolute terms:

1) the record and field delimiters are each defined as a particular byte in the character set
2) every tag must be three bytes long and
3) the label must be twenty-four bytes long, with specified data in fixed locations therein (some bytes in the label are left undefined; a local use may be defined).

The record must contain a record directory. Three kinds of variable-length fields follow the label and directory:

1) one record-identifier field bearing the tag 001
2) one or a very few fields called *reserved fields* in ISO2709 but known in North America (and in this book) as *control fields* (these bear tags numbered up to 009) and
3) any number of bibliographic-data fields (tag numbers permitted for this part of the record run from 010 through 999)

The latter are the fields containing the descriptive areas and elements of ISBD, the controlled-vocabulary name and subject access points, and additional fields for retrieval codes: essentially the entire bibliographic record as described so far in this book and a bit more. ISO2709 is silent on how data elements are to be expressed in these fields since that depends on the type of document or object listed and the cataloguing or other rules applied to govern data selection and arrangement.

Non-MARC ISO2709 Bibliographic Formats

There are ISO2709-based formats for bibliographic data outside the MARC group, two of them important enough to note. The UNISIST reference manual was designed for A&I services. It incorporates its own set of cataloguing rules, which differ in some respects from the international consensus developed around ISBD and AACR2. Its use is not widespread. The Common Communication Format (CCF) began as an attempt to bridge differences between the A&I community and the library community.[5] It is being used especially in parts of the world where the two groups have not become totally separated from one another by history or by economics. It is little known in the developed countries where MARC formats have become entrenched.

Technically, the CCF represents a major advance in formatting because it provides for different levels of description within the same record as these are defined later in this chapter. It thus distances itself considerably from the origin of machine-readable bibliographic formats in the manual file where each record is an indivisible physical unit. It remains a significant failing of MARC formats that a record must remain a whole for all linking purposes so that a link can only be established between one complete record and another complete record. In the CCF, this is not the case.

The MARC Family of Formats

With the acceptance of ISO2709 and the proliferation of variants of the original MARC format, the Library of Congress soon called its version LCMARC. Other versions tended to be national or regional, for example, CANMARC, UKMARC, and Latin American MARC. The MARC family consists of nearly fifty siblings with no identical twins! All are similar enough that they can be translated into one another using a fairly simple program. However, IFLA sponsored a "universal" MARC format (UNIMARC) for international record exchange, first published in 1977. It is the version most consciously divorced from the appearance of the manual catalogue card. When it is used as an intermediate format, each national agency need only provide a translation program for its records into and out of UNIMARC.

Globalization is overtaking this intended structure for international record sharing. The European Community MARC users are pursuing a USEMARCON Project for simple translation programs under Windows or UNIX. Meanwhile, LCMARC, later officially designated US-MARC, probably remains the best maintained and constantly improved version, backed by the American resources which once spread the Library of Congress catalogue card worldwide. The increasing dominance of the library software market by American firms is another factor causing individual libraries and national agencies elsewhere to adopt US-MARC and abandon their attempts to maintain a local version. Some are already calling USMARC the international version: IMARC.

THE PARTS OF A MARC RECORD

This section is a closer examination of the structure of a record in any of the MARC formats. In the appendix, the application of this structure to a particular cataloguing code (AACR2R) and particular examples is shown in the context of USMARC.

The Label

The ten types of information encoded in the label are not easily summarized. They include (1) bytes common to all records within a file, (2) elements, such as the total record length, which are calculated by the input program, not the cataloguer, and (3) four one-byte codes specific to the item being catalogued and therefore decided by the cataloguer. In every ISO2709-based format, the label comprises twenty-four characters, in character positions 0 through 23 (this is the compromise length with which every type of hardware and operating system known in the mid-1960s was compatible). The label tells a DBMS much about how to locate pieces of information within the record. Since this must work for every ISO2709-based format regardless of its internal file structure, the individual-record label specifies such information even if it does not vary from record to record within the format. A processing format may bypass this redundancy by treating the information as common to all and ignoring it in the individual record. This includes how many bytes are assigned to the second and third segments of the record directory (four and five, respectively, in every MARC format), how many one-byte indicators (see below) are used per field (two in most MARC formats), and how many bytes are reserved for each subfield code (again, two).

Content Designators (Tags, Subfield Codes)

The DBMS counts from a reference point unambiguously identifiable by it (the delimiter marking the end of the previous field) and treats the next three characters as a *tag* specifying the nature of the following field. ISO2709 specifies a uniform tag length of three characters so that a tag can be distinguished from the field's content this easily. It does not specify what kind of characters the tag should consist of; MARC uses numbers. In many in-house processing systems and in much user-interface display, mnemonic tagging is taken for granted so the system translates the numbers into, say, *AUT* or even *AUTHOR*. A DBMS does not know what an author is; it simply takes the information following this tag and indexes or prints it as specified by the human programmer for that tag. No two different types of field may therefore be identified by the same tag, but if a record contains repetitions of the same type of field, each repetition is identified by the same tag.

A subfield is a single element within a field, identified by its own content designator, a *subfield code*. The first byte of this code must be the third delimiter described on page 323; since the number of possible types of subfield within the same field is limited, one additional byte suffices to identify the type of each possible subfield. The same actual subfield code can be used with a different meaning in each different field. That is, in a name-access-point field, subfield *c* is a title of honour while, in a physical description field, subfield *c* is the size of the item. This is the same as using a space-colon-space for several purposes in ISBD but only one purpose within any one field, or giving many telephone lines the same seven-digit calling code but never two lines within the same country-and-area code. The first subfield in a field is by convention almost always designated *a*. Additional ones may be designated in alphabetic sequence (*b, c, d,* etc.) or mnemonically (*v* for *volume number; l* for *language*). In ISBD area 4, the place is coded as subfield *a*, the name of the publisher as *b*, and the date as *c*; in the name-title access point **Mozart, Wolfgang Amadeus, 1756-1791. Concerto, piano, K.466, D minor**, the personal name is coded as subfield *a*, dates of birth and death as *d*, the title (*Concerto*) as *t*, the medium (piano) as *m*, and the Köchel number as *n*. The expected designation *k* for the key signature was pre-empted for a now obsolete purpose which it must still serve in older records, so the key-signature subfield was rather arbitrarily assigned the unmemorable designation *r.*

The Record Directory

Delimiters and content designators suffice to enable a program to locate the beginning and the end of any desired unit of data in a variable-field record provided it scans each character in each record. Searching is more efficient if at least the major content designators (the tags) can be scanned separately in a kind of table of contents or index to the record. This is the record directory. An operating system or word-processing program creates a directory to a storage medium in which every file's name and size are associated with its location(s) on the storage medium. In the same way, the record directory indexes each field in the record by giving (1) its tag, (2) its length, and (3) its address relative to a fixed point of departure. With the directory as an index, the various fields in a record need not occur in any particular sequence. This makes record revision and additions technically simple, since an additional field tacked onto the end does not upset the address of any existing field relative to the *base address of data,* the character position of the content of the necessary first tag, 001.

The directory consists of as many units as there are variable fields in the record. Each unit is of equal length so that a program can count past any number of them in equal increments. The input portion of the DBMS, which assembles, indexes, and stores the completed records on tape or disk, does all this counting and addressing; the human cataloguer is not bothered with it. Nor does the DBMS go through a process of directory-matching and address-searching every time someone consults the file. It does so only when required to create (or update) its indices to the content of the file, a time-consuming batch job usually done overnight or on a weekend according to the requirements of the people who designed the search parameters and user interface described in chapter 4. These indices, not the actual records, are the basis for all subsequent searching. Since the DBMS uses the directory to create its indices, however, the most efficient indexing of the record is based on separate fields, a fact with major consequences for interactive searching. In practice, it requires the searcher to select the field(s) to be searched. The single-sequence dictionary catalogue is therefore not the model on which the interactive catalogue can efficiently be based.

Record-Identifier and Control Fields

The record-identifier field contains only one data element: a unique character string programmers call a control number, by which a DBMS recognizes all the parts of a record as belonging together. All inter-record links to and from related records, access-point links to authority files, etc. use this identifier. It does not matter what this identifying character string is: it can be all numeric, all alphabetic, or a combination, but no two records under the control of the same DBMS can have the same record identifier. Each Library of Congress Control Number (LCCN, formerly "card number") is a record identifier in that Library's in-house systems. A local processing system generates a number at random as a record identifier, so any record identifiers retained with their records from other systems (including those of the Library of Congress and of national bibliographies) must be put into a different field. The record-identifier field is often treated as if it were of fixed length, although in theory it need not be. ISO2709 prescribes that its tag be 001: the first variable-length tag in the record.

Several control fields are defined in MARC. They are so called because they contain data useful for processing and searching. Confusingly, they are often called the *fixed fields* because they contain coded data which can be stated in a fixed-field structure. Information is given in this group of fields both (1) in coded form for efficiency in storage and (2) in a fixed location relative to the beginning of the field for efficiency in searching. There is much potential for post-coordinate searching in the very large number of these codes which are defined in MARC. This potential has yet to be realized in most libraries. Some do not even bother coding all of them. The date of publication is stated in one of these fields as well as in the appropriate bibliographic-data field because it is more efficiently searched in a fixed field. Much of what is coded here is implicit, not explicit, in the rest of the record. The computer cannot determine which items listed are in the Farsi language by interpreting the meaning of title words as a human would, so if language is ever to be a search parameter, a program must locate an explicit language code. A fixed field is an efficient place to put such a code of a few bytes.

There follow a few examples of other coding provided, in one or a very few bytes, in these fields:

- —places of publication (in three bytes: *txu* for Texas, USA)
- —physical characteristics (in one byte per characteristic: *b* for super-8 mm. film)
- —types of content (*a* for autobiography)
- —technical characteristics of content (*j* for digitized stereophonic sound)
- —types of publication (*s* for a provincial-level government document, *1* for a conference proceedings)
- —audience level (*v* for a secondary-school textbook)

—types of illustrative material contained (*c* for portraits, *e* for architectural plans)
—housekeeping data: the date of cataloguing, a code for the cataloguing agency.

Each of these control fields is, as a whole, a variable field. More codes may be added to the format provided they do not alter the character position of anything already defined in the field. There are also no subfields because the character position of each code, not its placement in a subfield, reveals its identity. The appendix shows a fully coded control field for a published monograph.

Indicators

Tags and subfield codes identify the parts of a record. Processing these parts may depend on defining to a program certain characteristics of the data such as which controlled vocabulary a subject access point comes from or, in a bilingually indexed database, whether the subject access point recorded in a field is in one language or the other (without explicit identification, the computer cannot distinguish an LCSH from a MeSH access point or a French from an English one). It is possible to do much identification of this kind using a single-byte code attached to a field.

As another example, a person recognizes and ignores an initial article in any known language almost unconsciously when filing or searching a title. It is inefficient to program a computer to recognize every article in every language but a one-byte numeral associated with a title field can constitute an explicit instruction to the filing program to skip up to nine characters at the beginning of the title when placing that title in an alphanumeric sequence. A one-byte code used for such a purpose as those described here is called an *indicator.* Each variable-length field of bibliographic data begins with two one-byte indicators, even though one or both are often left uncoded (blank). Neither the record-identifier field nor any control field contains indicators. An indicator is only associated with an entire field, never with an individual subfield.

BIBLIOGRAPHIC ENTITIES (LEVELS)

The monographic bibliography and the library catalogue of recent centuries are not merely collections of isolated records, each providing information about one document or publication. They deliberately show relationships among different works and documents by means of

1) the controlled vocabularies of their name and subject access points which link works related to the same person, subject, etc.
2) notes of many types, discretionary with the bibliographer/cataloguer, which mention the existence of other works or documents bibliographically related to the one being described, even if these are not evident in separate access points and
3) the principal access point and other name-title and uniform-title access points which relate the various manifestations of the same work to each other.

This section examines an additional kind of linkage provided for in bibliographic formats: a linkage among the different records which either do exist or could exist for the *same* document when that document can have more than one bibliographic identity. Some formats accommodate this linkage better than others, as noted in the mention of the CCF above, but all permit it to some degree.

What Does a Title Entitle?

Every bibliographic description must begin with a title, even if the cataloguer has to invent one ad hoc for a document lacking one. This cliché is almost as valid from the opposite point of view: every title has a home at the beginning of area 1 of a bibliographic description—provided a cataloguer has decided to create that description. What different kinds of entities have titles? The critical distinction between a work and a document is emphasized throughout this book. If a work is published in different editions, translations, etc., a uniform title collocates these in the file. If variant wordings of the title of a document appear on its title page, running heads, spine, etc., they are mentioned in an area 7 note and possibly warrant additional access points. The problem raised in this section is different: it is that of a document issued with more than one title, each representing a different bibliographic guise of the same publication. Together, its several titles pose an identity crisis for both the document in hand and for the work(s) it embodies.

The title pages reproduced in figure 28 illustrate this problem. They are the first and last title pages of the six volumes of Churchill's war history as published in both its North American and its British edition. They raise a number of questions which may at first seem like pedantic hair-splitting but whose answers are significant in revealing how a user will search for any or all of the six either as physical documents or as intellectual works:

1) Did Sir Winston write one work in six volumes or six works constituting a series?

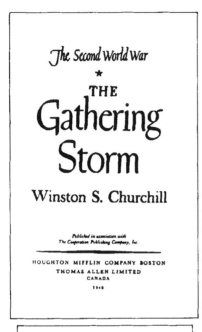

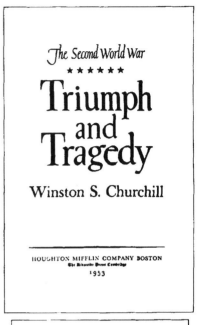

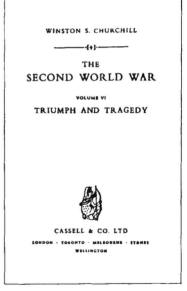

FIGURE 28.   Two pairs of title pages for the same works, showing the effect of typography in emphasizing titling at different levels.

2) Is the user more likely to search for Sir Winston's history of the war knowing the title common to the six parts (that is, at an access point beginning with S) or knowing each of the six

separate titles (that is, at G, T, etc.)? The answer that the user would search under C for **Churchill** does not resolve the issue; the large number of records accessible via his name must still be distinguished by individual titles.

3) Whether the user's information about Churchill's history of the war comes from references heard in conversation or from citations seen, how much are those conversational or citation-based references influenced by the wording, layout, and typography of the title pages of the documents in which they originate—that is, to what degree are a Briton and an American likely to search for, or cite, Churchill's history differently from one another because of the type of title which predominates typographically in the different editions shown in the figure?

4) In choosing which title to use as the basis of a footnote or other bibliographic record—that is, the title of the part (one particular volume) or that of the whole (all six volumes)—should one be influenced by whether one has read, bought, or consulted all six or only one or a few of them? (If it seems unlikely that a library would buy only one of the six Churchill volumes, such a decision is possible in another bibliographically identical situation.)

5) To describe all six volumes, should one prepare one bibliographic record (for the six volumes as a unit), six records (one for each volume), or seven? This last alternative is doubtless ideally preferable but
   a) it inevitably costs more money and
   b) it begs the question of how data elements will be presented for output or searching: each of the seven possible descriptions can begin with only one particular title in its area 1, and it is a different title in each case.

6) Would it have been easier or more difficult to arrive at a decision regarding questions (4) and (5) above when only the part first published existed or after all six had appeared?

To complicate matters further, all these questions have somewhat different implications for searchers in the environment of the interactive catalogue than they do in that of the manual catalogue.

Multiple Entities

This set of questions illustrates the problems involved in dealing simultaneously with two different things: (1) a multivolume set or series and (2) a monograph in that series. Each of the two is a distinct bibliographic entity identified by its own title proper, but both comprise the same physical item(s). The word *entity,* not a familiar part of bibliographic jargon in this context, is used, if reluctantly, here because neither of two more familiar terms, *work* or *level,* seems adequate. AACR2 uses the word in the sense intended here, but only in the glossary definition of "Main entry".

Level is used with the meaning intended here (1) in ISBD's section on the Multilevel Description, (2) throughout the Common Communication Format mentioned above, and (3) in AACR2R rule 13.6. However, among North American cataloguers, *level* normally serves only in the quite different sense discussed on page 198, that of a level of completeness in description. *Work* is also a less than satisfactory term here because of its other meanings. The Churchill case is not that of a single work which as a whole bears many titles; rather, as an entity to be catalogued, the six-volume history of the war is a different work than the one-volume history of its final year. Neither the problem nor the bibliographic solution is the same as in case of the Saint Matthew Gospel example at the beginning of chapter 6.

Some of the problems implicit in the above six questions seriously limit the possibility of retrieving what is wanted in a search of a manual file with its typically limited range of access points and its rigid display of records based on the cataloguer's determination of which of several possible bibliographic entities should be the basis for a record. In an interactive file, the possibility of searching each significant word of a title removes many of these limitations but only if the file includes and the search covers *every* title element possible, not only a supposed title proper. There are a number of reasons why this may not be as easy, or even possible, as it seems. One, which is striking in this particular example, is that almost every one of the title words involved is quite common. A search for *storm, tragedy, war,* etc. may prove confusing and discouraging when thousands of hits result.

A variant of this same problem occurs when the author, as in this case, appears in the file in relation to many different records rather than just one or two. Most user interfaces show only a few truncated data elements on a monitor as the initial response to a search request. Even if the searcher approaches a query involving this example in a theoretically sound way, by searching under the author's name, titles appearing as series or notes rarely appear on the screen until a fuller display is specifically requested. How is the user to know for which records to request this fuller display as the large number of Churchill's works are scrolling by and the initial display of their area 1 titles proper shows nothing which, *prima facie,* seems relevant?

The other two reasons show how keyword access may be a practical solution in particular cases when boolean operators can be applied in conjunction with keyword searching. However, this is never a theoretically sound approach to identifying the desired item. Both are based on the fact that a title may appear in one of several areas of the ISBD and therefore with different MARC tagging, as explored more fully in the next example.

One of these areas is a contents note, where titles of parts appear. The difficulty here is that no cataloguing code requires contents notes. Whether or not to include one is only suggested by the likelihood that a user might be helped in choosing a document through a fuller indication of what it contains. Cataloguers' judgement and libraries' policy on whether to include a contents note can therefore be expected to vary. Traditionally, therefore, contents notes serve the primary function of identification, not searching. They are not necessarily formulated as access points, especially not of a controlled vocabulary (as would be demanded if any personal or corporate name or uniform title were involved). The processing and memory capacity of modern search systems has encouraged librarians to make all contents notes searchable on a keyword basis within a title index, the basic natural-language index of any bibliographic system. This may or may not be either cost-effective or productive for any one given search. It is a blunt use of what could be a refined search strategy if full authority control were applied to all the names involved.

The final theoretical issue is that formatting can determine the index in which a title is searchable in an OPAC. In whatever fashion the volumes shown in figure 28 are catalogued, one or another of the titles involved will appear in area 6 or area 7, either or both of which may not be indexed for searching in a way the individual searcher expects, as discussed further below.

A Serial as One of the Entities

The title of a *serial*, like that of its very close bibliographic relative, a *series*, is subject to variation and also to linkage (whether in actual title wording or at least in the minds of searchers) with the name of an issuing body. A monographic series, as distinguished from a multivolume set bearing a series title, is also a serial because its publisher intends to issue titles in the series indefinitely. Historically, the two very similar types of title have been treated differently in library cataloguing less on the basis of sound theory than because of conventions based on the traditional maintenance of separate manual files (bibliographies, union lists, etc.) for serials. This has only resulted in unresolved argument and indecision among librarians as to whether monographic series, which include many proceedings of recurring conferences, should be treated primarily as serials or as monographs.

Despite this, despite the typical end-user's lack of awareness of any distinction between these two multivolume publication formats, and despite the file integration resulting from automation, the historical differences were unfortunately perpetuated in the MARC coding and OPAC search routines relevant to series and serials. A series title is typically added to a name authority file along with links to variant title(s) and usually also to the name of a noncommercial issuing agency. On the contrary, a serial title is not included in an authority file. Its variants and the name of any issuing agency are made additional access points directly in the bibliographic file. This can make a significant difference in how the two are located in an OPAC search, depending on the particular OPAC's user-interface programs.

The title page reproduced in figure 29 is more complex than that of the Churchill title pages because one of the three entities it explicitly identifies is a serial. The entities are represented by their titles:

1) *Sublevel Caving in Relation to Flow in Bins and Bunkers*
2) *Analysis of Bulk Flow of Materials under Gravity Caving Process* and
3) *Colorado School of Mines Quarterly.*

The sixty pages in this single-piece physical item contain other titles, too: titles of chapters, sections, and subsections of the text. Those may be important to the person quoting or indexing a particular passage within the document, but are of no importance in listing it as a whole. Or are they? Near the end of this perhaps overlong treatise on the bibliographic record, its author is less able than ever to offer the most significant definition related to access (*What is a work?*) or to answer the most important question for the future of bibliographic control (*Should the work replace the document as the basis of bibliographic description?*). That the answers to both these fundamental questions remain problematic is the thrust of this necessarily difficult section, which the beginner may wish to skip.

However one chooses to cite, to catalogue, or to index this publication, none of the three titles appearing on the title page reproduced in figure 29 can simply be ignored. Ideally, all three should appear in any record for the item. The following discussion explores

1) how the format embodied in ISBD, AACR, and MARC locates and relates the three titles in records of various kinds which should, or at least could, be created for the item
2) which kind of record is most appropriate under certain circumstances and
3) why in some cases one or more of these titles does *not* appear on a given record.

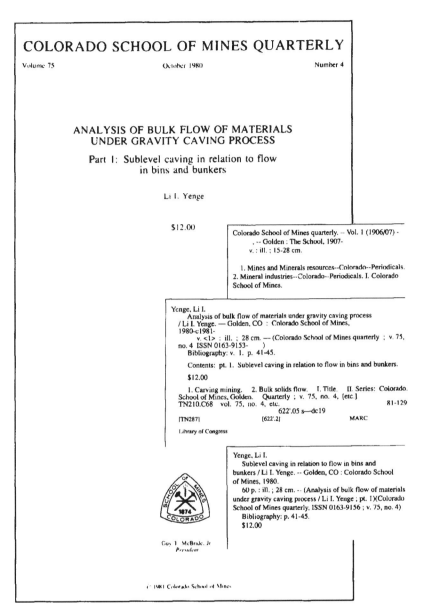

FIGURE 29. The title page of a single issue of a journal and some bibliographic records relevant to it.

The relationship of each entity to the other two is explicit and unambiguous. The entities are described below, beginning with the physically smallest and therefore least comprehensive one.

1) *Sublevel Caving* . . . comprises sixty pages issued by its publisher as one physical piece. It is part 1 of *Analysis of Bulk Flow* . . . and is, at the same time, the whole of the October 1980 issue (volume 75, number 4) of *Colorado School of Mines Quarterly.*

2) *Analysis of Bulk Flow* . . . comprises (1) the entity described immediately above *plus* (2) either the whole or part of some later issue(s) of the *Quarterly.* The appearance of *Part 1* on the title page in the figure implies that the publisher intended to issue one or more additional parts later, but neither its (their) eventual existence, titling, nor relationship to the *Quarterly* could be predicted with certainty. Bibliographic good intentions—even promises—remain unfulfilled, if perhaps not as often as some other ones. *Analysis of Bulk Flow* . . . was in fact subsequently completed by the appearance of a second piece which also bears three titles: (1) *Analysis of Bulk Flow* . . . , (2) *Theoretical and Physical Modeling of Gravity Flow of Broken Rock,* and (3) *Colorado School of Mines Quarterly,* of which it is the whole of the July 1981 issue (volume 76, number 3). Two of these three titles are therefore common to both parts of this entity.

3) *Colorado School of Mines Quarterly* was published continually under that title from 1906 to 1992 when *Review of Engineering* was added to the title (a fact ignored in the following discussion). Its hundreds of separate issues tend to be preserved in four-to-a-volume rebindings in libraries.

While it is not very common for a quarterly journal to devote each separate issue to a single separately titled contribution by a single person, this practice is spreading. To compare it with the Churchill example is to see how little difference it makes to the *work* (in this case, what Mr. Yenge wrote) whether it be published

1) as a single independent publication—something simple both to list and to search in a bibliographic file and for which the simplest of formats suffices

2) as a publication in a monographic series

3) as a single contribution gathered together into a monograph with other independently created contributions (one type of such publication is the anthology; another is the conference proceedings) or

4) as an article in, or the whole of, an issue of a serial publication.

Which of these modes of publication actually takes place may seem to concern only the work's author and publisher. These people tend to forget that it also makes a great deal of difference to anyone who must list the work in an A&I service, a bibliography, or a library catalogue and therefore also to anyone searching for it because each of these tools treats the entities it lists and indexes in a somewhat different context. It would simplify bibliographic control enormously if every work, however one defines that word, occupied the whole of, and only, one physical piece with only one title! There would then be no such thing as a serial, multivolume work, series, anthology, conference proceedings, etc. There would also be many unemployed indexers, cataloguers, and reference librarians because clerks could do much more of the bibliographic work and end-users could find much more of what they need without professional assistance.

Record Formats for Emphasizing Different Entities

The focus of each bibliographic record is the title proper chosen for its area 1. The formatting of every other data element in the record and the coherence and intelligibility of the record as a whole depend on how the other data elements are made to relate to that title proper. Each of the three records shown in figure 29 describes in some way the one physical piece whose title page is reproduced in that figure; two of them originated at the Library of Congress. Each record begins with the title proper of a different one of the item's three entities, and therefore gives prominence to the entity primarily identified by that title proper. The records show how ISBD areas 1, 6, and 7 are used to clarify the trinitarian nature and relationships of the one physical document. These three records are now analyzed separately.

The record with the title proper *Colorado School of Mines Quarterly* is a serial record. There is no area 6 because this is the most comprehensive entity involved in this case. One could conceivably list the titles of the individual issues of this serial, either totally or selectively, in area 7 as a contents note but to do so is rare in the case of a continuing serial because the note would be of uncontrollable length, a concern even with digital records. The record is incomplete because the serial is still being published. Blank spaces occur in areas 3, 4, and 5 to signal that information not yet knowable will be added when the serial ceases to be published. This type of record is still sometimes called an *open entry*. In its manual card form, it showed much empty space so that when the entity was added to or completed, the record could be updated with data inserted in manuscript or by typewriting without rewriting or retyping the entire record.

The cataloguer who anticipates problems of identifying separately titled single issues of a serial may choose, ad hoc, to analyze some or all of them as described in the next subsection. Even that is rare because it is normally expected that any citation will inform a searcher when the cited work is a part of a serial, thus shunting the entire search-and-retrieval process toward the A&I publication (whose very purpose is to analyze serials) and away from the library catalogue (whose focus is the monographic publication)—or, in an OPAC, toward A&I databases and away from the files describing the library's own collections. One might view the records in any A&I publication as contents notes linked to the records for whole serials which appear in library catalogues. The caution is that the two routes sometimes merge and that some bibliographic entities manage not to get onto either retrieval route.

The record in figure 29 entitled *Analysis of Bulk Flow* . . . describes a multivolume work not all of which existed at the time this record was made for its first part. The serial title *Colorado School of Mines Quarterly* appears in area 6 as the title of a series, a more comprehensive entity of which this is a part. The title of the least comprehensive entity, *Sublevel Caving* . . . , appears in a contents note in area 7 because it identifies part of the entity named in area 1. When this record was initially produced, only part of this entity existed, so like the serial record described in the previous paragraph, this one contains blanks in areas 4 and 5 in anticipation of later data. This is not, however, a serial record and therefore has no area 3. The Library of Congress eventually revised this record, completing it as shown in figure 30.

The final record in figure 29, the one with the title proper *Sublevel Caving* . . . is the only one whose focus, that is, the title in its area 1,

```
Yenge, Li I.
   Analysis of bulk flow of materials under gravity
caving process / Li I. Yenge. -- Golden, CO : Colorado
School of Mines, 1980-1981.
   2 v. : ill. ; 28 cm. -- (Colorado School of Mines
quarterly, ISSN 0163-9153 ; v. 75, no. 4, v. 76, no. 3)
   Bibliography: Vol. 1, p. 41-45; v. 2, p. 63-67.
   Contents: Pt. 1. Sublevel caving in relation to flow
in bins and bunkers -- pt. 2. Theoretical and physical
modeling of gravity flow of broken rock.
   $12.00 (per vol.)

   1. Caving mining. 2. Bulk solids flow. I. Title.
II. Series: Colorado School of Mines quarterly; v. 75,
no. 4, [etc.]

TN210.C68  vol. 75, no. 4, etc.     622'.05 s --dc19
[TN287]                             [622'.2]
                                            81-129
```

FIGURE 30.   The same record-identifier number shows this to be the same record as one of those in figure 29. The record in figure 29 has been completed and also revised to correct the error in the first subject heading in the earlier version.

is the single physical piece whose title page started this bibliographic journey. It is unlikely that any library would prepare this record because this entity is so self-evidently dependent on one or more other entities that citation to it in isolation would seem unlikely; in other words, a user is not likely to seek this title as such in a catalogue or A&I publication. Why this is self-evident, however, has more to do with the typography of the title page than with the wording of this title, which in itself is neither dependent nor unusual. There is probably a citation in some mining journal to this title, lacking adequate identification of its more comprehensive guises and therefore ready to trap some unwary searcher into looking for this entity, which lies buried without access in many a library. Despite the hypothetical nature of this record, it is worth noting with respect to the format that starting area 1 with this title makes it necessary to record not one but two more comprehensive entities as series in area 6. Since this record represents the least comprehensive entity of the three under discussion, any area 7 contents note on this record could only mention chapter or section captions from the text. This is always possible in theory but rare in practice.

Component Parts: Analytics and Multilevel Description

In the briefest description permitted by AACR2 rule 1.0D, no area 6 is required even if the title in area 1 is a part of a larger entity. Regardless of how brief or full the record, whether or not it includes a contents note is optional. For these reasons, any title identified above as belonging in area 6 or area 7 may not be included in the record produced by one or another agency. Even if a title is recorded in area 6 or 7, making it searchable in an OPAC is a separate issue. While it is normal to index all titles, the local user interface governs access parameters. Area 6, an area of controlled format and access vocabulary, is typically treated differently in interface programs from area 7, an area whose format is much less rigidly controlled.

The fact that interfaces still vary considerably from one to another can thus complicate a search for the user who routinely searches the catalogues of different libraries. Z39.50 interface software is not a magic remedy in this situation because the basis of accessibility is still the content and coding included by the library where the record originates. The user of any OPAC who does not know or bother about the distinction between a serial title, a series title, and a title appearing in a contents note is also ill served by their essentially technical distinction in the practice of cataloguing.

If full description and greater certainty of access is wanted for *each* entity involved, two ISBD/AACR-authorized formats are available, known as (1) the analytic and (2) the multilevel description. Analysis is the production of a bibliographic record for a *component part* of a *host item* when the latter (in this case, the *Colorado School of Mines Quarterly*) has its own record in the same file.[6] The Library of Congress records in figures 29 and 30 bearing the title *Analysis of Bulk Flow . . .* in area 1 are therefore *analytic records* or just *analytics*. In this example, the component part is a separately published document with its own title page, so the analytic record is indistinguishable from a record for a separate publication which is part of a series. However, *any* work, or part thereof, within a document can be analyzed provided it has its own title; for example, a single hymn in a hymnal or even (although probably not wisely) a chapter of a textbook where each chapter is by a different author.

A document has publication details; a work as such has none. The formatting described so far in this chapter accommodates bibliographic relationships among documents. A slight variation, the *In-analytic* format, shows the relationship between a work and a publication of which it is only a part. The word *In* introduces a very brief description of the host item because the latter is not the focus of the record in question. Its full description can be found elsewhere in the file, in a record to which the analytic is linked in the MARC format. The Chicago Manual of Style prescribes the following, in its humanities style, as the citation format for one of the plays in the anthology whose title page appears as figure 2 on page 50:

> Coward, Noel. *Hay Fever.* In *Modern Plays,* ed. John Hadfield. London: Dent, 1939, 141-98.

Although ISBD and AACR provide for a very similar catalogue format for the analytic, the advent of automated searching has curtailed its use. It is now more common to include searchable contents notes in records for host items notes than to create, at greater cost, separate analytic records for component parts. This limits access to the part. Access to a part in an "unstructured" contents note is limited to the natural vocabulary of the brief wording of the note. Although a "structured" contents note is possible, including, for example, an author's name in controlled-vocabulary form, full (including subject) access to a part, on the same basis as to its host item, is only possible when a separate analytic record is created for it.

Multilevel description is a method of displaying *full* information about each of several entities within a single record, as shown in figure 31. Access points can be derived from elements presented for any of the entities. Although part of ISBD, multilevel description is unfamiliar in Anglo-American practice. To take full advantage of it requires links from *parts* of a record, for example, a series field of one record to a contents field of another or to a title subfield of a third.

```
The Second World War / Winston S. Churchill. --
Boston : Houghton, Mifflin, 1948-1953.
   6 v. ; 23cm.

   1: The gathering storm. -- Boston : Houghton,
Mifflin ; Toronto : T. Allen, 1948. -- xvi,
784 p. : maps. -- Published in association with
the Cooperative Publishing Co.

   2:
      [etc.]

   6: Triumph and tragedy. -- 1953. -- xvi,
800 p. ; maps
```

FIGURE 31.   A multilevel description for the volumes of the Churchill item illustrated in part in figure 28 on page 334.

This essentially hypertext linkage, a familiar feature in the World Wide Web and possible in the Common Communication Format and in relational file structure, may seem an obvious and desirable feature of the library catalogue, but individual records formatted in MARC and assembled as units in an inverted file structure are not easily amenable to such linkage. The community of CCF users is still so small that programs to manipulate and search records in that format are not well developed.

Which, and How Many, Entities to Emphasize?

Whether the focus of a bibliographic record should be the work or the document is raised as a theoretical question throughout this book. It is in this area where its practical resolution is the most troublesome. Neither cataloguing codes nor record formats prescribe which of several possible entities represented in the same physical item the cataloguer must feature by recording its title proper in area 1—nor should they. Almost every record in an A&I publication is, in cataloguers' terms, an analytic record because its focus is the work: the individual journal article, conference paper, etc. The host document, the published journal issue, is treated only as a locator for the work. A bibliography of poetry, plays, songs, or festschrift papers is similarly based on the component parts of anthologies, not on the anthologies per se.

Despite its basic orientation to documents, AACR rule 1.1G contains the option of making a separate record for each of several works in a collection lacking a collective title—although only in closely circumscribed situations. It was a requirement in some situations in earlier rules. Until about 1980, the Library of Congress routinely applied this option in the case of sound recordings. The option is now almost universally ignored. Creating several shorter records is more costly than creating one longer one with a contents note. Cooperative/distributed cataloguing and resource sharing also focus attention on the document. If each of many cataloguers determines on an item-by-item basis which of several entities present within the same document should be the basis for a record, consistency among those contributing to a multilibrary database is highly unlikely.

Objective factors such as a library's size and type and the publication history of the work in question remain valid considerations. The user who wants Thornton Wilder's *Our Town* neither knows nor cares if it comes in a separate book, a three-volume anthology of American drama, or a magazine of play scripts. A large library typically buys a separately published play or longer poem as a monograph, but a smaller library must often rely on having it only as part of an anthology. Reference collections still include published indices of works included in anthologies. At an OPAC, it is ever more likely that a searcher can find an item published in an anthology through a search of contents notes or A&I files, but this is hardly a predictable and user-friendly response to a well-known need.

In the case of a part of a serial publication, another local factor in the decision as to which entities should be represented in the catalogue is whether or not the library acquires all of the serial or series. If it subscribes to the *Colorado School of Mines Quarterly,* the two parts of *Analysis of Bulk Flow* . . . are separated from each other by the two intervening issues of the *Quarterly;* in fact, they are probably bound into separate physical volumes. Nevertheless, its users are more likely to be directed by citations to the title of the whole journal. If, on the contrary, the library does *not* subscribe to the *Quarterly,* it has acquired *Analysis of Bulk Flow* . . . explicitly to serve an independent subject need. This should dictate that it bind the two thin parts together and treat them as one separate unit for cataloguing and shelving, giving priority to their intellectual content (the work) rather than to their origin in a journal (the document). If the same library acquires occasional other parts of the *Quarterly* and treats them in the same way, their origin in the serial is still revealed in the series area in their descriptions and retrievable at a series access point. It is reasonable for different cataloguing and shelving decisions to apply in different libraries, but as mentioned above, this leads to inconsistency within any multilibrary database.

To buy an A&I publication or a monographic bibliography has always been essentially the same as purchasing derived cataloguing. They give a library bibliographic access to essential parts of its own collection as well as indicating the existence of things it does not own. Yet their cost is almost always charged to a different part of the library's budget than its cataloguing function, and they are rarely thought of as integral parts of that function. When administrators decide that creating analytic records is too costly to continue, they ignore the fact that the bibliographic coverage of external databases such as A&I services does not quite meet the need for access to works contained within documents of larger scope in the collection. Analysis remains justifiable when the astute reference librarian can predict that such a work will be hard to locate unless given its own description and access points. It is the reference librarian, not the cataloguer, who should make such ad hoc decisions. Cataloguers and administrators should be willing to act on them.

If the creation of analytic records is no longer routine in general libraries, it still characterizes the cataloguing of special collections. The results find their way into the databases of the bibliographic utilities and onto the Internet, where they are welcomed for resource sharing. It is no surprise that a library which analyzes its collections thoughtfully gets requests for items other libraries actually own but have not adequately revealed to their own users in their catalogues. Sharing analytics has a major drawback, however: the variety of formatting options described in this discussion of bibliographic entities almost ensures inconsistency, even at times confusion, in identifying those entities. Deciding whether and by what technique to deal with the work, as distinguished from the document, remains the least standardized aspect of bibliographic control.

9
■ ∙ ■

Alphanumeric Arrangement

The arrangement of data elements is highly significant both in searching for a bibliographic record and then in interpreting the information displayed. The most meaningful juxtapositions within single records and files of them are therefore the ones predetermined by the cataloguer, even though user interfaces make it increasingly easy for a searcher to pick these apart, or not even to notice them when scanning a record or file display.

That different meanings result from different arrangements of data elements within a record is illustrated in the example on page 307. The consequences of juxtaposing elements in various possible pre-coordinate arrangements are seen in the example on page 142. The order of the words and parts of a single subject access point is of concern throughout chapter 7. All of classification consists of meaningful and helpful arrangement. To make the most effective possible search for information is to take advantage of all the work that has gone into these careful arrangements. However, it takes almost as much background knowledge and judgement to do so as it took the bibliographer to record and format them.

Many searchers lack the relevant knowledge or organizational skill, or just the time, to make this most effective kind of search, and many seek a quite simple unifacetted fact. These are comforted by the fact that single access points are almost necessarily arranged, whether for a manual or an interactive search, in alphanumeric order—that is, without regard to meaning, context, judgement, knowledge, etc. That *M* follows *L* and 5 follows 4 is neither rational nor logical. Unlike any other possible arrangement, it is universally both acceptable and useful precisely because it is both arbitrary and conventional. It is not, unfortunately, totally independent of language. Semantic elements have crept into almost every filing rule ever devised, although they are not essential to one. The inevitable linguistic problem in alphanumeric arrangement is the fact that there are hundreds of forms of the alphabet, among them the arabic, cyrillic, devanagari, hebrew, and roman forms. There are also several forms of numeric symbols, among them the arabic, chinese, roman, and thai forms. Few people know the characters or numerals and their conventional arrangement in many of these forms.

Because roman letters and arabic numerals are associated with a number of the world's most widely spoken languages and with the expansionist empires of Europe, they have been in the ascendency for centuries and are widely known, in both form and traditional sequencing, even where they are not much used to convey the vernacular. The spread of computer hardware and software from English-speaking countries also means that the twenty-six-character roman alphabet without diacritics is still favoured, despite developments in digital character sets for nonroman scripts and modified roman letters. The principles applied in *romanization*—converting characters of every other writing system into roman letters—are discussed at the end of this chapter.

Language intrudes somewhat into the sequential ordering of characters; for example, the Japanese have two ways of arranging their phonetic hiragana/katakana syllabary even when romanized, neither being the roman A–B–C order. A basic alphabetic character can become a problem when modified, as with a diacritic, because single-language conventions exist concerning the order of certain modified characters. Danes, for example, traditionally file ø after *z*; Germans traditionally file ü as if it were *ue*. Computerization has become a significant influence on the reassessment of the use of modified characters. For example, in German, the umlaut is now often ignored in filing, and a proposal to drop the β entirely is being debated; the Académie française is also investigating simplification of the use of diacritics, including the elimination of some.

Roman is one of the few scripts in which linguistic, not merely aesthetic, distinctions are conveyed by different forms of the same character such as upper- and lowercase. Fortunately, most of these distinctions are ignored in alphabetic arrangement. So, increasingly, is punctuation. Access-point indices are therefore usually converted into, stored, and searched in only one case and without punctuation.

This facilitates error-free keying of search requests and simplifies the writing and running of sorting programs, but the resultant loss of linguistic distinctions as a browse of access points is displayed can cause confusion and misinterpretation of those access points.

PHILOSOPHIES OF ARRANGEMENT

There is universal agreement on the sequence of the roman letters and therefore of the arrangement of single words. However, few access points consist of only a single word each. Details of arranging multiword and multielement bibliographic access points have been in dispute among librarians for generations. Internal consistency in the arrangement of any one file is of paramount importance, but a library's manual card catalogue exists in only one place so while this was the normal catalogue format, almost no force favouring standardization was available to stifle the ingenuity of the librarians as those in each library sought the perfect filing rule. Numerous differing filing rules resulted.

As stated at the beginning of this chapter, *meaningful* arrangement is the basis for the most fruitful searching of a bibliographic file. Librarians have traditionally attempted to bring meaning into essentially nonmeaningful alphanumeric filing by adding complications to the basic A–Z and 0–9 order on the basis of the meaning conveyed in the bibliographic function of each part of the access point being filed. Charles Ammi Cutter's influence in fostering classification—meaningful grouping of like things—is as strong in filing (and persisted as long) as in the matters discussed in chapters 6 and 7.

In what follows, it will be clear that meaning has not been erased from consideration. People, even file clerks, are accustomed to thinking about what they do and are easily trained to make judgements at the level for which they are recruited and paid. Programming judgement into a computerized operation is, however, costly and complex and results in significantly slower and less reliable operation. A meaningful arrangement brings more satisfaction and probably better results to a thinking, experienced searcher, but if it does not immediately appear simple and straightforward, it deters someone less at ease with bibliographic searching, less prepared with a search strategy, and less patient. The person or computer in a hurry has no time to puzzle out the intricacies of the increasingly complex filing-by-meaning common in library catalogues by the mid-twentieth century. Academic libraries in particular tended to follow the model of the Library of Congress, whose internal filing rules were never intended to be used except in the very largest of manual files and by the most experienced searchers; to apply it in, say, a college library was unwise.

Now that virtually all filing is done by a computer program, now that a searcher sees the results of a *BROWSE* command only a screenful at a time, now that end-user searching of bibliographic files is more the norm than ever before, the philosophy of filing has had to change from "Make It Meaningful" to "Keep It Simple, Stupid!" Librarians did not do this in isolation from the needs of even their experienced users. Those users were quickly becoming familiar with the simplified arrangement automation brought to virtually every directory, index, and other reference tool the library acquires in print as well as in digital form. It also brought the major benefit of a standardization previously unknown, not least because filing arrangement typically comes to a library with the DBMS it purchases.

BASIC FILING RULES

The most basic decision in alphanumeric filing is whether alphabetic and numeric characters should be interfiled or separated. Every "meaningful" filing sequence eventually involves filing "as if." In almost every manual bibliographic file (and most others), arabic numerals are interfiled with words as if they were being spoken as words in the language of their context. The attempt to continue this in early computer filing was short-lived. Numerals are now filed for what they are: characters different from letters and therefore to be arranged in their own sequence, either all before (the norm) or all after the sequence of letters.

This is not trouble-free. If each numeral is arranged as a separate character, the resulting order is 1, 15, 161, 18, 253, 36, 6. . . . Arithmetic meaning can be imposed on the sequencing, but it is not easy. The program must recognize the complete number as a unit, identify a decimal point if one exists, ignore commas, and arrange the result working to the left and to the right of the decimal point. In usages where thousands are separated by periods and a decimal is introduced by a comma, this too must be taken into account. In usage where thousands are separated by spaces, the very identification of the complete number is compromised. Then what does one do with roman numerals? Is the title of Shakespeare's play *Henry IV* to appear between *Henry Is Coming* and *Henry Misses Out*? Some problems admit no simple solution.

In the following examples, different types of access point are distinguished by the typographic conventions used throughout this book, but in them, the capitalization of titles is that prescribed by AACR. The most basic issue in the arrangement of words is whether or not the space which separates them constitutes a significant character for filing. The first example below shows *letter-by-letter* sequence. A space is ignored, and therefore *Newfoundland* precedes *New York* because *f* precedes *Y*. Punctuation is also ignored in letter-by-letter filing, but some punctuation is also ignored in other filing arrangements.

The example includes a range of access-point types: authors, titles, and subjects are interfiled in the "dictionary" arrangement now obsolete in the library catalogue but still typical of the back-of-the-book index. Since different access-point types are now almost invariably searched in a library OPAC in separate indices, the example is a bit unfair to an arrangement which works quite satisfactorily when used to arrange instances of only one type of access point. This is why, for example, telephone directories, whose filing elements are all names, and many encyclopaedias, where they are primarily subject words, retain letter-by-letter filing. The Chicago Manual of Style still recommends this arrangement for back-of-the-book indexing, although the latest version of the ANSI/NISO indexing standard Z39.4 recommends the word-by-word arrangement shown in the second example below.

Full capitalization shows the first access point in the example to be a one-word subject heading and italicization shows the second to be a one-word title. For filing purposes, the two are identical access points, so a rule or filing program must go outside the form of the access point itself to determine which precedes the other—for example, to the MARC content designator which reveals its function. Cutter assigns priority to a personal name, a place name, a subject, and a title in that order when the *entire* access points in question (not merely their first words) are identical. The simplest type of program for filing by computer arranges these in whatever order the access points are presented to the program, typically in the order of the control number for the whole record, which has no other meaning.

> **WOOD**
> *Wood*
> **WOOD—BIBLIOGRAPHY**
> **WOOD CHIPS INDUSTRY—CANADA**
> *Wooden shoes and windmills*
> *Wood frame construction*
> **Wood, Henry Angus**
> **Wood Lake (Neb.)**
> **Woodlawn Cemetery**
> **Wood (Pa.)**
> **WOOD—PRICES**
> **Wood-Rogers, Frank**

Wood's function in interior design
Wood, Sir Daniel
Wood, stone, and glass as building materials
The woodturner's craft
Wood-turning as an art
Woodward Stores and retailing in Western Canada
Woodward Stores, Ltd.
Wood, William

Letter-by-letter filing destroys the integrity of the word, the most basic meaningful unit of language. Few bibliographic access points consist of a single word. Cutter established word-by-word arrangement as the most basic principle of bibliographic filing, and it still is. It offers no problem in the operation of a computer program. Word-by-word filing is sometimes called *nothing-before-something* filing: a space (nothing, a blank) is treated as a twenty-seventh character of the alphabet and assigned a filing location preceding *A* (something). Thus *New York* precedes *Newfoundland* because the space after the *w* precedes *f*. A mark of punctuation is normally converted into a space, and no distinction is made between a single space and two or more spaces together. An apostrophe is, however, ignored—that is, removed and not replaced with a space. The special problem of hyphens is discussed after the example. This is now the most common arrangement in library catalogues, monographic bibliographies, and A&I publications, with few differences among individual ones.

The following example uses the same access points as in the letter-by-letter example above, again combining names, titles, and subjects.

WOOD
Wood
WOOD—BIBLIOGRAPHY
WOOD CHIPS INDUSTRY—CANADA
Wood frame construction
Wood, Henry Angus
Wood Lake (Neb.)
Wood (Pa.)
WOOD—PRICES
Wood-Rogers, Frank
Wood, Sir Daniel
Wood, stone, and glass as building materials
Wood-turning as an art
Wood, William
Wooden shoes and windmills
Woodlawn Cemetery
Wood's function in interior design

The woodturner's craft
Woodward Stores and retailing in Western Canada
Woodward Stores, Ltd.

The hyphen, two of which occur in this example, is more of a problem than other marks of punctuation. Here, it is converted into a space with the result that *woodturning* is separated from *wood-turning,* or *wood turning,* although all three are orthographically acceptable forms. When dealing with natural language, this situation arises frequently as in *on-line* and *online; co-operation* and *cooperation/coöperation.* Manual filing rules require the filer to make an ad hoc judgement based on the separability of the parts before and after the hyphen. For computer filing, it is only practicable to treat hyphens all one way (changing them into spaces) or another (removing them and not inserting a space). Because they are more troubled by hyphens in title words than in names, many database vendors choose the latter course, which would cause *Wood-Rogers* to appear almost at the end of this sequence, filed as *woodrogers.*

Punctuation and the Structure
of Access Points

That the hyphen is typically changed into a space while the apostrophe is ignored indicates that to program either effect is not difficult and that punctuation is not in itself a problem in arranging displays generated by a DBMS. However, there is no standardization in the effect of punctuation on searching or display. A search for **Smith John** in some systems generates the unexpected response "Nothing found" because the comma following the surname in the index must be matched as well as the other characters and spaces. It is much more common for punctuation to be ignored in searching and not to be displayed when access points are browsed. In that case, the search for **Smith John** in the same database would result in many hits. Problems with the hyphen, indicated above for manual searching, prevail also in interactive searching because of the several ways the designer of the DBMS and the coding manual for input can treat this troublesome mark.

Punctuation is discretionary with the cataloguer in any natural-language elements of a record, including title (but not uniform-title) elements. In filing such elements, punctuation is therefore invariably ignored. In every rule for constructing controlled-vocabulary access points, however, punctuation is meaningful. It serves as a kind of content designation, is exactly matched by the subfield coding of access points in the MARC format, and is intended to make the different elements separately manipulable. Cutter specified what punctuation is to be used within name and subject access points, then wrote a filing rule making use of it. A period divides a corporate subheading from the name of the parent body. A subject subdivision follows a dash (not a hyphen). In some filing rules, the period is still the signal that all corporate subdivisions of one body (from **Ohio. Assessment Board** through to **Ohio. Youth Assistance Agency**) must precede a different body (**Ohio General Insurance Co.**). Even when the punctuation no longer serves an explicit purpose in arranging, it still aids in interpreting the access point. Cutter's punctuation pattern is continued even more consistently in AACR.

The complex filing rules developed at the Library of Congress by the 1950s as extensions of Cutter's "meaningful" type of arrangement represent both the ultimate stage and the death-rattle of interpretive considerations once thought beneficial to trained searchers using a huge manual catalogue.[1] People came to call it filing *as if* because of its deviation from the strict order of the words and characters present in the filing element. When computer-based filing was forced on librarians by the abandonment of manual card files, they first pursued the writing of programs which would accomplish what they were doing manually. It quickly became evident that the necessary programs would be far too complex and their execution time too lengthy.[2]

COMPUTER-BASED FILING RULES

As librarians, as well as their patrons, became familiar with the results of computer-based filing all around them, the simplification, and also the separation of name, title, and subject indices, came to appear more beneficial than detrimental to effective searching. Many of the amendments to AACR over its thirty-year development have been occasioned by the consequences for computer-based filing of how an access point is structured. Three major English-language rules for computer-based filing were finally published in 1980, one written by a committee of the American Library Association, one at the Library of Congress, and one at the British Library.[3] These rules are designed for computer application in more than one way; for example, they identify how data elements are to be arranged both in words and by their MARC tags and subfield codes.

The American Library Association rules depart most completely from the Cutter tradition in that they ignore almost all the distinctions among different parts and types of access point signalled by punctuation marks. In contrast, Library of Congress and British Library rules retain the traditional grouping of access points by type (surnames, jurisdictions with subdivisions, etc.). **Canada Bank Note**

Co. files before **Canada. Census Division** in the ALA rules, while the other two preserve the Cutter principle of the *Ohio* example above. There are advantages and disadvantages to either approach, but two assumptions underlie the greater complexity of the latter:

1) more attention to logical groupings is needed in searching a very large catalogue, where it is harder to see the forest for the trees, and
2) the catalogue of a national institution is more likely to be searched by persons well versed in bibliographic practices than by casual untrained users.

It seems unlikely that these rules will ever need to be extensively reviewed. Filing principles, and a model result of using them, have also gone through the process of ratification by ISO. The former are expressed as standard ISO7154: "Documentation — Bibliographic Filing Principles." Since only limited agreement could be reached on the latter, it appears as an ISO technical report, TR8393: "Documentation — ISO Bibliographic Filing Rules." These two documents constitute an excellent study of the component parts of any type of access point inasmuch as they can influence filing at any level of complexity.

A review of the two 1980 American rules examines the human interpretation and judgement still required to implement them and the resulting programming complications.[4] That *Sir* is ignored when it is a title of honour in a name access point but not when it appears in a title is one of the few related to controlled-vocabulary access points. In a controlled vocabulary, the authority file provides for linkages so that searcher who fails to locate the preferred form directly may do so using a link at a different search key or file location:

> **A One Carpet Cleaning Ltd.**
> *search under* **A-1 Carpet Cleaning Ltd.**

Authority control also operates with uniform titles. Orwell's *1984* was also published with the title-page wording *Nineteen Eighty-Four,* so accepting one of these as the uniform title and creating an equivalence link with the other is totally in keeping with the rules. However, it is impracticable routinely to provide links for all possible number forms (from *Nineteen Sixty-Eight* to *1968*) when the only edition of the work bears only one of these on its title page. It is even more awkward to deal with abbreviated and symbolic forms embedded within, rather than beginning, a data element, for example, *&* for *und, et, and,* etc., or × for *times, by,* etc.

Computer-based filing therefore continues to burden the searcher with the need to think, sometimes imaginatively, about what exact form a natural-language access point might take because the computer does not group forms similar in meaning but visually different. It helps if one knows when it may be necessary to search in two places for a possible hit. Now that the searching of abstracts and the full text of articles, etc. is routine, a searcher may regularly deal with more natural than controlled language. Some A&I services have a policy of requiring clerical input operators to change selected elements of natural-language text into a consistent form for searching according to directives they can implement without exercising judgement. Complex programs can also be used for this purpose. Numbers, acronyms, initialisms, and abbreviations are prime candidates for such modification. No library cataloguing rule has ever countenanced changing any character (except for punctuation or capitalization) in a title. Nor, to date, has any library rule specified the wording of natural-language cataloguers' notes with a view to retrieval, but the wise cataloguer now makes a greater attempt at consistency when composing such notes.

RECORD DISPLAY SEQUENCE

A searcher first locates access points, whether controlled or in natural language, according to any of the above relatively simple principles or rules. The hits sought, however, are not those access points, but the complete or partial records to which they are linked. When the search key is a title, a single such hit is the norm. When it is a name access point, this is also usually the case, but a searcher looking for, say, **Shakespeare, William** should not be surprised if hundreds of hits result. It is the very purpose of a controlled-vocabulary subject access point to group many individual items. Finally, the number of records retrieved using any single natural-language word or term as a search key can rarely be predicted and is often very large. To be able to tailor such keys to particular requests and retrieve a limited amount of highly relevant material is a mark of a searcher's intelligence, experience, and skill.

Whether the number of records displayed on a monitor screen or the number of cards found in a card file at the same access point is two or hundreds, the records appear in some determinable sequence. It may be no more meaningful than the order in which the records happen to have been added to the file: a control-number order is typical of the simplest computer-based systems. Since a searcher has no control over the sequencing within a manual file, it is particularly important that it be the most useful order to the greatest number of searchers. Filing and cataloguing rules ensure a bibliographically meaningful sequence of records in a manual file through what is essentially pre-coordination: prescribing which two or more access points or data elements are considered sequentially in the file arrangement.

Fifty different items bearing a common name access point are subarranged or displayed in alphanumeric order by their titles. What other order could be more useful? At a subject access point, the author in general and the individual work in particular are traditionally considered the most significant attributes of the hits. Critiques of Shakespeare's work are best subarranged to group those of Bradley separate from those of Kittredge, etc., and it is good to have all editions of any one of these authors' works presented together. Every filing rule including the 1980 ones cited above express, in their rules for subarrangement, the continuing importance of the principal access point (main entry heading)—in principle, an author plus a uniform title—as the single most generally useful means for both identifying and isolating the work in question regardless of what other access points are involved in the search.

However, just as access by many different characteristics is preferable to access by only one, no one method of subarranging the records retrieved at a single access point suits all purposes equally well. Searchers for material in the sciences and technologies are more concerned to retrieve the most recent documents than those searching in the humanities. In some libraries, filing even in the card catalogue was changed to make the date the element of primary subarrangement, *then* the author, within a subject access point. That this subarrangement is likely to separate different editions of the same work seems more of a disadvantage to some searchers than to others. It is not feasible, however, to adopt a particular subarrangement only in some subject areas: how can one objectively define, say, a "science" access point?

Interactive searching is not based on a fixed file, nor necessarily on one filing rule. A user interface can be programmed to arrange a hit list on the basis of any formatted data element(s). It is increasingly common for the searcher to be given some control over how the results of any particular search are arranged for display, bypassing the default order of one of the standard filing rules. Librarians once discussed and disputed filing in detail among themselves. It now seems an issue only when a library evaluates integrated processing systems in preparation for buying and installing a new one. It buys the filing routines along with all the other functions of the system's DBMS and is unlikely to reject an entire system solely on the basis of how it deals with this matter. Filing is usually not even mentioned in the vendor's promotional material. Information supplied to end-users at an OPAC about either the default arrangement or alternative ones available is often scanty. Even strict conformity with one of the filing rules cited above is not usually assured.

NONROMAN SCRIPTS

European academic and national libraries commonly keep records for material in nonroman scripts (for example, arabic, cyrillic, hangul) in separate catalogues, each arranged according to the filing conventions peculiar to itself. In most North American libraries, records for material in different scripts are consolidated in a combined file, which requires the use of romanized forms of names (including all titles)—anything used as an access point—even if the remainder of the record is in the vernacular script. Romanization (sometimes, but more loosely, called transliteration) is the conversion of nonroman characters into characters of the roman alphabet. It is not translation. Converting 日本放送協会 into **Nihon Hōsō Kyōkai** (or into NHK) is romanization; changing it into **Japanese Broadcasting Corporation** is translation. Romanization is not an issue only for large, academic, or automated libraries. Names of nonroman-script origin are regularly encountered in everyday library work in English in even the smallest libraries:

Peter Tchaikovsky: *originally* **Пётр Ильич Чайковский**
Anton Chekhov: *originally* **А. П. Чехов**
Sholem Asch: *originally* **שלום אש**
Yukio Mishima: *originally* 三 島 由 紀 夫

Existing Romanization

The surname of the author of *The Cherry Orchard,* shown above in its original cyrillic form, appears in print on some title page in each of the romanizations shown below, the language of the title page being indicated in brackets.

Anton Čechov [English, German, Italian]
Anton Čechow [German]
Anton Čexov [English]
Anton Chehov [English]
Anton Chekhov [English]
Anton Czechow [Polish]
Anton Tchehov [English]
Anton Tchekhoff [English]

Anton Tchekhov [English, French]
Anton Tchékhov [French]
Anton Tchekoff [English]
Anton Tschechov [German]
Anton Tschechow [German]
Anton Tsjechov [Dutch]

As a modern example from another script, the surname of the Libyan head of state appears in various English-language news-media headlines with the initial letter **G**, **K**, or **Q**. Each of the above forms is called an existing romanization because it appears in some existing roman-alphabet publication. If a library collects materials in many languages, a few cases are sure to arise of differing existing romanizations of the same name, if not cases as extreme as those involving Mr. Chekhov and Colonel al-Qadhdhafi (the Libyan leader's name as found in one English-language title).

Romanization is based on phonetics: it attempts to reproduce in the roman alphabet the sound of the character in the other script as it is pronounced by a native speaker of the language in question. It almost inevitably involves some distortion of the sound of both the original language and of the language (or dialect) of the person who imposes the romanized form. Many roman characters, singly or in combination, are pronounced differently by native speakers of different languages—often even among speakers of the same language. Romanization also involves orthography, a very imprecise art in most languages but particularly in English, which is notoriously inconsistent in its rendering of roman characters in sound and vice-versa.

Multiple existing romanizations arise from the fact that cultural exchanges between, say, the slavic and the arab worlds (on the one hand) and speakers of various Western European languages (on the other) began early; sometimes before the stabilization of orthography brought about by print. Speakers of each Western European language romanized the foreign words by sound and passed on their romanizations in diaries and published writings, often ignorant of different romanizations of the same words adopted by others. Thus a German hearing a particular sound made by a Russian visualizes an equivalent German word which begins *tsch* or *tch;* at the same time, an American bystander hearing the same person visualizes an equivalent English word which begins *ch.*

Throughout the nineteenth century, the English-speaking world got most of its nonindigenous musical tradition via Germany, the source of most printed scores, so English speakers accepted the Russian composer's surname as Tschaikowsky or (now more often) Tchaikovsky. For the most part, the literary and theatrical traditions came directly from Russia to Great Britain, so the surname of the

Russian writer only begins with a *T* in an English-language source in the increasingly rare case of a publication directly influenced by Germans. In their original cyrillic script, the surnames of both the composer and the writer begin with the same character: Ч.

Systematic Romanization

In the ethnocentric world of colonization and imperialism, it was expected that the owners of the roman script, the European and Anglo-American community, would determine how to romanize other scripts. The previous paragraph shows that this process cannot solve the problem. Using existing romanizations as access points therefore still requires authority control, since there may be different ones for the same original characters. It pleases a librarian or a user interested only in music, or only in literature, because it matches ingrained expectations. However, library databases are rarely limited to a single subject area. The compromise born of convenience and long adopted in libraries is to use a *systematic romanization:* an automatic equating of a given nonroman character with one or more specific roman characters. Applying this principle to the cyrillic-script surnames of the composer and the writer named in the previous paragraph means that the same initial roman letter must begin both surnames, whether that be C or T. This makes the matching of character sets possible through computer programs and facilitates international communication of names.

Librarians have long been involved in efforts toward international agreement on ISO-authorized systematic romanization tables. Although these exist for a number of scripts, they are not widely used because of the entrenched interests of people in business, government, and libraries with large existing files which would have to be thoroughly revised, staff which would need to be retrained, and users potentially mystified by the appearance of, say, Colonel al-Qadhdhafi's name even when they have reached it automatically after keying **Kadafi**. In most North American libraries, and to a high degree in the international English-language library community, the tables applied when systematic romanization is used are those devised at the Library of Congress for its own use. These are presented to the American Library Association for review and sanction and are the tables used in the examples in AACR.[5]

In the 1950s, the government of the People's Republic of China decided, in conjunction with other language initiatives, to create a new systematic romanization, pin-yin, and to dictate its use in all roman-script publications issued within its jurisdiction. This romanization differs substantially from the Wade-Giles system previously prevalent among English-language sinologists, journalists, etc. That the initiative came from within China marked a break from the previously almost universal practice of romanization imposed by those outside the language area in question. It took the Chinese government more than a generation of continual cultural and diplomatic pressure to have pin-yin adopted abroad, but the result is a greater worldwide standardization in the romanization of Chinese characters than is the case with other nonroman scripts. In 1979, a person was identified on the cover of *Time* magazine as Mr. Teng. Ten years later, the same person was Mr. Deng on another *Time* cover. The pronunciation by a native Mandarin speaker of both his name and that of the country's capital city never changed, but *Peking* also virtually disappeared from sight, just as *Pei-ching,* a form printed in many earlier English-language books, slipped from currency a century ago.

Systematic romanization was required by Cutter and by subsequent rules applied in library catalogues until 1980. With the implementation of AACR2, in which it is optional, the Library of Congress decided to use either existing or systematic romanization depending on specified circumstances, in order best to meet the expectations of the scholarly community in different fields. Those consulted by the Library of Congress on this matter still consist primarily of people who have learned to read a nonroman script as scholars, not those who write in it as natives. It took until 1996 for that library to begin adopting pin-yin. The Russian musical composer was moved in 1981 from C, where he languished hidden for so long, to T, while Chekhov remained where he was. The revival of interest in a common authority file for the Library of Congress and the British Library, mentioned in chapter 5, requires them to review their differing practices in romanization as well as in other areas where they have hitherto followed different options in AACR2. Perhaps now attention can shift to another form already firmly established in English-language writing: *Qu'ran* instead of *Koran.*

APPENDIX

▬ ▪ ▬

The MARC Format

The characteristics of variable-field formatting in general and of both ISO2709-based formats and the subset of these known as MARC formats are described in chapter 8. MARC must accommodate every possible data element considered useful in any size or type of library and for a search of any complexity, no matter how esoteric or infrequently encountered. Libraries digitize old manual records without necessarily upgrading their content to current cataloguing codes, so MARC still includes content designators applicable to obsolete cataloguing practices. As items in new media need to be described and more specialized search options are made possible in processing software, new content designators are added, and some changed, as committees keep MARC under constant review. Like a cataloguing code, the digital format will never be finished.

For these reasons, a complete MARC coding manual is a bulky loose-leaf publication internally repetitious and including many details which a practising cataloguer requires only infrequently. That one can catalogue a very high proportion of current materials in the most usually collected media using only a fraction of all the available content designators was acknowledged in the publication of a "concise" version of USMARC. More recently, the Library of Congress prepared an even more simplified version for the novice.[1] The latter publication makes it unnecessary for this appendix to be a full "teaching version" of MARC of the kind featured in this book's first two editions. This appendix is therefore limited to a discussion of MARC's scope and its essential technical structure, so that the reader can understand how it functions, and enough of its history to explain the seeming anomalies and illogicalities which are carry-overs from its origins and early development.

Conceptually, cataloguing may be a single intellectual operation, but in practice, each of its many stages involves the application of a different set of rules, policies, lists of prescribed codes, etc. Even the two most basic and most nearly universally applied codes of practice, AACR and the MARC format, are maintained by separate committees in each of several countries. It is therefore an achievement that they remain in conformity with one another. Summaries of MARC now exist with explicit references to AACR rule numbers, but AACR is not yet published with mention of MARC content designators—nor are lists, such as LCSH, of controlled-vocabulary subject access points. It is even more unfortunate that MARC and ISBD were introduced separately to local cataloguing operations (ISBD rather later than MARC in North America) and that, for a long time, retrospective conversion of non-ISBD records into the MARC format also kept the practical application of the two formats separate to a degree.

Each local library and consortium adds its overlay of policies and some local MARC coding to the published standards. The cataloguing aids and interpretations issued by the Library of Congress have been consolidated onto one CD-ROM sold as the *Cataloger's Desktop* and because the CD-ROM edition of AACR2R uses the same software, the two can be linked in use. Despite the greater technical ease of using the published documentation, the practising cataloguer now faces so much and such varied information to apply that it is virtually impossible to rely, as one routinely did in simpler days, on personal experience and memory.

INPUT AND OUTPUT CONVENTIONS

In the environment of digitized records, all cataloguing operations are eventually expressed through the MARC format. A cataloguer

1) decides on the data elements to appear in the record by examining the document in the context of rules for descriptive cataloguing and name access (AACR2) and controlled-vocabulary subject analysis practices (DDC, LCC, LCSH)

2) codes each resultant data element or separately defined part thereof with the appropriate MARC content designators: tags, indicators, and subfield codes (this is called *tagging* the record)

3) adds codes in one or more control fields to make certain pieces of information explicit and more easily searchable

4) codes for the label (called *leader* in USMARC) a few elements describing the record as a whole and finally

5) adds any required local data with the appropriate coding.

In the first step, for example, the cataloguer uses AACR to compose the following principal access point and ISBD area 1:

```
Roland, J.H. (John Harvey), 1943-
The Kennedy days / John H. Roland and Ralph
Beacock.
```

In the second step, the cataloguer determines the appropriate content designators for each of these two separate fields of data:

1) one tag: for the access point, 100; for area 1, 245
2) two indicators: for the access point, a 1 (because the person has a single surname) and a 0; for area 1, a 1 (because a title access point is desirable) and a 4 (because its first four bytes must be ignored when it is filed) and
3) a two-byte subfield identifier preceding each subfield, the first being the standard subfield delimiter printed throughout this appendix as ‡.

When this is input, something like the following appears on the monitor screen:

```
100 10 ‡aRoland, J.H. ‡q(John Harvey), ‡d1943-
245 14 ‡aThe Kennedy days /‡cJohn H. Roland
       and Ralph Beacock.
```

In the third step, the cataloguer realizes that this title implies that the book includes biographical information and looks up the appropriate one-byte code to indicate this fact in field 008, where it it is possible to search for it in isolation or in boolean combination with other sought factors.

In the fourth step, the cataloguer might code that this is a revised record replacing a previously incomplete CIP record used for acquisitions purposes in the same system, and that it describes a monographic textual item: these are among the facts about the record itself (not about the item being catalogued) needed for file management. Another byte in the leader carries a code to identify the type of material to which the item being catalogued belongs; for example, a computer file or a sound recording. Because some bibliographic-data fields are only relevant to certain types of material and much coding in the control fields (tags 006, 007, and 008) is specific to a type of material, that byte controls format management by determining which of different possible meanings is to be associated with a particular code or piece of data.

In the final step, the cataloguer might add, in a MARC field reserved for local uses, the code for each branch to which a copy of the book is assigned.

Professional cataloguers now routinely work directly at a keyboard rather than filling out work sheets manually for clerks to input. This is because from the same workstation, the cataloguer locates a large proportion of all the information needed in the process: existing records from a variety of bibliographic and authority databases, policy decisions and interpretations, even reference information on authors, answers to queries posted on Internet bulletin boards, etc. The exercise a cataloguer once got from repeatedly rising to go to check a manual file or publication must be replaced by jogging or swimming after hours!

What the cataloguer sees on the monitor, like what the end-user sees at an OPAC, is governed by the interface incorporated into the library's processing system. Many systems make it possible for the individual cataloguer (or searcher) to customize this. Some prefer an automatic prompt for the next expected data element in sequence by automatic display of its content designation—this may be manually overridden if it is not appropriate in the particular case. Others prefer a complete screen of expected content designators as a kind of spreadsheet to be filled in. By adding information available as constants, counting bytes, etc., the software completes the structuring of the keyed data as a MARC (or MARC-compatible) record in the local system and indexes it for searching—all according to the parameters the library chose when it installed the software.

For efficiency, software is designed to minimize repetitious routine keying. Any data or code which can be generated by a program should be provided as a constant. For example, library cataloguing rules based on Cutter require the enclosure of a series description (ISBD area 6) within parentheses, and there are MARC tags unique to this area. A program can therefore recognize the appropriate tag and supply the parentheses as a display constant without the need to key them into the record. The dash required in the ISBD area separator but not found on a keyboard can also be input automatically, along with its surrounding spaces, as the program identifies each relevant tag. The area separator has been rendered largely irrelevant in OPAC output, which is now typically "labelled" so that a field's name appears as a display constant before the data in the field (see the third version of the example below).

When the first processing programs were written in the 1960s and early 1970s, it was common for a record to be displayed on a monitor screen in the manner in which it would have appeared on a 3-by-5-inch card. The Z39.50 interface protocol described at the end of chapter 4 is the culmination of a long process of separating the way data are input by the cataloguer from the many different ways the same data can be made to appear to the searcher. Yet many of the cataloguers' input conventions fixed decades ago are still applied, even ones no longer necessary or even logical. For example, with one exception which could easily be resolved with a little goodwill, *all* ISBD punctuation could be generated from MARC content designators and would not need to be keyed.

Computer programs for automatic format recognition are now common in many applications. Such a program not only digitizes optically scanned data, but identifies the nature of its elements according to their appearance, location within the visual image, and/or internal context, and can therefore supply the appropriate content designation. Banks process cheque clearance and bill payments using such programs. Automatic formatting of a scanned title page to produce a MARC record is still experimental, but its operation with a satisfactorily low error rate is anticipated.

Patterns and Mnemonic Features

Throughout MARC, content designation was chosen for mnemonic value where possible. For example, when a personal name is chosen as (or as the first element of) a principal, added, or subject access point, its tag always ends in two zeros (100, 600, 700, 800). Furthermore, one of its indicators and many, if not all, of its subfield codes are identical in all these fields. Much subfield coding expresses alphabetically the order of the elements of the field in question as they are usually displayed, for example, *a, b,* and *c* for the place, publisher, and date in area 4. In fact, it is rare for the first-displayed subfield to be coded anything but *a* even when the rest is not an alphabetic sequence. In other cases, subfield codes were chosen mnemonically (for example, *l* for *language*). Their relative alphabetic position does not, therefore, necessarily express the usual display order of the elements in question. That is governed by the cataloguing rules, list of subject headings, etc.

Many a field or subfield is repeatable. Repeating a field means repeating its tag, its two indicators, and all relevant subfields as many times as necessary. This is usually the case only with access points. There can only be one principal access point per record, but there may be many added, subject, and number-identifier access points of the same type. Repeating a subfield means repeating only that subfield, along with its two-byte subfield code, *within* the field. A great many subfields are repeatable.

AN EXAMPLE

A hypothetical complete record is now shown, first in the traditional manual unit-card format.

```
Smith, Jean, 1943-
     Collecting Canada's past / Jean &
Elizabeth Smith ; photography by Bob Bell. —
Scarborough, Ont. : Prentice-Hall of Canada,
c1995.
     220 p. : ill. (some col.) ; 27 cm. —
(The Hobbyist's handbooks, ISSN 1523-5071 ;
no. 5)
     ISBN 0-13-140467-9 : $39.95.
     1. Collectors and collecting. 2.
Material culture—Canada. 3. Canada—Social life
and customs. I. Smith, Elizabeth, 1947- II.
Bell, R. K. III. Title. IV. Series.
NK1125.S687      745.1'0971      95-102301
```

The same data are given below with MARC content designators, presented in columns with the different types of content designators separated from each other. This is one of many possible ways of displaying either a newly created record or one received from an external database so that personnel in the cataloguing department can verify both text and content designation at a glance. The first line shows only the six bytes the cataloguer inputs for the leader. (Although the leader bears no tag, it is often displayed as if it bore the tag *000*). The second line is the record-identifier number in the receiving library's database, a number generated by that library's input program, which then transfers the record-identifier number of the sending institution into a different field. The double dagger stands for the subfield delimiter; the field and record terminators are typically not displayed.

```
000              nam*a*
001              38657410
008              950328s1995****onca**********001*0*eng*1
010    **    ‡a  ***95102301*
020    **    ‡a  0131404679 :
             ‡c  $39.95.
050    0*    ‡a  NK1125
             ‡b  .S687
082    **    ‡a  745.1'0971
             ‡2  20
100    10    ‡a  Smith, Jean,
             ‡d  1943-
245    10    ‡a  Collecting Canada's past /
             ‡c  Jean & Elizabeth Smith ; photography
                 by Bob Bell.
260    0*    ‡a  Scarborough, Ont. :
             ‡b  Prentice-Hall of Canada,
```

```
           ‡c   c1995.
300   **   ‡a   220 p. :
           ‡b   ill. (some col.) ;
           ‡c   27 cm.
440   *4   ‡a   The Hobbyist's handbooks,
           ‡x   15235071 ;
           ‡v   no. 5
650   *0   ‡a   Collectors and collecting.
650   *0   ‡a   Material culture
           ‡z   Canada.
650   *0   ‡a   Canada
           ‡x   Social life and customs.
700   1*   ‡a   Smith, Elizabeth,
           ‡d   1947-
700   1*   ‡a   Bell, R. K.
```

How this record appears to any subsequent searcher is under the control of the user interface as described at the end of chapter 4. The following is one of many possible "labelled" (or "tagged") displays, in which MARC codes are changed into words to name the displayed fields. OPACs vary greatly in the selection of elements and their labelling, but some local holdings and location information is a necessary part of it. Modern interfaces link circulation data with the bibliographic file so that the location field not only states the normal branch and shelf location of every copy of the item owned by the library but also provides up-to-the-minute information about its circulation status.

```
     TITLE:      Collecting Canada's past
     AUTHOR:     Jean & Elizabeth Smith
     DATE:       c1995
     PUBLISHER:  Prentice-Hall of Canada
     SERIES:     The Hobbyist's handbooks
     LOCATION:   copy 1: Main Library, REF 745. 10971
                 SMI (Reference)
                 copy 2: Holly Branch, 745. 10971 SMI
                 (available)
                 copy 3: Myrtle Branch, 745. 10971 SMI
                 (out on loan)
FOR RELATED MATERIAL SEE SUBJECT FILE UNDER:
                 Collectors and collecting.
                 Material culture—Canada.
                 Canada—Social life and customs.
```

Stored on a length of tape, the record (without the locally added data) looks like the binary equivalent of the alphanumeric version shown in figure 32.

0 0 7 4 3 n a m * * 2 2 0 0 2 1 7 * a * 4 5 0 0	0 0 1 0 0 0 9 0 0 0 0 0	
0 0 8 0 0 4 1 0 0 0 0 9	0 1 0 0 0 1 7 0 0 0 5 0	0 2 0 0 0 2 6 0 0 0 6 7
0 5 0 0 0 1 8 0 0 0 9 3	0 8 2 0 0 1 9 0 0 1 1 1	1 0 0 0 0 2 4 0 0 1 3 0
2 4 5 0 0 8 2 0 0 1 5 4	2 6 0 0 0 5 8 0 0 2 3 6	3 0 0 0 0 4 0 0 0 2 9 4
4 4 0 0 0 4 9 0 0 3 3 4	6 5 0 0 0 3 1 0 0 3 8 3	6 5 0 0 0 3 0 0 0 4 1 4
6 5 1 0 0 3 7 0 0 4 4 4	7 0 0 0 0 2 9 0 0 4 8 1	7 0 0 0 0 1 6 0 0 5 1 0

$F_{217=0}$ 3 8 6 5 7 4 1 0 F_{009} 9 5 0 3 2 8 s 1 9 9 5 * * * * o n c a * * * * * * *

* * * 0 0 1 * 0 * e n g * 1 F_{050} * * ‡ a * * * 9 5 1 0 2 3 0 1 * F_{067} * * ‡ a

0 1 3 1 4 0 4 6 7 9 * : ‡ c $ 3 9 . 9 5 . F_{093} 0 * ‡ a N K 1 1 2 5 ‡ b . S

6 8 7 F_{111} * * ‡ a 7 4 5 . 1 ' 0 9 7 1 ‡ 2 2 0 F_{130} 1 0 ‡ a S m i t h , * J e

a n , ‡ d 1 9 4 3 - F_{154} 1 0 ‡ a C o l l e c t i n g * C a n a d a ' s * p

a s t * / ‡ c J e a n * & * E l i z a b e t h * S m i t h * ; * p h o t

o g r a p h y * b y * B o b * B e l l . F_{236} 0 * ‡ a S c a r b o r o u g h

, * O n t . * : ‡ b P r e n t i c e - H a l l * o f * C a n a d a , ‡ c

c 1 9 9 5 . F_{294} * * ‡ a 2 2 0 p . * : ‡ b i l l . * (s o m e * c o l .)

* ; ‡ c 2 7 * c m . F_{334} * 4 ‡ a T h e * H o b b y i s t ' s * h a n d b o

o k s , ‡ x 1 5 2 3 5 0 7 1 * ; ‡ v n o . * 5 F_{383} * 0 ‡ a C o l l e c t o

r s * a n d * c o l l e c t i n g . F_{414} * 0 ‡ a M a t e r i a l * c u l t

u r e ‡ x C a n a d a . F_{444} * 0 ‡ a C a n a d a ‡ x S o c i a l * l i f e

* a n d * c u s t o m s . F_{481} 1 * ‡ a S m i t h , * E l i z a b e t h , ‡

d 1 9 4 7 - F_{510} 1 * ‡ a B e l l , * R . * K . R

FIGURE 32. A MARC record as the computer "sees" it. The vertical lines are not part of the digitized record; they indicate (1) the end of the twenty-four-byte leader, the end of each twelve-byte unit of the record directory, and the end of each variable field. *F* stands for the field terminator, *R* for the record terminator, and the double dagger for the subfield delimiter, all hexadecimal characters prescribed as mentioned in chapter 8. These delimiters are included in all byte counts made by the input program to be included in the label and the record directory.

The Record Directory

The record directory comprises the sixteen twelve-byte units following the leader, plus its one-byte field terminator. One of these sixteen units is present for each variable field in the record, and each begins with the three-byte tag for that field. The following four bytes are the count of the number of bytes in that individual field, including its two indicators, its field terminator, and all subfield identifiers (of two bytes each) which it includes. The final five bytes of each unit of the record directory give the "address" of that variable field in the record, counting from the *base address of data,* which is the character position immediately following the entire record directory. It is shown in figure 32 with the subscript annotation "217=0." That is, the figure 3 there occupies character position 217 in the entire record, but also character position 0 of a new numbering sequence. This is the base address of data where the variable fields of bibliographic data begin. Like all addresses, it is calculated by a program.

The record is thus divided into two parts: (1) the data needed to process the record as a whole (leader and directory) and (2) the fields of bibliographic data, each with its own processing codes. The division makes it possible to add or subtract entire fields in a revision or local processing of the record with the addition of record-directory units but a change of only that base address of data, which is thus so important that it is stored in character positions 12 through 16 of the leader. The record directory is thus the "mystery" part of the MARC format, almost never displayed for human viewing. The input program composes it automatically, and the DBMS is its only user.

The Bibliographic-Data Fields: Tags 010 through 899

These comprise the data for which the record ultimately exists. Since the tag of each one appears in the directory, the field itself, following the base address of data, begins with its required two indicators, followed by the required first (or only) two-byte subfield identifier, then the text of the field (including any further subfield identifiers), and finally its field terminator.

The example shows how few fields and subfields of bibliographic data are relevant in a reasonably complete record for an average trade monograph. Yet over a hundred fifty different fields are now defined in the format, to cover data relevant to all types of printed, audiovisual, archival, and electronic documents, whether as serials or as monographs. In the original draft version of MARC three decades ago, a two-digit tag was proposed but as this would have restricted all future uses to well under a hundred data fields, this was wisely seen as potentially insufficient. Since only a few dozen are used with any frequency, the cataloguer inevitably becomes familiar with those few. Still, in many processing formats, these are displayed to the cataloguer as mnemonic two- or three-letter alphabetic codes; for example, *DA* for *date.*

Tag-Number Order as a Carry-Over
of the Unit-Entry Card Format

Not surprisingly, the tag-number sequence fixed in the 1960s followed the order of the elements on a Library of Congress "main entry" in its manual format. The principal access point comes first, so this appears in tags whose numbers begin with *1*—that is, the 1XX fields. The *body of the entry* is the paragraph containing the transcription of the title page (or other chief source of information), hence 2XX tags are assigned to ISBD areas 1 through 4. The physical description (the 3XX tags; ISBD area 5) is followed by series data within parentheses (the 4XX tags; area 6), both comprising a paragraph printed in smaller type on the Library of Congress card. An unpredictable number of different notes follow, each occupying a separate paragraph (the 5XX tags; area 7). Non-ISBD elements complete the record. On a card, these are printed at the bottom. The most prominent of these are the *tracings,* the access points (other than the principal one) at which a copy of the card is filed in a manual file. Tracings are given in two groups, each sequentially numbered. The first of these, with arabic numbering, comprises the controlled-vocabulary (LCSH) subject access points (the 6XX tags). In the second, a roman numeral identifies each "added" (that is, not principal) access point for filing in the author-title part of a divided catalogue (the 7XX tags, through 740); the last in this sequence are any series access points requiring a filing form different from the form in a 4XX tag (the 8XX tags, through 830).

Identification and access codes in the form of numbers or combinations of letters and numbers include the international standard numbering (ISBD area 8), subject access points consisting of classification notation, other codes related to the intellectual content of the item, and codes (such as the Library of Congress Control Number) to identify the bibliographic record itself, not the document it describes. These codes appear in various places on a unit-card record; all bear MARC tags in the 0XX range from 010 through 089. Fields tagged from 090 through 099 are reserved for local call numbers and appended holdings information such as branch location, etc. The numeric sequence of tag numbers has no technical significance. A DBMS locates any specified field in the entire record via the record directory, not the relative position of the content of the desired field.

The issue of a principal access point, particularly when it involves a uniform title, is treated at the end of chapter 6. It is important enough that its MARC coding, reflecting a now forgotten manual card format, warrants further explanation. A principal access point consisting of a personal, corporate, or conference name is tagged as 100, 110 or 111 respectively. A principal access point consisting of a uniform title with no other associated name is tagged as 130. Only these four tags in the 1XX range are used, so if the principal access point is the title proper, no 1XX field exists in that record, and by default the 245 (title proper) field is also the principal access point. When a uniform title *follows* a personal, corporate, etc. name as part of the principal access point identifying a work, that uniform title does not share the same field as the name but is tagged as 240.

Conversely, and confusingly, when a work is identified in a name-title *subject* or *added* access point, its two identifying elements do form subfields of a single MARC field. This may occur in fields 600, 610, 611, 700, 710, 711, 800, 810, or 811. Thus the subject access point for a book about Beethoven's Rasumovsky Quartets is tagged *600*, the tag for a personal name as a subject, with the uniform title for the quartets in a series of subfields:

```
600 10 ‡a Beethoven, Ludwig van, ‡d 1770-1827.
       ‡t Quartets, ‡m strings, ‡n no. 7-9, op. 59
```

Some important data are not necessarily part of the unit-record card once distributed by central agencies. Their tag numbering appears almost random; for example, fields 760 through 787 contain links to other records, and those from 850 through 886 contain both local holdings data (see below) and such newly significant information as the document's URL at an Internet site.

THE FAMILY OF USMARC FORMATS

As noted in chapter 8, an ISO2709-based format can be used to store, search, exchange, and display any kind of variable-length data, bibliographic or other. MARC, the first such format, became operational in the late 1960s only to encode the data on a manual Library-of-Congress-type catalogue card. The implications of digital formatting and processing described in chapters 3 and 4 for bibliographic file structure and searching were yet to be explored. As they were, separate MARC-like formats were devised first for name-authority records and then for the more complex subject-authority records.

Since the original MARC was devised only to facilitate data exchange, not local data processing, there was initially no reason for it to accommodate data needed only in a library's in-house system for local uses such as acquisitions, pricing, copy-specific and branch-specific locations. However, as soon as members of a consortium contributed to a common database in which one record for an item identifies the holdings of all members, local data had to be input in a standardized format using content designation compatible with that of the rest of the record. The result was a MARC "holdings format." Archivists saw enough similarities between the data elements recorded in their finding aids and those in library catalogues that they adapted library cataloguing practices to their needs and devised MARC(AMC): MARC for Archival and Manuscript Control. The most recent addition to the MARC family is a format for classification schemes. The Dewey Decimal Classification has been digitized using it; digitizing the Library of Congress Classification will soon follow.

That these additional formats share the basic MARC structure and mnemonic features means that their content designators appear familiar to anyone who knows the basic MARC for bibliographic description. To the degree possible, similar tag numbering and subfield coding is used for similar data throughout this family of formats. A name authority record is shown in manual format as figure 13 on page 119, a uniform-title authority record for a work is shown as figure 21 on page 250, and subject authority records from two printed vocabularies are shown in figure 24 on page 290. Figure 33 shows a subject authority record labelled for visual display and in the full MARC authorities format. The latter includes data of primary value to the cataloguer and therefore not included in initial OPAC display or in printed output, such as the sources of information for the creation of the record.

```
ACCESS UNDER: Night people (May Subdivide Geographically)
USED FOR:     Night owls (Persons)
              Nighttime people
              Nocturnal people
BROADER TERM: Persons
_ _ _ _ _ _ _ _ _ _ _

000  00532nz***2200181n**450b
001  sh*86006451*
005  19861211161704*8
008  860930i**anannbab***********a*ana******
040  **  ‡a DLC ‡c DLC
150  *0  ‡a Night people
450  *0  ‡a Night owls (Persons)
450  *0  ‡a Nighttime people
450  *0  ‡a Nocturnal people
550  *0  ‡wg ‡a Persons
670  **  ‡a Work cat.: Melbin, M. Night as frontier.
670  **  ‡a Web. 3  ‡b (Nocturnal; Nocturnalism; Night owl)
670  **  ‡a Hennepin ‡b (Night--Social aspects)
675  **  ‡a NYT Index; ‡a Thes. Psych. Index
```

FIGURE 33.   A subject authority record showing the content designation of the USMARC authorities format.

. . ▬

Notes

Chapter 1

1. Charles A. Cutter, *Rules for a Dictionary Catalog*, 4th ed., rewritten, U.S. Bureau of Education, Special Report on Public Libraries, Part II (Washington: Government Printing Office, 1904), p. 6. [Reprint: London: Library Association, 1935.]

2. Roy Stokes, *The Function of Bibliography*, 2nd ed. (Aldershot, Hants.: Gower, 1982) expands on the various uses of what is encompassed in the term.

3. Cutter, loc. cit.

Chapter 2

1. In 1993, ISDS adopted the name ISSN Network. Its database now contains identifications of some three quarters of a million serial titles. See *ISDS Manual* (Paris: ISDS International Centre, 1983). Its records are much less detailed than those in the CONSER database mentioned at the end of chapter 5.

2. The example is from Philip Gaskell, *A New Introduction to Bibliography* [1st ed.], repr. with corr. (Oxford: Clarendon Press, 1979), p. 374.

Chapter 3

1. In manual catalogues following Library of Congress practice, access was sometimes provided to a word of a title other than the first for quasi-subject access. This could be effective in a dictionary catalogue where authors, titles, and subjects are interfiled, and the practice was restricted to cases where no subject heading was yet authorized for a new concept specified in a title word.

2. When either typing time (on multiple copies of cards) or space occupied (in book-form files and indices) is a major cost factor, the abrupt forms *see . . .* and *see also . . .* were once almost universal. Automation brought more gentle expressions such as that shown here.

3. See *Guidelines for the Construction, Format, and Management of Monolingual Thesauri,* standard Z39.19-1993 of the National Information Standards Organization. This is a more recent statement of essentially the same standard as the International Organization for Standardization's ISO2788 and the British Standards Institution's BS:5723.

Chapter 4

1. *Library of Congress Subject Headings* does not treat this as a valid pre-coordination although it does allow **IONIZATION OF GASES**. Examples in this chapter are used to illustrate theory, not to prescribe practical application. This one has been chosen partly because comparison with the LCSH treatment of the topic would help the reader to understand the theory as well as the LCSH practice discussed further in chapter 7.

2. See *Commands for Interactive Text Searching,* standard ISO8777: 1993 of the International Organization for Standardization. This is essentially the same as *Common Command Language for Online Interactive Information Retrieval,* standard Z39.58-1992 of the National Information Standards Organization.

3. See *Information Retrieval Application Service Definition and Protocol Specification,* standard Z39.50 of the National Information Standards Organization. This is also issued by the International Organization for Standardization as standard DIS23950.

Chapter 5

1. *LC Cataloging Newsline: Online Newsletter of the Cataloging Directorate, Library of Congress* 4, no. 13 (October 1996).

2. Dorothy May Norris, *A History of Cataloguing and Cataloguing Methods, 1100–1850, with an Introductory Survey of Ancient Times* (London: Grafton, 1939), p. 132.

3. Other than ASCII, the standards still most widely accepted are summarized in the International Organization for Standardization's ISO5426 (2 parts): *Extension of the Latin Alphabet Coded Character Set for Bibliographic Information Interchange.* ISO6630, *Bibliographic Control Characters* and ISO6862, *Mathematical Coded Character Set for Bibliographic Information Interchange* supplement this.

4. See the International Organization for Standardization's *Open Systems Interconnection* standards, ISO10160–10163.

5. Cutter, op. cit., p. 11.

6. *Cataloging Service Bulletin,* no. 36 (spring 1987): 40–53, describes the minimal level in detail. Statistics for fiscal 1996 published in *LC Cataloging Newsline,* loc. cit., show that something over fifteen percent of the approximately 275,000 items catalogued at the Library of Congress during that year were accorded minimal-level cataloguing and another fifteen percent were described at the collection level, with an average of some fourteen items per collection. The Library of Congress now also defines a "core" level of cataloguing, not quite full but more than minimal.

Chapter 6

1. All editions of AACR, as well as Cutter's code and those of 1908 and 1941 (the latter not mentioned in this sketchy history), include rules for describing publications (the topic of chapter 8 of this book) as well as rules for the choice and form of name and title access points (the topic of this chapter). A 1949 code, which was not generally implemented in the U.K., is limited to the issues treated in this chapter. Only Cutter's code deals with the entire record, including subject access points and filing (the topics of chapters 7 and 9). The titles of the English-language codes between Cutter's and AACR are: 1908 (American edition): *Catalog Rules, Author and Title Entries;* 1908 (British edition): *Catalogue Rules, Author and Title Entries;* 1941: *A.L.A. Cataloging Rules, Author and Title Entries,* preliminary 2nd edition; 1949: *A.L.A. Cataloging Rules for Author and Title Entries,* 2nd edition. The proceedings of the Paris Conference referred to on the next page were published in 1963 by the Conference Organizing Committee with the conference name as title. Its twelve principles are separately published in *Statement of Principles Adopted at the International Conference on Cataloguing Principles, Paris, October, 1961,* annotated edition with commentary and examples by Eva Verona [et al.] (London: IFLA Committee on Cataloguing, 1971). The 1967 AACR appeared in separate British and North American editions with some notable differences between them. To reconcile these, the Joint Steering Committee for Revision of the Anglo-American Cataloguing Rules, representing agencies in Canada, the United Kingdom, and the United States, was created in 1974 (Australian representation was added later). This committee wrote the second edition of AACR for publication in 1978 by national library associations in the three countries then involved. AACR2 was generally implemented on January 1, 1981. Its current (1988) version is

called the "second edition, revised" (AACR2R). Periodic amendments to both versions of AACR2 have been published; in 1997, the library associations in the U.S., the U.K., and Canada jointly published the current state of AACR2R on CD-ROM. The Joint Steering Committee called a conference for late 1997 to explore how it should approach future rule revision. In this book, reference to *AACR* means that the rule or practice in question is the same according to all three codes of that title; if *AACR2* is specified, the rule or practice is only authorized by the two versions of that edition. *AACR2R* is used to refer to the current code as such and to any rules unique to it.

2. See, for example, *Names of Persons: National Usages for Entry in Catalogues*, 3rd ed., compiled by the IFLA International Office for UBC (London: The Office, 1977), and its 1980 Supplement. Government agencies in countries with many immigrants take a similar interest in documenting naming patterns. See, for example, *Naming Systems of Ethnic Groups: A Language Guide for Departmental Staff*, Department of Social Security, Migrant Services Section (Canberra: AGPS Press, 1990).

3. The name of this body is Akron Public Library, but Cutter's requirement to use the name of the place alone as the main heading takes precedence over his rule for a name beginning with a proper word. As with the Yale University Library example on pages 233–34, *Akron* is not repeated in the subheading. The city name appearing as the main heading in each of these examples is shown in the form prescribed by the latest Cutter-type rules, that is, followed by the name of a larger jurisdiction except for a city as "famous" as Paris. This is another considerable complication for filing—and in deciding what constitutes fame. Current practice is described in the section on place names, pages 234–36.

Chapter 7

1. Cutter, op. cit., p. 23.

2. Francis Miksa, *The Subject in the Dictionary Catalog from Cutter to the Present* (Chicago: American Library Association, 1983). Current policies governing the application of LCSH are described in great detail in Library of Congress. Subject Cataloging Division, *Subject Cataloging Manual: Subject Headings,* 4th ed. (Washington: Cataloging Distribution Service, Library of Congress, 1991) [2 v., loose-leaf]. Changes of both policy and individual headings appear in the quarterly *Cataloging Service Bulletin.*

3. Each is described briefly in Timothy C. Craven, *String Indexing,* Library and Information Science Series (Orlando: Academic Press, 1986).

4. This book, by Tom McArthur (Cambridge, University Press, 1986), deals with the matter of this chapter (subject analysis and its alphabetic and classified display) and is highly recommended as a nonlibrarian's analysis and historical presentation of the topic.

5. Cutter, op. cit., p. 80.

6. *Free-Floating Subdivisions: An Alphabetical Index,* prepared by the Office of Subject Cataloging Policy (Washington: Cataloging Distribution Service, Library of Congress) [annual editions]. *Subject Cataloging Manual: Subject Headings* is cited in note 2 to this chapter. These, as well as other rules and interpretations frequently consulted by a cataloguer, appear on the CD-ROM *Cataloger's Desktop,* published by the Library of Congress.

7. Cutter, op. cit., p. 68.

8. *Cataloging Service Bulletin,* no. 41 (summer 1988): 83.

Chapter 8

1. *Reference Manual for Machine-Readable Bibliographic Descriptions,* 2nd rev. ed., comp. and ed. by H. Dierickx and A. Hopkinson (Paris: Unesco General Information Programme and UNISIST, 1981). PGI-81/WS/2. Two hundred twenty-six English-language style and reference manuals, each at least five pages long and published between 1970 and 1983, are cited in John Bruce Howell, *Style Manuals of the English-Speaking World: A Guide* (Phoenix: Oryx Press, 1983). Howell's brief history of the style manual dates its first appearance to 1608.

2. The classic analysis of this kind of description remains Fredson Bowers, *Principles of Bibliographical Description* (Princeton: Princeton University Press, 1949).

3. *Poole's Index to Periodical Literature,* rev. ed. (Boston: Houghton, Mifflin, 1882), v.1, pt.1:[iii]. On the other hand, Poole observes a difference between issue dating and imprint dating, which is rarely done any longer.

4. Some background knowledge of formats for computer processing is assumed in the very concise technical summary of the next few paragraphs. Comprehension may be facilitated by reference to the appendix, particularly the single fully visualized MARC record in figure 32 on page 370.

5. *CCF/B: The Common Communication Format for Bibliographic Information,* ed. by Peter Simmons and Alan Hopkinson (Paris: Unesco General Information Programme and UNISIST, 1992). PGI-92/WS/9. The *Reference Manual* is cited in note 1 to this chapter.

6. These are the terms used in the *Guidelines for the Application of the ISBD's to the Description of Component Parts* (Munich: Saur, 1988),

where details of using techniques of multilevel description and analysis are illustrated. The terms are used to describe a whole-to-part hierarchic relationship between any two bibliographic entities.

Chapter 9

1. Library of Congress, Processing Department, *Filing Rules for the Dictionary Catalogs of the Library of Congress* (Washington: Library of Congress, 1956).

2. See, for example, William R. Nugent, "The Mechanization of the Filing Rules for the Dictionary Catalogs of the Library of Congress," *Library Resources & Technical Services* 11 (spring 1967): 145–66.

3. *ALA Filing Rules* [by the] Filing Committee, Resources and Technical Services Division, American Library Association (Chicago: ALA, 1980). *BLAISE Filing Rules,* by the British Library Filing Rules Committee (London: British Library, 1980). *Library of Congress Filing Rules,* prepared by John C. Rather and Susan C. Biebel (Washington: Library of Congress, 1980).

4. John K. Knapp [Review of both rules], *Journal of Library Automation* 14 (June 1981): 126–29.

5. See *ALA-LC Romanization Tables: Transliteration Schemes for Non-Roman Scripts Approved by the Library of Congress and the American Library Association,* ed. by Randall K. Barry (Washington: Cataloging Distribution Service, Library of Congress, 1991). Revisions appear from time to time in *Cataloging Service Bulletin.*

APPENDIX

1. *USMARC Concise Formats for Bibliographic, Authority, and Holdings Data* (Washington: Cataloging Distribution Service, Library of Congress, 1988). The current full CANMARC and USMARC bibliographic formats are: *Canadian MARC Communication Format for Bibliographic Data* (Ottawa: Canadian MARC Office, National Library of Canada, 1994) [1 v., loose-leaf] and *USMARC Format for Bibliographic Data: Including Guidelines for Content Designation* (Washington: Cataloging Distribution Service, Library of Congress, 1994) [2 v., loose-leaf]. Lists of codes for languages, countries, etc. used in records are published as separate pamphlets in the USMARC documentation. The simplified version is *Understanding MARC: Bibliographic* by Betty Furrie, 4th ed. reviewed and ed. by the Network Development and MARC Standards Office, Library of Congress (Washington: Cataloging Distribution Service, Library of Congress in collaboration with The Follett Software Co., 1994).

Index

Please refer to the Contents for a systematic survey of the topics treated in this book.

The arrangement is word-by-word; an acronym or initialism is unpunctuated and treated as a single word. An acronym which has assumed independent status in the library literature is so indexed with a cross-reference or duplicate indexing at the spelled-out form.

Unless otherwise specified, library practice is the context of every term; hence library and librarian are unindexed as such. The following concepts, treated integrally throughout the book, are only indexed to locate the pages on which they are defined: A&I publications, access, access points, bibliographic records, bibliographies, bibliography, catalogues, citations, database management systems, databases, files, index, OPACs, records, standards. A page number on which any term is merely defined, without further exploration, is printed in italics. Definitions of obsolete/obsolescent terms are indexed in this way, but a cross-reference leads to the term(s) where substantive discussion of the related concept appears.

To ignore Charles Ammi Cutter seemed strange. However, this book is not an historical, but a conceptual survey of its field with selected examples. Therefore, no personal, and few corporate, names are indexed. Examples and figures are only indexed if a significant concept or definition is expressed only in it; *fig.* denotes the figure on the page.

Ronald Hagler is professor at the School of Library, Archival and Information Studies, the University of British Columbia in Canada. He has been on the faculty since its inception in 1961, teaching in the areas of publishing and information, historical bibliography, and bibliographic control. In the school's archival studies programme, he has taught description and indexing of archival material.

Hagler's professional activities have focused on bibliographic control. He has been involved with the development of the Anglo-American Cataloguing Rules from 1964 through the publication of *AACR2, 1988 Revision* (CLA, LA, & ALA, 1988). He was also involved in the preparation of the two concise versions, the latest being the *Concise AACR2, 1988 Revision* (ALA, CLA, & LA, 1989), and their French translations, as well as the 1978 *Where's That Rule?*, a guide to implementing the change from AACR1 to AACR2. For this work he was awarded the ALA-ALCTS-CCS Margaret Mann Citation in 1990. In addition to this new edition of BRIT, he is doing detailed bibliographic investigation for published catalogues of the University of British Columbia's Arkley Collection of Historical Children's Literature.

ISBD 319